War,
Morality,
and the
Military
Profession

Other Titles of Interest

†Available in hardcover and paperback.

About the Book and Editor

War, Morality, and the Military Profession
edited by Malham M. Wakin

This anthology appropriately brings together material on two major topics: the military as a profession, and morality and war. The articles in the first section stress the ethical dimensions of the military profession and juxtapose the positions of well-known scholars. Themes include the inextricable association of human values with the military profession, and the resolution required when crucial military values are at odds with those of the parent society.

The agonizing issues associated with modern warfare are confronted with hard-hitting realism in the essays on morality and war. These selections provide some acquaintance with classical "just war" theory; discussions of the laws of war and war crimes; distinctions between questions of the morality *of* war and those related to morality *in* war; and considerations of the complexities generated by modern warfare possibilities.

Malham M. Wakin is associate dean of the faculty and professor and head of the Department of Philosophy and Fine Arts, U.S. Air Force Academy. He is in his twentieth year of teaching philosophy at the academy.

War, Morality, and the Military Profession

and the

Military Profession

edited by
Malham M. Wakin

Westview Press / Boulder, Colorado

All royalties accrued from the sale of this book are disseminated to the U.S.A.F. Academy Association of Graduates and to the U.S.A.F. Academy Academic Support Fund. Through these two instrumentalities support is provided for a number of Academy programs.

THIRD PRINTING, 1981

Copyright © 1979 by Westview Press, Inc.

Published in 1979 in the United States of America by
Westview Press, Inc.
5500 Central Avenue
Boulder, Colorado 80301
Frederick A. Praeger, Publisher

Library of Congress Cataloging in Publication Data
Main entry under title:
War, morality, and the military profession.
   1. Military ethics—Addresses, essays, lectures.
2. War and morals—Addresses, essays, lectures.
3. Armed Forces—Addresses, essays, lectures.
I. Wakin, Malham M.
U22.W36   301.5'93   79-12893
ISBN: 0-89158-670-9
ISBN: 0-89158-661-X pbk.

Printed and bound in the United States of America

Contents

Part 2
War and Morality

Preface

This volume brings together under a single cover two major topics: reflections on the military as a profession and issues relating to morality and war.

Selections for Part 1 were made with specific focus on the ethical dimensions of the military profession which themselves have obvious connections to the moral issues associated with warfare.

If there are discernable themes to be found in the variety of discussions of the military profession collected here, the following seem most clearly included:

1. Important human values are inextricably associated with the military profession in such a fashion as to make the proper pursuit of the military function impossible without their institutional inculcation.

2. The line between incompetence and immorality is a thinner one in the military profession than in almost any other human vocation.

3. The crucial military values (essentially conservative) may not always receive equal emphasis in the value system of the parent society; and if this is so, some understanding and resolution of the divergence becomes imperative.

4. If there are trends away from the traditional professional values and toward an "hourly work for pay" framework in the American military, this is an occasion for very serious concern and study.

The selections dealing with morality and war provide some acquaintance with classical just war theory, extensive discussions of the laws of war, discussions of war crimes, distinctions between the issues involved in questions related to the morality *of* war and those related to morality *in* war, and important considerations of the complexities generated by modern warfare possibilities.

The need for this book has long been felt by the philosophy teaching staff at the United States Air Force Academy, where these issues receive extensive treatment in our ethics courses. Although Colonel Mal Wakin is the principal editor, all department members assisted in selecting the materials and testing them in the classroom, and several wrote introductory summaries for the articles on morality and war. Mal Wakin wrote the introductions to Parts 1 and 2, an article in Part 1, and the introductory summaries to the articles in Part 1. Special thanks go to Professor Robert Cunningham for his encouragement and scholarly assistance in bringing this work to fruition during his year as Distinguished Visiting Professor of Philosophy at the Academy.

The following department members wrote introductory summaries for articles in Part 2:

Professor Robert Cunningham (identified by R. C. as author of introductory summaries)

Major John Bois (J. B.)

Major James Parsons (J. P.)

Major William Stayton (W. S.)

Major Kenneth Wenker (K. W.)

Captain Michael Biggs (M. B.)

In addition, Captains Ken MacDonnell and Donald Fawkes assisted with selecting appropriate materials and other details associated with publication.

Special thanks are due to Celeste Parsons for her expert manuscript preparation and to Frederick A. Praeger and his competent staff at Westview Press for their sincere interest and efficient assistance.

We are grateful to the Association of Graduates of the United States Air Force Academy, who loaned the funds for copyright permissions and manuscript preparation. Their interest in supporting this publication and similar endeavors affirms their commitment to education and research associated with the profession of arms.

—M.M.W.

Part 1
Ethics and the Military Profession

Introduction to Part 1

Malham M. Wakin

In a post-Vietnam and post-Watergate era we find in the United States a great deal of attention being paid to professional ethics. Congressional ethics committees have received considerable publicity for their investigations of various conflict-of-interest issues affecting members of Congress. Much attention has been given to the fact that many lawyers were involved in the events surrounding the Watergate affair—subsequently we find many law schools providing a forum for searching inquiry in required courses in legal ethics. The many contemporary moral issues in medicine—test-tube babies, abortion, DNA research, etc.— command media attention almost daily and have generated courses and concerned writings in medical ethics and bioethics. The business world has its special area of moral sensitivity with world attention being directed to alleged bribery of international political figures by multinational corporations and other versions of influence buying. Many firms and business colleges are developing and teaching courses in business ethics. Professional educators find themselves caught up in these issues both as spectators and participants. Higher costs and reduced enrollments tempt teachers to woo students with easier work and higher grades in order to guarantee teacher job security with a resultant diminishing of educational standards. Perennial concern for student cheating has heightened. In 1973 Karl Menninger reported that "studies at Cornell University have tended to show that the average child of ten in the United States has already developed a noncondemning attitude toward cheating."[1]

Yet, at the height of public revelations of ethical misdeeds in the many professions already mentioned, a poll taken by *U.S. News and World Report* in 1976[2] suggests that these ethical lapses must be aberrations and are certainly not signals that our moral ideals have changed substantially. When 1,400 key Americans were queried concerning the three most important characteristics of leadership, 76.1 percent listed "moral integrity," 55.2 percent listed "courage," and 52.9 percent listed "common sense." Surprisingly, "charisma" was listed by only 5.5 percent. Perhaps what we witness here is the classical conception of wishing to appear noble and good while in reality acting in ways we believe to benefit our own self-interest (what we do is different from what we say), but this is too easy and certainly too pessimistic a view of human conduct. Indeed, from the perspective of 1978 we might wish to conclude that a society's concern for moral behavior tends to be cyclical and that we are experiencing the high part of such a cycle. One can discern extreme emphasis currently being placed on honesty in all human relationships and less embarrassment by institutions in insisting that moral character "counts" as both a job requirement and an educational goal. In the 1960s educational and even some military institutions were scurrying to deny responsibility for the personal behavior of their constituents; all were abjuring any responsibility "in loco parentis." In the late 1970s student behavior codes are once more returning to college campuses and a host of American bureaucratic organizations are returning to the more conservative values in their employee codes, written or unwritten.

These reflections on societal trends are relevant to our considerations of ethics in the military profession because, like the other professions, the military constituency is drawn from the present society. Those concerned with education and training in the military must see their mission in the context of that parent society. However much we may wish to agree with Samuel Huntington in the lead articles of this section of the text that military professionalism flourished in this country partly as a result of the alienation of the military from civilian society, we cannot extend that alienation totally to our moral values. Indeed, there seems to be a special sense in which the society as a whole looks to the military profession as a final reservoir of its most precious human values (the selections in this volume by General Sir John Winthrop Hackett are especially supportive of this view). Evidence for this may be seen in the public reactions to the most recent service academy cheating episode at West Point. One can easily imagine a professor at a civilian institution calling her local newspaper to report that several of her students had cheated on a homework assignment, only to be disappointed by the editor's reaction that her story was not newsworthy. But a service academy cheating episode makes headlines, causes national investigative committees to be appointed, precipitates reassignments for superintendents and commandants, and may even generate massive curriculum changes. One interpretation of these events may well be that we perceive the military function as necessarily involving moral integrity in such a crucial fashion that any hint of dishonesty in the services must become a matter of paramount concern. Another interpretation may be that our military leadership represents the heroic for all of us and we must sustain the moral qualities of this heroic image or perhaps accept the depressing conclusion that it exists nowhere. Please notice that our expectations are specific: military knowledge and competence are not enough; we insist that they be conjoined with courage, loyalty, obedience, subordination of the self to the greater whole, and most importantly, with moral integrity. Perhaps this is because the knowledge and competence of military leadership already include some inextricable relationship with moral values. Many of the authors in Part I of this text provide support either directly or indirectly for this position.

Perhaps there are two main discernible ties between moral virtue and the military profession: first, as mentioned above, some important virtues (loyalty, obedience, selflessness, integrity) are crucial to carrying out the military function and not merely "nice to have" as they might be in some other endeavors; second, the profession itself can be noble because its ultimate purpose in a morally sound nation must involve one of mankind's highest values.

Several of the authors included in the first part of this volume argue for the first of these ties between ethics and the profession. I would like to provide some reflections here which have a strong bearing on the second point.[3] As a preliminary assumption, I assert that human beings generally have among their many needs a strong and critically important need to "accomplish"—we are purposive beings. We must find within ourselves some sense of meaningfulness, some reason for our existence. The plethora of self-help literature currently available seems aimed at aiding each of us in finding some sense of personal importance through a sort of introspective celebration of the ego. Perhaps a sensible approach to this need to "find ourselves" is to examine our attitudes toward our work: how do we view ourselves in the context of our daily routines? One contemporary attitude might well view "work" as that activity for which we strive to be paid more and more for doing less and less in order to have more time in which to do nothing. If this characterization of work brings a smile to our lips it may be because we recognize it as being more accurate than we wish it to be. We are uncomfortable with this view of work precisely because it takes away the significance of the activity to which we devote the majority of our waking hours. This activity is in reality our life's work no matter what it may be.

We may view our work as a *job*. Everyone knows that a job is what you do from eight to five; you get a paycheck for doing it, and when you leave the office or the garage or the factory each day, you leave your job there and become a different kind of person. Many of us have "jobs," that is, we have that attitude toward our daily work which makes it impossible to achieve the sense of accomplishment or personal fulfillment that is so essential to us. But often we stay in this line of work because the pay is acceptable, the security is comforting, or for some other reason not related to the need to find meaningfulness in our major human activities.

A second attitude we may take toward that activity to which we devote the majority of our waking hours is to view it as a profession. Several writers have analyzed carefully the attributes of professions. Samuel Huntington, in the first chapter of *The Soldier and the State*, suggests that expertise, corporateness, and responsibility are three important characteristics which distinguish the professions from other endeavors. To gain the expertise of a given profession one must have had extensive education and training in the special skill. The knowledge unique to the professional activity is not normally available to laymen (those not engaged in that line of work). The "corporateness" grows from the shared employment of the special skills and the interest in maintaining high standards of plying the skill. "Responsibility" grows out of the obvious service that this type of work provides to the society, thus making those who provide the professional service responsible to the entire society for the manner in which they provide the service. One who views his work as a profession is not so likely to place emphasis on pay and conditions of employment as the person who views his work merely as a job. Huntington is especially concerned to point out that military officers qualify as professionals because their skill involves expertise, responsibility, and corporateness in a fashion similar to the respected professions of medicine and law.

Huntington, Moskos, and several others fuse the notion of professionalism with that of a "calling," but it appears better to distinguish the concept of a "calling" from both "job" and "profession." To view one's work as a calling or a *vocation* is to add a dimension beyond that of either job or profession. When one feels his daily work constitutes a vocation, he gives to it not merely the majority of his time; he in a real sense becomes identified with his work; his whole personality development is associated with what he does and how he does it. It is this added dimension of viewing one's work as a vocation that holds out the most promise for finding the answer to our need for fulfillment in our work. This attitude can be held toward any ordinary human endeavor; one can have a vocation, for example, to repair shoes (a clear memory from my childhood of the neighborhood cobbler easily comes to mind), to teach school, to manufacture automobiles, to serve in the ministry. Furthermore, viewing one's work as a vocation seems most likely to permit us to find in that work the meaningfulness, the sense of accomplishment, that all human beings require. Those who do not satisfy that need in their work will seek it elsewhere; those who do not find it at all will fall short of what humanity promises and will find their existence empty of meaning.

When the notion of vocation is lost or replaced by a framework which reduces all work to the status of a job, not only do the persons involved suffer as individuals; those whom they serve will also be deprived. These reflections may provide the basis for the concern generated by Charles Moskos in "From Institution to Occupation," which is included in this anthology. His great concern is that a possible turn toward viewing the military function as a job will very negatively affect the effective carrying out of the military mission.

If we pursue the question of vocations further and ask which are the noblest callings in our society, the responses we are likely to get are easy to predict. In fact, when I have asked diverse groups to identify the prestige professions for me their answers have been remarkably uniform: medicine and law invariably are listed first. There may be a number of explanations why this is so depending upon the composition of the group one asks, but there is one analysis that seems most correct. When we examine what the doctor does *qua* doctor (not as wage earner) we see easily that his essential function is directed at something we value very highly: life itself. The same is true of law; we value what lawyers and judges do because they too are charged with providing society with something it treasures: justice. Please note that we do not value merely being alive; we are interested in the *quality* of life. We do not wish to be in ill health or in pain. Similarly, justice is a quality of a life style that we value.

If we return now to the question that initiated these considerations of the concept of human work, we are in a position to inquire about the military as a profession or a vocation. Does the military profession offer a noble function analogous to those of medicine and law? Clearly, the purpose of the military establishment of any nation must be evaluated in terms of that nation's purposes. If the nation's posture in the international context is responsible, if its constitution and governmental structure are aimed at providing a dignified lifestyle for each of its citizens, then the institution charged with defending that life style must have a noble purpose—a moral purpose. Both historical experience and philosophical wisdom inform us that not all life styles are worth defending. In Plato's *Apology,* Socrates reminds us that "the just man concerns himself far more with whether he does right or wrong than with whether he lives or dies." This, of course, seems an additional affirmation of our previous reflection that we are concerned with the quality of our lives more than with merely staying alive—we are critically interested in health and justice. On this accounting it seems to follow that if we judge professions by their functions, the military profession in an ideal state is clearly among the most noble; its function involves preservation of our highest human values, collectively referred to as our way of life.

It is important to observe that the military function may be accomplished in the modern world when fighting is limited and maintained at the lowest levels of the use of force. Just as medicine serves us best when it prevents the outbreak of an epidemic, so too the military in a deterrent posture may serve us best when it prevents or limits the use of violence in the international environment. Hackett's remarks on this topic in *The Profession of Arms* and Janowitz's conception of a constabulary function for modern military forces seem to reach the mark correctly on this issue. But this has serious implications for those who seek to find in the military profession the crucial sense of fulfillment we spoke of earlier. The doctor may derive a great sense of accomplishment from fulfilling medicine's ultimate function almost every day as he deals with and cures successfully his patients' ailments. The lawyer and judge may well involve themselves with justice very frequently in the routine involvement of their daily work. But, except in times of dire crisis, the military professional will find it more difficult to see his daily activities in the direct context of the military's ultimate function: preservation of a worthwhile way of life. In a real sense, his work is done best if he never fights; yet it is only when he fights that society generally acknowledges the importance of his function. This special difficulty needs to be understood both by those who would make the modern military their chosen profession and by the larger society from which they come. Unless the profession captures the full dedication of those who are competent both morally and intellectually to meet its challenges, unless it becomes for the most talented a complete and fulfilling vocation, it is likely to fall on hard times. In the hands of the mediocre or the morally insensitive, the vocation of arms could find its noble purpose distorted with tragic consequences for all humanity.

Notes

1. Karl Menninger, *Whatever Became of Sin* (New York: Hawthorne Books, Inc., 1973), p. 159.

2. *U.S. News and World Report,* 19 April 1976, p. 29.

3. The reflections which follow are the latest versions of views I have published previously, e.g., in "The Vocation of Arms" written with Paul Briand which appeared in *Air Force Magazine,* July 1963. Similar reflections appeared in *Notre Dame Magazine,* February 1974, in a brief article entitled "The Military—A Noble Profession?"

1

Officership as a Profession

Samuel P. Huntington

Military scholars already view The Soldier and the State *as a classic examination of the military as a profession. In this opening chapter, Huntington posits the thesis that modern military officership is a profession in an analogous sense to medicine and law. He provides defining characteristics of a profession (expertise, responsibility, and corporateness) and argues convincingly that military officers meet the criteria of professionalism. He identifies the central skill of military leadership, describes the special knowledge required of military leaders, and suggests the type of education and training appropriate to the profession. He makes illuminating comments concerning the realm of the military officer's competence, his relationships to the state, and the role ideally played by rank and bureaucratic structure. A central theme to be pursued in this text is his view that "the profession thus becomes a moral unit positing certain values and ideals which guide the members in their dealings with laymen."*

—M.M.W.

Professionalism and the Military

The modern officer corps is a professional body and the modern military officer a professional man. This is, perhaps, the most fundamental thesis of this book. A profession is a peculiar type of functional group with highly specialized characteristics. Sculptors, stenographers, entrepreneurs, and advertising copywriters all have distinct functions but no one of these functions is professional in nature. Professionalism, however, is characteristic of the modern officer in the same sense in which it is characteristic of the physician or lawyer. Professionalism distinguishes the military officer of today from the warriors of previous ages. The existence of the officer corps as a professional body gives a unique cast to the modern problem of civil-military relations.

The nature and history of other professions as professions have been thoroughly discussed. Yet the professional character of the modern officer corps has been neglected. In our society, the businessman may command more income, the politician may command more power, but the professional man commands more respect. Yet the public, as well as the scholar, hardly conceives of the officer in the same way that it does the lawyer or doctor, and it certainly does not accord to the officer the deference which it gives to the civilian professionals. Even the military themselves are influenced by their image in the public mind and at times have refused to accept the implications of their own professional status. When the term "professional" has been used in connection with the military, it normally has been in the sense of "professional" as contrasted with "amateur" rather than in the sense of "profession" as contrasted with "trade" or "craft." The phrases "professional army" and "professional soldier" have obscured the difference between the career enlisted man who is professional in the sense of one who works for monetary gain and the career officer who is professional in the very different sense of one who pursues a "higher calling" in the service of society.

The Concept of Profession

The first step in analyzing the professional character of the modern officer corps is to define professionalism. The distinguishing characteristics of a profession as a special type of vocation are its expertise, responsibility, and corporateness.[1]

Expertise

The professional man is an expert with specialized knowledge and skill in a significant field of human endeavor. His expertise is acquired only by prolonged education and experience. It is the basis of objective standards of professional competence for separating the profession from laymen and measuring the relative competence of members of the profession. Such standards are universal. They inhere in the knowledge and skill and are capable of general application irrespective of time and place. The ordinary skill or craft exists only in the present and is mastered by learning an existing technique without reference to what has gone before. Professional knowledge, however, is intellectual in nature and capable of preservation in writing. Professional knowledge has a history, and some knowledge of that history is essential to professional competence. Institutions of research and education are required for the extension and transmission of professional knowledge and skill. Contact is maintained between the academic and practical sides of a profession through journals, conferences, and the circulation of personnel between practice and teaching.

Professional expertise also has a dimension in breadth which is lacking in the normal trade. It is a segment of the total cultural tradition of society. The professional man can successfully apply his skill only when he is aware of this broader tradition of which he is a part. Learned professions are "learned" simply because they are an integral part of the total body of learning of society. Consequently professional education consists of two phases: the first imparting a broad, liberal, cultural background, and the second imparting the specialized skills and knowledge of the profession. The liberal education of the professional man is normally handled by the general education institutions of society devoted to this purpose. The second or technical phase of professional education, on the other hand, is given in special institutions operated by or affiliated with the profession itself.

Responsibility

The professional man is a practicing expert, working in a social context, and performing a service, such as the promotion of health, education, or justice, which is essential to the functioning of society. The client of every profession is society, individually or collectively. A research chemist, for instance, is not a professional man because the service he renders, while beneficial to society, is not essential to its immediate existence and functioning: only Du Pont and the Bureau of Standards have a direct and immediate interest in what he has to offer. The essential and general character of his service and his monopoly of his skill impose upon the professional man the responsibility to perform the service when required by society. This social responsibility distinguishes the professional man from other experts with only intellectual skills. The research chemist, for instance, is still a research chemist if he uses his skills in a manner harmful to society. But the professional man can no longer practice if he refuses to accept his social responsibility: a physician ceases to be a physician if he uses his skills for antisocial purposes. The responsibility to serve and devotion to his skill furnish the professional motive. Financial remuneration cannot be the primary aim of the professional man *qua* professional man. Consequently, professional compensation normally is only partly determined by bargaining on the open market and is regulated by professional custom and law.

The performance of an essential service not regulated by the normal expectation of financial rewards requires some statement governing the relations of the profession to the rest of society. Conflicts between the professional man and his clients, or among members of the profession, normally furnish the immediate impetus to the formulation of such a statement. The profession thus becomes a moral unit positing certain values and ideals which guide its members in their dealing with laymen. This guide may be a set of unwritten norms transmitted through the professional educational system or it may be codified into written canons of professional ethics.

Corporateness

The members of a profession share a sense of organic unity and consciousness of themselves as a group apart from laymen. This collective sense has its origins in the lengthy discipline and training necessary for professional competence, the common bond of work, and the sharing of a unique social responsibility. The sense of unity manifests itself in a professional organization which formalizes and applies the standards of professional competence and establishes and enforces the standards of professional responsibility. Membership in the professional organization, along with the possession of special expertise and the acceptance of special responsibility, thus becomes a criterion of professional status, publicly distinguishing the professional man from the layman. The interest of the profession requires it to bar its members from capitalizing upon professional competence in areas where that competence has no relevance and likewise to protect itself against outsiders who would claim professional competence because of achievements or attributes in other fields. Professional organizations are generally either associations or bureaucracies. In the associational professions such as medicine and law, the practitioner typically functions independently and has a direct personal relationship with his client. The bureaucratic professions, such as the diplomatic service, possess a high degree of specialization of labor and responsibilities within the profession, and the profession as a whole renders a collective service to society as a whole. These two categories are not mutually exclusive: bureaucratic elements exist in most associational professions, and associations frequently supplement the formal structure of bureaucratic professions. The associational professions usually possess written codes of ethics since each practitioner is individually confronted with the problem of proper conduct toward clients and colleagues. The bureaucratic professions, on the other hand, tend to develop a more general sense of collective professional responsibility and the proper role of the profession in society.

The Military Profession

The vocation of officership meets the principal criteria of professionalism. In practice, no vocation, not even medicine or law, has all the characteristics of the ideal professional type. Officership probably falls somewhat further short of the ideal than either of these. Yet its fundamental character as a profession is undeniable. In practice, officership is strongest and most effective when it most closely approaches the professional ideal; it is weakest and most defective when it falls short of that ideal.

The Expertise of Officership

What is the specialized expertise of the military officer? Is there any skill common to all military officers and yet not shared with any civilian groups? At first glance this hardly seems to be the case. The officer corps appears to contain many varieties of specialists, including large numbers which have their counterparts in civilian life. Engineers, doctors, pilots, ordnance experts, personnel experts, intelligence experts, communications experts—all these are found both within and without the modern officer corps. Even ignoring these technical specialists, each absorbed in his own branch of knowledge, just the broad division of the corps into land, sea, and air officers appears to create vast differences in the functions performed and the skills required. The captain of a cruiser and the commander of an infantry division appear to be faced with highly different problems requiring highly different abilities.

Yet a distinct sphere of military competence does exist which is common to all, or almost all, officers and which distinguishes them from all, or almost all, civilians. This central skill is perhaps best summed up in Harold Lasswell's phrase "the management of violence." The function of a military force is successful armed combat. The duties of the military officer include: (1) the organizing, equipping, and training of this force; (2) the planning of its activities; and (3) the direction of its operation in and out of combat. The direction, operation, and control of a human organization whose primary function is the application of violence is the peculiar skill of the officer. It is common to the activities of the air, land, and sea officers. It distinguishes the military officer *qua* military officer from the other specialists which exist in the modern armed services. The skills of these experts may be necessary to the achievement of the objectives of the military force. But they are basically auxilliary vocations, having the same relation to the expertise of the officer as the skills of the nurse, chemist, laboratory technician, dietician, pharmacist, and X-ray technician have to the expertise of the doctor. None of the auxiliary specialists contained within or serving the military profession is capable of the "management of violence," just as none of the specialists aiding the medical profession is capable of the diagnosis and treatment of illness. The essence of officership is embodied in the traditional admonition to Annapolis men that their duty will be to "fight the fleet." Individuals, such as doctors, who are not competent to manage violence but who are members of the officer corps are normally distinguished by special titles and insignia and are excluded from positions of military command. They belong to the officer corps in its capacity as an administrative organization of the state, but not in its capacity as a professional body.

Within the profession itself there are specialists in the man
agement of violence on sea, on land, and in the air, just as there
are heart, stomach, and eye specialists within medicine. A military
specialist is an officer who is peculiarly expert at directing the
application of violence under certain prescribed conditions. The
variety of conditions under which violence may be employed and
the different forms in which it may be applied form the basis for
subprofessional specialization. They also form the basis for
evaluating relative technical competence. The larger and more
complex the organizations of violence which an officer is capable of
directing, and the greater the number of situations and conditions
under which he can be employed, the higher is his professional
competence. A man who is capable of directing only the activities
of an infantry squad has such a low level of professional ability as to
be almost on the border line. A man who can manage the
operations of an airborne division or a carrier task force is a highly
competent professional. The officer who can direct the complex
activities of a combined operation involving large-scale sea, air,
and land forces is at the top of his vocation.

It is readily apparent that the military function requires a
high order of expertise. No individual, whatever his inherent
intellectual ability and qualities of character and leadership, could
perform these functions efficiently without considerable training
and experience. In emergencies an untrained civilian may be
capable of acting as a military officer at a low level for a brief period
of time, just as in emergencies the intelligent layman may fill in
until the doctor arrives. Before the management of violence
became the extremely complex task that it is in modern
civilization, it was possible for someone without specialized
training to practice officership. Now, however, only the person
who completely devotes his working hours to this task can hope to
develop a reasonable level of professional competence. The skill of
the officer is neither a craft (which is primarily mechanical) nor an
art (which requires unique and nontransferable talent). It is
instead an extraordinarily complex intellectual skill requiring
comprehensive study and training. It must be remembered that
the peculiar skill of the officer is the management of violence, not
the act of violence itself. Firing a rifle, for instance, is basically a

mechanical craft; directing the operations of a rifle company requires an entirely different type of ability which may in part be learned from books and in part from practice and experience. The intellectual content of the military profession requires the modern officer to devote about one-third of his professional life to formal schooling, probably a higher ratio of education time to practice time than in any other profession. In part this reflects the limited opportunities of the officer to acquire practical experience at the most important elements of his vocation. But to a large degree it also reflects the extreme complexity of the military expertise.

The peculiar skill of the military officer is universal in the sense that its essence is not affected by changes in time or location. Just as the qualifications of a good surgeon are the same in Zurich as they are in New York, the same standards of professional military competence apply in Russia as in America and in the nineteenth century as in the twentieth. The possession of a common professional skill is a bond among military officers cutting across other differences. The vocation of the officer also possesses a history. The management of violence is not a skill which can be mastered simply by learning existing techniques. It is in a continuous process of development, and it is necessary for the officer to understand this development and to be aware of its main tendencies and trends. Only if he is aware of the historical development of the techniques of organizing and directing military forces can the officer expect to stay on top of the profession. The importance of the history of war and military affairs receives sustained emphasis throughout military writing and military education.

The military skill requires a broad background of general culture for its mastery. The methods of organizing and applying violence at any one stage in history are intimately related to the entire cultural pattern of society. Just as law at its borders merges into history, politics, economics, sociology, and psychology, so also does the military skill. Even more, military knowledge also has frontiers on the natural sciences of chemistry, physics, and biology. To understand his trade properly, the officer must have some idea of its relation to these other fields and the ways in which these other areas of knowledge may contribute to his own purposes. In addition, he cannot really develop his analytical skill, insight, imagination, and judgment if he is trained simply in vocational duties. The abilities and habits of mind which he requires within his professional field can in large part be acquired only through the broader avenues of learning outside his profession. The fact that, like the lawyer and the physician, he is continuously dealing with human beings requires him to have the deeper understanding of human attitudes, motivations, and behavior which a liberal education stimulates. Just as a general education has become the prerequisite for entry into the professions of law and medicine, it is now also almost universally recognized as a desirable qualification for the professional officer.

The Responsibility of Officership

The expertise of the officer imposes upon him a special social responsibility. The employment of his expertise promiscuously for his own advantage would wreck the fabric of society. As with the practice of medicine, society insists that the management of violence be utilized only for socially approved purposes. Society has a direct, continuing, and general interest in the employment of this skill for the enhancement of its own military security. While all professions are to some extent regulated by the state, the military profession is monopolized by the state. The skill of the physician is diagnosis and treatment; his responsibility is to the health of his clients. The skill of the officer is the management of violence; his responsibility is the military security of his client, society. The discharge of the responsibility requires mastery of the skill; mastery of the skill entails acceptance of the responsibility. Both responsibility and skill distinguish the officer from other social types. All members of society have an interest in its security; the state has a direct concern for the achievement of this along with other social values; but the officer corps alone is responsible for military security to the exclusion of all other ends.

Does the officer have a professional motivation? Clearly he does not act primarily from economic incentives. In western society the vocation of officership is not well rewarded monetarily. Nor is his behavior within his profession governed by economic rewards and punishments. The officer is not a mercenary who transfers his services wherever they are best rewarded, nor is he the temporary citizen-soldier inspired by intense momentary patriotism and duty but with no steadying and permanent desire to perfect himself in the management of violence. The motivations of the officer are technical love for his craft and the sense of social obligation to utilize this craft for the benefit of society. The combination of these drives constitutes professional motivation. Society, on the other hand, can only assure this motivation if it offers its officers continuing and sufficient pay both while on active duty and when retired.

The officer possesses intellectualized skill, mastery of which requires intense study. But like the lawyer and doctor he is not primarily a man of the closet; he deals continuously with people. The test of his professional ability is the application of technical knowledge in a human context. Since this application is not regulated by economic means, however, the officer requires positive guides spelling out his responsibilities to his fellow officers, his subordinates, his superiors, and the state which he serves. His behavior within the military structure is governed by a complex mass of regulations, customs, and traditions. His behavior in relation to society is guided by an awareness that his skill can only be utilized for purposes approved by society through its political agent, the state. While the primary responsibility of the physician is to his patient, and the lawyer to his client, the principal responsibility of the military officer is to the state. His responsibility to the state is the responsibility of the expert adviser. Like the lawyer and physician, he is concerned with only one segment of the activities of his client. Consequently, he cannot impose decisions beyond his field of special competence. He can only explain to his client his needs in this area, advise him as to how to meet these needs, and then, when the client has made his decisions, aid him in implementing them. To some extent the officer's behavior towards the state is guided by an explicit code expressed in law and comparable to the canons of professional ethics of the physician and lawyer. To a large extent, the officer's code is expressed in custom, tradition, and the continuing spirit of the profession.

The Corporate Character of Officership

Officership is a public bureaucratized profession. The legal right to practice the profession is limited to members of a carefully defined body. His commission is to the officer what his license is to a doctor. Organically, however, the officer corps is much more than simply a creature of the state. The functional imperatives of security give rise to complex vocational institutions which mold the officer corps into an autonomous social unit. Entrance into this unit is restricted to those with the requisite education and training and is usually permitted only at the lowest level of professional competence. The corporate structure of the officer corps includes not just the official bureaucracy but also societies, associations, schools, journals, customs, and traditions. The professional world of the officer tends to encompass an unusually high proportion of his activities. He normally lives and works apart from the rest of society; physically and socially he probably has fewer nonprofessional contacts than most other professional men. The line between him and the layman or civilian is publicly symbolized by uniforms and insignia of rank.

The officer corps is both a bureaucratic profession and a bureaucratic organization. Within the profession, levels of competence are distinguished by a hierarchy of ranks; within the organization, duties are distinguished by a hierarchy of office. Rank inheres in the individual and reflects his professional achievement measured in terms of experience, seniority, education, and ability. Appointments to rank are normally made by the officer corps itself applying general principals established by the state. Assignments to office are normally somewhat more subject to outside influence. In all bureaucracies authority derives from office; in a professional bureaucracy eligibility for office derives from rank. An officer is permitted to perform certain types of duties and functions by virtue of his rank; he does not receive rank because he has been assigned to an office. Although in practice there are exceptions to this principle, the professional character of the officer corps rests upon the priority of the hierarchy of rank over the hierarchy of office.

The officer corps normally includes a number of nonprofessional "reservists." This is due to the fluctuating need for officers and the impossibility of the state maintaining continuously an officer corps of the size required in emergencies. The reservists are a temporary supplement to the officer corps and qualify for military rank by education and training. While members of the corps, they normally possess all the prerogatives and responsibilities of the professional in the same rank. The legal distinction between them and the professional is preserved, however, and entrance into the permanent corps of officers is much more restricted than entrance into the reserve corps. The reservists seldom achieve the level of professional skill open to the career officers; consequently, the bulk of the reservists are in the lower ranks of the professional bureaucracy while the higher ranks are monopolized by the career professionals. The latter, as the continuing element in the military structure and because of their superior professional competence as a body, are normally charged with the education and indoctrination of the reservists in the skills and the traditions of the vocation. The reservist only temporarily assumes professional responsibility. His principal functions in society lie elsewhere. As a result, his motivations, values, and behavior frequently differ greatly from those of the career professional.

The enlisted men subordinate to the officer corps are a part of the organizational bureaucracy but not of the professional bureaucracy. The enlisted personnel have neither the intellectual skills nor the professional responsibility of the officer. They are specialists in the application of violence, not the management of violence. Their vocation is a trade not a profession. This fundamental difference between the officer corps and the enlisted corps is reflected in the sharp line which is universally drawn between the two in all the military forces of the world. If there were not this cleavage, there could be a single military hierarchy extending from the lowest enlisted man to the highest officer. But the differing character of the two vocations makes the organizational hierarchy discontinuous. The ranks which exist in the enlisted corps do not constitute a professional hierarchy. They reflect varying aptitudes, abilities, and offices within the trade of soldier, and movement up and down them is much more fluid than in the officer corps. The difference between the officer and enlisted vocations precludes any general progression from one to the other. Individual enlisted men do become officers but this is the exception rather than the rule. The education and training necessary for officership are normally incompatible with prolonged service as an enlisted man.

Notes

1. This author has discovered only one volume in English which analyzes officership as a profession: Michael Lewis, *England's Sea Officers: The Study of the Naval Profession* (London, 1939). More typical is the standard history of the professions in Great Britain which omits mention of the military "because the service which soldiers are trained to render is one which it is hoped they will never be called upon to perform." A. M. Carr-Saunders and P. A. Wilson, *The Professions* (Oxford, 1933), p. 3. Sociological studies, following Max Weber, have usually analyzed the military as a bureaucratic structure. See H. H. Gerth and C. Wright Mills (eds.), *From Max Weber* (New York, 1946), pp. 221-223; C. D. Spindler, "The Military—A Systematic Analysis," *Social Forces* (October 1948):83-88; C. H. Page, "Bureaucracy's Other Face," *Social Forces* (October 1946):88-94; H. Brotz and E. K. Wilson, "Characteristics of Military Society," *American Journal of Sociology* (March 1946):371-375.

While bureaucracy is characteristic of the officer corps, it is, however, a secondary not an essential characteristic. Other writers have followed the liberal tendency to identify the military with the enemies of liberalism and have stressed the feudal-aristocratic elements in militarism. See Alfred Vagts, *A History of Militarism* (New York, 1937), and Arnold Rose, "The Social Structure of the Army," *American Journal of Sociology* 51 (March 1946):361-364. For definitions of professionalism, see Carr-Saunders and Wilson, *The Professions*, pp. 284-285, 298, 303, 365, 372; A. M. Carr-Saunders, *Professions: Their Organization and Place in Society* (Oxford, 1928), p. 5; Talcott Parsons, "A Sociologist Looks at the Legal Profession," *Essays in Sociological Theory* (Glencoe, Ill., rev. ed., 1954), p. 372, and *The Social System* (Glencoe, Ill., 1951), p. 454; Abraham Flexner, "Is Social Work a Profession?" *Proceedings*, National Conference of Charities and Correction (1915), pp. 578-581; Carl F. Taeusch, *Professional and Business Ethics* (New York, 1926), pp. 13-18; Roy Lewis and Angus Maude, *Professional People* (London, 1952), pp. 55-56, 64-69, 210; Roscoe Pound, *The Lawyer from Antiquity to Modern Times* (St. Paul, 1953), pp. 4-10; R. H. Tawney, *The Acquisitive Society* (New York, 1920), p. 92; Graham Wallas, *Our Social Heritage* (New Haven, 1921), pp. 122-157; M. L. Cogan, "The Problem of Defining a Profession," *Annals* of the American Academy 297 (January 1955):105-111.

Professional education is discussed in T. Parsons, "Remarks on Education and the Professions," *International Journal of Ethics* 47 (April 1937):366-367, and Robert M. Hutchins, *The Higher Learning in America* (New Haven, 1936), pp. 51-57. The ups and downs of the legal profession in the United States may be traced in terms of the liberal education requirement. See Pound, *Lawyer from Antiquity to Modern Times*, p. 229; M. Louise Rutherford, *The Influence of the American Bar Association on Public Opinion and Legislation* (Philadelphia, 1937), pp. 46ff.

On professional ethics, see Taeusch, *Professional and Business Ethics;* Benson Y. Landis, *Professional Codes* (New York, 1927); R. D. Kohn, "The Significance of the Professional Ideal: Professional Ethics and the Public Interest," *Annals* of the American Academy 101 (May 1922):1-5; R. M. MacIver, "The Social Significance of Professional Ethics," ibid., pp. 6-7; Oliver Garceau, *The Political Life of the American Medical Association* (Cambridge, 1941), pp. 5-11; James H. Means, *Doctors, People, and Government* (Boston, 1953), pp. 36-40; George Sharswood, *An Essay on Professional Ethics* (Philadelphia, 5th ed., 1907, first published 1854); Samuel Warren, *The Moral, Social, and Professional Duties of Attornies and Solicitors* (Edinburgh and London, 1848); Henry S. Drinker, *Legal Ethics* (New York, 1953); "Ethical Standards and Professional Conduct," *Annals* of the American Academy 297 (January 1955):37-45. For the origins of occupational values in general, see E. C. Hughes, "Personality Types and the Division of Labor," *American Journal of Sociology* 33 (March 1928):762.

2

The Military Mind: Conservative Realism of the Professional Military Ethic

Samuel P. Huntington

The "military mind" has often been stereotyped, frequently unattractively. Huntington provides an idealized form of a professional military ethic as a model that he proposes as a useful device for determining the professionalism of any officer corps: the closer to his model, the more professional the military leadership. His description of a military ethic is drawn from his view of the appropriate military function and not from empirical observation. Values of the military ethic include commitment to military security of the state, a pessimistic view of a static and weak human nature, subordination of the individual to the group, loyalty, obedience, civilian control, alienation from political activity, and the military's essentially instrumental function in the state. The model drawn here of military values is described as "conservative realism." This picture of the military mind is deserving of careful analysis with special attention to the claim that it provides a measure for the level of professionalism in military organizations.

—M.M.W.

The Meaning of the Military Mind

The unique or functional aspect of the military has often been discussed in terms of the "military mind." This chapter attempts to define this concept precisely enough so that it may serve as a useful tool of analysis. The military mind may be approached from three viewpoints: (1) its ability or quality; (2) its attributes or characteristics; and (3) its attitudes or substance.[1]

Reprinted by permission of the publisher from *The Soldier and The State* by Samuel P. Huntington, Cambridge, Mass.: The Belnap Press of Harvard University Press, Copyright © 1957 by the President and Fellows of Harvard College.

Writers employing the first approach have normally emphasized the low caliber of the "military mind." The intelligence,
scope, and imagination of the professional soldier have been
compared unfavorably to the intelligence, scope, and imagination
of the lawyer, the businessman, the politician. This presumed
inferiority has been variously attributed to the inherently inferior
talents and abilities of the persons who become officers, the
organization of the military profession which discourages individual initiative, and the infrequent opportunities which an officer
has actively to apply his skill. This general approach deals with one
feature of the military mind, but it does not help to define the
peculiarly "military" aspects of that mind. The mere fact that the
military mind occupies a particular point on the intelligence scale
says nothing about its distinctive characteristics. The point might
well be the same one occupied by the engineering or dental minds.

The second approach holds that the uniqueness of the military
mind lies in certain mental attributes or qualities which constitute
a military personality. Military and civilian writers generally seem
to agree that the military mind is disciplined, rigid, logical,
scientific; it is not flexible, tolerant, intuitive, emotional. The
continuous performance of the military function may well give rise
to these qualities. Intuitively one feels that these descriptions, also
intuitive, come close to the mark. But until more knowledge is
accumulated about the personality traits of military men and other
politically significant groups and also about the relation between
personality, values, and behavior in social situations, this approach
will not be very useful in analyzing civil-military relations.

A third and more fruitful approach is to analyze the substance of
the military mind—the attitudes, values, views of the military
man. This has customarily been done through one of two
techniques: to define the military mind in terms of content, or to
define it in terms of source. The former method describes certain
values and attitudes as military in content, and then asserts that
these values and attitudes are widely prevalent among military
men. Emphasis has generally focused upon two sets of attitudes
assumed to be characteristically military: bellicosity and authoritarianism. The military man is held to believe that peace is
stultifying and that conflict and war develop man's highest moral
and intellectual qualities; he favors aggressive and bellicose

national policies. He is also thought to be opposed to democracy and to desire the organization of society on the basis of the chain of command. Irrespective of whether these conclusions are accurate, the method used in arriving at them is both subjective and arbitrary. The a priori assumption that certain values are military and that military men therefore hold those values may or may not be true, but there is nothing in the procedure which requires it to be so.

An alternative approach is to define military values by source. This is to assume that any expression of attitude or value coming from a military source reflects the military mind. But the difficulty here is that everything that comes from a military source does not necessarily derive from its character as a military source. Military men are also Frenchmen and Americans, Methodists and Catholics, liberals and reactionaries, Jews and anti-Semites. Any given statement by a military man may not reflect his attitudes *qua* military man but may instead stem from social, economic, political, or religious affiliations irrelevant to his military role. This difficulty could be overcome if it were possible to cancel out these accidental characteristics of military men by surveying a broad, representative sample of communications from military men from all walks of life, all countries, and all times. The magnitude of such an undertaking, however, makes it desirable to find an alternative path to the military mind: to arrive at the substance of *l'idée militaire* by defining it as a professional ethic.

People who act the same way over a long period of time tend to develop distinctive and persistent habits of thought. Their unique relation to the world gives them a unique perspective on the world and leads them to rationalize their behavior and role. This is particularly true where the role is a professional one. A profession is more clearly isolated from other human activity than are most occupations. The continuing objective performance of the professional function gives rise to a continuing professional *Weltanschauung* or professional "mind." The military mind, in this sense, consists of the values, attitudes, and perspectives which inhere in the performance of the professional military function and which are deducible from the nature of that function. The military function is performed by a public, bureaucratized profession expert in the management of violence and responsible for the military security of the state. A value or attitude is part of the professional military ethic if it is implied by or derived from the peculiar expertise, responsibility, and organization of the military profession. The professional ethic is broader than professional ethics in the narrow sense of the code governing the behavior of the professional man toward nonprofessionals. It includes any preferences and expectations which may be inferred from the continuing performance of the military occupational role.

The military mind is thus defined abstractly as a Weberian ideal type in terms of which the beliefs of actual men and groups can be analyzed. Obviously, no one individual or group will adhere to all the constituent elements of the military ethic, since no individual or group is ever motivated exclusively by military considerations. Any given officer corps will adhere to the ethic only to the extent that it is professional, that is, to the extent that it is shaped by functional rather than societal imperatives. Few expressions of the ethic by an officer corps indicate a low level of professionalism, widespread articulation of the ethic a high degree of professionalism. The professional military ethic, moreover, is "non-dated and non-localized" just like the profession of which it is the intellectual expression. So long as there is no basic alteration in the inherent nature of the military function there will be no change in the content of the professional ethic. Simple changes in military technique, such as developments in weapons technology or the increased importance of economics in military affairs, do not alter the character of the military ethic any more than the discovery of penicillin altered medical ethics. The military ethic consequently is a constant standard by which it is possible to judge the professionalism of any officer corps anywhere anytime. For the sake of clarity, this ideal model may be referred to as the "professional military ethic." The views actually held by a concrete group of officers at some specific point in history may be termed the "nineteenth-century German military ethic" or the "post-World War I American ethic."

In the sections that follow an attempt will be made to elaborate the professional military ethic with respect to (1) basic values and perspectives, (2) national military policy, and (3) the relation of the military to the state. The accuracy of this definition of the ethic depends upon the extent to which the views stated are necessarily implied by the performance of the military function. These deductions as to the nature of the ethic will be illustrated by occasional references to typical expressions drawn from military literature. Since the historical evolution of the military ethic in the United States will be described in some detail in later chapters, the citations from American sources will purposely be limited. These references, moreover, are just examples; they do not prove that the views expressed are part of the professional military ethic any more than a completely contradictory statement from a military man would invalidate their inclusion in the ethic. The sole criterion is relevance to the performance of the military function.

The Professional Military Ethic

Man, Society, and History

The existence of the military profession presupposes conflicting human interests and the use of violence to further those interests. Consequently, the military ethic views conflict as a universal pattern throughout nature and sees violence rooted in the permanent biological and psychological nature of men. As between the good and evil in man, the military ethic emphasizes the evil. Man is selfish. He is motivated by drives for power, wealth, and security. "The human mind is by nature one-sided and limited."[2] As between the strength and weakness in man, the military ethic emphasizes the weakness. Man's selfishness leads to struggle but man's weakness makes successful conflict dependent upon organization, discipline, and leadership. As Clausewitz said, "All war presupposes human weakness, and against that it is directed." No one is more aware than the professional soldier that the normal man is no hero. The military profession organizes men so as to overcome their inherent fears and failings.[3] The uncertainty and chance involved in the conduct of war and the difficulty of anticipating the actions of an opponent make the military man skeptical of the range of human foresight and control. As between reason and irrationality in man, the military ethic emphasizes the limits of reason. The best schemes of men are frustrated by the "friction" existing in reality. "War is the province of uncertainty," Clausewitz said; "three-fourths of the things on which action in war is based lie hidden in the fog of greater or less uncertainty." Human nature, moreover, is universal and un-changing. Men in all places and at all times are basically the same.[4] The military view of man is thus decidedly pessimistic. Man has elements of goodness, strength, and reason, but he is also evil, weak, and irrational. The man of the military ethic is essentially the man of Hobbes.

The existence of the military profession depends upon the existence of competing nation-states. The responsibility of the profession is to enhance the military security of the state. The discharge of this responsibility requires cooperation, organization, discipline. Both because it is his duty to serve society as a whole and because of the nature of the means which he employs to carry out this duty, the military man emphasizes the subordination of the will of the individual to the will of the group. Tradition, esprit, unity, community—these rate high in the military value system. The officer submerges his personal interests and desires to what is necessary for the good of the service. As a nineteenth-century German officer put it, the military man must "forego personal advantage, lucre, and prosperity. . . . Egotism is beyond all doubt the most bitter enemy of the qualities essential to the officer-corps."[5] Man is preeminently a social animal. He exists only in groups. He defends himself only in groups. Most importantly, he realizes himself only in groups. The "weak, mediocre, transient individual" can only achieve emotional satisfaction and moral fulfillment by participating in "the power, the greatness, the permanence and the splendour" of a continuing organic body.[6] The military ethic is basically corporative in spirit. It is fundamentally anti-individualistic.

The military vocation is a profession because it has accumulated experiences which make up a body of professional knowledge. In the military view, man learns only from experience. If he has little opportunity to learn from his own experience, he must learn from the experience of others. Hence, the military officer studies history. For history is, in Liddell Hart's phrase, "universal experience," and military history, as Moltke said, is the "most effective means of teaching war during peace." The military ethic thus places unusual value upon the ordered, purposive study of history.[7] History is valuable to the military man only when it is used to develop principles which may be capable of future application. The military student of history constantly tries to draw generalizations from his study. Yet the military ethic is not bound to any specific theory of history. While it rejects monistic interpretations, it also emphasizes the importance of force as contrasted with ideological and economic factors. The permanence of human nature makes impossible any theory of progress. "Change is inevitable. Progress is not inevitable."[8] Insofar as there is a pattern in history, it is cyclical in nature. Civilizations rise and fall. War and peace alternate, and so also does the supremacy of offensive and defensive warfare.[9]

National Military Policy

The military view toward national policy reflects the professional responsibility for the military security of the state. This responsibility leads the military: (1) to view the state as the basic unit of political organization; (2) to stress the continuing nature of the threats to the military security of the state and the continuing likelihood of war; (3) to emphasize the magnitude and immediacy of the security threats; (4) to favor the maintenance of strong, diverse, and ready military forces; (5) to oppose the extension of state commitments and the involvement of the state in war except when victory is certain.

The Primacy of the Nation State. The existence of the military profession depends upon the existence of nation-states capable of maintaining a military establishment and desiring to maintain such an establishment because of threats to their security. There is no necessary reason why nation-states should be the only socio-political groups maintaining professional forces. But with a few peripheral exceptions, this has been true. The military man consequently tends to assume that the nation-state is the ultimate form of political organization. The justification for the maintenance and employment of military force is in the political ends of the state. The causes of war are always political. State policy aimed at continuing political objectives precedes war, determines the resort to war, dictates the nature of the war, concludes the war, and continues on after the war. War must be the instrument of political purpose. The purpose of the state cannot be its own destruction. Consequently "total war" or "absolute war" is to be avoided if it is likely to produce the mutual devastation of the combatants.[10]

The Permanency of Insecurity and the Inevitability of War. In a world of independent nation-states, the problem of military security is never finally solved. Competition among the states is continuous, and war is only an intensification of this competition which brings to a crisis the ever present issue of military security. War is always likely and is ultimately inevitable. Its immediate causes spring from conflicting state policies, but its fundamental causes lie deep in human nature where exist the sources of all human conflict. "To abolish war we must remove its cause, which lies in the imperfection of human nature."[11]

If the causes of war are in human nature, the complete abolition of war is impossible. Consequently, the military mind is skeptical of institutional devices designed to prevent war. Treaties, international law, international arbitration, the Hague Court, the League of Nations, the United Nations are of little help to peace. The decisive factor is always the power relation existing among the states. "In the last analysis the action of States is regulated by nothing but power and expediency."[12] Diplomacy itself only provides a superficial covering for the existence and uses of power. Treaties and other international agreements have meaning only insofar as they reflect the realities of international power. A state can achieve little by diplomacy unless it has the strength and the will to back up its demands with force. As Nelson once said: "A fleet of British ships of war is the best negotiator in Europe."

The Magnitude and Immediacy of the Security Threats. The military man normally views with alarm the potency and immediacy of the security threats to the state. As Lord Salisbury once remarked: "If you believe the doctors, nothing is wholesome: if you believe the theologians, nothing is innocent: if you believe the soldiers, nothing is safe." The military man recognizes the continuing character of threats to the state, but he also stresses the urgency of the current danger. The goal of professional competence requires the military man to estimate the threat as accurately as possible. But the military man also has a professional interest and a professional duty to stress the dangers to military security. Consequently, the objective realities of international politics only partially determine the military estimate of the situation. The military man's views also reflect a subjective professional bias, the

strength of which depends upon his general level of profession-
ism. This professional bias, or sense of professional responsibility,
leads him to feel that if he errs in his estimate, it should be on the
side of overstating the threat. Consequently, at times he will see
threats to the security of the state where actually no threats exist.

In estimating the security threats the military man looks at the
capabilities of other states rather than at their intentions.
Intentions are political in nature, inherently fickle and changeable, and virtually impossible to evaluate and predict.[13] The
military man is professionally capable of estimating the fighting
strength of another state. But judging its policies is a matter of
politics outside his competence. Human nature being what it is, a
stronger state should never be trusted even if it proclaims the
friendliest intentions. If a state has the power to injure one's own
security, it is necessary to assume that it will do so. Safety requires
attributing to other powers the worst intentions and the shrewdest
abilities. It is a military responsibility to be prepared for any
eventuality. The military "opinion must never be coloured by
wishful thinking. . . . The military man will be dealing with
military fact, hard figures, grim realities of time and space and
resources."[14] Military planners of one country may prepare
elaborate plans for a war with another country without necessarily
indicating that it is the purpose of the first country to attack the
second.

The Level and Sources of Military Strength. The concern of military
men with the dangers to national security leads them to urge the
enlarging and strengthening of the military forces available to
protect the security of the state. The most common manifestation
of this is the demand for a larger share of the national budget. The
same concern also leads the military to desire the conversion of
military resources (the economic and human potential of the state)
into actual military strength. The military man typically prefers
regular troops to reserve forces and stockpiles of weapons to
factories capable of building weapons. He wants force in being, not
latent force. He also desires forces capable of meeting virtually
every possible contingency. The limitations of human foresight
make it dangerous to assume that security threats will necessarily
take one particular form. Consequently, the military man favors
maintaining the broadest possible variety of weapons and forces

provided that each weapons system is kept sufficiently strong so that it is capable of dealing with the threat it is designed to meet. Since the state normally is incapable of maintaining forces to meet all or most possible threats, the military man is usually required to establish a ladder of military priorities. Theoretically he should do this in terms of the objective requirements of military security. In reality, of course, he tends to stress those military needs and forces with which he is particularly familiar. To the extent that he acts in this manner he becomes a spokesman for a particular service or branch interest rather than for the military viewpoint as a whole. No matter what hierarchy of priorities he establishes, however, his military instincts lead him to urge the state to go as far down the ladder as possible.

The military man also favors protecting the state through guarantees and alliances, provided that these arrangements increase the strength of the state more than they increase its commitments. Weak, unstable, and adventurous allies are a liability rather than an asset. Allies should be selected purely on the basis of mutuality of national security interests regardless of ideological and political concerns. "Alliances between States should be regarded entirely from the point of view of might [power] policy."[15] The author of this dictum was a German monarchist but he had no more compunctions about military cooperation with communist Russia in the 1920s than American military leaders had about cooperating with fascist Spain in the 1950s. National strength may also be increased by the expansion of national territory and the acquisition of foreign bases. Here too, however, it is essential that the expansion of territory result in a real increase in power and not simply an overextension of commitments. The military man has no desire to acquire isolated, overseas territories which are vulnerable to attack and difficult to defend.

The Restriction of Commitments and the Avoidance of War. The military man has no concern with the desirability or undesirability of political goals as such. He is, however, concerned with the relation between political goals and military means since this directly affects the military security of the state. The politician must beware of overcommitting the nation beyond the strength of its military capabilities. Grand political designs and sweeping political goals are to be avoided, not because they are undesirable but because they are impractical.[16] The military security of the state must come first. Moral aims and ideological ends should not be pursued at the expense of that security. The political object is the goal, but in Clausewitz's words, it "is not on that account a despotic lawgiver; it must adapt itself to the nature of the means at its disposal. . . ." The statesman furnishes the dynamic, purposive element to state policy. The military man represents the passive, instrumental means. It is his function to warn the statesman when his purposes are beyond his means.

The military man normally opposes reckless, aggressive, belligerent action. If war with a particular power is inevitable at a later date with decreased chances of success, the military man may favor "preventive war" in order to safeguard national security. Normally, however, he recognizes the impossibility of predicting the future with certainty. War at any time is an intensification of the threats to the military security of the state, and generally war should not be resorted to except as a final recourse, and only when the outcome is a virtual certainty.[17] This latter condition is seldom met except in the case of a powerful state fighting an isolated minor or backward nation. Thus, the military man rarely favors war. He will always argue that the danger of war requires increased armaments; he will seldom argue that increased armaments make war practical or desirable. He always favors preparedness, but he never feels prepared. Accordingly, the professional military man contributes a cautious, conservative, restraining force to the formulation of state policy. This has been his typical role in most modern states including fascist Germany, communist Russia, and democratic America. He is afraid of war. He wants to prepare for war. But he is never ready to fight a war.

This pacifist attitude may well have its roots in institutional conservatism as well as concern for state security. The military leader is at the top of one of the great power structures of society. He risks everything if that society becomes engaged in war. Whether victorious or not, war is more unsettling to military institutions than to any others. A Tsarist officer once said that he hated war because "it spoils the armies," and American naval officers complained that the Civil War "ruined the navy."[18] This attitude reflects an orientation about means to the point where means become ends, to where, in Merton's terms, the latent function supersedes the manifest function. The military man in his concern with power may come to consider the accumulation of power as an end in itself irrespective of the uses to which it may be put. He may become most reluctant to dissipate that power in any manner.

The military man tends to see himself as the perennial victim of civilian warmongering. It is the people and the politicians, public opinion and governments, who start wars. It is the military who have to fight them. Civilian philosophers, publicists, academicians, not soldiers, have been the romanticizers and glorifiers of war. Military force as such does not cause wars. The state which desires peace must be well armed to enforce its desire. Weak states invite attack. The tendency of the civilian politician is to court popular favor by curbing the arms budget and simultaneously pursuing an adventurous foreign policy. The military man opposes both tendencies. The military ethic thus draws a sharp distinction between armed strength and bellicosity, the military state and the warlike state.[19] The former embodies the military virtues of ordered power: discipline, hierarchy, restraint, steadfastness. The latter is characterized by wild, irresponsible excitement and enthusiasm, and by the love of violence, glory, and adventure. For the professional military man, familiar with war, this type of mentality has little appeal. Believing in the ultimate inevitability of war, he raises the strongest voice against immediate involvement in war.

The Military and the State

The military profession is expert and limited. Its members have specialized competence within their field and lack that competence outside their field. The relation of the profession to the state is based upon this natural division of labor. The essence of this relationship concerns the relative scope of competence of the military expert and political expert or statesman. Before the professionalization of military science in the nineteenth century, the same person could be simultaneously qualified in both fields. Now this is impossible. Napoleon embodied the old unity of military science and politics. He was replaced by Bismarck and Moltke who symbolized the new dichotomy.[20] The exact character of the relationship which should exist between statesman and military officer cannot be defined precisely. But it is possible to state some of the principles which should govern that relationship.

Military science is an area in which specialized competence acquired by professional training and experience is necessary for decision and action. This field, which concerns the implementation of state policy by armed force, is divided into constant and variable components. This division was recognized only after the emergence of the military profession. The constant element reflects the permanency of human nature and physical geography. This may be called strategy, and so distinguished from the variable elements, tactics and logistics, or it may be formulated into a set of "fundamental," "immutable," "eternal," "unchanging and unchangeable" principles of war. Military historians differ as to the number and content of these principles but they do not question their existence as the fundamental core of military science. Their application, however, is constantly changing with changes in technology and social organization. The ideal military man is thus conservative in strategy, but open-minded and progressive with respect to new weapons and new tactical forms. He is equally expert in both the constant and variable aspects of military science. The essence of his art may indeed be defined as the relation between the two: "the unchangeable fundamental conditions of good generalship in their relation to changeable tactical forms."[21] It is this area within which the statesman must accept the judgments of the military professional.

Politics deals with the goals of state policy. Competence in this field consists in having a broad awareness of the elements and interests entering into a decision and in possessing the legitimate authority to make such a decision. Politics is beyond the scope of military competence, and the participation of military officers in politics undermines their professionalism, curtailing their professional competence, dividing the profession against itself, and substituting extraneous values for professional values. The military officer must remain neutral politically. "The military commander must never allow his military judgment to be warped by political expediency."[22] The area of military science is subordinate to, and yet independent of, the area of politics. Just as war serves the ends of politics, the military profession serves the ends of the state. Yet the statesman must recognize the integrity of the profession and its subject matter. The military man has the right to expect political guidance from the statesman. Civilian control exists when there is this proper subordination of an autonomous profession to the ends of policy.

The responsibilities of the military man to the state are threefold. He has, first, a representative function, to represent the claims of military security within the state machinery. He must keep the authorities of the state informed as to what he considers necessary for the minimum military security of the state in the light of the capabilities of other powers. The extent to which he may carry the presentation of his views is difficult to define but he must recognize and accept the fact that there are limits. In general, he has the right and the duty to present his views to the public bodies, whether executive or legislative, which are charged with the appointment of resources between the military and other claims. Secondly, the military officer has an advisory function, to analyze and to report on the implications of alternative courses of state action from the military point of view. If the state leaders are weighing three possible policies, the military man, of course, cannot judge which is the most desirable. He may, however, say that the first policy could easily be carried out with the military strength currently available, that the second policy would involve serious risks unless there is a considerable augmentation of military forces, and that the third policy is simply beyond the military capability of the state to implement effectively. Finally, the military officer has an executive function, to implement state decisions with respect to military security even if it is a decision which runs violently counter to his military judgment. The statesmen set the goal and allocate to him the resources to be used in attaining that goal. It is then up to him to do the best he can. This is indeed the meaning of military strategy in relation to policy: "the practical adaptation of the means placed at a general's disposal to the attainment of the object in view."[23]

Obviously a considerable area exists where strategy and policy overlap. In this realm the supreme military commander may make a decision on purely military grounds only to discover that it has political implications unknown to him. When this turns out to be the case, considerations of strategy must then give way to considerations of policy. The military man must recognize that a wide number of conceivably purely military decisions, such as the selection of a theater of war, also involve politics, and he must be guided accordingly. As Clausewitz said, "the art of war in its highest point of view becomes policy, but, of course, a policy which fights battles instead of writing notes." The top military leaders of the state inevitably operate in this intermingled world of strategy and policy. They must always be alert to the political implications of their military attitudes and be willing to accept the final decisions of the statesmen. When required in his executive capacity to make decisions involving both military and political elements, the military man ideally should formulate his military solution first and then alter it as needs be on the advice of his political advisers.

The military profession exists to serve the state. To render the highest possible service the entire profession and the military force which it leads must be constituted as an effective instrument of state policy. Since political direction comes only from the top, this means that the profession has to be organized into a hierarchy of obedience. For the profession to perform its function, each level within it must be able to command the instantaneous and loyal obedience of subordinate levels. Without these relationships military professionalism is impossible. Consequently, loyalty and obedience are the highest military virtues: "the rule of obedience is simply the expression of that one among the military virtues upon which all the others depend."[24] When the military man receives a legal order from an authorized superior, he does not argue, he does not hesitate, he does not substitute his own views; he obeys instantly. He is judged not by the policies he implements, but rather by the promptness and efficacy with which he carries them out. His goal is to perfect an instrument of obedience; the uses to which that instrument is put are beyond his responsibility. His highest virtue is instrumental not ultimate. Like Shakespeare's soldier in *Henry V,* he believes that the justice of the cause is more than he should "know" or "seek after." For if the king's "cause be wrong, our obedience to the King wipes the crime of it out of us."

An officer corps is professional only to the extent to which its loyalty is to the military ideal. What appeals politically one day will be forgotten the next. What appeals politically to one man will inspire the hatred of another. Within the military forces only military loyalty to the ideal of professional competence is constant and unifying: loyalty of the individual to the ideal of the Good Soldier, loyalty of the unit to the traditions and spirit of the Best Regiment. The most effective forces and the most competent officer corps are those which are motivated by these ideals rather than by political or ideological aims. Only if they are motivated by military ideals will the armed forces be the obedient servants of the state and will civilian control be assured. In the modern army the professional motivation of the officers contrasts with that of the temporary citizen-soldiers who are conscripted or who enlist because of economic or political appeals. The professional officer corps is the instrument of the state in insuring the obedience of the enlisted personnel. The latter, of course, can never develop professional motivation and the sense of professional responsibility characteristic of the West Point or St. Cyr graduate. Nonetheless, the difference between the professional officers and the enlisted personnel is minimized to the extent that the enlisted personnel become indifferent to outside motivations and influences. The professional army which fights well because it is its job to fight well is far more reliable than the political army which fights well only while sustained by a higher purpose. The United States Marine Corps and the French Foreign Legion serve their governments with unvarying and impartial competence whatever the campaign. The military quality of the professional is independent of the cause for which he fights.

The supreme military value is obedience. But what are the limits of obedience? This question arises in two separate connections. The first concerns the relation between military obedience and professional competence, the moral and intellectual virtues of the officer. The second concerns the conflict between the military value of obedience and nonmilitary values.

Military Obedience versus Professional Competence. The conflict between military obedience and professional competence usually involves the relation of a military subordinate to a military superior. It arises in two broad senses: operational and doctrinal. The former concerns the execution by a subordinate of a military order which in his judgment will result in military disaster. Assuming he has made his views known to his superior and the superior persists in his order, or assuming he does not have the opportunity to present his views, does the subordinate nonetheless obey? The purpose of obedience is to further the objective of the superior. If the subordinate is thoroughly acquainted with this object, and circumstances unknown to the superior make it possible to achieve the object only through a disobedience of orders, the subordinate may then be justified in disobeying. Only rarely, however, will this be the case. Normally the disruption of the military organizations caused by disobedience to operational orders will outweigh the benefits gained by such obedience. The greater competence and knowledge of the superior officer must be assumed. In operations, and even more particularly in combat, ready obedience cannot conflict with military competence: it is the essence of military competence.[25]

The second possible manifestation of the conflict of military obedience with professional competence involves nonoperational doctrinal issues. Rigid and inflexible obedience may well stifle new ideas and become slave to an unprogressive routine. It is not infrequent that a high command has had its thinking frozen in the past and has utilized its control of the military hierarchy to suppress uncomfortable new developments in tactics and technology. In a situation of this sort, to what extent may a junior officer be justified in disobeying his superiors to advance professional knowledge? There are no easy answers to this question. The authority of superior officers is presumed to reflect superior professional ability. When this is not the case, the hierarchy of command is being prostituted to nonprofessional purposes. Yet the subordinate officer must tread judiciously in pushing doctrines which seem to him to be manifestly superior to those embodied in the manuals. In particular, the subordinate must consider whether the introduction of the new technique, assuming he is successful in his struggle, will so increase military efficiency as to offset the impairment of that efficiency caused by the disruption of the chain of command. If it does, his disobedience is justified. Ultimately, professional competence must be the final criterion.[26]

Military Obedience versus Nonmilitary Values. The second set of problems concerns the relation of military obedience to nonmilitary values. What is the responsibility of the officer when he is ordered by the statesman to follow a course which he knows will lead to national disaster? Or when he is ordered to do something which manifestly violates the law of the land? Or when he is ordered to do something which is an equally clear transgression of commonly accepted standards of morality? It appears possible to divide these issues into four groups.

First, there is the conflict between military obedience and political wisdom. We have already said that a military subordinate may be justified in forcing upon military leaders new developments which will increase professional efficiency. Should not the same relationship exist between the higher commander and the statesman? If the statesman is pursuing a course which seems to be sheer political folly, is not the military commander justified in resisting it by appeal to the standards of political wisdom? The subordinate officer "bucking" his superiors defends himself by appealing to professional wisdom. There is, however, a vast difference between these two cases. The criteria of military efficiency are limited, concrete, and relatively objective; the criteria of political wisdom are indefinite, ambiguous, and highly subjective. Politics is an art, military science a profession. No commonly accepted political values exist by which the military officer can prove to reasonable men that his political judgment is preferable to that of the statesmen. The superior political wisdom of the statesman must be accepted as a fact. If the statesman decides upon war which the soldier knows can only lead to national catastrophe, then the soldier, after presenting his opinion, must fall to and make the best of a bad situation. The commanding generals of the German army in the late 1930s, for instance, almost unanimously believed that Hitler's foreign policies would lead to national ruin. Military duty, however, required them to carry out his orders: some followed this course, others forsook the professional code to push their political goals. General MacArthur's opposition to the manner in which the government was conducting the Korean War was essentially similar. Both the German officers who joined the resistance to Hitler and General MacArthur forgot that it is not the function of military officers to decide questions of war and peace.

Second, and at the other extreme, there is the conflict between military obedience and military competence when that competence is threatened by a political superior. What does the military officer do when he is ordered by a statesman to take a measure which is militarily absurd when judged by professional standards and which is strictly within the military realm without any political implications? This situation, provided that the last qualification holds and that it is completely removed from politics, represents a clear invasion of the professional realm by extraneous considerations. The presumption of superior professional competence which existed in the case of a military superior giving a questionable order does not exist when the statesman enters military affairs. Here the existence of professional standards justifies military disobedience. The statesman has no business deciding, as Hitler did in the later phases of World War II, whether battalions in combat should advance or retreat.

Third, and between these two extreme cases, there is the conflict between military obedience and legality. What does the military officer do when he receives an order which his civilian superior does not have the legal authority to issue? Presumably, the military officer as the servant of the state is the servant only of the legitimately constituted authorities of the state. If the statesman in ordering his action recognizes himself that he is acting illegally, then the military officer is justified in disobeying. If the statesman claims to be acting legally, but the action seems illegal to the officer, then the issue is one of the relative competence of the officer and the statesman to judge what is legal and illegal. Most modern states which have military professions also have a group of specialized experts, the judiciary, whose function it is to decide such issues. If their judgment can be obtained, the military officer is bound to accept it. If this is not possible, either because of the urgency of the situation or because the legality of the judiciary itself is in doubt, the military officer can only study the law applicable to the situation and arrive at his own decision. The standards of law are generally far more precise than those of politics but less definite than those of military science. In any event, the officer is bound to give a considerable presumption of validity to the opinion of the statesman. If there are two governments in the state, each claiming to be duly constituted and to be deserving of military obedience, the military officer cannot escape the political choice between them.

Finally, there is the conflict between military obedience and basic morality. What does the military officer do if he is ordered by the statesman to commit genocide, to exterminate the people of an occupied territory? So far as ability to judge and apply ethical standards are concerned, the statesman and the soldier are equal. Both are free individuals morally responsible for their actions. The soldier cannot surrender to the civilian his right to make ultimate moral judgments. He cannot deny himself as a moral individual. Yet the problem is not as simple as this. For politics as well as basic morality may be involved here. The statesman may well feel compelled to violate commonly accepted morality in order to further the political interests of the state. That this is frequently the case, there is no denying. If the statesman rejects the private claims of conscience in favor of the *raison d'état*, is he also justified in implicating the military man too, in subordinating, in effect, the military man's conscience as well as his own? For the officer this comes down to a choice between his own conscience on the one hand, and the good of the state, plus the professional virtue of obedience, upon the other. As a soldier, he owes obedience; as a man, he owes disobedience. Except in the most extreme instances it is reasonable to expect that he will adhere to the professional ethic and obey. Only rarely will the military man be justified in following the dictates of private conscience against the dual demand of military obedience and state welfare.

Summary: Conservative Realism

The military ethic emphasizes the permanence, irrationality, weakness, and evil in human nature. It stresses the supremacy of society over the individual and the importance of order, hierarchy, and division of function. It stresses the continuity and value of history. It accepts the nation-state as the highest form of political organization and recognizes the continuing likelihood of wars among nation-states. It emphasizes the importance of power in international relations and warns of the dangers to state security. It holds that the security of the state depends upon the creation and maintenance of strong military forces. It urges the limitation of state action to the direct interests of the state, the restriction of extensive commitments, and the undesirability of bellicose or adventurous policies. It holds that war is the instrument of politics, that the military are the servants of the statesman, and that civilian control is essential to military professionalism. It exalts obedience as the highest virtue of military men. The military ethic is thus pessimistic, collectivist, historically inclined, power oriented, nationalistic, militaristic, pacifist, and instrumentalist in its view of the military profession. It is, in brief, realistic and conservative.

Notes

1. For discussion of the military mind, see Walter Bagehot, *Physics and Politics* (New York, 1948), p. 83; Alfred Vagts, *A History of Militarism* (New York, 1937), pp. 11-21; Herbert Richmond, "The Service Mind," *Nineteenth Century and After* 113 (June 1933):90-97; R. P. Patterson, "The Military Mind," *Infantry Journal* 61 (July 1947):13; W. R. Kintner, "Sound Thinking in the Army," ibid., 63 (October 1948):17-22; "The U.S. Military Mind," *Fortune* 45 (February 1952):91ff.; A. M. Schlesinger, Jr., "Generals in Politics," *Reporter* 6 (April 1, 1952):33-36; Drew Middleton, "The Enigma Called 'The Military Mind,' " *New York Times Magazine*, April 18, 1948, pp. 13ff; J. P. Marquand, "Inquiry Into the Military Mind," ibid., March 30, 1952, pp. 9ff.; L. B. Blair, "Dogs and Sailors Keep Off," U.S. Naval Institute *Proceedings* 76 (October 1950):1095-1103; Burton M. Sapin, Richard C. Snyder, and H. W. Bruck, *An Appropriate Role for the Military in American Foreign Policymaking: A Research Note* (Foreign Policy Analysis Series No. 4, Organizational Behavior Section, Princton University, July 1954), pp. 24-33, 42-51. W. R. Schilling's contrasts between civilian and naval thinking in World War I may also be extended into general patterns. "Civil-Naval Politics in World War I," *World Politics* 7 (July 1955):578-579. For pungent attacks on the quality of the military mind, see David Lloyd George, *War Memoirs* (Boston, 6 vols., 1933-37), 6:338-344; J. F. Dobie, "Samples of the Army Mind," *Harper's* 193 (December 1946):529-536; and *contra* J. J. McCloy, "In Defense of the Army Mind," ibid., 194 (April 1947):341-344. On the military personality, see Hanson Baldwin in Lester Market (ed.), *Public Opinion and Foreign Policy* (New York, 1949), pp. 118-120; W. T. Colyer, "The Military Mind," *Independent* 89 (January 1, 1917):22; Field Marshal Earl Wavell, *The Good Soldier* (London, 1948), pp. 27-28; Field Marshal Viscount Montgomery, *Military Leadership* (London, 1946), pp. 15-16; Commander H. E. Smith, "What is the Military Mind?" U.S. Naval Institute *Proceedings* 79 (May 1953):509ff.; *The Officer's Guide* (Harrisburg, Penn., 19th ed., 1952), p. 270. For a priori definitions of the substance of the military mind, see W. O. Douglas, "Should We Fear the Military?" *Look* 16, (March 11, 1952):34; Albert Salomon, "The Spirit of the Soldier and Nazi Militarism," *Social Research* 9 (February 1942):95; Quincy Wright, "The

Military and Foreign Policy," in Jerome Kerwin (ed.), *Civil-Military Relationships in American Life* (Chicago, 1948), pp. 116-120; Louis Smith, *American Democracy and Military Power* (Chicago, 1951), pp. 111-13. For literary portrayals, see Tolstoy, *War and Peace;* Stendahl, *Lucien Leuwen;* and Proust, *The Guermantes Way.* Among contemporary fiction, there is Norman Mailer, *The Naked and the Dead;* James Gould Cozzens, *Guard of Honor;* James Jones, *From Here to Eternity;* and, most especially, John P. Marquand, *Melville Goodwin, USA.*

2. Friedrich von Bernhardi (General, Germany), *On War of To-day* (London, 1912), pp. vi. On the universality of conflict, see Sir Reginald Bacon (Admiral, Great Britain) and Francis E. McMurtrie, *Modern Naval Strategy* (London, 1940), pp. 15-16; W. D. Bird (General, Great Britain), *The Direction of War: A Study of Strategy* (Cambridge, 1920), p. 1; Hermann Foertsch (Colonel, Germany), *The Art of Modern Warfare* (New York, 1940), p. 3; Stewart L. Murray (Major, Great Britain), *The Peace of the Anglo-Saxons* (London, 1905), p. 9.

3. J. F. C. Fuller (General, Great Britain), *The Foundations of the Science of War* (London, 1926), pp. 34-35; Ardant du Picq (Colonel, France), *Battle Studies: Ancient and Modern Battle* (New York, 1921), pp. 48-51, 96-97, 111, 118; U.S. Department of Defense, *The Armed Forces Officer* (Washington, 1950), p. 131.

4. *On War* (New York, 1943), pp. 32-33, 53-55; Foertsch, *Modern Warfare,* p. 24; U.S. Department of Defense, *Armed Forces Officer,* p. 131; Ardant du Picq, *Battle Studies,* pp. 39-40; U.S. Department of War, *Field Service Regulations: Operations* (FM 100-5, June 15, 1944), p. 27.

5. Colmar von der Goltz (Lieutenant Colonel, Germany), *The Nation in Arms* (London, 1887), p. 37.

6. Charles de Gaulle (General, France), *The Army of the Future* (Philadelphia, 1941), pp. 115-116; Clausewitz, *On War,* pp. 128-131; Auguste Frederic Marmont (Marshal, France), *The Spirit of Military Institutions* (Philadelphia, 1862), pp. 243-256, 271.

7. B. H. Liddell Hart (Captain, Great Britain), *The Strategy of Indirect Approach* (London, 1941), chapter 1; von Moltke, quoted in Spenser Wilkinson, *The Brain of an Army* (London, revised edition, 1913), pp. 164-165; Sir H. W. Richmond (Admiral, Great Britain), *National Policy and Naval Strength and Other Essays* (London, 1928), pp. 255-293; A. T. Mahan (Admiral, United States), "Subordination in Historical Treatment," *Naval Administration and Warfare* (Boston, 1918), pp. 245-272.

8. Field Marshal Viscount Montgomery, quoted in *Combat Forces Journal* 4 (July 1954):14.

9. J.F.C. Fuller, *Armament and History* (New York, 1945), pp. 11-14, 20-21.

10. The classic formulation of course is Clausewitz, *On War*, pp. 594-601. See also Jomini, *On War of To-Day*, 2, 182-202; Foertsch, *Modern Warfare*, pp. 6-8; B. H. Liddell Hart, *Paris or the Future of War* (London, 1925), pp. 91; von der Goltz, *Nation in Arms*, p. 117. On the limitation of war, see Fuller, *Armament and History*, pp. 35ff., 343ff., and Vagts, *A History of Militarism*, pp. 397, 410.

11. Liddell Hart, *Paris*, p. 8; Lopez Valencia (General, Spain), quoted in *Military Review* 29 (January 1950):83; J. J. Graham (Lieutenant Colonel, Great Britain), *Elementary History of the Progress of the Art of War* (London, 1958), p. 1; J.F.C. Fuller, *The Reformation of War* (London, 1923), p. 7; von der Goltz, *Nation in Arms*, p. 386.

12. Murray, *Peace of the Anglo-Saxons*, p. 13; Bacon and McMurtrie, *Naval Strategy*, p. 30; Moltke quoted in Vagts, *History of Militarism*, p. 427; von der Goltz, *Conduct of War*, p. 2; Liddell Hart, *Paris*, pp. 7ff.; Cecil Battine (Major, Great Britain), "What is Militarism?" *Fortnightly* 111 (March 1919):378-379.

13. See U.S. Army, *Field Service Regulations: Operations* (FM 100-5, June 15, 1944), p. 36.

14. Sir Richard Gale (General, Great Britain), "The Impact of Political Factors on Military Judgment," *Journal* of the Royal United Service Institution 99 (February, 1954):37.

15. See von Seeckt (General, Germany), *The Future of the German Empire* (New York, 1930), pp. 151-53.

16. "The duty of a professional military man obliges him to be a pessimist. He must be the 'no' man for idealism and wishful thinking. Unpopular as it makes him during periods of peace and prosperity he must assume that such conditions are transient, and that the pendulum of history will eventually swing back to the point where the country must risk its well-being and possibly its survival on the final arbitration of armed force." R. A. Hall (Captain, United States), "The Peacetime Duties of the Armed Services," U.S. Naval Institute *Proceedings* 80 (June 1946):781.

17. See Bird, *Direction of War*, p. 8; Walter H. James (Lieutenant Colonel, Great Britain), *Modern Strategy* (Edinburgh, 1907), p. 10. For the attitudes of the military and others on preventive war, see Alfred Vagts, *Defense and Diplomacy: The Soldier and the Conduct of Foreign Relations* (New York, 1956), chapter 8.

18. Quoted respectively in Vagts, *History of Militarism*, p. 13, and Carlos G. Calkins (Lieutenant, United States), "How May the Sphere of Usefulness of Naval Officers Be Extended in Time of Peace with Advantage to the Country and the Naval Service?" U.S. Naval Institute *Proceedings* 9 (1883):178. See also De Tocqueville's comments, *Democracy in*

America (Cambridge, 2 vols., 1863), 2:333-35.

19. See Ashton, *Nineteenth Century and After* 136:633-34; Vagts, *History of Militarism,* p. 15; Ardent du Picq, *Battle Studies,* pp. 14, 224; V. Derrécagaix (Colonel, France), *Modern War* (Washington, 3 vols., 1888), 1:81.

20. "Interchangeability between the statesman and the soldier passed for ever, I fear, in the last century. The Germans professionalized the trade of war; and modern inventions, by increasing its technicalities, have specialized it. It is much the same with politics, professionalized by democracy. No longer can one man hope to exercise both callings, though both are branches of the same craft, the governance of men and the ordering of human affairs." Field Marshal Earl Wavell, *The Good Soldier* (London, 1948), pp. 27-28.

21. Moltke, quoted in Wilkinson, *Brain of an Army,* p. 165. Prior to the nineteenth century the word "strategy" was generally employed in the sense of stratagem. Since then it has been used to identify the permanent core of military science. See Admiral Castex (France), *Théories Stratégiques* (Paris, 5 vols., 1929-1935), 1:3-27; A. R. Maxwell (General, United States), "This Word 'Strategy' " *Air University Quarterly Review* 7 (Spring 1954):66-74. For the principles of war, see Cyril Falls (Captain, Great Britain), *Ordeal by Battle* (London, 1943), chapter 5; Bernhardi, *On War of To-Day,* 1:30-43; Alfred Higgins Burne (Lieutenant Colonel, Great Britain), *The Art of War on Land* (London, 1944); C. R. Brown (Admiral, United States), "The Principles of War," U.S. Naval Institute *Proceedings* 75 (June 1949):621-33; Marshal Foch, *Precepts and Judgments* (London, 1919), pp. 215-18; Sir F. Maurice (General, Great Britain), *British Strategy* (London, 1919), chapter 2; and for a critical discussion, Bernard Brodie, "Strategy as a Science," *World Politics* 1 (July 1944):466-88.

22. Gale, *Journal* of the Royal United Service Institute 99:37.

23. Von Moltke, quoted in Liddell Hart, *Strategy of Indirect Approach,* p. 185.

24. A. T. Mahan, "The Military Rule of Obedience," *Retrospect and Prospect* (Boston, 1902), p. 283; Derrécagaix, *Modern War,* 1:78. For an excellent statement by a civilian, see T. V. Smith, "Ethics for Soldiers of Freedom," *Ethics* 60 (April 1950), 157-68.

25. The classic instances of the disobedience of operational orders involve Lord Nelson, who justified his behavior in one case on the grounds that "I find few think as I do but, to obey orders is all perfection. What would my superiors direct, did they know what is passing under my nose? To serve my King and to destroy the French I consider as the great order of all, from which little ones spring, and if one of these little ones militate

against it, I go back to obey the great order." See A. T. Mahan, *The Life of Nelson* (Boston, 2 vols., 2d ed. rev., 1900), 1:56-63, 189-91, 445-51, 2:80-92, and *Retrospect and Prospect* (Boston, 1902), pp. 255-83.

26. See B. H. Liddell Hart, *The Ghost of Napoleon* (New Haven, 1934), pp. 171-77; Richmond, *National Policy and Naval Strength,* pp. 217-30.

3

The Future of the Military Profession

Morris Janowitz

Although it was written several years ago (1960), this final chapter from Morris Janowitz's The Professional Soldier *contains many insights regarding the values and the future of the American military profession. Janowitz almost prophetically introduces the conception of a constabulary force that "is continuously prepared to act, committed to the minimum use of force, and seeks viable international relations, rather than victory." Like Huntington he stresses the military's need for understanding the principle of civilian control but unlike Huntington he does not see a loss of professionalism as the military officer moves closer to civilian values and becomes less alienated from the parent society. He predicts a number of trends and emphasizes the need for military officers to study international relations at the very outset of their careers. His discussion of the roles of military technologists, heroic leaders, and military managers has made these terms part of the standard terminology of military scholars. He stresses the need for a more realistic understanding of practical politics as distinguished from the "moralistic exhortations regarding ideal goals." His distinction between the intellectual officer and the military intellectual rings true, as do his assessments of the tasks facing these different types of military leaders. The trends he noted in 1960 toward the study and uses of social sciences and away from engineering obviously materialized, but such trends may well be cyclical since the current experience suggests a return to technical emphasis.*

—M.M.W.

As in the past, the future of the military profession rests on a balance between organizational stability and adaptation to rapid technological and political change. Military leaders must be prepared to solve, or perhaps more accurately, to live with a series of dilemmas. First, they must strive for an appropriate balance between conventional and modern weapons. New types of warfare do not eliminate older and even primitive forms. During the period in which the superpowers have developed atomic mass destructive weapons, the tempo of limited warfare, irregular warfare, and armed revolutionary uprisings in politically unstable areas has been intense. Perhaps the deepest dilemma is whether conventional military formations can be armed with tactical atomic weapons, and still operate without employing them.

Second, military leaders must be prepared to assist in accurately estimating the consequences of the threat or use of force against the potentials for persuasion and conflict resolution. The industrialized nations of the West cannot take for granted that mutual security systems against Soviet expansionism will receive mass political support, if these systems are viewed as increasing the threat of mass destruction. Moreover, as a basis for their national security, many political leadership groups in the new nations prefer "neutrality" to military alliance with the West. Historically, the threat and use of violence to influence international relations has operated within definite limits, and the development of mass weapons of destruction has drastically narrowed these limits.

Third, military leaders must make the management of an effective military force compatible with participation in political and administrative schemes for arms inspection and control that may emerge in the future. Any system of nuclear arms control would probably enhance the importance of conventional arms. In fact, some analysts have urged a return to a mass militia system in areas of Western and Central Europe, as part of the process of denuclearizing these zones. Finally, dilemmas of the military profession include the assumption that in the event of an unthinkable general atomic war—the so-called "broken-back war"—the final military decision might well rest with the side which is prepared and committed to continuing the struggle with very primitive methods of warfare.

Professional Requirements

To meet these continuing dilemmas, the officer corps has been seeking to redefine its professional requirements. The military profession, however, also requires a new set of self-conceptions. The use of force in international relations has been so altered that it seems appropriate to speak of constabulary forces, rather than of military forces. The constabulary concept provides a continuity with past military experiences and traditions, but it also offers a basis for the radical adaptation of the profession. The military establishment becomes a constabulary force when it is continuously prepared to act, committed to the minimum use of force, and seeks viable international relations, rather than victory, because it has incorporated a protective military posture. The constabulary outlook is grounded in, and extends, pragmatic doctrine.

The constabulary force concept encompasses the entire range of military power and organization. At the upper end are the weapons of mass destruction; those of flexible and specialized capacity are at the lower end, including the specialists in military aid programs, in para-military operations, in guerrilla and counter-guerrilla warfare. To equate the management of mass destructive weapons with strategy, and the management of low destructive weapons with tactics, has been and remains a source of professional and public confusion. The constabulary concept recognizes that there are day-to-day decisions from the management of community relations at overseas bases to the timing of political-military pronouncements by national leaders. On the other hand, strategic decisions regarding limited warfare involve far-reaching policies about the size, control, and allocations of military units.

No longer is it feasible for the officer corps, if it is to be organized effectively for strategic deterrence and for limited war, to operate on a double standard of "peacetime" and "wartime" premises. Since the constabulary force concept eliminates the distinction between the peacetime and the wartime military establishment, it draws on the police concept. The professional soldier resists identifying himself with the "police," and the military profession has struggled to distinguish itself from the internal police force. In this sense, civilian supremacy in the United States has rested on the assumption that its national military forces were organized and controlled separately from the local and more decentralized police forces. The military tends to think of police activities as less prestigeful and less honorable tasks, and within the military establishment the military police have had relatively low status.

In the early history of the United States, the army, as an internal police force, was called on to enforce the authority of the central government. As the authority of the central government became paramount after the Civil War, the internal police activity of the army was required to enforce laws strained by opposing social and economic groups—strikes and race tension in particular. In modern times, the army has been reluctant to become involved in such disputes, except as the ultimate source of sanctions. Such intervention, which often involves the army in short-run political conflict, is seen as detracting from its ability to perform as a guardian of the nation. When called on to intervene in support of the Supreme Court decisions on desegregation of the public school system, the army found itself relatively unprepared for such police work. While as a public servant the military automatically and vigorously complied with orders, such duty ran counter to their self-conceptions.[1] The constabulary concept does not refer to police functions in this historical role. On the contrary, extensive involvement of the military as an internal police force—except as the reserve instrument of ultimate legitimate force—would hinder the development of the constabulary concept in international relations.

The officer in the constabulary force is particularly attuned to withstand the pressures of constant alerts and tension. He is sensitive to the political and social impact of the military establishment on international security affairs. He is subject to civilian control, not only because of the "rule of law" and tradition, but also because of self-imposed professional standards and meaningful integration with civilian values. Moreover, civilian control over the military, as it moves in the direction of a constabulary force, cannot be based on outmoded assumptions that it must merely prod the military into modernization or prevent a Bonapartist uprising.

Instead, the problems of civilian control consist of a variety of managerial and political tasks. As a requisite for adequate civilian control, the legislature and the executive must have at their disposal both criteria and information for judging the state of readiness and effectiveness of the military establishment in its constabulary role. The formulation of the standards of performance the military are expected to achieve are civilian responsibilities, although these standards cannot be evolved independent of professional military judgment.[2] In this respect, the conventional aspects of warfare and military activities at the lower end of the destructive range present difficult problems for civilian leaders. The adequacy of forces for strategic deterrence and the conditions for atomic inspection and control have come to be posed as scientific questions over which the military have no monopoly of professional expertise, a fact which they recognize. The adequacy of limited war forces facilities, the management of military assistance, and the conduct of irregular warfare are questions over which segments of the military seek to perpetuate an exclusive professional jurisdiction.

Until the constabulary concept is firmly established, civilian authorities must also be prepared to respond to the pressures generated by the military definition of international relations. In varying degree, military responsibility for combat predisposes officers toward low tolerance for the ambiguity of international politics, and leads to high concern for definitive solutions of politico-military problems. Military management—of strategic deterrence or limited war—involves risk taking according to one set of premises; conflict resolution, nuclear test suspension, and arms inspection involve risk taking based on another calculus.

Finally, civilian control of the constabulary must be fashioned in terms of the kind of military service required of the citizen population. Three alternatives are available: First, citizen service could be eliminated by relying on a complete professional and voluntarily recruited military force. Second, a system of universal public service could be enacted in which military service would be but one alternative to civilian defense, community service, or human and natural resource conservation duty. Third, the present mixed system of a predominantly professional armed force and a limited system of selective service, which must necessarily operate without equality or clarity, could be continued. All three arrangements are compatible with the constabulary force conception, although each presents different problems of political supervision.

While one may argue that a system of universal public service is most appropriate for the consensus of a political democracy, there is no reason to assume that a completely professionalized constabulary force would necessarily be incompatible with democratic political institutions. The technological necessities of warfare weaken the citizen-soldier concept, at least in its traditional form. The constabulary officer corps must be composed of highly trained personnel, ready for immediate operations. Citizen reservists must be organized on a standby basis. Short-term, active-duty officers will be more and more replaced by men who are available for periods of five to ten years of professional service. Longer and more continuous service will be required for enlisted personnel as well. The trend is toward a military force of career professionals, although strong arguments, both military and political, can still be offered against such a development.

In considering the development of a voluntary career service, political leaders tend to pose the question of professional officer motivation more and more in economic terms. How much money will be required to raise the necessary officer and enlisted personnel? Studies have been launched by defense-supported research groups to determine the price and costs of converting the military establishment into an occupation competitive with civilian occupations. What will it cost to make a military pilot competitive with the pilot of a commercial air line? In the short run, the military profession, like other public service careers, becomes more and more effective as salaries are raised. Yet it remains an open question whether a political democracy should have a constabulary force motivated purely by monetary incentives. In the long run, it is doubtful whether the military establishment, like other public agencies, could maintain its organizational effectiveness merely by raising monetary rewards, and by making the conditions of employment approach those found in civilian enterprise. Monetary rewards might work most effectively for those officers engaged as military technologists. Even if salaries were to become truly competitive, the incentive system would not necessarily produce the required perspectives and professional commitments. Men can be motivated by money to undertake dangerous and irksome tasks, but the result would be to weaken essential heroic traditions. In a private enterprise society, the military establishment could not hold its most creative talents without the binding force of service traditions, professional identifications, and honor.

The shift from the contemporary partial selective service system to a fully voluntary recruited and professional military establishment is likely to be a slow process. Although selective service operates only to supply directly the manpower needs of the military establishment, military leaders see the system as essential because young men become short-term duty officers and reservists in all services as an alternative to meeting the obligations of selective service. Political leaders are reluctant to increase military appropriations to the point of making military salaries more attractive, if not fully competitive. Thus, the constabulary force concept in the United States will have to be built on the contemporary system of citizen military service, although in the long run a completely professional service is likely to emerge.

The initial hypotheses of this study concerning military authority, skill structure, officer recruitment, career patterns, and political indoctrination were designed to highlight the characteristics unique to the military profession. Each of these dimensions is crucial in assessing the potentials of the military to modify itself. The technological and organizational revolution narrowed the gap between the "military" and the "civilian" so that it appears to be less than in any other period in modern history. But the overriding conclusion points in the very opposite direction. In the end, it is still necessary to return to the original point of departure; namely, the military establishment has a special environment because it alone has the organizational responsibility for preparing and managing war and combat.

First, there is the problem of military authority. The long-term trend has been a shift from military authority based on domination toward a greater reliance on techniques of group control and consensus. The complexity of military technology prevents a return to older forms if initiative is to be maintained. But there must be limits on the newer forms of indirect control if military organization is to be effective. What these limits should be remains an area of controversy. When military leaders operate successfully, they use their organizational skills to produce stable and purposeful participation at each level in the hierarchy of ranks. This is true for all managerial leaders, except that in the military the threat of danger and the need to endure the tensions of constant alert complicate the tasks of managerial authority. As a result, the military profession is vulnerable to organizational rigidity, ceremonialism, and overprofessionalization.

Although it can draw on the experiences of other organizations, the military establishment must find its own authority equilibrium. The style of management offered by university schools of business that emphasizes cost-accounting, budgeting, and "human relations," and that has considerable vogue in military circles, is probably not adequate for the combat formations of the constabulary forces. But it is possible to assess whether the military are evolving a form of "fraternal authority"—the recognized equality of unequals—which, theoretically, would permit initiative and creativity within a hierarchical command structure. Such a fraternal-type authority would be characterized by two elements: One, the formal superordinate and subordinate roles, with little or no attempt to hide the facts of power and authority. Two, from the highest to the lowest levels, technical and interpersonal skill plus group loyalty qualify subordinate personnel for effective but circumscribed participation in the decision-making process.

Human beings cannot operate effectively if they find themselves under the pressures of conflicting authority. Therefore, the constabulary forces must function as an integrated whole under unified command. The great divide in styles of authority is between the logistical support formations and the constabulary forces. The military profession has been slow to learn that the accumulation of those logistic and engineering functions that can be performed by a civilian Department of Supply weaken the effectiveness of military styles of management. The profession seems only dimly aware that the elimination of many of these research and supply operations would, in effect, unify the military establishment and reduce the strains on authority. However, it is evident that military authority, in the most combat-oriented units at both the lower and higher end of the destructive range, has become compatible with the values of a civilian society which emphasizes technical achievement, rationality, and pragmatic ethics.

The second problem in transforming the military profession into a constabulary force is its skill structure. Skill changes in the military profession have narrowed the difference between military and civilian occupations. The professional soldier must develop more and more skills and orientations common to civilian administrators. Yet, the effectiveness of the military establishment depends on maintaining a proper balance between military technologists, heroic leaders, and military managers.

The constabulary force will depend on the military manager to maintain this appropriate balance. He is better equipped today than in the past, not only because of the improved quality of military education, but also because his day-to-day tasks develop broader administrative skills. He will have to demonstrate considerable skill in segregating the constabulary functions from those of logistical and engineering support, although they are obviously interdependent. Even more important, military managers will have to prevent the constabulary from being dominated or defined by either the military technologist or the heroic leader. The military technologists tend to thwart the constabulary concept because of their essential preoccupation with the upper end of the destructive continuum and their pressure to perfect weapons without regard to issues of international politics. The heroic leaders, in turn, tend to thwart the constabulary concept because of their desire to maintain conventional military doctrine and their resistance to assessing the political consequences of limited military actions which do not produce "victory."

Because the military establishment is managerially oriented, the gap between the heroic leader and the military manager has also narrowed. At the lower levels, to be a company commander, an aircraft commander, or an officer in command of a small vessel requires administrative expertise. At the middle and upper levels, the same office must often fuse both roles, as the most routine operations become enmeshed in political-military tasks. By contrast, the greatest gap in the skill structure of the contemporary military establishment rests between the military technologist and the military manager. The technologist is likely to be most concerned with means, the manager with the purposes of military policy.

The contents of a military career for the multiple tasks of the constabulary force becomes a third problem. The military profession has traditionally placed heavy emphasis on a prescribed career involving a rotation through various assignments in order to train for top-ranking leadership posts. In the future it will require more extensive general competence from its military managers and more intensive scientific specialization from its military technologists.

Many military technologists will be drawn from civilian universities; even now the purpose of university-based Reserve Officers' Training Corps (ROTC) programs is changing from that of supplying reserve officers to that of recruiting technical career officers. The extensive programs of sending officers to civilian technical graduate schools operate in the same direction. Higher technical specialization will result as the undergraduate curriculum of the military academies becomes more differentiated and permits some students to engage in more extensive scientific specialization. The academies will learn that liberal education is compatible with some degree of professional specialization, if students have adequate secondary education.

But the education and career development of future military managers also present the crucial problem of redefinition. Presently, the military academies are deeply concerned with whether they can adequately present an image of a "whole man," who, realistically, is both a modern heroic leader and a military manager. Can the curriculum infuse into the potential candidates for the military elite the skills of military organization and, at the same time, emphasize the traditions required for the fighter spirit?

Moreover, one of the basic findings of this study is that the strategic leaders of the past often prepared themselves for emerging tasks, not merely by following closely the prescribed career, but by their own initiative and efforts. Therefore, the problem of future career development is two-fold: adaptation of the prescribed career line to the needs of the constabulary force, especially in fusing the roles of heroic leader and military managers; and maintaining and increasing professional tolerance for those who seek to develop innovative careers by their own initiative.

The prescribed career of the future is one that will sensitize the military officer to the political and social consequences of military action. It is not true that all officers need to be broadly educated in political-military affairs, although this is a desirable objective. However, all officers must be trained in the meaning of civilian supremacy. Under the constabulary concept, even the most junior officer, depending on his assignment, may be acting as a political agent. Political-military education cannot be delayed until the middle of the officer's career, when he enters the war college. Officer education in politico-military affairs should start in the military academy where tactical training must be related to the requirements of international relations, and continue at higher levels of education and professional experience.

To develop a broad, detached, and strategic perspective, career rotation cannot be limited to any single service, if the officer is to gain understanding, by actual experience or observation, of the full range of the military spectrum. Unification of the armed forces realistically involves creating career lines which will permit selected officers to familiarize themselves with a greater variety of military weapons systems. In addition, it is doubtful whether the future constabulary officer can get all of his essential professional experiences within the military establishment. He will probably require duty in civilian agencies, at home and abroad, or with military agencies engaged in civilian enterprises, such as the Corps of Engineers who provide technical assistance to underdeveloped countries.

Rotation through a wide range of military assignments is compatible with a greater degree of geographical specialization. In order for the military manager of the future to operate effectively in foreign areas, ten to fifteen years of experience may be required. With the development of air transport, a counterpart of the old regimental system seems feasible by which an officer can rotate periodically from continental duty to overseas duty in the same area. Overseas duty would permit him to accumulate geographical and language expertise, while his career development would be influenced and molded by his continental assignments.

Such a career is fully compatible with a second career after the completion of military service. Under these circumstances, even the contemporary rates of officer resignation would not be considered unduly high, if they were not concentrated among those with the most superior talents. Rotation out of the military establishment, like professional mobility in civilian life, becomes a common feature of organization life and, in fact, assists in integrating the profession with the larger society.

Fourth, the military profession, because it has broadened its recruitment from a narrow, specialized, relatively high-status social base to a broader, lower status and a more socially representative one, has conformed to the requirements of a political democracy. Even if the military profession increases the percentage of sons of officers in its ranks—as there is every reason to believe it will—there is little likelihood that the profession will become predominantly self-recruited. On the contrary, in order to meet its personnel needs, the military will continue to expand the social base of its recruitment by relying more heavily on enlisted personnel as sources of officer personnel.

Because of the greater heterogeneity of officer recruits, social background emerges as progressively less important than professional experiences and personal alliances in fashioning the outlook of the military elite. But this does not mean that social background is of no consequence, for it still plays an important part in the complex issues of career motivation. The armed forces must continue to tap those social groups most likely to predispose young men toward a public service and a military career. Sons of military officers enter the military with an outlook appropriate for perpetuating military traditions and the heroic ideal. The military profession will continue to recruit heavily from more rural areas—although geographic concentration in the South has declined—since from this background personal inclination for a military career persists, and the military remains a significant avenue of social mobility.

Since there are no valid psychological instruments for selecting military leaders, social background from a military family or a rural setting are still meaningful criteria. Moreover, as the importance of social pedigree declines as a criterion of recruitment, the academies have resisted, when possible, the application of purely academic criteria as the basis of selection.[3] The social basis of recruitment is likely to continue to operate in selecting persons with a conservative orientation toward life styles and human nature. The organizational milieu of the military profession is likely to re enforce such belief patterns. But, in the broadest terms, the internal indoctrination system, rather than social origins, will determine the political orientations of the military profession.

Therefore, the fifth program for the military profession centers on the increased importance of these indoctrination procedures. For the constabulary force, the officer must be given a candid and realistic education about political matters. But it would be in error to assume that contemporary political education in the armed forces serves all the needs of a political democracy. Since 1945, the increase in advanced political-military education has been impressive, particularly because of the military's efforts to draw on civilian resources. But this system has had a strong built-in tendency to produce conformity to a service point of view. Masland and Radway conclude that, despite the broadened consequences, "most military schools remain service-oriented and in this respect the intangibles—the traditions, slogans, and unwritten customs—are of more significance than the formal programs."[4]

Much of the study of politico-military affairs deals with the most general policy issues in international affairs, and, in this sense, it provides an indispensable general education. Higher military education, as well as actual military experience, presses the military professional to become more rational; that is, he becomes more interested in the relationship between military means and political objectives. But this is not an unmixed advantage. The professional officer may come to exaggerate his competence in judging alternative political goals. His new knowledge may increase his professional frustration, unless it sufficiently emphasizes the limits on violence in influencing international relations. All evidence indicates that both absolutists and pragmatists—in varying degree—over-emphasize the potentials of force. The realistic study of international relations involves an appreciation of the limits of violence. Military education does not continually focus on these issues, as it relates both to nuclear and limited conventional warfare. Paradoxically, military education does not emphasize the potentialities of unconventional warfare and political warfare, since these are at the periphery of professionalization.

There is little in the curriculum to prepare the officer for the realities of participating in the management of politico-military affairs. While the case study and war game approaches give the officer a direct understanding and "feel" for the logistics and organizational apparatus that must be "moved" for military operations, there is no equivalent training for the political dimensions of international relations. The military establishment, especially the ground forces, operates a variety of special schools, dealing with military government, psychological warfare, and strategic intelligence, which are relevant, but which have as their student body staff specialists rather than future members of the military elite. No arrangement exists for giving officers an integrated training in politico-military administration.

Moreover, military education at all levels fails to give the officer a full understanding of the realities of practical politics as it operates in domestic affairs. Because it is constrained in exploring the strength and weakness of the democratic political process, military education does not necessarily develop realism and respect for the system. Its content is still dominated by moralistic exhortations regarding ideal goals. Equally important, military education has little interest in discussing the standards that should govern the behavior of officers vis-à-vis civilian appointees and Congress. There is little emphasis on the complex problems of maintaining administrative neutrality.

Finally, the constabulary concept would be facilitated by an effective unification of the military and organization of the military establishment along more functional lines. The present military organization does not permit adequate appraisal of the relative allocation of resources on the various tasks of strategic deterrence, versus limited warfare, versus the management of international security affairs. But in developing unification, each service faces a different set of problems in moving toward the constabulary concept. The air force, in particular, as constituted at the end of the 1950-60 decade, was confronted with the deepest crisis. Its organization was dominated by heroic leaders, who had risen to the top by accumulating managerial skill. The imbalance in the future will come from the larger concentration of military technologists who will rise to the very top. The training of future military managers for the air force remains a most problematic issue. In adapting themselves to future requirements, both the army and the navy will be confronted with the same issue, but not to the same extent.

Military Intellectuals

In the military profession, as in any profession, self-criticism is an essential prerequisite in effecting change. But if it is to be more than self-castigation, self-criticism must have significant intellectual content. Intellectual ferment very often means stimulation from "the outside," even though the "outsider" may be found within the profession. The rise of the military manager has meant that greater effort has been exerted among officers to keep abreast of intellectual currents outside the profession. Ironically, the military profession seems to be vulnerable to new fashions in intellectual life, even before they have been submitted to adequate scrutiny.

Although military leaders do not think of themselves as intellectuals, their approach toward intellectual activity is a curious mixture. The military profession, because it emphasizes education and schooling, has a formal respect for intellectual achievement. The military manager must be prepared to make use of intellectual accomplishments, because he is so concerned with producing scientific solutions to complex administrative and organizational problems. Since the destructive capacities of weapons have virtually eliminated trial and error, military commanders are required to do their military planning more effectively. In such a setting, the products of intellectual efforts are deeply respected, to the measure of their practical worth.

Moreover, the educated man is seen as having an intrinsic merit as well. The military leader believes that the research scientist and university professor is a dedicated public servant like himself, and, as such, is immune to the excesses of sheer commercial pursuits. The military stand in respect for those men in civilian society who devote their lives to intellectual pursuits, although there are important service differences. Of the services, the navy displays the least respect for intellectuals—civilian or military.

Negativism toward intellectual pursuits is rooted partially in the fear that unguided intellectualism produces irresponsibility. Clearly, action and responsibility for one's action are more valued than reflection in any organization where combat is the basic goal. Thus, despite its propensity to introduce technological change, the military establishment remains resistant to sudden innovations or brilliant insights which might cause doubt and temporary paralysis. Among professional soldiers, anti-intellectualism can also express itself in an uncritical veneration of the military treatises of the past which, with almost metaphysical reverence, are taken as permanent contributions to military doctrine. Another manifestation of anti-intellectualism is the reduction of complex problems to technical formulations. Ideas are judged as practical or impractical after there has been a staff study by men who can exaggerate the power of their "generalist" thinking.

In describing intellectual pursuits among officers, the intellectual officer can be distinguished from the military intellectual. The intellectual officer is the soldier who brings an intellectual dimension to his job. His intellectual quality is held in check by the needs of the profession. He sees himself primarily as a soldier, and his intellectuality is part of his belief that he is a whole man.

The military intellectual is a markedly different type. Although he is a professional soldier, his attachments and identifications are primarily with intellectuals and with intellectual activities. he would have no trouble shifting from military to university life, for his orientations are essentially scholarly. He is generally denied or unequipped for the highest command posts, as would be the case with intellectuals in civilian society. His position is essentially advisory, but in the military setting, the advisory post is institutionalized and accepted.

Both the army and navy point with pride to a past succession of military thinkers and theoreticians. More often than not, these men were recognized for their achievements long after the fact. Up until World War II, they served mainly as self-appointed critics, usually located at the military academies or the war colleges. They had relatively limited contact with civilian intellectual life, for the problems of conducting war or the role of violence in international relations were not the central concerns of university professors. As the source of their analytic approach, military intellectuals drew heavily upon history, but their outlook was derived essentially from the engineering sciences.

In the army the first figure of distinction was Dennis H. Mahan, father of Alfred T. Mahan, the naval theoretician and ideologist. The elder Mahan served for many years before the Civil War as professor of engineering and the art of war. Among his students were commanding generals on both sides of the Civil War. His conception of military operations as a complex engineering undertaking supplied the intellectual background for the emergence of the military manager. The line of intellectual succession in the army included such names as Emory Upton, Charles W. Larned, Tasker H. Bliss, and John McCauley Palmer, each of whom was preoccupied with the organizational problems of converting the ground forces from a collection of regiments into a large-scale military establishment. In retrospect, their contributions appear pragmatic, mainly professional, and relatively devoid of political content.

Alfred T. Mahan became the leading naval intellectual, and rose to prominence during the Spanish-American War period. Although Mahan was concerned with professional and strategic problems, he was more patently a publicist and ideologist. Mahan's ideas represented a mixture of Christian doctrine, social Darwinism, and nationalism. Although he led an intolerable existence as a naval officer, he became the foremost champion of naval power in support of national expansion.

Between World War I and World War II no military intellectuals rose to professional or public eminence.[5] Since 1945, the intellectual ferment within the military profession has been continuous. Military intellectuals have emerged as a distinct and visible type. Their training, their activities, and their tasks are different from those of the older military intellectuals, however, for intellectual activity within the military has become organized.

First, the traditional intellectual isolation of the military profession has broken down. One of the major tasks of the contemporary military intellectual is to maintain contacts outside the military establishment. This task is complicated because the universities have lagged in their efforts to integrate the study of military affairs. Whereas the medical and legal professions find their direct counterparts in the university community, the military does not.

Secondly, intellectual life within the military is no longer the work of self-appointed spokesmen, but, rather, is carried on by trained professionals. In both civilian and military life, intellectual activities have become more and more group and staff activities. This involves sending the brightest and most articulate military officers to civilian universities for advanced professional training. As a result, the services have a small cadre of their own Ph.D. intellectuals.

Thirdly, a shift has been under way from engineering as a center of intellectual ferment toward the social sciences, and particularly toward the study of international relations. This shift reflects a change from a concern with the purely "hardware" aspects of the military establishment toward an interest in the broader political implications of military affairs.

The relevance of social science as a basis for the military intellectual remains problematic. Social science can be a tool of detached intellectual inquiry, or it can be merely a device for supporting existing policies. In any organization as large and complex as the military establishment, social science is assured a measure of acceptance as a managerial device, for personnel selection, for intelligence research, or for internal management. But the aspirations of military intellectuals are beyond these housekeeping tasks. They are concerned with applying social science to the strategy of national security.

The most ambitious claims of general social science are put forth in the name of game theory as the basis of a general theory for managing international conflict. Game theory was originally devised as a form of mathematics, different from traditional theories of probability, which found its most fruitful application in the area of economics. The essential idea in mathematical game theory is that, by taking into consideration our own reactions to our opponent's response to our moves, we can evolve a strategy designed to make him involuntarily choose a course of action favorable to us. Such a theoretical framework seems most appropriate for international relations.

But a social science theory of international relations based on game theory appears to be an unfulfilled promise, for it has not produced hypotheses and understanding beyond common sense.[6] The point has been reached where the drive for a general theory of international relations and a general theory of conflict resolution has become a rigid act of faith and ideology, rather than a problem-solving effort.[7] There is reason to believe that the relevance of social science for the military intellectual rests with its contribution to understanding the specific consequences of force (and other agents of social change) in molding behavior; that is, in helping to clarify the relations of means to ends in a variety of concrete settings.

The ability of the military intellectual to use social science hinges upon organizational arrangements, because intellectual activity has become a complicated group activity. On the one hand, the military intellectual requires detachment from immediate policy questions in order to produce new ideas and new solutions. On the other hand, he requires access to the military elite in a staff capacity if his endeavors are to be realistic and if they are to be brought to bear on the professional life of the military establishment. Attempts to utilize the social sciences for strategic issues in the military establishment have not been conspicuously successful, in part because of an inability to achieve a proper balance between detachment and involvement.[8] Some of the most conspicuous efforts have been tied too closely to immediate operational problems. At the war colleges, including the National War College, advanced research groups have been established to draw upon developments in the social sciences. These enterprises have not been considered highly successful, partly because expectations were too great and partly because the armed forces have been reluctant to underwrite sufficient long-term support. Nor have efforts to utilize social science by means of semi-independent research groups, under military sponsorship, been profoundly successful, except in the field of economics, where these enterprises have been effectively linked with both the military establishment and the most competent university-based social scientists. The efforts of the military intellectual will remain hampered until the university community develops a more organized and more sustained concern with the social science study of military and national security affairs.

Control of Frustration

The evolution of the constabulary concept is obviously more than an intellectual accomplishment—military or civilian. In a pluralistic society, the future of the military profession is not a military responsibility exclusively, but rests on the vitality of civilian political leadership. The constabulary force concept is designed both to insure the professional competency of the military and to prevent the growth of a disruptive sense of frustration. To this end, the following requirements must be met by authorities: one, to limit military goals to feasible and attainable objectives; two, to assist in the formulation of military doctrine, so that it becomes a more unified expression of national political objectives; three, to maintain a sense of professional self-esteem in the military; and four, to develop new devices for the exercise of democratic political control.

With regard to the first requirement, from 1945 to 1960 the American military were not confronted with prolonged limited warfare and policing assignments which might have produced pervasive frustration, although there has been an accumulation of considerable professional discontent. In this respect, United States experience has paralleled that of Great Britain, in contrast to that of France. During the post-war period, the British forces demonstrated considerable resourcefulness in developing a constabulary concept to deal with their policing missions. As a result, they have contributed to the political stability of the members of the British Commonwealth and associated states. In part, the British forces have been able to draw on their colonial traditions, which sensitized them to the tasks of political warfare. The intervention at Suez, with inadequate resources, internal mismanagement, and conflicting and unclear objectives strained the British armed forces to its professional limits. But ultimately, political solutions have saved the British Army from undertakings which would have been profoundly disruptive of its professional ethic. By contrast, French political direction assigned its military such tasks that professional frustration and direct involvement in domestic politics were the most likely outcomes.

In Korea, the United States armed forces were tested to the utmost in limited warfare and, in the end, performed effectively. This is not to overlook the sense of discontent generated among many officers and nourished by military budgets which they believe are inadequate for limited warfare responsibilities. In the absence of colonial possessions, the direct tasks of policing politically unstable areas seem more limited, if not more manageable, for the United States, although commitments in the Far East present potential areas of involvement. Alliance politics may, of course, force the United States into policing actions in other areas of the world, particularly in Africa, where the United States has guaranteed, for example, the security of Liberia.

In the future the major source of potential professional frustration will center around the management of strategic nuclear deterrence. Since many responsible officers are committed to an absolutist doctrine, they still seek to perpetuate notions of military superiority in strategic weapons. An added dimension is the effort of military technologists to emphasize the suggestion that biological and chemical weapons can restore the "initiative" and "superiority" of the United States. Although the idea of extensive disarmament is likely to remain illusive, important segments of the military establishment are reluctant to take the steps that are required to inhibit the arms race. The de facto, or negotiated, suspension of massive nuclear tests within the earth's atmosphere is increasingly likely, either because they are no longer technically necessary, or because of both the political liabilities and radiological hazards they create. Some measure of limited arms control in very specified geographic areas also appears likely. Resistance to disarmament schemes among professional officers, especially of the absolutist persuasion, is not mainly an expression of career interests, although this operates. It is an expression of a belief that in such negotiations the United States is likely to come out "second best."

In part, arms control constitutes a constabulary task, and the operational code of the military must be adapted to these requirements. The assumptions of the original Baruch-Lillienthal proposals that peacetime nuclear production and arms control be joined together were unrelated to the realistic tasks of international relations. Implicitly, these proposals assumed that the policing function could not attract the requisite human resources to be effective and creative. But the detection and control of radiation became scientific problems for radiologists and other health scientists. For the constabulary force, too, policing the suspension of nuclear tests and arms control is a positive function. It will require a division of labor between civilian and military personnel;

and it will also require a division of labor between the United
States, the Soviet Union, and the United Nations. In fact, these
new tasks will involve the expertise of the military technologist, the
military manager, and even the heroic leader—for there is much
that is heroic in the assumption that these systems can be effective.
Stated in other terms, civilian leaders, in order to prevent a sense of
professional frustration, must make clear the new responsibilities
that will accrue to the military in an inhibited arms race.

The second goal cannot be accomplished unless there is less
divergence in the operational codes of the competing factions in the
military establishment. There is every reason to believe that a more
unified code will emerge because of the realities and pressures of
international relations. The actuality of direct negotiations with
the Soviet Union may force the absolutists to modify their goals;
the pragmatists will learn of the narrow limits within which their
recommendations can be implemented. Since the actuality of
general nuclear war is remote, the question of the military
operational code has real meaning in the day-to-day conduct of
"international security affairs" particularly in strengthening
mutual security alliances and in communicating protective
military intentions.

The pressure of the differing military doctrines has operated as a
form of countervailing power. During the decade 1950-1960, while
the American military posture became more absolutist, public
criticism by pragmatic military leaders was extensive, and not
without real effect. However, if these political activities of the
military served national interests, they did not necessarily
contribute to the strengthening of civilian control. In the next
decade the pressure from the military is more likely to oppose
pragmatic trends in civilian political leadership. To strengthen the
civil service concept of anonymity, discretion, and subservience to
political direction does not deprive the military of an active policy-
recommending role.

By the same token, the effectiveness of the constabulary concept,
during a period of active diplomacy, does not depend on ill-
conceived and exaggerated "psychological warfare." The growing
sense of frustration which leads the military to a search for a
comprehensive ideology also contributes to the belief that the
professional soldier should be a self-appointed publicist.[9] The

military establishment must have an active public information role—both domestic and foreign. To remain completely silent is to invite confusion. However, the constabulary concept, especially as it relates to strategic deterrence, rests on a self-conception of the older naval tradition of the "silent service."

Three, the maintenance of self-esteem in the military profession requires that civilian leadership be constantly aware of the conditions of employment in the military. The constabulary force obviously requires an adequate standard of living and a style of life appropriate to its tasks. Uninhibited criticism of this style of life by political leaders is deeply resented. A feeling of injustice similarly arises when the profession feels that the basic terms of its contractual relations with the government have been violated, as some have come to believe since passage of the 1958 legislation on retirement pay, which discriminates between retired officers on the basis of the arbitrary criterion of date of retirement. Because the military career has become the first step in a two step career, greater concern with the mechanics of transfer is likely to emerge. Officers enter private industry, in part, because Congress has passed the Dual Compensation Act that deprives the officer of his pension if he enters government service after retirement. Since many officers wish to continue a public service career, university based programs for retraining officers for educational administration, teaching, and social welfare services appear to be likely alternatives.

However, the self-esteem of the military will require a clearer public image of the constabulary concept. It is not enough for the civilian population to recognize its dependence on the military profession. It must recognize the worth and meaningfulness of the professional career, since such recognition is an essential component of the self-esteem of the soldier. To some extent, the worth of the military profession has been historically rooted in the importance of its nonmilitary functions. In the past its exploration and engineering activities have enhanced its self-esteem and given it an alternative role in civilian society. Exploration has been broadened to include outer-space and undersea activities of almost boundless scope. The military engineer can become part of the international technical assistance and military assistance programs. The constabulary force concept is also compatible with a social education and social welfare function at home for the conservation of human and natural resources.

On the basis of a professional redefinition, toward the constabulary concept, new devices of civilian control become feasible. Foremost would be a congressional review of the adequacy of its own procedure of legislative oversight. In the executive branch changes would center around a stronger notion of a permanent higher civil service, and a system of longer tenure for political appointees seems in order. But the formulation by both Congress and the executive branch of acceptable limits for pressure group activities and domestic public information activities of the armed forces is not unimportant. Bold experimentation in the political education of the officer corps is also required. It is impossible to isolate the professional soldier from domestic political life, and it is undesirable to leave the tasks of political education completely to the professionals themselves, even though they have been highly responsible in this assignment. The goal of political education is to develop a commitment to the democratic system and an understanding of how it works. Even though this task must rest within the profession itself, it is possible to conceive of a bipartisan contribution by the political parties.

The political control of the military cannot be separated from the control of the activities of the Central Intelligence Agency, especially since Congress has avoided any such supervision. In 1959 a report of the Senate Foreign Relations Committee, concerning the views of retired senior foreign service officers, included the following statement: "It is true that there is little accurate information available, but every senior office of the Foreign Service has heard something of the CIA's subversive efforts in foreign countries and probably most of them have some authentic information of this nature in some particular case. Unfortunately, most of these activities, if not all of them, seem to have resulted to the disadvantage of the United States and at times in terrible failure."

Ultimately, political control of the military profession hinges on the answer to the question: Why do officers fight? In a feudal society political control is civilian control only because there is an identity of person and interest between aristocratic groups and military leaders. The officer fights because he feels that he is issuing the orders. Under totalitarian control, the officer fights because he has no alternative. As they emerge into power, totalitarian political leaders make temporary alliances with military leaders, but, finally, they destroy the autonomy of the military profession.

Political democracies assume that officers can be effectively motivated by professional ethics alone. The officer fights because of his career commitment. The strain on democratic forms under prolonged international tension raises the possibility of the garrison state under which the military, in coalition with demagogic civilian leaders, wield unprecedented amounts of political and administrative power. In the garrison state the officer fights for national survival and glory.

But the constabulary force is designed to be compatible with the traditional goals of democratic political control. The constabulary officer performs his duties, which include fighting, because he is a professional with a sense of self-esteem and moral worth. Civilian society permits him to maintain his code of honor and encourages him to develop his professional skill. He is amenable to civilian political control because he recognizes that civilians appreciate and understand the tasks and responsibilities of the constabulary force. He is integrated into civilian society because he shares its common values. To deny or destroy the difference between the military and the civilian cannot produce genuine similarity, but runs the risk of creating new forms of tension and unanticipated militarism.

Notes

1. When they have intervened in domestic civil disorders, federal troops have encountered little opposition, except for the Pullman strike. In the past, the presence of a limited number of troops, for there were usually no more than a limited number available, has been sufficient to restore order and prevent further disturbance. By contrast, General MacArthur engaged in a relatively large-scale operation when 500 troops were used, with more than 1,000 held in reserve, in order to evict the 8,000 bonus marchers on Washington, D.C. during the administration of President Herbert Hoover. The cavalry led the way, followed by tanks, machine gunners, and infantry. The troops wore gas masks, and in a few minutes tear gas completely cleared the "Fort," where the bonus army lived in makeshift huts. Apparently, the army had been requested to

move into the troubled area without firearms, but the military authorities decided that if soldiers were to be involved, they would use guns, not sticks. However, this episode stands in contrast to the typical behavior of the army in civil disorders. When properly trained, equipped, and commanded, it has sought to limit the display and use of force. See Reichley, M. S., "Federal Military Intervention in Civil Disturbances" (Ph.D. dissertation, Georgetown University, 1939).

2. Despite the growth of reporting and control devices, it is the infrequent real tests which lay bare the state of the military establishment. The small-scale landing in Lebanon in 1958, undertaken under most favorable conditions, was considered by observers to have been a defective military operation, aside from its political dimensions. See, in particular, Baldwin, Hanson, "Concern Over Defense," *New York Times,* 1958, p. 14. Such disclosures constitute the basis for fundamental civilian review of the adequacy and organization of constabulary forces, although, in actuality, this particular instance was not used either by Congress or by executive leadership.

3. In February 1959, the United States Naval Academy announced that it was changing its system of selecting midshipmen who entered by the reserve channels of noncongressional appointment and examination. While in the past the results from entrance examinations were the only determining factor for these candidates, thereafter, school records, leadership potentials, and recommendations from principals and others would be considered. (*New York Times,* February 11, 1959.)

4. John W. Masland & Laurence I. Radway, *Soldiers and Scholars* (Princeton: Princeton University Press, 1957).

5. One noteworthy figure was Colonel Herman Beukema, who taught social science at West Point and anticipated post–World War II intellectual trends.

6. See, in particular, Thomas C. Shelling, *Toward a General Theory of Conflict Applicable to International Relations* (Santa Monica: Rand Corporation, March 19, 1959), Publication No. 1648.

7. Much of game theory, and other general theories of international relations, makes it possible for the analyst to think about international relations without constantly returning to the content of the real world. See Harold Guetzkow, "Limits and Potentialities of Inter-Nation Relations Through Complex Organizations" (International Relations Conference, Northwestern University, 1959). The task of social science is not simply to produce theories, but to increase the understanding that might come from a theory. The purpose of social science is to enhance the rationality of political leadership, but it is clear that this purpose is not necessarily achieved by developing theories which assume that

international relations are guided by rationality.

8. See Morris Janowitz, *Sociology and the Military Establishment* (New York: Russell Sage Foundation, 1959).

9. A naval commander, without previous political-military experience, served on the United States truce team at the Israeli-Arab border. Instead of maintaining detached discretion, shortly thereafter he wrote a book in which he issued a bitter attack on the Israeli government, although such an outburst by a truce officer could hardly contribute to the constabulary image of the United States armed forces. See Commander E. H. Hutchison, *Violent Truce: A Military Observer Looks at the Arab-Israeli Conflict, 1951-1955* (New York: Devin-Adair, 1956).

A rear admiral, annoyed with the impasse of the activities of the Joint Military Armistice Commission in Korea, sought to throw the "spotlight on Communist tactics," by inviting United States Embassy and service wives to observe the proceedings, although it is difficult to infer what objectives were involved. (*New York Times*, January 22, 1959).

4

Society and the Soldier: 1914-18

Sir John Winthrop Hackett

In this brief lecture, General Hackett points up the critical moral qualities necessary for carrying out the function of military service. He emphasizes that virtues such as courage, fortitude, and loyalty are moral virtues for all human beings, but that in the military profession they take on special functional significance. He examines poor examples of military leadership on the part of both the French and the British, in World War I, highlighting the responsibility of military leaders to develop imaginative approaches and to become current in technological development of weapons and tactics. Clearly he believes that many French and British soldiers who died in World War I did so needlessly on the command of incompetent military leaders. Incompetence in this field seems in this view to be immoral.

—M.M.W.

I come now in these lectures to the twentieth century, in which reflection upon the profession of arms soon compels us to face critical issues of our time. Before discussing the grave dilemma created by the introduction into war of weapons of mass destruction, there is one thing I wish to say about the purpose of armed forces, the characteristics of armed service and of those who embrace it as a calling, and the relation of these institutions and men to their parent societies.

It is the business of armed services to furnish to a constituted authority—a government—the greatest possible number of options in situations where force is or might be used. The greater the strength and variety, and the better the equipment and training of its armed forces, the higher will be the number of options open to a government willing to pay for them.

There are, of course, always limits to the amount any government will spend on defense. "How great can the number of standing soldiers become," asked a German critic of the 1880s, "in comparison with the number of working subjects, before neither have anything to eat?"[1] The same question arises today in somewhat different forms.

As long as sovereign states exist, however, the constituted authority of any one of them would be unwilling and unwise to abandon all power to direct the application of force in any situation where conflict between groups of men has resulted, or is likely to result, in violence. It must decide for itself how much it will spend, that is, how many options it will pay for.

Man normally lives in a group; he is a social animal, a πολιτικον ζωον.[2] The phrase is Aristotle's and the argument can be developed on something approaching Aristotelian lines. Anything can be called better or worse if it discharges a specific and distinguishing function more or less well. A good knife cuts well. A less good knife cuts less well. It is a distinguishing function of man, the πολιτικον ζωον to live in a society. The better able he is to do this, other things being equal, the better he is as a man. The better he is able to live in a city, the more civilized he is. But living in a group demands some subordination of the interests of self to the interests of the group. The military contract demands the total and almost unconditional subordination of the interests of the individual if the interests of the group should require it. This can lead to the surrender of life itself. It not infrequently does. Thus in an important respect the military would appear to be one of the more advanced forms of social institution.

This argument may appeal little to the average young officer. Since I am suggesting, however, that it is not only more important now than ever before for intelligent men to join the military, but that it is the act of a rational man to do so, I think I am bound to set the argument out.

The military life is lived in order that an authority properly constituted over a significant group of men (such as a tribe, city, nation, state, or federation) may be furnished with professional armed forces. If those bearing arms act in ways not consonant with the interests of the constituted authority, if they usurp its powers or dominate it, or in important ways put their own interests first, we have militarism. The proposition that militarism is suicidal has been described as "almost a truism."[3]

But although militarism may be a suicidal perversion, though war may be bad, fighting may be bad, application of physical force among men may be bad (none of which is self-evidently true, but assuming it to be so), the military life, which would disappear if violence vanished among men, is in many important respects good.

Why this should be so is not difficult to see if we look at what have been called the military virtues. These, to quote an impartial witness in Toynbee, "confront us as a monumental fact which cannot be whittled down or explained away." But the military virtues are not in a class apart; "they are virtues which are virtues in every walk of life . . . none the less virtues for being jewels set in blood and iron." They include such qualities as courage, fortitude, and loyalty.

What is important about these qualities in the present argument is that they acquire a functional as well as moral significance in the military context. The essential function of an armed force is to fight in battle. Given equally advanced military techniques, a force in which the qualities I have mentioned are more highly developed will usually defeat a stronger force in which they are less. Thus, while you may hope to meet these virtues in every walk of life and a good deal of educational effort is spent on developing them as desirable qualities, in the profession of arms they are functionally indispensable. The training, the group organizations, the whole pattern of life of the professional man at arms is designed in a deliberate effort to foster them, not just because they are morally desirable in themselves, but because they contribute to military efficiency. A digest of Cicero's *De Officiis* might well figure as a military training manual.

In consequence, the moral tone in a military group tends to be higher than in a professional group where the existence of these qualities is desirable but not functionally essential, where their presence will make life for the members of the group more agreeable but will not necessarily make the group functionally more efficient. This is one reason why officers do not always find it easy at first to settle down and earn a living in civilian life, where the functional aspects of moral obligation are less apparent and the ex-officer is distressed to find, for reasons he cannot always comprehend, a moral tone lower in some important respects than that to which he is accustomed.[4]

Mussolini said in the early 1930s: "War alone brings all human energies to their highest tension, and sets a seal of nobility on the peoples who have the virtue to face it."[5] This is rubbish, and dangerous rubbish at that. War does not ennoble. Kant's view that war has made more bad people than it has destroyed is probably nearer the mark.[6] But the interesting thing is that although war almost certainly does not ennoble, the preparation of men to fight in it almost certainly can and very often does.

Men have joined armed forces at different times for different reasons.[7] I do not see many young men joining for the philosophical reasons I have suggested earlier, though I believe that reflections of the sort outlined then may help officers to realize the nature and the value of the life they lead. Almost always the desire for an active life has been prominent among reasons for taking up the profession of arms, but there have usually been contributory motives. These have often been ephemeral in value, and accidental rather than essential in kind. Sometimes the terms of reference have changed and disappointment has resulted.

Young Frenchmen of good family joined the armies of the *ancien régime* often because they had nothing else to do, or because they were expected to do so, but very often there was also a real attachment to the concept of monarchy and some desire for distinction in the service of the king.

Young Prussian Junkers might have been similarly motivated in entering the service of Frederick the Great. Frenchmen joined the revolutionary and Napoleonic armies on a surge of national spirit. Young Englishmen took commissions as Britain's empire grew thinking that it was worthwhile doing something for the empire, and hoping to have an exciting life into the bargain.

But the scene can change. Alfred de Vigny, of royalist family though he was, joined for *gloire* in Napoleon's time, but Napoleon vanished into exile and *gloire* faded. De Vigny was left seeking a more enduring cause for the real satisfaction he and others about him derived from the soldier's life, and finding in it abnegation.

The British empire had dwindled too, and some who joined the British armed forces when the sun still had not set on government house found little comfort in the rising Commonwealth.

I suppose there are some, in western countries, who have become professional fighting men to fight communism, just as there may be some, in eastern countries, who have become professional fighting men to fight capitalism, though I hope this is not so in either case. Certainly east-west divisions are likely to persist, and if a young man has reasons such as these for joining armed forces today they are unlikely to go cold on him, as poor de Vigny's *gloire* did.

Are these reasons valid, then, or do they suggest a faulty distribution of emphasis between essence and accident? I cannot help thinking the latter. Officers in the British service do not always fully understand their own reasons for taking the shilling, and are happily reluctant to discuss the more important ones. I know one undergraduate who went on record in 1932 as saying that since a second world war was inevitable he would take a regular commission because he found it tidier to be killed as a professional than as an amateur. I hope you will be glad to learn that this logically minded man, though wounded in World War II, is very much alive (and still serving) today.

The military institution is a persistent social form. The essential reasons which induce rational men to devote their adult lives to it, with its well-understood demands and accepted risks, are unlikely to be discreditable. Our difficulty here lies in identifying reasons of constant validity and separating them from others of temporary and often dubious worth; any officer who honestly tries to do this will not, I think, be disillusioned.

I want to take up the thread again now at the point I reached in my last lecture in giving an account of the rise of professionalism in Europe at the beginning of the twentieth century.

On the ground in Europe the chief powers had four million men under arms, eight times the numbers in the early eighteenth century. Before long they would mobilize nearly ten times as many.

Wars are not started by military commanders. De Tocqueville said more than a century ago, "in a political democracy the most peaceful of all people are the generals."[8] Events since then suggest that this may be true under other forms of government as well. The advice given by the German general staff to the Kaiser before

World War I, for example, was on the cautious side. A quarter of a century later, Hitler's generals received with dismay the führer's proposals for a war against France and his willingness to accept a war on two fronts. And, in no country are the professional men at arms less likely to push us into war than in Britain, where civilian control has become by evolution fairly complete.

Even when a war has begun, it is still the politicians who play the biggest part in conducting it. But whatever responsibilities the politicians may have to bear, the social consequences of intellectual inadequacy in high military command have been appalling in this century.

While the French were ordering national defense with the urgency born of their recent humiliation by Prussia, a new and visionary trend in military thinking began to appear in France. There were protests, like those Nietzsche had already raised in Germany, against a materialistic view of war. Writers like Ardant du Picq echoed and developed them in France, and evoked wide response when they spoke of the spirituality of war. Clausewitz had already promoted the sovereign virtues of the will to conquer and the unique value of the offensive, delivered with unlimited violence. A military voluntarism began to develop in France. When General Colin emphasized the importance of material factors he was laughed at. The business of the intellect was to overcome and rule out all consideration of losses, to bring about a disregard of all material obstacles to the offensive.

Engels was one of those who knew better than to underrate material factors: "Force is no mere act of will but calls for . . . tools . . . the producer of more perfect tools, *vulgo* arms, beats the producer of more imperfect ones."[9]

Already by 1894 the basis of all French tactics was once more the mass attack. Foch, who became head of the École de Guerre in 1908, taught that the tactical fact of battle is the only argument in war and that battle demands, above all, offensive action *à outrance*.[10] In 1912, Grandmaison (more extreme even than Foch and, in Liddell Hart's words, the precipitator of disaster in 1914) said that the French army no longer knows any other law than the offensive, which can only be carried through at the expense of bloody sacrifice.[11]

Napoleon said in 1805, "All my care will be to gain victory with the least shedding of blood." How far he may have meant what he said is doubtful, but Napoleon was only quoted by the French military in the 1900s when he was useful, and this observation was ignored.

The impact of modern techniques was misunderstood or disregarded. In the eighty years between Clausewitz and 1911 the rate of rifle fire had increased from three rounds a minute to sixteen, the range of guns from one thousand yards to five or six. Of artillery one responsible French officer said, "We have rather too much of it."[12] Arrangements for ammunition failed to take into account "the appetites of quick-firing guns." In spite of the experiences of the American Civil War, Foch argued that a greater volume of small-arms fire favored the attack. Of aviation and "all that sport," he said, "It's zero."[13]

After the war Foch was to say, "We then believed morale alone counted, which is an infantile notion." Before it, the elderly theorist who had never been in a major battle taught that victory is won by a single supreme stroke at one point. Later, when he had himself risen to supreme command of the Allied armies on the western front and contributed more than any other single man to Allied victory, Foch was to say that "victory is won by bits and scraps." "I have only one merit," he said quite early in the war, "I have forgotten what I taught, and what I learned."[14]

From the very outset, however, in 1914, the French were totally committed to a policy of attack. General Joffre, the commander in chief, pressed on under what was known as Plan 17 with an all-out offensive eastwards in Lorraine. He had plenty of evidence that the Germans were doing exactly what the general he had replaced was dismissed for saying they would do, that is, enveloping the French northern flank. He disregarded this and pressed on to the east.

The offensive in Lorraine failed. Within three weeks the French had been thrown back everywhere with the loss of 300,000 men and the Germans were threatening Paris. Plan 17 was in ruins and with it the French prewar army. Very soon and for the rest of the war the western front was dominated, as the Russo-Japanese war had already indicated would probably happen, by entrenchment, barbed wire, and bullets from automatic weapons.[15]

As the war dragged on, French devotion to the all-out offensive died hard. Many men died with it, often fighting only to gain ground in accordance with the sterile doctrine that ground, simply in and for itself, gave an advantage. The French dead in World War I amounted to nearly one and a half million. Four and a half million were wounded. Three-quarters of the eight million men mobilized in France were casualties. They were mostly young men. The memorial tablet in the chapel of the French officer cadet school at St. Cyr, destroyed in World War II, contained one single entry for "The Class of 1914."[16] The population of France had not doubled between Valmy and the Marne[17] but the number of lives lost in defending the Ile-de-France had been increased one hundredfold. The social results to the nation of these losses, which make themselves more powerfully felt as time goes by, are still incalculable.

Very many of these deaths were the direct consequence not only of failures in management and faults of technique but also of error in the formulation of general principles. The French came into World War I the slaves of an abstract military concept that was totally invalid but from which they only painfully struggled free.

The British also made costly errors, not so much of abstract thought as of practical applications. The commander in chief in 1914, Field Marshal French, was a cavalryman like many other senior commanders in World War I, including Douglas Haig, who was first a corps commander and then the field marshal's successor as commander in chief. Both French and Haig had shown marked ability as administrators, trainers, and commanders of troops, with distinguished records in the South African War. Neither had the intellectual capacity to evaluate the importance of new techniques, or the imagination to break the bonds of his own experience.

French was often quite plainly out of his depth, besides being a little suspicious of his allies. "*Au fond,* they are a low lot," he wrote, "One always has to remember the class these French generals mostly come from."[18] Both he and Haig planned to use large masses of cavalry in exploitation of infantry success, even when conditions on the western front had long condemned mounted troops, used as such, either to idleness, in a phrase of Michael Howard's, or suicide. Ian Hamilton had reported from the Russo-Japanese war, when bullet, wire, and trench became dominant, that the only use for cavalry there had been to cook rice for the infantry, but he was thought by some to be insane. Haig had said earlier that artillery was effective only against demoralized troops. He had written in a memorandum to the Army Council in April 1915 that the machine gun was a much overrated weapon, and two per battalion were more than sufficient.[19] The number fortunately increased a little later on to eight and then, largely due to civilian pressure, to sixteen.

Examples could be multiplied of the failure of the professionals to realize the "terrible transformation in the character of War which," says Toynbee, "took our generation by surprise in 1914."[20] The sad tale of what took place on the second day of the battle of Loos has recently been written again. It is worth citing here as an example of what could happen.

Two new infantry divisions were committed on the morning of September 26, 1915, to the continuation of a mass attack on German positions, of which the front lines had been penetrated the day before. The barbed wire of the reserve positions was heavy and intact. For the British attack there was nothing that could be called artillery preparation. Twenty minutes of desultory shell fire, which appears to have caused the Germans no casualties, was followed by a pause of about half an hour. Then, on a clear morning, twelve battalions (10,000 men) advanced in columns up a gentle slope toward the enemy's trenches. The wire in front of the trenches was still unbroken.

The British advance met with a storm of machine-gun fire. Incredulous, shouting in triumph, the Germans mowed the attackers down until, three and a half hours later, the remnants staggered away from the "Leichenfeld von Loos," having lost 385 officers and 7,861 men. The Germans, as they watched the survivors leave, stopped firing in compassion. Their casualties in the same time had been nil.

> "Good-morning; good-morning!" the General said
> When we met him last week on our way to the line.
> Now the soldiers he smiled at are most of 'em dead
> And we're cursing his staff for incompetent swine.
> "He's a cheery old card," grunted Harry to Jack
> As they slogged up to Arras with rifle and pack.
> . . . .
> But he did for them both with his plan of attack.[21]

It is not only the battle of Loos that these lines of Siegfried Sassoon, written in 1917, call to mind. The lives at Loos were thrown away. Nothing was gained at all except a painful lesson we could do without. But there are many other occasions in four years of war which included Neuve Chapelle, the Somme, the battles around Ypres and Passchendaele, when inadequacy in command caused grievous loss of life for no return. The total of British dead was around the million mark, about half that of France where the productive and creative capacity of a whole generation was pretty well eliminated.

Let us not minimize the responsibilities of others besides the military commanders, but these have much to bear. In the examples I have chosen the French and the British each made cardinal errors in spheres peculiarly their own: the French in their failure to evolve a valid concept, the British in their failure to evaluate current techniques.

These generals were not all wicked men nor always stupid men, and they were very rarely cowards themselves. Their errors were more those of blindness than malignity. Where they failed was in understanding the techniques of their time; in consequence they could not formulate sound principles, and their handling was faulty. Sometimes, as in Foch's case, they found they had to modify radically in practice what they once had preached. Whatever their many good qualities they were often unequal to their task, and when they made mistakes the results were often appalling, with the most serious consequences for western society.

What thought, in our own society in Britain, was given in the late nineteenth and early twentieth centuries to preventing these mistakes? The army was left largely where it was. Its other-rank personnel was improving with a rising standard of living; but its officer corps was still the preserve of young men of good social standing who had the outlook of amateurs and usually were. They were ill-paid, with "half a day's pay for half a day's work," and so had to be of independent means. This meant that most were hard to teach and many were unteachable. They were not well trained and were expected to be neither industrious nor particularly intelligent. From men such as these came the commanders of World War I. As a foreign observer has put it, among the officers of the British army bravery often had to compensate for lack of ability.[22]

What a society gets in its armed services is exactly what it asks for, no more and no less. What it asks for tends to be a reflection of what it is. When a country looks at its fighting forces it is looking in a mirror: if the mirror is a true one the face that it sees there will be its own.

Notes

1. W. Wenck, *Deutschland vor Hundert Jahren* (1887), Vol. 1, p. 61, quoting a writer of 1785.

2. Aristotle, *Politics*, trans. Jowett (Oxford: 1905), Bk. 1, Chap. 2 and Bk. 3, Chap. 6.

3. A. Toynbee, *A Study of History* (1939), Vol. 4, p. 640.

4. It is going too far to suggest, as Evelyn Waugh does in *Men at Arms*, that where there are gentlemen in charge in military operations conducted under stress there will be order and where there are not there will be none. To maintain this is to adhere to the eighteenth century notion that the qualities essential in the good officer will only be found in "gentlemen," using the term, as Waugh seems to, in its eighteenth-century connotation.

5. Toynbee, *A Study of History*, Vol. 4, p. 644.

6. Immanuel Kant, *Zum Evigen Frieden*, trans. M. Campbell Smith (London: 1903), p. 57, quoting an unnamed Greek.

7. M. Janowitz, *The Professional Soldier* (Free Press of Glencoe: 1960), pp. 108-121.

8. Ibid., p. 223.

9. G. Mayer, *Friedrich Engels*, trans. G. & H. Highet (London: 1936), Vol. 2, p. 436, cit. A Vagts, *A History of Militarism* (London: Allen and Unwin, 1938), p. 227.

10. B. H. Liddell Hart, *Foch*, (1931), p. 474.

11. Ibid., p. 67.

12. J. Monteilhet, *Les Institutions Militaires de la France 1814-1924)* (Paris: Librarie Felix Alcan, 1932), p. 262.

13. Liddell Hart, *Foch*, p. 47.

14. Monteilhet, *Les Institutions Militaires*, p. 321.

15. Major-General J. F. C. Fuller, *The Conduct of War 1789-1961* (1961), p. 142.

16. Barbara W. Tuchman, *August 1914* (London: Constable, 1962), p. 425.

17. J. U. Nef, *War and Human Progress* (London: Routledge and Kegan Paul, 1950), p. 367.

18. Tuchman, *August 1914,* p. 241.

19. Cit. Alan Clark, *The Donkeys* (London: Hutchinson, 1961), p. 163. The memorandum is dated 14th April, 1915.

20. Toynbee, *A Study of History,* Vol. 4, p. 153.

21. S. Sassoon, *Collected Poems* (1947), p. 75.

22. *Deutsche Vierteljahrschrift,* 1859, No. 2, p. 69, cit. Vagts, *A History of Militarism,* p. 242.

5

Today and Tomorrow

Sir John Winthrop Hackett

Sir John reflects on the nature of war and the role of the military profession in this lecture, suggesting that Clausewitz's view of total war must today be revised. He anticipates that the role of the military must become that of containing violence in the sense of Janowitz's constabulary conception and that total war must be avoided. He calls for talented minds to handle tomorrow's military challenges and emphasizes the positive personal rewards of competent military service. He perceives the military and civilian society as moving closer together but predicts that the military calling will always maintain its unique professional character because of its special function and its unlimited liability.

—M.M.W.

After World War I, in England, we did better. A conscious effort was made in the 1930s to build up a more professional and modern army and there was progress. A more professional outlook developed, with better pay and brighter promotion prospects leading to harder work and higher efficiency. The British commanders of the second German war were, in consequence, generally much better at their jobs than those in the first, even if they were not better, braver, finer men, which on the whole they were possibly not. Most knew their business, not as of yesterday, like some of the senior commanders in the first war, but as of today.

It has, in our time, been customary to think of war and peace as though one must be at war if one is not at peace and vice versa. This

Reprinted by permission of Harold Ober Associates Incorporated. Copyright © 1962 by General Sir John Winthrop Hackett.

is nearly always wrong, and certainly so at any time when war is not total, as it was not in the mid-eighteenth century. When Sterne set out from England on his Sentimental Journey in 1762 he had forgotten that England was at war with France. He had no passport and was given one at Versailles by, it was said, the foreign minister himself, who was then actively prosecuting the Seven Years War against England. "Un homme qui rit," said the minister, "ne sera jamais dangereux."[1] When England and France were in a state of war most people continued to be unaffected, and very many would never even have heard about it at all.

All of that changed with the French Revolution and Napoleon's unmannerly intrusion into a world of limited war.[2] Through the nineteenth century, even in times of deceptive peace, forms of political thought and of professional military practice continued to develop along lines leading straight towards total national war.

We owe a great deal here to the Germans. The response to the Napoleonic challenge, which had led to the collapse at Jena, was the overhaul of German military institutions and the development at the same time of a national frame in which to house them. The movement towards national unity and sovereignty gathered strength as the Prussian army became more formidable. A military philosophy, that of Clausewitz, appeared just when it was most wanted. The Germany of our time was founded in war in the nineteenth century and tested in war as the century progressed. Bismarck's three wars of Prussian aggression established the German state as we came to know it in our time. The two great world catastrophes of the first half of the twentieth century revolved around Germany as the central figure.

Just as the last of these two world wars ended, the missing piece dropped into place and the pattern was complete; the concept of total war between sovereign national states was now matched with a technique of total destruction.

As a result, if by war we still mean total war, as Clausewitz did, war can no longer be what Clausewitz called it—the continuation of policy by other means. It is difficult to argue, though I know some do (e.g., Herman Kahn in *On Thermonuclear War*), that unrestricted war between powers of high and roughly equal nuclear capability can possibly be brought about by a rational act of deliberate policy. General war can result, it seems to me, from miscalculation, or aberration, or mischance. It just possibly might come back into play as a rational act of policy, for a short time, in the very unlikely event of a radical technical advance which gives one power an overwhelming, if temporary, superiority over the rest. War in the sense of general unrestricted war, however, can no longer be regarded as a normal continuation of foreign policy or an alternative to peace.

Unfortunately we are often the prisoners of terms like "war" and "peace." Forms of national organization are still closely related to this outworn dichotomy. In Great Britain, as elsewhere in Western Europe and in the United States, much legislation and many administrative arrangements (particularly those relating to the armed forces) are comprehensible only in terms of it. Confusion and inefficiency readily result.

What is required (in addition to whatever preparations may be thought necessary for total war) is the ability to deploy that degree of warlike effort that the circumstances demand, in gentle gradation from something very small to something that, though large, is still short of general mobilization. This is more easily contrived in the United States than in Britain. Here we are still burdened with a system distinguishing between war and peace, on the assumption that each is an identifiable and uniform state excluding the other. We have made a few makeshift adjustments, but we are still far from a smoothly working concept of partial war and partial peace in varying degrees of either.

Even if it were universally accepted that total war had disappeared entirely as a valid act of deliberate national policy, this would still do nothing to lessen tensions between men or the causes of conflict between sovereign states. War, total war, we have to avoid. Warfare, acts of organized violence between groups of men which in sum amount to less than total war, which we are unlikely to be able entirely to prevent, we must do something about.

How do we avoid total war? One widely supported suggestion is that general war could not take place if we all agreed to do away with the means to wage it. General and complete disarmament is therefore put forward as the answer, perhaps with nuclear disarmament first. Others argue that, so long as sovereign states exist, no such agreements, even with far better guarantees than the great powers are at present likely to agree upon, can be foolproof. The argument goes as follows: there is now a high degree of transferability between civil and military skills. Since techniques cannot be abolished, an attempt to lock the weapons up is not a very sensible way of trying to prevent conflict. An agreement for general and complete disarmament would probably raise more problems than it would solve. The prevention of total war, therefore, can best be approached through arms control.

I mention these arguments not to take sides but to make a rather obvious point. In the prevention of total war, whatever means are chosen, the state will rely heavily upon professional agencies in the military sphere. Neither a working system of arms control nor an effective state of general disarmament is possible without the military agent.

Still less can you dispense with the military if some discriminate form of nuclear warfare emerges. The search for it, the study of it, its conduct if it were to take place, would make heavy demands on the capacity of military professionals.

It must be admitted that warfare of some sort cannot be seen as anything but quite inevitable. No one can say in advance when or how armed conflict between groups of men will emerge. What goes on at this moment—in November, 1962? An armed force of a Commonwealth country, India, is fighting the Chinese. A United Nations force is fighting in the Congo. There is civil war in the Yemen. United States federal troops have recently intervened to enforce at bayonet-point the enrollment of an unwelcome undergraduate in the state of Mississippi. Praetorian states exist in many places and have their own troubles. Kashmir, Berlin, Indonesia, Angola, Quemoy—to name only a few—are among many places lying under the threat of force if not suffering its immediate impact.

Who could have predicted all this a year or two ago, when there was already fighting in the Trucial States, in Algeria, Cyprus, Malaya, and Kenya, or a year or two before that when there was already fighting or soon would be in Hungary, in eastern Germany, in the Suez Canal zone, and coups d'état had taken place or were about to in Syria, Pakistan, Iraq, the Sudan, and Burma? Who will predict with any confidence what the pattern of violence may be in the next few years, or the next half-century?

The mathematical resources of the social scientist may be of help here in the long run, but they are not yet sufficiently reliable to furnish much guidance to makers of policy. It is difficult to say how conflict will emerge or what form it will take. All we can say with confidence is that it will occur.

Edward Gibbon in the late eighteenth century predicted the early disappearance of warfare between nations.[3] He was wrong. World War I was "the war to end war." It was followed by World War II. World War III cannot be allowed, but its prevention will make little if any difference in the tendency toward minor outbreaks of violence, except perhaps to increase their frequency. For if you can take a club to your neighbor without bringing down a thunderbolt you will club him the more readily.

Now, since fighting is bound to take place, situations are easily conceivable in which the only hope of avoiding something worse may lie in taking a hand in it. We may well be working towards a position in which the main purpose of the profession of arms is not to win wars but to avoid them; that is to say, by timely warfare to lessen the risk of general war. In my opinion we are already there.

If this is so, the chief function of the armed forces maintained by properly constituted authorities, whether these are nation-states or something else, now becomes the containment of violence. We may thus be moving towards what Janowitz calls a constabulary concept. Within such a concept the function and duty of the military professional remain the same. His function is the orderly application of armed force. His duty is to develop his skill in the management of violence to the utmost and to act as the true subordinate of the properly constituted authority, whatever this may turn out to be.[4]

Engels drew attention to the close reflection of the dominant political characteristics of nineteenth-century states in their military establishments.[5] This correspondence has not been confined to the nineteenth century, as I have suggested in these lectures, and it is not only the political structure of a society but its social characteristics as well that are reflected in the pattern of its armed forces.

The pattern of society in Great Britain is evolving and the pattern of her armed forces will evolve in conformity with it, whether we in this country like it or not. Some of an older generation possibly do not. They may like it as little as the Duke of Wellington liked the proposals to abolish purchase. But it is the business of those in responsible positions in our armed forces today to see that modification of structure to a changing pattern in society is facilitated, while careful attention is paid to the preservation of what is worth preserving.

Where does the "gentleman" stand in the officer establishment today? I have no time to pursue this at length. A view set out in the United States in 1950 in an official publication seems reasonable: "The military officer is considered a gentleman . . . because nothing less . . . is truly suited for his particular set of responsibilities."[6] In relations between young officers and men, when consistency, firmness, and sincerity are important and warmth of personal feeling must be tempered with some degree of detachment, the implications of what is said here are just. They are above all important where disciplinary questions arise, as happens inevitably under the terms of the military contract. These make heavy demands on the young officer, who has to be made to remember that only a person of liberal mind is entitled to exercise coercion over others in a society of free men.

It is worth remarking here that as an officer rises higher in his profession the demands made upon him in the administration of justice increase. The machine is efficient but must be most jealously watched. A senior officer who confirms punishments often has the power to modify or lessen them. He will not do so without careful inquiry, to which he will also bring compassion and common sense. This can tax a whole mind and it brings its own rewards.

Whatever may be thought now about "officers" and "gentlemen," a change of critical importance in our time is in the rejection of the assumption that the qualities required of an officer are to be found only in one stratum of society. Criteria of social standing in deciding a man's suitability for officership, which have been applied for close to 2,000 years in western society, with only rare and short-lived challenge, are now being modified.[7]

The vestiges of the eighteenth-century distinction between gentle and simple, as reflected in relationships between officers and nonofficers, are vanishing. An article in a popular weekly paper[8] pointed out recently that the disappearance of what it calls the old feudal relationship, "typical of the prewar professional," is not without disadvantages. "Many officers today," says *The People*, "are nine-to-five types." The problem is to retain group coherences and a rational pattern of discipline and command without relying on moribund features in the social structure. This is a problem that the British army, as the paper points out with considerable penetration, is trying to solve.

The distinction between officer and noncommissioned officer (NCO) is unlikely to disappear. There is, however, much to be said for a reexamination of the pattern of distribution of responsibilities between officers and NCOs. It probably still takes too little account of the results of rising standards in living, education, and general information amongst people almost everywhere in the western world. The better and maturer minds required among officers in armed service today, moreover, will not be so readily attracted to it if the demands made upon the junior officer are too low. A consequent tendency has been evident to increase the responsibilities of the NCO and to liberate the junior officer from some of the duties which make few demands on the mental qualities expected in him. This tendency is likely to continue. If it results in further significant adjustment of areas of responsibility it could bring about a modification of the numerical relationship of officers to noncommissioned officers as well as of patterns of promotion and discipline.

On the officer side an interesting distinction is emerging in the British army between those who are likely to become competitors for the higher posts and those who are not. A double career structure is being set up to take account of it.[9]

A distinction is worth pointing out here between professional education in the profession of arms and that in some others, such as medicine or the law. In these, emphasis is placed on a single, long, and concentrated dose, after which the practitioner, though he has very much to learn, is recognized as qualified. In armies and to a lesser degree in navies and air forces the initial professional educational dose is only enough for the earliest stages. Thereafter the officer who gets on in the service frequently goes back to school. In specialist courses, in staff and command schools, and in advanced courses he spends not less than one-fifth of his professional life on studies intended to prepare him for an extension of his experience or for greater responsibilities. This is vastly greater than the amount of time spent in this way in the law and rather more than in medicine.

The pattern of professional education in the armed services is progressive. There is consequently no intolerable waste of preparatory effort in the policy announced by the War Office in 1960 under which those who are unlikely to rise high in their profession or are unwilling to stay in it long may leave early in order to reestablish themselves elsewhere while they are still young enough to do so. It is hoped to make their sojourn in the service attractive and to bring them out of it not less well placed to start somewhere else than if they had never joined.

Whether we have succeeded in the British army in a policy that has admittedly only lately been introduced has recently been questioned by a Cambridge sociologist. Dr. Abrams[10] says with some justification that the resettlement both of the officers who leave in their thirties and those who serve on to fifty-five years of age "remains the outstanding challenge to those who would create a modern military profession in Britain."[11]

The military profession in Britain is changing in pattern as the parent society changes. Officer qualities are now sought in a deeper section of society than they were. Educational standards at entry and at various stages thereafter are rising. Command by domination has in significant degree given way to command by management. Professionalism is more respected. In the army, the least technical (in a nonmilitary sense) of the three services in Britain, the requirements for technical awareness in ambitious officers have risen steeply in the last few years and are still rising. Material rewards are not unsatisfactory during an officer's service and although pillage now plays no part in his expectations he can look forward to a pension when he retires that compares very favorably with what he could put by in other professions. Career prospects in terms of promotions are rational and the criteria for advancement are sensible.

Improvements such as these have long been urgent. I hope, and believe, they have been made in time. Others must follow: the social results of inadequacy in the management of violence in two world wars have already been enormous and remain incalculable. Since war became total we have acquired weapons that can destroy mankind. The penalty of inadequacy was high before;

now it could be final.

We struggle to escape from this situation. Opinion tends to move between two absolutist extremes. At one end are those who are convinced that total war must come, that it should be prepared for as a matter of the highest priorities, that a favorable opportunity for it should be welcomed and even sought. Such unlikely companions as the pure Marxist-Leninist and the champion of unrestricted capitalist free enterprise (both rather old-fashioned types) can easily find themselves together here. At the other extreme are all those who see no hope for mankind except in the rejection and suppression of *all* means of war, starting with the most destructive and making a brave and desperate gesture of voluntary surrender, if need be, in the hope that others will follow.

Somewhere between these two positions you will find most of the more intelligent professional soldiers. They are more pessimist than optimist in that they see little cause to suppose that man has morally advanced so far as to be able to refrain from violence. They tend to be more pragmatic than absolutist in that they reject the inevitability of total war at one end as totally intolerable, while they regard the notions of the total disarmers at the other as scarcely practicable. They do not, in sum, see why man, in spite of his ineradicable tendency towards violence, should be unable to manage the affairs of the world without blowing it up, even though he now knows how to do it and cannot be forced to forget; but they realize that the solution to these problems demands more good minds in the profession of arms than have been found there in the past.

The regularization of the profession was accompanied by a marked rise in the threshold between the military and civilian areas of activity. Barrack life, uniforms, increased specialization in military skills, and the growth in extent and complexity of formal military administration were among the factors contributing to set the soldier more apart from the civilian. The distinction between the specialist in warfare on land and at sea also grew more marked.

As the profession grew more professional, first at sea and then on land, the sailor and the soldier moved further apart from each other, and the functional area in which both operated, the military, grew ever more sharply distinct from the nonmilitary. The development of aerial warfare in the early twentieth century led to the specialization of a third type of armed service whose relations to the other two has varied from time to time and country to country and whose future locus and function are at present obscure. All that can be said is that they are likely to be largely determined by technical developments.

As professionalization proceeded the professional was allowed more of a prescriptive right to authoritative judgment in his own sphere. Not unnaturally this was most noticable where the rate of advance in professionalism was highest, that is, in nineteenth-century Germany. Here the success of the military in ordering their own affairs and the obvious national advantages which resulted led to a widespread belief in a capacity in the military for successful organization in nonmilitary areas. They claimed the expertness of the initiate and were accorded as well a discretionary right of judgment in spheres other than their own. In mid-twentieth-century Germany the area of activity within which the military establishment is encouraged to operate has been sharply curtailed. Conversely, in other states of which all too many instances will come to mind, the effectiveness of the military in maintaining an orderly structure when civil political constitutions prove too frail to do so has resulted in assumption by the military of civil functions. Praetorianism is widespread: its growth must be watched with deep misgiving.

It is worth saying here that the degree of recognition of what might be called purely military factors seems to vary roughly with the degree of freedom of the military from civilian control. It remained high in Germany until World War II. It was higher in France in 1912 than it is now fifty years later. It is higher now in the United States than it was in 1912. It has never been high in Britain.

The movement of the military away from the civil has now in general been reversed. They have come closer together. Military skills are less exclusively specialist. The military community lives less apart. Uniforms are less worn in civilian society. The working clothes of a general in the field are very like those of a machine minder, though he still has something rather more grand put by for special occasions. All soldiers like to put on pretty clothes now and then, but I should prefer not to pursue the topic of dressing up too far, here, where I am a guest in an ancient university.

How far will this tendency toward reintegration go? Not, I am sure, as far as a complete merger. The special nature of the military calling will persist, and although the threshold between civil and military has in recent years gotten lower, and may get lower still, it is unlikely in my opinion to disappear. It is the task of those in charge to determine its optimum height, or, to put it another way, to see how close the military can be brought to the civilian without destroying the value of the soldier to society. One thing is recognized as particularly important: to minimize the difficulty of reintegration when the soldier wishes to cross the threshold and become a civilian.

I have mentioned this before and do so again only to emphasize its importance, which has risen sharply in the last two decades. Probably in no country has the requirement yet been fully met, but in every one the effort is being made. A civilian qualification for every military intellectual, or at least skills saleable in civil life, is the ideal. In this country where currently more than 200 young officers out of a small army are reading for university degrees on the army's time and payroll, and the other services are certainly doing no less in other ways, we have at least made a start.

How then does the military calling look to one who has all his adult life followed it? It is one of the fundamental pursuits. There are occupations whose demands on those who pursue them cannot be entirely regulated by contracts between men. The compulsions exerted in these occupations arise mainly from the nature of the task itself. They include those of the priest, the healer, the lawgiver, the craftsman, the teacher, the scholar, the seaman, and the farmer. They are not merely mechanical pursuits.[12] The profession of arms is prominent among them.

The essential basis of the military life is the ordered application of force under an unlimited liability. It is the unlimited liability that sets the man who embraces this life somewhat apart. He will (or should) always be a citizen; as long as he serves he will never be a civilian.

There are many ways of looking at a soldier. He can be regarded as no more than a military mechanic: a military operation can be considered as just another engineering project. This is a mistake. It can lead to unfortunate results when the unlimited liability clause in the unwritten contract is invoked as the operation unfolds.

He can be regarded, rather emotionally and too simply, as a

hired assassin. Only those who do not know many soldiers can maintain this view with confidence. If soldiers were only paid killers their calling would have done something to them that you can look for in vain.

The soldier can be thought of as one of de Vigny's great shaggy dogs of grenadiers—mournful, sweet-tempered, and doomed. He has been romanticized, reviled, esteemed, and derided.

He has been the target of some of the best invective: Voltaire's[13] for example, or Shaw's. I particularly recommend the preface to *John Bull's Other Island (Down with the soldier)* as sane and refreshing reading for the regular officer. To see how far Shaw is wrong today is as important as to see how far he is still right, and to make sure we continue to steer the profession of arms away from his picture of it. Shaw is as angry as Voltaire and for the same reason: man obstinately remains what he is and declines to become what the radical reformer thinks he ought to be. The very existence of the profession of arms is a constant reminder that this is so and the rancor it sometimes arouses in the radical breast is easily understood.

The man at arms is different things at different times to the same people. "Our God and soldiers we alike adore/Ev'n at the brink of danger; not before."[14] He can be looked at in a thousand different ways, for he is an inevitable phenomenon in human society. More poetry has been written about him and his doings than about anything else on earth.

In his professional environment he lives an ordered life. It is the sort of life which Cicero admired, lived *ordine et modo*.[15] Its orderliness is liberating rather than oppressive. It is far from incompatible with Christianity. The record of the actions of Jesus Christ in the gospels shows him forbearing to soldiers, even kind. He was rough with politicians, lawyers, financiers professors, and divines.

There is a satisfaction in service, in an ordered life, in the progressive mastery of complex skills, and in professional association with men of a high average level of integrity. But the service has to be service to what is worthwhile, and the ordered life has to lead somewhere. The professional skills must be interesting and around them must be a wide area of choice in other pursuits. It is upon these points that the young man considering armed service must satisfy himself. I do not think he will be disappointed.

The primary function of an armed force is to fight in battle. This is nowadays impossible without a highly complex system of supporting activities. Among these a man may find not only the chance of self-fulfillment in a closely coherent group of human beings, where confidence is generally high and everyone receives from others what he is prepared to give; he will also be offered an opportunity for nearly every pursuit that appeals to the rational man.

I know only one general now serving on the Army Council who has had a picture hung in the academy, but there are many generals who paint. I do not know any generals who are first class interpreters in Russian, Arabic, or classical Cantonese, but almost any young officer able and willing to do so may study a language for two or three years and will often spend some of this time abroad at his employer's expense. If he is of unusual capacity as a scientist he might find himself, after a first at Cambridge or London, reading for a doctorate. The young officer can paint, sail boats, play a musical instrument, join an expedition, learn mathematics, bundle down the Cresta—help himself in short to a variety of pursuits active or reflective, not as things he has to struggle to do but as things the system in which he has made his life encourages and sometimes even helps to pay for.

Make no mistake about it: the military establishment is not a philanthropic body. It has good reason to encourage these pursuits. First, there are skills (and a very wide range of them) whose availability in armed forces is deemed important. Secondly, there are activities that develop the mental, moral, and physical qualities required in the efficient fighting man. Thirdly, the life must be attractive to the right young men if the function of armed forces is to be efficiently discharged. The things I speak of as examples fall under one or more of these heads, most under all three.

Some men are dissatisfied if they are too far separated from the earth upon which they live and what happens on and around it. I realized myself as a young officer that I should not have been content doing anything for a living in which it was never important to me what time the sun rose. Dawn, dusk, moonrise and moonset, what the wind does, the shape and size of woodland, marsh, and hill, currents and tides, the flow of rivers and the form of clouds, whether the leaf is on the tree or the branches are bare, the seasons, the weather, and the stars—these are matters of compelling importance in the lives of sailors, soldiers, airmen, some of more importance to one, some to another; and so, too, at all times and above all, are people.

In measuring the worth of any way of life a study of its average products will not tell you what you want to know. Those who display its essential characteristics in exceptional degree are more informative, a Colonel Newcombe, let us say, or a Jos. Sedley. Perhaps even more misleading than to regard the average is to look only at the worst. To see how bad men can be in any profession is to learn little about it worth knowing. Ask instead what opportunities it gives the μεγάθυμοι.

The profession of arms is an essential social institution offering an orderly way of life, set a little apart, not without elegance. "The performance of public duty is not the whole of what makes a good life," said Bertrand Russell, in language that would have pleased Cicero; "there is also the pursuit of private excellence."[16] Both are to be found in the military life. It gives much and takes more, enriching freely anyone prepared to give more than he gets. It will remain with us for as long as man continues to be what he is, too clever and not good enough. This looks like a long time yet.

Notes

1. Sterne, *A Sentimental Journey* (1768), p. 120 ff.

2. "It was reserved to the genius of Napoleon to make unmannerly war." Bulow, cit. Alfred Vagts, *A History of Militarism* (London: Allen and Unwin, 1938), p. 91.

3. See Edward Gibbon, *The History of the Decline and Fall of the Roman Empire,* ed. Smith (1854), Vol. 4, p. 405 ff.

4. It would be idle to pretend that a dilemma cannot arise here. After the fall of France, the French forces in Syria and Lebanon, the Troupes françaises du Levant, fought the British, their former allies, who were prosecuting the war against Germany. They did this on the orders of a metropolitan government: it had capitulated, but their duty as professionals still lay to a government whose legitimacy they could not question. Many German professional officers who detested Nazism were

unable to deny that legitimate authority in Germany lay with the Nazis. They therefore continued to fight against the allies, in whose victory lay the only hope for Germany, as many knew. They were, of course, much helped in their confusion by the insistence of the allies that the German nation, and not only the German government, was their enemy.

5. *Putnam's Monthly* (New York: 1855), Vol. 6, pp. 193-206 and 306-331. Cit. Rapoport, "A Comparative Theory of Military and Political Types," in *Changing Patterns of Military Politics*, ed. S. P. Huntington (Glencoe, Ill.: Free Press of Glencoe, 1962), p. 71.

6. *The Armed Forces Officer* (Washington: Department of Defense, 1950), p. 4, cit. Morris Janowitz, *The Professional Soldier* (Glencoe, Ill.: Free Press of Glencoe, 1960), p. 219.

7. Janowitz, *The Professional Soldier*, p. 79 is interesting on this point.

8. *The People*, July 1, 1962, p. 10.

9. Defense White Paper, 1960.

10. "Democracy, Technology, and the Retired British Officer," in Huntington, *Changing Patterns*, p. 150.

11. Dr. Abrams has offered an interesting and valuable comment on the new pattern of retirement of the British officer; he suggests that the sort of occupations found for the admittedly impressive numbers of officers already resettled is unlikely to attract young men to join the armed forces, and draws the conclusion "that there is no better way to get to the top of English society than to start there." But useful though this analysis is, it has neglected to emphasize that the policy has been in operation for a very short time, and the material for resettlement is pretty well exclusively the product of an earlier period, when less thought was given to resettlement. He has gone, as it were, for evidence on animal behaviour more to the dead animal than the living, more to South Kensington than Whipsnade.

12. I should be inclined to describe them as *abanausic*.

13. See *Candide*, passim.

14. Francis Quarles, *Epigram*.

15. Cicero, *De Officiis*, Bk. 1, Chap. 5, Sec. 15-17.

16. Bertrand Russell, *Authority and the Individual* (Reith Lectures, 1948-49), 1949, p. 111.

6

The Military in the Service of the State

Sir John Winthrop Hackett

This paper by Lt.-General Sir John Winthrop Hackett was delivered as the Harmon Memorial Lecture at the United States Air Force Academy in October 1970. Hackett pursues the theme here that the relationship between the military and the state in the twentieth century must be analyzed in terms of the nature of war and peace in this century. He suggests that previous American conceptions of the nature of war and the role of the military in the state were anti-Clausewitzian, but the structure of war from the Korean conflict on has required a different view. He points up the various consequences that ensued in World War II as a result of differing philosophies regarding war and politics. He maintains that the world situation today is such that total war must not be allowed to occur but that limited wars will continue to occur; war and peace will once more coexist. He reflects on the controversy between MacArthur and Truman, reaffirming the principle of civilian control of the military and making a number of astute observations about the proper placement of loyalty. He describes the ethical strains that military professionals must encounter and offers important reflections on the role that moral qualities play in the very function of the military.

—M.M.W.

I am much honored by the invitation to address this distinguished gathering tonight, and my wife and I are deeply indebted to our hosts for their hospitality and for the opportunity to visit this beautiful and remarkable place. My topic tonight is one upon which much has already been said. It might reasonably be asked whether anything omitted from the distinguished writings of men like Samuel Huntington, Hanson Baldwin, Spanier, Clark, Legere, Coles, Ralston, Higgins, to name only a few, as well of course as those very distinguished men, Theodore Ropp and Forrest C. Pogue, and my own good friend and countryman Michael Howard, who have also enjoyed your hospitality on similar occasions—whether anything omitted by them has sufficient importance to justify a transatlantic journey to say it. But times and perspectives change. It is perhaps worthwhile to ask, from a point in time now well advanced in a century that has seen swifter change in human affairs than any since the world began, what the relationship between the military and the state looks like today, what changes have taken place in it in our time, and what factors are at work leading to further change. To try to be exhaustive would be to succeed only in exhausting patience. I propose therefore only to outline a basic position and suggest broadly how it has developed up to our time, to point to some of the factors bearing in a novel way upon the relationship between the military and the state in the second half of our century and to ask what their effect might be, and finally to consider some ethical aspects of the relationship.

Until man is a great deal better than he is, or is ever likely to be, the requirement will persist for a capability which permits the ordered application of force at the instance of a properly constituted authority. The very existence of any society depends in the last resort upon its capacity to defend itself by force.

"Covenants without swords are but words," said Thomas Hobbes 300 years ago. This is no less true today. Government thus requires an effective military instrument bound to the service of the state in a firm obligation.

The obligation was at one time uniquely personal. Later it developed into an obligation to a person as the recognized head of a human group—a tribe, a clan, a sect, or a nation. The group develops in structure, acquires associations and attributes (including territoriality) in a process occurring in different ways at different times in different places. The polis emerges in ancient Greece. King John is found in medieval England describing himself on his seal, the first of English kings to do so, as Rex

Angliae, King of England, and no longer Rex Anglorum, King of the English. The state is born. In western Europe statehood had by the mid-thirteenth century largely replaced the concept of an all-embracing Christendom as the basic political structure. Military service continued, however, to be rendered as an obligation to a person, to the single ruler, or to the monarch, and the personal link has persisted in one form or another right up to today.

As we leave the Middle Ages behind, the military profession emerges, clearly distinguished from other institutions. Continuous service, regular pay, uniforms, segregation in barracks, the revival and improvement of ancient military formations such as the Roman Legion, the development of tactics, the introduction of better materials and techniques and of firearms, more attention to logistics—these and other developments had by the early eighteenth century given to the calling of the man-at-arms a clearly distinguishable profile as the lineal antecedent of the military profession we know today. The eighteenth century regularized this calling; the nineteenth professionalized it. From the late nineteenth century onwards, armed force was available to the governments of all advanced states through the medium of military institutions everywhere broadly similar in structure and essentially manned—and wholly managed—by professionals. The soldier and the statesman were by now no longer interchangeable, the subordination of military to civil was, in theory everywhere and in your country and mine in fact as well, complete.

The Napoleonic experience led not only to the complete professionalization of the military calling; by reducing to a system the basic concept of the French revolutionary armies, it opened up the era of the nation-in-arms and thus of total war. In the eighteenth century, wars were conducted by a relatively small sample of the nation's manpower applying a relatively small proportion of the nation's wealth. The nineteenth century led to the situation in which the totality of a nation's resources in men and materials was applied to conflicts that similarly mobilized all other belligerents. In the eighteenth century, war and peace could to some extent coexist. England and France were at war when the writer Sterne received his passport to travel in France from the French ambassador in London himself, with the words, "A man who laughs is never dangerous."[1] Odd vestiges of the coexistence war and peace persisted even into the nineteenth century: George Washington's investment account was handled by Barings of London throughout the Revolutionary War; and Russia, seventy years later, helped to finance the Crimean War against France, Turkey, and Britain by means of loans raised in London. But by quite early in the twentieth century, war and peace had come to be mutually exclusive concepts and could coexist no longer.

A century and a half after Napoleon we seem to have reverted in some respects to the position evident before him. Total war is now unacceptable, total peace is apparently unobtainable. The world lives in a state between the two: war and peace again now coexist.

With the military institution professionalized, regularized, and seen to be subordinate to the civil power, what was its sphere of operation and to what or whom was it ultimately responsible? Clausewitz declared that war was the continuance of policy by other means. Military action in war must always be governed by political requirements.

But some who have accepted that the state is master have not always accepted that the statesmen are the masters, or have done so with extreme reluctance. "I can't tell you how disgusted I am becoming with those wretched politicians," said General George McClellan in October 1861[2]—a sentiment that has possibly been echoed more than once since then. On at least one important occasion in recent years, hostility and distrust have erupted into something near open insubordination.

The principles formulated by Clausewitz have not been accepted as binding at all times everywhere. In Germany in World War I, the army under the control of Hindenburg and Ludendorff, became "a state within the state claiming the right to define what was or was not to the national interest."[3] The supreme command reserved to itself the right of defining Germany's war aims.

The history of the United States in our time has also afforded instances of tendencies to operate in a sense opposed to the concepts set out by Clausewitz. The case of General MacArthur is important here and I shall return to it later. But in quite another respect the approach of the United States to military/civil relationships up to the middle of our century could be described as anti-Clausewitzian.

Let us look at the spring of the year 1945 as events drove swiftly on to military defeat of Germany. In spite of agreement between the Allies on postwar areas of occupation, "It was well understood by everyone," as Winston Chruchill wrote, "that Berlin, Prague, and Vienna could be taken by whoever got there first."[4] The Supreme Allied Commander, writes Forrest C. Pogue, "halted his troops short of Berlin and Prague for military reasons only." As General Eisenhower himself said of this time, "Military plans, I believed, should be devised with the single aim of speeding victory."[5]

General Eisenhower recognized that Berlin was the political heart of Germany. General Bradley, however, in opposing the British plan for an all-out offensive directed on the capital, described Berlin as no more than "a prestige objective," though he frankly conceded later that: "As soldiers we looked naively on the British inclination to complicate the war with political foresight and nonmilitary objectives."[6]

Here lies the crucial difference between two philosophies. The one holds that war *replaces* politics and must be conducted by purely military criteria towards purely military ends. When war has been ended by the enemy's military defeat, political action can once more take over from the military. The other maintains that war *continues* policy and is conducted *only* to a political end, that in grand strategy purely military criteria and objectives do not exist, and that military action must at all times be governed by political considerations arising out of clearly defined war aims. Under the first concept the only war aim is to win the war and to do this as quickly as possible. Under the second the prime aim in war is to win the peace. A policy of unconditional surrender is not a war aim at all, but the acknowledgement of the lack of one.

There were of course towards the end of World War II problems of national sensitivity within the alliance which complicated issues. It would be wrong now to oversimplify them. Nevertheless, whereas Churchill asked at the time whether the capture of Berlin by the Russians would not "lead them into a mood which will raise grave and formidable difficulties for the future,"[7] the U.S. Chiefs of Staff were of the opinion that such "psychological and political advantages as would result from the possible capture of Berlin ahead of the Russians should not override the imperative military consideration, which in our opinion is the destruction and dismemberment of the German armed forces." There is no evidence whatsoever that General Eisenhower at any time put American national interests above those of the British. There is plenty of evidence that he acknowledged the complete priority in importance of the general political interest over the military. "I am the first to admit," he said, "that a war is waged in pursuance of political aims, and if the Combined Chiefs of Staff should decide that the Allied effort to take Berlin outweighs purely military considerations in this theater, I would cheerfully readjust my plans and my thinking so as to carry out such an operation."[8] The Combined Chiefs gave him no other instructions on this critically important point than to make his own dispositions. The new president of the United States, Harry S Truman, cabled Churchill on 21 April 1945 that "the tactical deployment of American troops is a military one."[9]

On 2 May 1945, with the Allied troops still halted according to their orders from SHAEF on or about the Elbe, the Russians completed the capture of Berlin. On 12 May, with the Allies halted on orders from the same source to the north and west of Prague, the Russians entered Prague too. I do not think I need dwell now on the consequences of these events or their effect upon the history of our own time. Let me only add a warning against oversimplification. The record stands as quoted. The Yalta agreement, however, is also on the record and it is not easy to see how the Allies could have stayed in Berlin and Prague even if they had got there first.

The decisions which led to the course of events I have outlined here were in general wholly consistent with U.S. attitudes up to the mid-twentieth century. The national ethic was not greatly in favour of the application of armed force to a political end. It is true that the United States had been involved in limited wars (like the Spanish-American and that of 1812-14 with Britain) and in wars against the Indians which could scarcely be justified on grounds either of absolute morality or of national survival. But the nation has in general been reluctant to fight except when there was clear and compelling danger of national overthrow or a violation of the moral code the nation followed—a violation so grave and flagrant as to demand correction. It has then suspended normal peacetime procedures wherever the military imperative demanded, thrown its whole weight into the crushing of opposing armed force as speedily as possible and, this accomplished, returned with relief to its own way of life.

From this concept there developed a division of responsibility of which a classic exposition is quoted by Morton from an Army War College statement of September 1915. "The work of the statesman and the soldier are therefore coordinate. Where the first leaves off the other takes hold."[10]

The middle years of our century, however, have seen changes that have profoundly affected the relations of military and civil and have set up a new situation. Of developments in military practice, the introduction of weapons of mass destruction is the most obvious, but it is not the only one. Improved and new techniques and materials abound and have been applied not only in all aspects of weaponry but over the whole range of tools for war. Developments in metals, ceramics, plastics; new sources of energy; new forms of propulsion; new techniques in the electric and electronic fields; laser beams and infrared; the startling developments in solid state physics which have revolutionized communications and control systems—these are only a few examples chosen at random from a list any military professional could almost indefinitely extend. What has been happening in space needs no emphasis, nor does the dramatic rise in powers of surveillance. The flow of information from all sources has vastly increased and the application of automatic processes to its handling has opened a new dimension.

There are other developments than those in the hardware departments. International alignments have changed. The United States has replaced Britain in important traditional roles; Russia has been reborn; China has emerged as a major power. The Third World has grown up out of disintegrating colonial empires— British, French, Belgian, Dutch—and stresses have developed in the international community no less than at home as the rich are seen to get richer much more quickly than the poor do. International relations have grown more complex with the demise of bipolarity. The Russians have moved further from strict Marxism at home and have developed a striking potential for armed action at a distance abroad. The failure hitherto of yet another attempt to establish a world community of nations in the

United Nations has been accompanied by a growing impatience worldwide with warfare as a means of settling social problems, while there has been no decline at all in the resort to warfare. There has been a surge of interest everywhere in the study of defense problems, an interest which springs, in my view, from a basic realization that what is at stake is nothing less than human survival. There has been much striving towards international agreement to take account of the new situation, and some of it not unpromising—the Test Ban Treaty, for instance, and SALT. The American relationship with Europe has changed and is changing further. These are only some of the more important developments in the field of external relations.

Here in the United States you have seen an increase in centralized authority and a closer scrutiny of the decision-making process in relation to national security. The risks of the nuclear age and the complexity of international issues have resulted in a day-to-day involvement of the executive in external affairs, with all their military implications, far greater than in the past. The reason for this, as well as for the development of defense analysis into a considerable industry, lies in the imperatives of nuclear weapon power. Armed forces cannot now be brought into being more or less at leisure after the crisis breaks, as was formerly possible for America beyond the oceans, and for Britain, protected by her navy, when Britain could afford to be content to lose every battle but the last. For in general and unrestricted war the last battle is now the first, and we know that it cannot be won. Thus it is vital not to let the war take place at all, and deterrence becomes the major element in defense. But deterrence demands an apparatus sufficient in size and performance, always up to date, always at a high state of readiness, but never used and never even fully tested. It is therefore quite inevitable that the military agency will be closely and continuously monitored by its civil masters.

From all these and other developments, the civil/military relationship now finds itself in a new frame of reference. I select two important elements in this new environment for further comment.

First of all there is the enormous rise in the cost of warlike material since World War II and the huge increase in the burden on national resource, in money, materials, and skilled manpower, which preparation for war demands. President Eisenhower spoke of the growing significance of a military/industrial complex. General MacArthur among others drew attention to the ruinous cost of preparation for war, as distinct from the cost of its conduct. The demands of the military upon national resource, in times when a world war is *not* being fought, can be so great that the whole orientation of national policy, not only abroad but at home as well, can be determined by them. The danger of the formal supersession of civil authority by the military can today in our two democracies be dismissed as negligible. National resource, however, whatever its size, is limited. Money spent on space exploration cannot be spent on slum clearance. Money spent on the containment of pollution cannot be used for an antiballistic missile system. Even if the usurpation of civil government by the military is no longer to be feared, the orientation of policies, particularly at home, which might be forced upon the state by demands upon material resource, money, and skilled industrial, technical, and other manpower, could place the military in a position of dominance scarcely less decisive in this event than formal usurpation of powers of government.

In a pamphlet published in Britain this month, J. K. Galbraith speaks of the growth of a huge bureaucratic organization of defense contractors and politicians acting with service advice. It began to grow, to use Galbraith's arresting phrase, before poverty was put on the national agenda. The danger that the military, through the demands upon resource of the military/industrial complex, would exercise too powerful an influence over the state was never high in postwar Britain. Professor Galbraith suggested to me last week in England that the British tradition of civil supremacy was probably too powerful to allow it. There are other, simpler reasons. The world wars which greatly enriched the United States greatly impoverished the United Kingdom. Britain was made very sharply aware at the end of World War II that drastic reduction in national resource demanded a drastic review of spending priorities. Over the postwar years Britain has asserted and confirmed priorities in which social spending went ahead of expenditure on defense. In the past few years, for the first time ever, less has been spent in Britain on defense, for example, than on education.

In the United States, where resource was so much greater, the realization came later that resource, however great, was not unlimited. Hard priorities have had to be drawn and as this disagreeable task was faced, perhaps a little reluctantly, the demands of some other claimants on national resources have had to be heard.

My own view is that the danger of unbalancing the relationship between military and state through inordinate demand upon national resource was never great in Britain; and now in the United States, as national priorities come under review, it is on the decline. There is, however, an aspect of civil/military relations to which we are not yet, I think, wholly accommodated.

Of crucial importance in this relationship between armed forces and the state is atomic weapon power. It is a commonplace now that total war is no longer a rational act of policy. George Kennan saw this earlier than most when he wrote in 1954, "People have been accustomed to saying that the day of limited war is over. I would submit that the truth is exactly the opposite: that the day of total wars has passed, and that from now on limited military operations are the only ones that could conceivably serve any coherent purpose."[11] The implications of this situation have not been fully accepted everywhere. The concept of the nation-in-arms is no longer viable in major powers and we have to think of national security in other terms. But in what terms?

The introduction of atomic weapons has thrown new light upon a hallowed principle of Clausewitz's. "As war . . .," he wrote, "is dominated by the political object the order of that object determines the measure of the sacrifice by which it is to be purchased. As soon, therefore, as the expenditure in force becomes so great that the political object is no longer equal in value this object must be given up, and peace will be the result."[12]

Into an equation that Clausewitz saw in relative terms, atomic weapons have now introduced an absolute. Can *any* political object be secured by the opening of a nuclear war which devastates both sides? Hence, of course, the whole language of brinkmanship in a situation in which one object—survival—has come to be common to all parties. In the context of general war we have here a completely new situation.

In the closing stages of World War II President Roosevelt showed much reluctance to impose a policy upon the Joint Chiefs of Staff. His successor, President Harry S Truman, was disinclined at a critical time in 1945, as we have seen, to instruct General Eisenhower to act in Europe on any other than purely military considerations. It was only five years later that this same presidential successor found himself roughly compelled to accept the logic of the new order and act in a diametrically opposite sense.

"The Korean War," says Samuel Huntington, "was the first war in American history (except for the Indian struggles) which was not a crusade."[13] I cannot quite accept this, but it certainly was for the United States a war of unusual aspect. It was a war conducted according to the main concept supported by Clausewitz and not at all according to the practice of Ludendorff. That is to say, the object from the beginning was clearly defined in political terms, and limited. There were variations from time to time in the war aim. After MacArthur's brilliantly successful amphibious operation at Inchon, the aim shifted from the simple reestablishment of the status quo in South Korea to the effecting of a permanent change in the whole Korean Peninsula. The chance was seen to reunite this at a time when China was thought to be too preoccupied with the danger from the old enemy Russia to be inclined to intervene by force of arms. But China did intervene and the administration reverted to its former aim, whose achievement would in their view run small risk of furnishing the USSR with excuse and opportunity for the opening of World War III before Europe was strong enough to resist.

General MacArthur could not accept this position in terms either of the limitation of means or of the restriction of ends. He challenged the administration on both counts. In criticizing the administration's desire to prevent the war from spreading, he declared that this seemed to him to introduce a new concept into military operations. He called it the "concept of appeasement . . . the concept that when you use force you can limit that force."[14]

"Once war is forced upon us," he told Congress, "there is no alternative than to apply every available means to bring it to a swift end."[15] He was not consistent here. He did not, in fact, advocate the use of every available means against China. He was strongly against the use of U.S. ground forces in any strength on the mainland, for example, and advocated in preference air bombardment and sea blockade with the possibility of enlarging Nationalist forces on the mainland out of Formosa. He did not, in my view, either convincingly or even with total conviction argue against the acceptance of limitations on hostilities. What he did insist on was that the limitations accepted should be those of his, the military commander's, choice and not those settled upon by his political superiors. But given the acceptance of limitation in principle, the identification of those areas in which specific limitations must be accepted is a clear matter of policy. Is that for soldiers to determine? MacArthur challenged the administration on this issue and appealed to the legislature and the American people over the administration's head. He lost. Perhaps he underestimated the character of the president and the degree to which experience had helped him to develop since the spring of 1945. Perhaps he overestimated the support that he could expect in the Joint Chiefs. The position taken by the Joint Chiefs, however, supported that of the president. It conveyed quite clearly that the instrumental nature of the military, as an agency in the service of the state, was not going to be forgotten. In the seven years between 1945 and 1952 there probably lies a watershed in civil/military relations in the United States, which future historians will see as of prime importance.

But another question arises, and this too was raised by the case of MacArthur, as it arose in the matter of the Curragh incident in Ireland in 1914 and with General de Gaulle in 1940. Where or by what is the allegiance of the military professional engaged? Personal service to an absolute monarch is unequivocal. But in a constitutional monarchy, or a republic, precisely where does the loyalty of the fighting man lie?

In Ireland just before the outbreak of World War I, there was a distinct possibility that opponents of the British government's policy for the introduction of home rule in Ireland would take up arms to assert their right to remain united with England under the crown. But if the British army were ordered to coerce the Ulster Unionists, would it obey? Doubts upon this score were widespread and they steadily increased. As it turned out, there was no mutiny, though the Curragh incident has sometimes been erroneously described as such. The officers in a cavalry brigade standing by on the Curragh ready to move into the north of Ireland all followed their brigade commander's example in offering their resignations from the service. The Curragh episode, all the same, formed an unusually dramatic element in an intrusion by the military into politics which seriously weakened the British government of the day and forced a change in its policy. As a successful manipulation of government by the military on a political issue, it has had no parallel in Britain in modern times. But it also raised the question of where personal allegiance lay and raised it more sharply than at any time since 1641, when the hard choice between allegiance to the king and adherence to Parliament, in the days of Thomas Hobbes, split the country in the English Civil War.

Essentially the same question was raised by MacArthur, for he challenged the administration on the fundamentals of policy—upon political ends, that is—as well as upon choice of military means. He also claimed that he was not bound, even as a serving officer, by a duty to the executive if he perceived a duty to the state with which his duty to the administration conflicted. His words to the Massachusetts legislature are worth quoting: "I find in existence a new and heretofore unknown and dangerous concept, that the members of our armed forces owe primary allegiance or loyalty to those who temporarily exercise the authority of the Executive Branch of the Government rather than to the country and its Constitution which they are sworn to defend. No proposition could be more dangerous."[16]

There is here a deep and serious fallacy. I do not refer to the possible violation of the president's constitutional position as commander in chief. I have more in mind a principle basic to the whole concept of parliamentary democracy as it is applied, with differences in detail but in essential identity of intention, in our two countries. It is that the will of the people is sovereign and no refusal to accept its expression through the institutions specifically established by it—whether in the determination of policies or in the interpretation of the constitution—can be legitimate. MacArthur's insistence upon his right as an individual to determine for himself the legitimacy of the executive's position, no less than his claim of the right as a military commander to modify national policies, can never be seen in any other way than as completely out of order. It is ironic that MacArthur, who himself might perhaps have been brought to trial for insubordination, should at one time have sat in judgment on another general officer for that very offense. General Mitchell, though possibly wide open to charges of impropriety in the methods he used, was challenging the correctness of the administration's policy decisions. MacArthur's act was the far graver one of challenging his orders in war, and of appealing to the legislature and people over the commander in chief's head.

It is worthy of note that in the wave of criticism of General MacArthur from non-American sources, some of it violent at times, General de Gaulle in France was almost alone among those of comparable importance who raised his voice in MacArthur's defense. De Gaulle himself, of course, had been there, too. He had declined to accept the wholly legitimate capitulation to a national enemy in war of a properly constituted French government. This is something for which France will always remain deeply in his debt. There is no doubt, however, of the correctness of the position taken by officers of the so-called Vichy French Forces after the fall of France. We fought them in Syria on account of it. The Troupes françaises du Levant had orders to defend French possessions in mandated territories against all comers and this they did.

I was wounded for the first time in the last war in that campaign, commanding a small force in an untidy little battle, which we won, on the Damascus road. After the armistice in Syria and the Lebanon, I was walking around Beirut with my arm in plaster when I met a French officer who was another cavalryman and a contemporary whom I had known before the war as a friend. He had the other arm in plaster and, I discovered, had been in this little battle as the commander on the Vichy French side. We dined together in the St. Georges Hotel while he explained to me with impeccable logic how professionally incompetent the command had been on our side. The fact that we had won was at best irrelevant and at worst aesthetically repugnant. But I do not recall that in the whole of our discussion either of us doubted the correctness of his action in fighting against the Allies and his old friends.

There is sometimes a purely military justification for disobedience. Britain's greatest sailor, Lord Nelson, exploited it. After Jutland, Admiral Lord Fisher said of Admiral Jellicoe that he had all Nelson's qualities but one: he had not learned to disobey. What I describe as military justification rests in the opinion of the officer on the spot that he can best meet the military requirement of his superiors if he acts in some way other than that prescribed by them. This is a matter of professional judgment, and of courage, for failure can prejudice a career. It is not a matter of morals. But there are also circumstances in which men or women find themselves under a moral compulsion to refrain from doing what is lawfully ordered of them. If they are under sufficiently powerful moral pressure and are strong enough and courageous enough to face the predictable consequences of their action, they will then sometimes disobey. This, I know, is terribly difficult ground. "My country right or wrong" is not an easy principle to reconcile with an absolute morality, even if we accept a Hegelian view that the state represents the highest consummation of human society. Early in World War I a brave English nurse called Edith Cavell, who had said that "Patriotism is not enough," was shot by her country's enemies for relieving human suffering where she found it, among people held by the enemy to be *francs tireurs* or partisans. Nurse Edith Cavell's statue stands in London off Trafalgar Square, around the corner from the National Gallery, and it is worth a look in passing. It bears the inscription I have quoted: "Patriotism is not enough."

In the half century since that time doubt has grown further, not only of the ultimate moral authority of the nation-state but also of its permanence as a social structure. The nation-state could at some time in the future develop into something else. States have before now been united into bigger groupings, and supranational entities are not impossible.

I do not see the nation-state disappearing for a long time yet, but already we have much experience of international political structures under which groups of national military forces are employed. The United States in the last third of a century, it has been said, has learned more about the operation of coalitions than ever before. Conflicts of loyalty are always possible where forces are assigned to an allied command. I have been a NATO commander in Europe, and as such I had on my staff an officer of another nation who was engaged in the contingency planning of tactical nuclear targets. This was less of an academic exercise for this particular officer than it might have been, say, for an American or even for a Briton, for the targets were not only in Europe but in this officer's own country and in parts of it he had known from boyhood. It was made known to me that this officer was showing signs of strain and I had him moved to other work, for the military servant of a nation-state can even now be put under moral strain in situations where conflicts of loyalties arise. The tendency towards international structures will almost certainly increase and the incidence of such situations is unlikely to grow less.

Let me draw together these thoughts upon the moral, as distinguished from the professional, aspect of obedience. The fighting man is bound to obedience to the interest of the state he serves. If he accepts this, as MacArthur certainly did, he can still, rightly or wrongly, question, like MacArthur, the authority of men constitutionally appointed to identify and interpret the state's interest. He could even, like de Gaulle, flatly refuse to obey these men. Those who consider general MacArthur open to a charge of insubordination may consider that General de Gaulle was probably open to a charge of no less than treason. Neither is constitutionally permissible. A case in moral justification might just possibly be made for both, though such a case is always stronger when the results of the act are seen to be in the outcome beneficial. "Treason doth never prosper," wrote Sir John Harrington in the days of Queen Elizabeth the First. "What's the reason? For if it prosper none dare call it treason." In the event, de Gaulle became in the fullness of time president of the French Republic. It was poor Pétain who was put on trial.

Finally there is disobedience on grounds of conscience to an order, lawfully given, whose execution might or might not harm the state but which the recipient flatly declines, for reasons he finds compelling, to carry out. This will be done by the doer at his peril; and the risk, which can be very great, must be accepted with open eyes.

Another possible cause of strain upon the military is divergence in the ethical pattern of the parent society from that of its armed forces. Samuel Huntington, in the book *The Soldier and the State,* which will always occupy a high place in the literature on this topic, spoke in the late 1950s of tendencies in the United States towards a new and more conservative environment, more sympathetic to military institutions. He suggested that this "might result in the widespread acceptance by Americans of values more like those of the military ethic."[17] The course of events since

Huntington wrote thus, in 1956, throws some doubt on the soundness of any prediction along these lines. The qualities demanded in military service, which include self-restraint in the acceptance of an ordered life, do not seem to be held in growing esteem everywhere among young people today. In consequence, where a nation is involved in a war which cannot be described as one of immediate national survival and whose aims, however admirable they may be, are not universally supported at home and perhaps not even fully understood there, strains can be acutely felt. Limited wars for political ends are far more likely to produce moral strains of the sort I have suggested here than the great wars of the past.

The wars of tomorrow will almost certainly be limited wars, fought for limited ends. The nation-in-arms has vanished; the general war is no longer a rational concept. But the nation-state will persist for a time yet and the application of force to its political ends will persist with it. These ends, however, will be limited and the means limited too—not by choice of the military but by choice of their employers, the constitutionally established civil agencies of the state. These employers will also be watching most carefully the level of military demand being made on national resource. If this level rises so high as to prejudice enterprises higher in the national scale of priorities than preparation for war, it will be resisted. There are signs that the very high priority given to the demands of the military on national resource in the United States in the third quarter of the twentieth century will not persist into the fourth.

Ladies and gentlemen, in addressing myself to the topic chosen for this memorial address, "The Military in the Service of the State," I have selected only a few aspects of a big and complex theme. Let me end with something like a *confessio fidei*—a confession of faith. I am myself the product of thirty-five years' military service—a person who, with strong inclinations toward the academic, nonetheless became a professional soldier. Looking back now in later life from a university, I can find nothing but satisfaction over the choice I made all those years ago as a student—a satisfaction tinged with surprise at the good sense I seem to have shown as a very young man in making it. Knowing what I do now, given the chance all over again, I should do exactly the same. For the military life, whether for sailor, soldier, or

airman, is a good life. The human qualities it demands include
fortitude, integrity, self-restraint, personal loyalty to other persons,
and the surrender of the advantage of the individual to the
common good. None of us can claim a total command of all these
qualities. The military man sees round him others of his own kind
also seeking to develop them, and perhaps doing it more
successfully than he has done himself. This is good company.
Anyone can spend his life in it with satisfaction.

In my own case, as a fighting man, I found that invitations after
World War II to leave the service and move into business, for
example, were unattractive, even in a time when anyone who has
had what they called on our side "a good war" was being demoted
and, of course, paid less. A pressing invitation into politics was also
comparatively easy to resist. The possibility of going back to
Oxford to teach Medieval History was more tempting. But I am
glad that I stayed where I was, in the profession of arms, and I
cannot believe I could have found a better or more rewarding life
anywhere outside it.

Another thought arises here. The danger of excessive influence
within the state to which I have been referring does not spring from
incompetence, cynicism, or malice in the military, but in large part
from the reverse. What is best for his service will always be sought
by the serving officer, and if he believes that in seeking the best for
his service he is rendering the best service he can to his country, it is
easy to see why. He may have to be restrained. He can scarcely be
blamed.

The military profession is unique in one very important respect.
It depends upon qualities such as those I have mentioned not only
for its attractiveness but for its very efficiency. Such qualities as
these make any group of men in which they are found an agreeable
and attractive one in which to function. The military group,
however, depends in very high degree upon these qualities for its
functional efficiency.

A man can be selfish, cowardly, disloyal, false, fleeting, perjured,
and morally corrupt in a wide variety of other ways and still be
outstandingly good in pursuits in which other imperatives bear
than those upon the fighting man. He can be a superb creative
artist, for example, or a scientist in the very top flight, and still be a
very bad man. What the bad man cannot be is a good sailor, or

soldier, or airman. Military institutions thus form a repository of moral resource that should always be a source of strength within the state.

I have reflected tonight upon the relationship between civil and military in the light of past history, present positions, and possible future developments and have offered in conclusion my own conviction that the major service of the military institution to the community of men it serves may well lie neither within the political sphere nor the functional. It could easily lie within the moral. The military institution is a mirror of its parent society, reflecting strengths and weaknesses. It can also be a well from which to draw refreshment for a body politic in need of it.

It is in the conviction that the highest service of the military to the state may well lie in the moral sphere, and the awareness that almost everything of importance in this respect can still be said, that I bring to an end what I have to offer here tonight in the Harmon Memorial Lecture for the year 1970.

Notes

1. Lodwick Hartley, *This is Lorence* (Chapel Hill, North Carolina: 1943), p. 153.

2. Bruce Catton, *The Army of the Potomac*, Vol. 1: *Mr. Lincoln's Army* (New York: 1962), p. 89.

3. Gordon A. Craig, *The Politics of the Prussian Army, 1640-1945* (Oxford: 1955), p. 252.

4. Forrest C. Pogue, "The Decision to Halt at the Elbe (1945)," *Command Decisions*, ed. Kent R. Greenfield (New York: 1959), p. 375.

5. Ibid., p. 377.

6. Ibid., p. 378.

7. Ibid., p. 380.

8. Ibid., p. 381.

9. Ibid., p. 385.

10. Louis Morton, "Interservice Co-operation and Political-Military Collaboration," *Total War and Cold War*, ed. Harry L. Coles (Columbus, Ohio: 1962), p. 137.

11. George F. Kennan, *Realities of American Foreign Policy* (Princeton: 1954), p. 80.

12. Karl von Clausewitz, *On War*, trans. O. J. Matthis Jolles (Washington: 1943), p. 21.

13. Samuel P. Huntington, *The Soldier and the State* (Cambridge,

Mass.: 1957), p. 387.

14. MacArthur's testimony before the Senate Armed Forces and Foreign Relations Committees quoted in Walter Millis (ed.), *American Military Thought* (New York: 1966), p. 481.

15. MacArthur's address to Joint Session of Congress, April 19, 1951, quoted in Douglas MacArthur, *Reminiscences* (New York: 1964), p. 404.

16. Douglas MacArthur, "War Cannot Be Controlled, It Must Be Abolished," *Vital Speeches* 17 (August 15, 1951):653. Speech before Massachusetts Legislature, Boston, July 25, 1951.

17. Huntington, *Soldier and the State,* p. 458.

7

Professionalism:
Problems and Challenges

Sam C. Sarkesian and Thomas M. Gannon

In this brief introduction to a series of articles on professionalism, Professors Sarkesian and Gannon sketch for us the scope of the issues central to an examination of the ethics of the military profession. On the question of whether military professionals and their values should be isolated from the parent society or fused with civilian society they suggest that the principle of civilian control can be properly maintained only if there is "a high degree of convergence between military and civilian values." They structure the problems for us into three categories: civilian-military relations, institutional criteria, and individual values. They highlight the critical connection they perceive between military ethics and military competence. Solutions to ethical dilemmas associated with the military role in a democratic society are to be found only by viewing the military as an integral part of the broader political system.

—M.M.W.

Ethics in public service has been a longstanding issue in the American political system. The Watergate affair and current examination of the role of the Federal Bureau of Investigation and the Central Intelligence Agency are only the latest in a long history of questionable activities and behavior on the part of administrative personnel and elected officials. There are parallels in the military profession, ranging from schemes to defraud the government by quartermasters in the Civil War to the impro-

Originally titled "Introduction: Professionalism: Problems and Challenges." Reprinted from *American Behavioral Scientist* 19, no. 5 (May/June 1976):495-510 by permission of the publisher, Sage Publications, Inc.

prieties of industrialists in concert with military men in producing military hardware, and the behavior of military men in Vietnam (My Lai, unauthorized bombing raids). Thus, while political ethics and corruption in government have become important questions for the American political system, military ethics has become a major concern of the military profession. The current debate began during the Vietnam experience and has been reinforced by the general public mood regarding the character of politicians and bureaucrats in general. At the same time, every profession—medicine, law, education, and so on—is debating ethical standards.

In such an environment, civilian control over the military—a fundamental premise of our political system—becomes suspect. Ethical behavior by military professionals as perceived by society is a basic ingredient to the legitimacy and credibility of the military institution. Furthermore, ethical behavior is fundamental to the military's cohesiveness and professional status. Thus, the perceived unethical behavior of military men not only erodes civilian control but also denigrates professionalism.

Although there is considerable concern by both civilians and military regarding ethics, there has been little success in dealing with the question in an analytical manner. This is particularly true in the military where ethical idealism, situational ethics, and careerism complicate the issue. In each instance, there is disagreement about the meaning and impact of ethical standards. This is compounded by the fact that military ethics and military competence are inextricably intermixed. Military ethics becomes the most important mark of military competence.

It was with this in mind that the Inter-University Seminar on Armed Forces and Society selected its theme and organized panels for its Biennial Conference in October, 1975, held at Loyola University of Chicago. The papers appearing in this volume are a sampling of the papers presented around the theme "Civilian Control and Military Ethics." These papers represent both "civilian" and "military" perspectives. However, the main emphasis is on the search for an analytical approach.

Our purpose in this introductory chapter is to seek to place these papers in a proper framework by providing some insights into the problems and challenges facing military professionalism. Doing this we also hope to stimulate and expand examination of the "new" military professionalism.

From our perspective, the subject of "Civilian Control and Military Ethics" cannot be viewed solely in terms of organizational norms and bureaucratic control. Ultimately, civilian control and military ethics are a function of professionalism as perceived by those in both the military and civilian sectors. The central questions revolve around the meaning of ethics, proper conduct, institutional and individual relationships, and civilian-military value systems. The general thrust of this volume focuses on these issues.

Fundamental Issues

The fundamental ethical problem facing the military profession is how to accommodate itself to its growing volunteer character and reinforce its links with society while maintaining its uniqueness as a profession. Within the context of these issues, the military must accommodate itself to the new international environment and maintain an effective combat capability. In the words of a soldier-scholar,

> Solutions to the dilemma facing the military profession fall somewhere between two unacceptable extremes: returning to traditional professionalism, involving withdrawal from society; or discarding traditional values and severely impairing cohesiveness and discipline. Obviously the two should be reconciled, but the prescription of preserving essential military values while maintaining a close relationship with civilian society is inordinately difficult.[1]

Answers to these questions will not be found in more elaborate technology, increased military discipline, isolation, or aloofness from society, but in understanding the role that the military plays in society and appreciating the "politics" of democratic systems. This requires a commitment to the idea that the military professional is part of the American political system and civilian value structure. The military must understand the political "rules of the game" not only of their own institution but those prevailing in the broader political system: this realignment calls for systematic study and serious discussion.

Using this approach, professional ethics takes on a wider meaning and is particularly sensitive to individual attitudes and behavior. More specifically, ethical questions become linked with the purpose and utility of military force, the degree of political influence of the military within the political system or nature of civil-military relations, the extent to which individual military officers can become involved in the "politics" of the political system, and the conflict between individual conscience and institutional demands.

Questions, for example, about the utility and purpose of military force require basic rethinking of professional purposes. Should military force serve society in other ways aside from preparation for and waging of war? There are a number of advocates of the peaceful uses of military force to include involvement in civic action, educational programs, and social-welfare roles. Indeed, some would argue that waging war is not sufficient to sustain professional purpose. A system of ethics, they would argue, cannot be based solely on a concept of "management of violence."

Concern over civil-military relations focuses on such problems as the influence of military men over political decisions. Equally important is the question of national priorities. Should military men include in their military calculus a concern over domestic priorities? Or should there be a purely military perspective based on the assumption that other branches of the government provide executive and legislative monitoring? To what degree should the military reinforce civilian value systems?

Much of the debate regarding these questions draws its content from the values of the larger society. This is clearly articulated in the recent literature. Hauser, for example, writes, "It seems almost simplistic to conclude that a disjuncture between the army and society has brought about this long litany of troubles, but that is what the evidence suggests. The army has been unable to isolate itself from society sufficiently to maintain its authoritarian discipline or to prevent the intrusion of such social ills as racial discord and drug abuse."[2] Thayer, on the other hand, notes that

"The concept of professionalism seems to demand that profes sionals themselves be constantly aware of the delicate balance they must maintain in their own behavior between autonomy and fusion. They cannot be so totally separated as to become the proverbial 'society within a society,' but neither can they afford total integration within the civilian overhead."[3]

From the individual point of view, military professionalism raises a number of questions regarding individual-institutional relations. For example, to what extent can military men express dissent without jeopardizing their careers? What are the boundaries of individual civil rights and liberties? Should military men be allowed to engage in political activity such as standing for elections? The recent furor over trade unionism in the military adds another dimension to questions about individual rights and liberties.

Within the profession there is also concern over the relationship between individual behavior and institutional norms. One of the most illuminating views comes from a study on military professionalism conducted at the U.S. Army War College. This states in part:

It is impossible to forecast future institutional climates with any degree of reliability. Nevertheless, it is not unreasonable to state as consequences of the present climate: it is conducive to self-deception because it fosters the production of inaccurate information; it impacts on the long term ability of the Army to fight and win because it frustrates young, idealistic, energetic officers who leave the service and are replaced by those who will tolerate if not condone ethical imperfection; it is corrosive of the Army's image because it falls short of the traditional idealistic code of the soldier—a code which is the key to the soldier's acceptance by a modern free society; it lowers the credibility of our top military leaders because it often shields them from essential bad news; it stifles initiative, innovation, and humility because it demands perfection or the pose of perfection at every turn; it downgrades technical competence by rewarding instead trivial, measureable, quota-filling accomplishments; and it eventually squeezes much of the inner satisfaction and personal enjoyment out of being an officer.[4]

This conclusion by a group of military professionals looking at their own profession has serious ramifications for the meaning of professional ethics. If such conditions are generally prevalent, what alternatives are available to rectify the problems? To what degree will the profession respond to—or allow—internal dissent? Can professionals refuse to carry out illegal orders? Are there institutionalized processes which foster reasoned dissent without implicit institutional retaliation against the dissenting officer?

Equally important, this conclusion points to an erosion of performance quality, as well as ethical imperfection. It also suggests the existence of a particular kind of professional working at the highest levels of military hierarchy symbolizing the profession to the community, and dictating the nature of the military value system and civil-military relations. What ethical standards are likely to prevail if those who consider career success the dominant norm become the professional elite?

Available Alternatives

In light of these considerations, the military profession is faced with three options. First, it can retreat into a rigid and narrow professionalism in which military men are unconditional servants of the state. This stance suggests a robotlike response to political leadership, once the military follows it unquestioningly.

Second, the profession can assume a civil service role in which civilian politics, unionization, salary concerns, and fringe benefits become the major motivation for individual officers. To civilianize the military this far would very likely erode its professional uniqueness and render it easily vulnerable to political manipulation. In the long run, this would create dangers not only for the profession but for the whole political system.

Third, the profession can develop a new rationale in which the military is seen as more than unconditional servants or simply paid employees of the state. This rationale would require that the military acquire political understanding and expertise, a sense of realistic and enlightened self-interest, and professional perspective transcending boundaries that we have traditionally associated with duty, honor, and country. The profession must accept political—not partisan—politics; it must be capable of dealing with environments that are not purely military, and recognize the professional military man's right to engage in politics within a domestic system, as long as he adheres to the rules of the game. In this third option, the profession would see itself as a political interest group trying to reach the civilian leadership and the public to explain its case and develop a consensus for its objectives. To implement this option requires a military leadership and profession which has specific, but limited, political posture.

We are not suggesting that military professionals should make political decisions regarding the goals of the political system, whether in peace or war. But surely they must be equipped to look beyond immediate exigencies and develop the intellectual tools and insights to appreciate the interdependence between war and politics. Such a perspective is not acquired in professional military schools—at least not in the present curriculum. In order to present the "military" point of view in a judicious and well-articulated manner, military professionals must understand the total concern of the political system. They must go beyond the simple loyalty of "managers of violence in the service of the state." Moreover, war itself raises questions of morality which require more than a "military" solution.

The first option of retreating to narrow professionalism is a more comfortable position, and has been the mythical basis for civilian-military relationships for some time. But this option relegates the professional military man to a robotlike role hardly adequate to the complexities of modern military life and present and future world politics. The second option would transform the military into a civil service in which self-interest rather than national purpose motivates action. The third option is clearly the most challenging and useful; yet it, too, has its dangers. Not only must the profession accept a political dimension to its ethical values, but it must always remember that it remains a servant of the state and is not an autonomous decision-making body. To take on this critical political dimension is only a short step away from assuming a self-righteous stance as the ultimate arbiter of society's political disputes. This third option provides a wider range of activity, mainly consultative, for the professional officer. Indeed, it requires an active, responsible self-interest and a nonpartisan involvement in the policy process and politics in general. The American political system is partially based on the assumption that groups and interests must have access to policy makers; articulation and aggregation of interests on a wide scale, unencumbered by government restrictions, are basic premises of democratic society. Even the military ought to be given the opportunity to argue its case within the accepted "rules of the game."

From the individual point of view, this third option requires that the profession recognize the limits to military institutional demands and individual subservience including combat situations. The institutionalization of healthy skepticism, reasonable inquiry, and legitimate dissent would do much to reinforce the worth of the "individual" while providing a momentum to innovation, imagination, self-examination. Obviously, this option requires substantive changes in professional ethics, and a different understanding of military professionalism.

Military Professionalism: Dimensions and Substance

There is little need to review the meaning of military professionalism.[5] Like all other professions, the military has a special expertise and technical competence. Its purpose is to wage war, and the exercise of its competence to achieve this purpose has been sanctioned by the community. The military's "client" is the whole community, yet the military way of life greatly isolates it from the community at large. As Bradford and Brown observe:

> Professionalism is more than simply belonging to the officers corps. It is a status determined jointly by the officer and his government. Neither the state nor the officers corps will grant professional standing to the man who lacks the necessary competence or who will not agree to make an unconditional commitment to duty if he is in the combat Army. The unconditional quality of this commitment is signified by the career length and life of selfless sacrifice, ranging from Melville Goodwin's "genteel poverty" to the Gettysburg "last full measure of devotion." Professionalism thus has both objective and subjective content. It is objective in that professional status is granted by the state if certain performance criteria are met by the officer. It is subjective in that the officer must feel a sense of duty to serve the lawful government "for the full

distance," even at the risk of his life. Mentally, he does not condition this obligation.[6]

The basic themes of military professionalism are integrity, obedience, loyalty, commitment, trust, honor, and service. Each of these is both self-evident and elusive—elusive because the application of any of these qualities to a particular situation is difficult to define. Equally puzzling are the criteria applying to "political" circumstances, whether these pertain to insurgency, war, or involvement in domestic issues. The concept of military ethics thus becomes increasingly complex when one adds to it the broader dimensions of military professionalism.

Central to the notion of military professionalism are the concepts of honor and trust. As Janowitz points out, military honor is a crucial part of the total professional ethics.[7] The traditional content of military honor can be described in the following categories:

Gentlemanly conduct. As long as members of the military elite consider themselves to be special because they embody the martial spirit, it is indispensable that they consider themselves gentlemen.

Personal Fealty. Personal allegiance, as a component of honor, has had to be changed to fit the growth of bureaucratic organization.

Brotherhood. In its contemporary form a major aspect of military honor comprises a sense of brotherhood and intense group loyalty . . . the sense of fraternity in the military is more than instrumental, it is an end in and of itself and for this reason it becomes suspect of the outsider.

Pursuit of Glory. The code of professional honor has had to be self-generating by drawing on its own historical achievement.

Equally important, honor and trust are the wellsprings of military ethics. Without honor and trust the professional soldier is merely a trained killer. With honor and trust, he becomes a man of "gentlemanly conduct," professing loyalty to a person or group, devoting himself to "expertise, responsibility, and corporateness of the profession of arms."[8] Honor and trust, therefore, provide the necessary link between the individual and the institution, between colleagues, and between the military institution and the community.

Over the past five years, however, honor and trust have eroded. Partly as a result of Vietnam, the denigration of such values in American culture, and increased professional concern about career success and the fear of failure, honor and trust have become purely symbolic concepts not realistically embedded in the professional military ethic. Former ethical standards, idealized as they may have been, no longer seem relevant and have been replaced by standards that are primarily situational and relative. That is, ethics has become associated with standards that insure success without violating institutional norms, regardless of how they may violate individual conscience.

Individual Ethics and Institutional Norms

Military men are prone to view the dilemma between individual conscience and institutional demands as unique to their profession. Yet this dilemma has a long history in western civilization. Sophocles, Socrates, and Thomas More give ample evidence that throughout history, men of conscience, committed to their principles of right and wrong, were willing to accept death rather than institutional demands. No one would argue that institutional demands and societal order are unimportant considerations. But what weight should individual values and conscience carry? As individuals, we are responsible for our own decisions and actions. But what is to be done when institutional expectations and individual demands of conscience conflict?

There are some who suggest that primacy should be given to institutional requirements and professional demands, regardless of individual preferences and attitudes. Institutional goals and success thus become the fundamental criteria for military professional behavior. These are the "absolutists" who would view individual dissent and resistance as "traitorous" to professional ethics. A modified version of this outlook is found among those who argue for situational ethics. The argument here is that individual conscience and "individuality" can be part of professionalism, but are clearly subordinate to particular policies and decisions of the institution.

In contrast, others argue that individual conscience and "individuality" comprise a basic ingredient of professionalism; otherwise the profession will become detached from society, and innovative and imaginative officers will leave the profession. The extreme position is taken by those who argue that institutional demands must always take second place to considerations of individual worth and conscience. We feel that there are few, if any, military men who realistically accept such a position.

Professional stress on integrity and achievement of institutional goals has made dissent or resistance illegitimate. Honesty and instant obedience are claimed to be unconditional requisites of military institutions. Nevertheless, the question of conscience versus institution persists and has become a particularly sensitive issue in today's military. Changing domestic values and the general skepticism of people towards the "establishment," the emergence of new attitudes after Vietnam, and the transition to an all volunteer system have all served to stimulate the military's restiveness about professional ethics.

An Analytical Perspective

It is always easier to discuss military professionalism in conceptual terms than to treat practical, concrete problems. Concepts of military professionalism must be "operationalized" if they are going to be both meaningful and useful in the everyday life of military men. In this context, conceptual frameworks for examining military professionalism sometimes run the danger of mixing theoretical assertions, institutional pragmatism, and metaphysics. Yet most would agree that there are certain basic norms essential to a professional ethic. The norms cluster around three major concerns: civilian-military relations, institutional criteria, and individual values. In each case, the substantive issues of professionalism include technical skills, ethics, standards, and political perspectives. The scope and dimensions of these issues must be assessed at the community, institution, and individual levels. At the individual level, professionalism may be studied in terms of an individual officer's competence as a military technician, his particular attitudes and conduct regarding professional ethics, and his political orientation and perceptions.

Taken together, these traits signify the quality of individual professionalism. But the total professional ethos is not merely an individual attribute, but must include both institutional norms and community expectations and values.

To examine military professionalism, therefore, one must view the individual officer in relation to both his own occupational institution and the wider society. Both demand that the officer is technically competent. Both expect him to obey norms and cherish certain values. There exists, in others, some consensus between military professionalism and community values—at least enough to reinforce the existing relationship. In the end, however, the really hard questions are posed in terms of individual values. At what point does a professional officer follow his conscience even if it means violating institutional norms? Can an individual be a professional officer and still not accept institutional demands? Can one be ethical and yet resist the institution?

Military professionalism must ultimately be grounded on the premise that military ethics converge with the ethical values of the larger society. A military system in a democratic society cannot long maintain its credibility and legitimacy if its ethical standards significantly differ from the civilian values of the larger society. Conversely, basic civil liberties, rights, privileges, and "individuality" of the person inherent in a democratic society must have some manifestation in *all institutions* of the political system. The ethical constructs of public service—military or civilian—must necessarily rest on this premise.

The study of military ethics and civilian control, therefore, must examine the prevailing value system of civilian society with particular emphasis on the roles expected of the military, assess institutional norms of the military, and investigate the individual values of the professional officer. By identifying the principal characteristics of each of these sets of values, we can determine the degree of convergence or divergence—the kind of relationship that links the civilian and military, and the extent of civilian control over the military. Equally important, we need to study political theory, philosophy, and history so that military men will understand and appreciate the dilemmas caused by the contradictions of conscience and institutional demands.

Our basic argument, then, is that a high degree of convergence between military and civilian values is essential for effective civilian control of the military. This argument rests on the general assumption that military ethics concerns more than the relationship between the institution and society, or the individual and institution. It also includes both individual value systems relating to personal conscience and perceptions about the norms of the military institution.

What is likely to be the result of this approach? First, we will be able to document in what ways the professional values and institutional norms that evolve in community-military interaction are crucial to the character and dimension of civilian control of the military. One measure of the effectiveness of this interaction will be the extent to which individual rights and liberties, the right of "legitimate" dissent and resistance, broadened political consciousness, legitimate political activity, and a pervasive sense of self-control have become recognized as essential attributes of military professionalism. The effect of this interaction will also be seen in increased legitimacy granted to the military. The military cannot bestow legitimacy upon itself; it must come from the larger society. This legitimacy will be based on the degree to which the military value system is perceived as reflecting the basic values of society.

Second, institutional norms will be subjected to more realistic scrutiny. We may find that "Duty, Honor, Country" no longer sufficiently explains military ethics. It is also conceivable that professional military men will become increasingly conscious of the inherent dilemma between an institution that demands total loyalty, total commitment, total obedience and individual conscience and perceptions regarding right and wrong.

Third, simple solutions regarding professional ethics will be recognized for what they are—a return to an "absolutist" ideal that is generally unworkable.

Finally, it should become clear that one must assume a developmental perspective regarding professional military ethics —the elusiveness of perfect answers for every question of ethics.

Our intent in this introduction has been to suggest directions for developing a "dynamic" professionalism in the military. It would be counterproductive to look now for some master plan that would provide a list of specific solutions. Rather, the kind of debate now taking place and expanding into the public domain is probably one of the best indices of the health of the military profession, assuming that the debate, as widely as possible, is itself a major component in fostering a "dynamic" military professionalism. There must always remain a peaceful yet adversary relationship between the military profession and society at large. Continually examining this relationship in light of the purpose of the military and the demands of democratic society is itself a valuable means to facilitate mutual accommodation.

> Through its government, the United States has told its soldiers for two centuries what it wants them to *do,* but it has seldom, if ever, told them what it wants them to *be.* As a result, the officers corps has largely depended on its own traditional assumptions. And if the old assumptions are wrong, they ask, what takes their place? It would seem that any philosophical redirection of the military must come from open, reasoned, and multi-sided public dialogue.[9]

Notes

1. R. G. Gard, Jr., "The Military and American Society," *Foreign Affairs* 49, 4 (July 1971), p. 707.

2. W. L. Hauser, *America's Army in Crisis* (Baltimore: Johns Hopkins University Press, 1973), p. 186.

3. F. C. Thayer, "Professionalism: the Hard Choice," in F. N. Trager and P. S. Kronenberg, eds., *National Security and American Society* (Lawrence: University of Kansas Press, 1973), p. 568.

4. U.S. Army War College, *Study on Military Professionalism* (Carlisle Barracks, Pa.: U.S. Army War College, 1970), pp. 28-29.

5. See B. Abrahamson, *Military Professionalization and Political Power* (Beverly Hills, Calif.: Sage, 1972); D. Bletz, *The Role of the Military Professional in U.S. Foreign Policy. Special Studies* (New York: Praeger, 1972); M. L. Cogan, "Toward a Definition of Profession," *Harvard Educational Review* 23 (Winter 1953); E. Greenwood, "Attributes of a Profession," *Social Work* 2, 3 (July 1957); Samuel P. Huntington, *The Soldier and the State* (New York: Free Press, 1964); Morris Janowitz, *The Professional Soldier* (New York: Free Press, 1960); Sam C. Sarkesian, *The Professional Army Officer in a Changing Society* (Chicago: Nelson-Hall, 1975).

6. Z. B. Bradford and F. J. Brown, *The United States Army in Transition* (Beverly Hills, Calif.: Sage, 1973), p. 223.

7. Janowitz, *Professional Soldier,* p. 218.

8. Bletz, *The Role of the Military Professional,* p. 6.

9. C. R. Kemble, *The Image of the Army Officer in America* (Westport, Conn.: Greenwood, 1973), pp. 202-203.

8

Duty, Honor, Country:
Practice and Precept

Lewis S. Sorley III

In this paper, Lewis Sorley provides a brief preliminary analysis of the concepts of "duty, honor, country" and proceeds to answer the question of their continuing usefulness as ethical standards for the military profession. He argues forcefully that ethical precepts are crucial to successful military leadership. After specific discussion of the ethical strains generated by certain institutional practices (reliance on quantitative measures in evaluating leadership, use of the body count and Hamlet Evaluation System in Vietnam, "zero defects"), Sorley concludes that "duty, honor, country" remain at an appropriate psychical distance to constitute continuing useful ideals, and the reforms needed are in institutional practices, not in the ideal standards.

—M.M.W.

Periodic examination of the ethical imperatives of the motto "duty, honor, country" and of the relationship of the military profession's precepts and its practices in light of these imperatives, is a necessary and rewarding experience. Such an examination has particular interest and relevance as part of an analysis and evaluation of the Vietnam era.

This paper will focus upon the officer corps of the United States Army. It will seek to define the meaning of "duty, honor, country" as it is taught and understood within the profession, to assess contemporary practice in ethical matters and how this relates to the standards espoused, to suggest some of the recent influences upon such practices, and finally to consider some of the derived

Reprinted from *American Behavioral Scientist,* Vol. 19, No. 5 (May/June 1976):627-646 by permission of the publisher, Sage Publications, Inc.

organizational imperatives for the future.

One necessarily commences any discussion of a topic such as this by admitting the influence of individual experiences and perceptions upon the judgments formed, and the difficulty of establishing generalizations that are in fact representative of diverse elements of the whole in different times and places. What can be asserted with some confidence is that there is continuing concern for the ethical standards of the officer corps of the army within the profession itself, an active debate as to the degree of disparity between practice and precept, and much discussion as to what to do about it.

The terms duty, honor, country derive, of course, from the motto of the United States Military Academy at West Point. Are they representative of an unattainable ideal of no utility in affecting ethical standards and shaping conduct, or are they a powerful statement of a workable, operative, valuable, and emotionally and intellectually gripping code of behavior which had and still retains contemporary relevance? That question, and an included concern as to the impact of certain management practices of recent years upon ethical standards and conduct within the army, are the central focus of this paper. Specifically, we will address the questions of whether the ethical precepts embodied in the motto are operative in the officer corps of the army at present, whether they exert a useful or detrimental influence, and whether their observance has been affected by specific evaluative techniques in recent years. The initial task is a definitional one, that of establishing what, for the purposes of this inquiry, we understand duty, honor, country to mean.

The Meaning of the Motto

Even before his arrival at the Military Academy, the prospective cadet is advised, by means of a special letter concerning the cadet honor code and system, and also through the catalogue, of the meaning of the West Point motto. The essence is loyalty, loyalty to ideals that transcend concern for self. The elements are "character, integrity, and . . . patriotism."[1] Character implies attention to duty, the willingness to make sacrifices, and the determination to perform to the utmost of one's ability. The familiar *Officer's Guide* describing the concept of duty quotes Abraham Lincoln: "I do the best I know how, the very best I can."[2]

Honor is perhaps the most discussed element of the motto, due to widespread interest in the honor code and its implementation through the honor system at West Point. A formulation of the concept of integrity, "the Honor Code has never outgrown its original and simple meaning—that a cadet will not lie, cheat, or steal, or tolerate those who do. The Code requires complete integrity in both word and deed of all members of the Corps and permits no deviation from those standards."[3] Honor is bound up in "the knowledge to determine right from wrong, and the courage to adhere unswervingly to the right."[4]

Country means patriotism, "the willingness to sacrifice and endure discipline for the welfare of the community."[5] The pamphlet entitled *The Armed Forces Officer*[6] is a source of guidance as to official views of the ethical aspects of an officer's responsibilities. There must have been many editions since, but I have kept the one promulgated by George C. Marshall when he was serving as secretary of defense. It points out that an officer's "ultimate commanding loyalty at all times is to his country, and not to his service or his superior," and sums the import of the motto by explaining that an officer is expected to conduct himself so that he will be "a worthy symbol of all that is best in the national character."[7]

Given West Point as the source of the motto, it should be observed that there are at the Military Academy today many who are concerned about the honor code and system—their health, viability and utility. There is increasing recognition in some quarters that in some senses, as a recent chairman of the cadet honor committee has said, "it is an impossible system." A precursor of this view is to be found in the official pamphlet on the honor code, which observes that "the Corps of Cadets is aware that . . . it would be possible to fall into the error of prescribing standards of ethics and honor for the cadet which would be unnaturally pietistic and dogmatic. The Corps abjures such an unrealistic and impractical view of human behavior."[8] But along with the admission by some that total compliance by all cadets is an unattainable ideal, there remains strong support for the code as a worthy goal of moral conduct for both cadets and the officer corps of the army. There has apparently come into practice a degree of discretion in application of the provisions of the code at West Point, and there is also some sentiment for the institutionalizing of the practice, thereby (in the view of those who favor doing so) more honestly coming to grips with the realities of human capacity for ideal behavior and enhancing the instructional aspects of the honor code in preparing cadets for future service as officers. Speaking of contemporary necessities in the broader context of the administration of government generally, Daniel Moynihan has suggested that "it would seem—conditional tense always!—that what we have to do is to create a secular morality, acceptable to the nonreligious, that accommodates itself to what man will actually do, which is to say, persists in the face of imperfection."[9]

It is impossible to predict at this point how or when these issues will be resolved, or the long-term impact they will have upon ethical performance in the army at large. Perhaps the answer will be, as one sincere and conscientious cadet who bore primary responsibility for administering the honor system suggested: "you know you won't be able to be all we say we'd like to be, but you set standards and try to be as good as you can, and hope to change things for the better. If our input [of ethical leavening to the army at large] were adjusted to what goes on there it wouldn't be input anymore."

Contemporary concern with the establishment and administration of ethical systems in educational institutions is not confined to the service academies. Johns Hopkins University, for example, recently abolished its academic honor code which had been in effect for more than 60 years, citing the breakdown of the system and the fact that "significant numbers of students have been using it as a license for cheating and plagiarism." The student council president was quoted as saying: "I think the whole concept of an honor system is sort of outdated."[10]

Such developments are undoubtedly traumatic indeed for the institution concerned. Were they to be even approximated at the Military Academy, given the indispensable part played by the integrity of its leadership in a democratic society's army, some very fundamental changes might be expected to result, and perhaps most importantly in the way in which the military establishment is regarded by the society it was created to serve.

As the sources of the previous definitions were chosen to underscore, the elements of the motto are not confined to, or perhaps even primarily concerned with, West Point. After all, graduates of the Military Academy compose only a small portion of the officer corps, and the ideals embodied in the motto, while stemming from the West Point experience, have never been considered the exclusive property of its graduates. Far from it: the principal justification for maintaining a national military academy has been to provide a nucleus of officers who can leaven and set standards for the entire officer corps in terms of dedication and ethical standards.

Utility of Ethical Precepts

It is essential, for individuals and organizations as well, that they have a meaningful frame of reference if they are to shape their behavior to approximate an ideal. Contemporarily, it could be argued that such a frame of reference is even more necessary as a corrective to the sense of futility and purposelessness that seems to afflict many in the society at large. There is a need to articulate the larger goal and the part one plays in helping to achieve it. Only, perhaps, in this way can one escape the cynicism manifested by a John Galbraith in his assertion that "it is in the nature of competition that the rewards of winning need not be examined."[11] There can be meaningfulness in striving to achieve a goal, even one that may be unsusceptible of complete achievement, and so perceived by the striver. In his Nobel Prize acceptance speech William Faulkner cited the poet's task "to help man endure by lifting his heart, by reminding him of the courage and honor and hope and pride and compassion and pity and sacrifice which have been the glory of the past." The code of the army also serves this purpose, and in a not unpoetic way. It is not disabled by the failure of imperfect men to perfectly observe its dictates. Arnold Toynbee has written that "it is characteristic of our human nature that we rebel against our human limitations and try to transcend them."[12] A meaningful ethical code gives coherence and direction to that rebellion.

Espousal of these values concerning duty, honor, and country is also a key element in the continuing confidence felt by the

American people in the reality and stability of civilian control of the military forces. The idealistic code is indeed at the very heart of the acceptance and trust of a military establishment in a free society. In many ways, ranging from fidelity to the officer's oath to "support and defend the Constitution of the United States" to his veracity in reporting to civilian leaders facts upon which they will base decisions, integrity plays a substantial role in maintaining the system. "During the long history of the profession of arms, strict adherence to professional, ethical, and moral codes has been essential if the power and influence of the military organization were to be an effective servant, rather than the arbitrary master of the state."[13]

A primary source of support for civilian control is the military establishment itself. Concepts of obedience, loyalty, and duty reinforce the security and effectiveness of civilian control. A recent example in the uneventful change of chief executives was commented upon by columnist Art Buchwald, delivering the commencement address at Vassar College:

> I was at the White House that night to hear [the president's] resignation speech, and what impressed me more than anything else was that while one leader of our country was resigning and another was taking his place, I did not see one tank or one helmeted soldier in the street and the only uniforms I saw that night were two motorcycle policemen who were directing traffic on Pennsylvania Avenue.[14]

Some Aspects of Current Practice

As a wise commander once pointed out, much of what we ask people to do in the army is either dull, dirty, difficult, or dangerous, and thus a high degree of willingness to subordinate individual concerns to those of the organization is essential. It is appropriate to ask, it seems to me, at this time and in this context, what the experience of the war in Vietnam has to tell us about the current impact of the theoretical standards of duty, honor, country. I suggest that it tells us quite a lot that is reassuring, and that the preponderance of evidence is that the ideal operated powerfully during the trauma of Vietnam. Perhaps three million Americans served in the Republic of Vietnam, or in adjoining waters or the sky above it, during the long course of the conflict. Many would probably not have chosen to do so, most were exposed to one or more of the hazards described above, and yet the vast majority performed not only competently, but often with courage and brilliance. It is not necessary to downplay the perplexing implications of the well-known deviations from high ethical and professional standards to recognize that most Americans who served in Vietnam did so substantially in consonance with a demanding institutional norm. Furthermore, they did so at considerable personal cost, and many derived increased commitment to the values they adhered to in the process.

Having said that, more detailed concern with the negative aspects of the experience is appropriate to the present inquiry. Throughout much of the last decade and a half, the dominant element of the "management revolution" in the Department of Defense has been the systems analysis/operations research approach. Implementation of such techniques was described by Charles J. Hitch and Roland N. McKean in their book *The Economics of Defense in the Nuclear Age*. While the authors were careful to point out, over and over again, the importance of taking into account the nonquantifiable factors which they described as intangibles, imponderables, and incommensurables, in practice all too often such factors seem to have been ignored, assumed away, or otherwise not given weight. Even more dangerously, attempts were sometimes made to get at the impact of such factors by means of intermediate quantifiable data said to represent them. When the hypothesized representational relationship did not in fact exist, but was nevertheless considered to, one had a surrealistic situation in which masses of data were being collected, analyzed, and used as the basis for decisions and policy formulation, but with no relevance to the situation at hand. Furthermore, crises of ethical values were induced by means of soliciting the quantifiable data from those whose performance would subsequently be judged by comparisons of their statistics with those submitted by their peers.[15]

Philip Geyelin has observed that:

the war, and the manner in which it was waged, asked too much, not only of the military but of the process of government of which the military is an essential element and a vital arm. For what was asked of military and civilian leaders alike was that they lend themselves to a kind of continuing, calculated deception—a conspiracy in restraint of candor required by the very nature of this new concept of limited war. . . . What this meant in practical terms . . . was that military progress reports were very nearly required to report progress.[16]

The distinguished military historian Russell Weigley has stated that "the principal impact of the quantitative approach upon the Vietnam problem seems to have been an unhappy propensity in the Defense Department to try to measure quantitatively successes and setbacks."[17] David Halberstam has asserted that "the only measure of the war the Americans were interested in was quantitative; and quantitatively, given the immense American fire power, helicopters, fighter-bombers and artillery pieces, it went very well. That the body count might be a misleading indicator did not penetrate the command; large stacks of dead Vietcong were taken as signs of success."[18] Officers as senior as Vice Admiral William P. Mack have conceded that "some military commanders purposely misrepresented the true battlefield situation in the reports they sent to superiors in Washington." In his view, "the military bears the same burden as everybody else for misrepresenting the situation on such things as body counts in Vietnam."[19] Some insight into the difficulties which occasioned these several views may be obtained by considering two significant attempts to measure progress in Vietnam, the body count and the assessment of hamlet security.

The Body Count

The body count may well be the most misguided attempt to devise a measure of progress that one could discover. This judgment could be made on any one of several grounds, to include both practical and philosophical. In retrospect, one can understand how we came to it, while still deploring the apparently unintended and unforeseen consequences.

Vietnam was a war unlike others in recent American experience. In World War II, for example, the archetypal war experience for most policy makers of recent years, measurement of progress was relatively simple. Well-defined front lines existed, and they either remained static or moved forward or back. If we pushed our lines forward, forcing the enemy's back, that was progress, clear and simple. Furthermore, it was progress that was easily explained and demonstrated. Schematic battle maps appeared in daily newspapers, with the front lines shown for that day and the previous day, and a cross-hatched area between highlighting the change. That cross-hatching represented progress (or loss) in a dramatic and graphic way. No agonizing over hearts and minds, no speculation over light at the end of the tunnel; you were moving the line forward or you were not, and you were therefore either winning or losing.

In Vietnam all that was changed. Probably no comparable situation had existed for United States forces, at least on a scale which characterized an entire campaign, since the Indian wars. There were, quite literally, no front lines. Enclaves were established and held, areas patrolled or searched, but nothing ever seemed clearly definable, much less permanent. Forces fought over the same ground two, three, a half dozen times. And won every time. And had nothing to show for it. At least nothing so clear and satisfying as advancement of front lines, acquisition of territory, and pushing back the enemy.

There was an ill-fated convergence of the frustration of this amorphous campaign with the advent of the managerial revolution, with all its emphasis on precision, scientific techniques, use of computer technology and, above all, its self-confidence. A way to measure and to demonstrate progress must be found, and it must be quantifiable. Perhaps someone knows (though I do not) the hard-pressed analyst struggling to meet this need from whose mind unfortunately there sprang the idea of the body count.

One of my colleagues has suggested that, when major policy decisions are being contemplated, there ought to be a requirement for some kind of ethical and moral impact statement, similar to the environmental impact statements now required in advance of major construction projects. It is hard to determine in retrospect whether such a statement, written before the fact, could have alerted us to the severe strains and widespread undercutting of ethical performance which were to result from institution of the body count as a "management tool," used to measure not only progress but also performance. But with benefit of hindsight these disastrous effects are all too readily apparent. Leaving aside the practical issue of whether the number of bodies produced had all that much to do with progress in such a war, on ethical grounds alone we might well have declared the body count unacceptable. Commanders at all levels, many of whom had only six months at most to prove themselves, were required to report their unit's body count, knowing full well that their performance would be judged based on the report.

The pressures were enormous, and they were virtually all in one direction (the Vietnam lore is conspicuously short on reports of commanders who came down to verify their subordinates' body count reports in order to insure that they were not being inflated). Some commanders, at various levels, caved in to fear or self-interest, and submitted exaggerated body counts, perhaps justifying them to themselves as "probable" after artillery or air strikes, or maintaining that the enemy had probably carried away that many bodies under cover of darkness. Knowledgeable staff officers learned to look at disparities between numbers of weapons captured (hard, verifiable evidence which could be turned in) and the body count as evidence of probable inflation of the latter. A reported body count of twenty, and three weapons turned in, made everyone feel uneasy.

Other officers refused to inflate the body count, or to allow their staff officers to do so, and risked paying the price in terms of being compared unfavorably with their peers. This was particularly risky inasmuch as statistical comparisons seldom took into account differences in assets made available to various commanders, so that lesser amounts of helicopter airlift, artillery, close air support, and so on were not often considered excuses for falling behind competing units in amassing high body counts. Many honest officers can recount visits from their superiors expressing dissatisfaction with reported body counts, suggesting that the estimate was too low, and employing other techniques of subtle and not so subtle pressure.

Still other officers were fortunate or skillful enough to consistently produce high actual body counts, so that they were able to prosper without agonizing over whether to inflate their reports. I think a minority were in this lucky category.

If there are any "lessons" to be learned from that war, one of the most important ought to be that it is unethical, impractical, self-deceiving, self-defeating, and potentially disastrous to extract from commanders statistical reports which are then compared with those of their peers and upon which are based the evaluation of their performance as commanders.

The Hamlet Evaluation System

A second, and in some ways even more interesting, supposed indicator of progress was later introduced, and it became known as the Hamlet Evaluation System. Based on a lengthy, complex, and superficially impressive list of factors to be evaluated and reported upon by the American advisor on the scene, it purported to give an analytical picture of the relative security of a given hamlet.

An official report once candidly observed that pacification is illusory in Vietnam. Experience bore this out as hamlets "pacified" in earlier years had to be pacified again, large proportions of the supposedly secure rural population lived with an active Viet Cong infrastructure, and assassinations and abductions of South Vietnamese officials showed major increases in the midst of the pacification program. Meantime, advisors struggled with hamlet evaluation worksheets and the numerous problems associated with them.

There remains the question as to whether the indicators were in fact valid measures of the true state of pacification. Even if they were honestly and accurately reported, there was major difficulty in independent determination by advisors as to the state of each indicator, and many relied heavily upon their Vietnamese counterparts to provide the information. The counterpart, of course, like the advisor, had a vested interest in the results. If he was newly assigned to the district, his tendency was to exaggerate the degree of enemy activity; subsequent reports could then plausibly reflect improvement of security on his watch. An incumbent who had been on the job long enough to be held responsible for the state of affairs experienced a contrary pressure to upgrade the security assessment, showing progress over previous periods. There was a calculus resulting from like pressures upon the advisor, whose tenure might or might not be in phase with that of his counterpart. Given the inherently conjectural nature of the evaluation process to begin with, and the strong but bewilderingly indeterminate influence of these individual factors, it is no wonder that the agglomerated results of numerous such evaluations provided little sound basis for making valid judgments of the state of progress or lack thereof.

The expanded version of the foregoing problem consisted of holding the American advisor responsible for the success or failure of those Vietnamese he advised. The corrupting aspects of such an approach are, at least in retrospect, fairly obvious. The advisor himself, having a vested interest in the success (or at least in his superior's view of the success) of his counterpart, became no longer able to deal with it objectively. In fact he became in many cases an advocate. This difficulty was compounded by the improbability that, in judging the advisor's performance, his superior would (or could, given what he probably knew) take into account such variables as the competence and experience of the advisee, the situation he inherited, the difficulty of the mission, the assets available to him, and the relative priorities he was being accorded by his higher headquarters. The consequences of this pheno- menon, in terms of inhibiting the training of counterparts to perform adequately on their own, are incalculable. One's visceral feeling is that it must have been enormous, possibly even decisive.

Institutionalizing the Problem

The debilitating effects of indiscriminate use of statistical comparisons is a lesson we have not yet learned. Young company commanders, afraid of the effects of too high an AWOL (absence without leave) rate in their units in comparison with other companies, sometimes place AWOL soldiers in a leave status rather than report them as absent without authority. Soldiers who should face courts martial or other disciplinary measures sometimes do not because their commanders feel they cannot afford to increase their statistic in that category. Commanders figuring their deadline rate on equipment sometimes forget, when estimating what jobs of controlled parts switching could put some items back in service, that not all jobs could be done simultaneously within the time allowed. Other similar practices occur all too often, all of them the product of evaluation by means of statistical comparisons, with the statistics derived from input extracted from those being judged by means of them.

Inherent in such depersonalized command and substitution of statistical "indicators" is intolerable pressure on lower echelons to be guided by how it will look on the charts rather than what is right in a given situation. The system also rewards relatively less meaningful and transitory accomplishments at the expense of more substantive and important (but probably less visible) building for the long haul well-being of the unit. This is especially unfortunate in the case of a unit which has been down on its luck. A competent commander could take it over, make quantum improvements, and not get the credit he deserves. In the unfootnoted statistical comparison, he could still come out behind, and yet have done more for his unit than any competitor. Furthermore, he would know this, and would have to struggle with his survival instincts as he submitted each statistical report to higher headquarters. Forced to operate in such an environment, to decide daily whether to opt for appearance over substance, and searching for some way to reconcile the contradictions, it is obvious that many will feel powerless to affect the ethical climate and will elect simply to leave the profession.

My impression is that it was once more nearly the custom to evaluate the performance of officers not in terms of statistical data in comparison to some abstract standard, but on such personal and highly individual assessments of what they accomplished with what they had to work with. Performance ratings took into account the assets provided a unit, the number and difficulty of missions assigned, the condition of the unit when the commander took it over, and other such highly variable factors. Success was then measured in terms of what the officer did accomplish as compared to what he might reasonably have been expected to do. This philosophy of evaluation underlay General Bruce Clarke's observation that "the outstanding officer is the one who gets superior results from average people." It was a good philosophy, particularly since it pitted people and units against the best that was in them instead of in counterproductive zero-sum competition with others, and it was worlds apart from evaluation by statistical comparison, in human as well as ethical terms.

Meanwhile someone, somewhere, did us the further disservice of institutionalizing the failure to assign priorities in the form of the "zero defects" philosophy. Apparently oblivious of the concept of diminishing returns, and also of the deadening effect on morale of guaranteeing failure for all (no one, and no organization, can honestly sustain zero defects over the long haul, nor is there any good reason in most cases why they should), we enthusiastically laid down zero defects as a legitimate goal. We got what we deserved. I hope it is clear by now how directly related to ethical standards and performance such matters really are.

In what may be a digression, but what seems to me a relevant one, perhaps it should be observed that, prior to the nuclear era, the typical peacetime American army was, in addition of course to being very small, scattered as well. Between the world wars elements of a division, for example, might be stationed at a number of widely separated posts, and both signal communications and the means of transportation available to higher commanders to physically get to subordinate units were much scarcer than today. I think this is important. Not only were subordinate commanders not subject to constant scrutiny by their superiors, but the means for deriving and utilizing statistical comparisons between units must have been substantially fewer.

My impression is that soldiering was more fun in those days. I recognize what a hazardous thing that is to say. I do not mean it casually, or as an evocation of the image of the "good old days," or as an expression of frustration with the more difficult and more complex problems of the day. Some of this perception may be due to the effects of our present crisis-coping interest in nostalgia, but not all. I think, though I could not begin to explain or document it, that there is a connection between an atmosphere where fun can flourish and the ethical climate of the profession.

There is evidence of the kind presented so gracefully by retired Major General A. S. Newman in his columns in *Army* magazine to establish that the between-wars army enjoyed rewarding interpersonal relationships, especially in terms of "loyalty down," and that this made it all both more satisfying in human terms and more fun. It did not, it should be noted, mean any degradation of professional standards. To the contrary, it also may well have made it more efficient. As Martin Landau has pointed out (citing Blau's research) in his essay "On the Concept of a Self-Correcting Organization," there seems to be "an inverse relationship between close supervision and productivity."[20] It would be difficult to establish by reference to present practice that this is much understood within the army today.

Utility of the Present Standards

Allowance for and, yes, tolerance of human shortcomings, ethical as well as practical, is essential to the health of an organization. Just as the "zero defects" concept has been so harmful in holding up an impossible (not to mention non-cost-effective) standard of achievement that insures that everyone is at all times *guaranteed* a sense of failure, so does expectation of impossible perfection in ethical matters undermine the very standards it seeks to enforce by causing hopelessness and lessened motivation to meet *any* standards on the part of those who are (understandably) unable to meet standards of perfection.

When success in human terms becomes impossible because anything short of perfection is by definition failure, unhealthy pressures build to define and strive for success in less admirable but more attainable terms, such as promotion or decoration. It is not that these latter goals are not reasonable; the problem arises when they become disproportionately important because normally more attainable goals of success in human terms are frustrated by demands for unrealistic perfection. It is a matter of institutional arrangements which undermine rather than provide support for the desired ethical standards.

We have observed that practice has fallen short of precept in important ways. This is certainly no cause for complacence or self-satisfaction. But it is also no cause for abandoning the profession of ethical standards because they have not universally been adhered to. There is, and one might say it is inevitable, a disparity between aspiration and attainment in the ethical realm. It could be argued that, were there not, the aspirations are too modest. George Santayana once observed, not flatteringly, that the American "dreams of helping to carry on and to accelerate the movement of a vast, seething, progressive society, and he actually does so. Ideals clinging so close to nature are almost sure of fulfillment."[21]

Ideals to be fully useful ought not be that sure of attainment. The gap or shortfall between aspiration and achievement might be described as producing a sort of creative tension, an important motivation for efforts to improve performance and to reach the ideal. While this gap, so far as I know, cannot be defined with any precision, I believe it is possible to determine when it is an operative factor by examining performance. When the gap becomes too large, when the disparity between aspiration and performance is too great, then the ideal no longer serves to motivate performance. There is instead resignation, hopelessness, a feeling that the ideal is so far beyond reach that efforts to achieve it are doomed to ignominious failure. Instead of producing a creative tension, the gap then inhibits effective action. We are, of course speaking in general terms, recognizing that there will be differences in the size of the gap which can be tolerated or made use of by individuals.

Now we ask whether the ethical precepts represented by the ideal of duty, honor, country are so far beyond the attainable performance for officers of our army as to be of no value in motivating ethical behavior. My sensing is that the gap is not so great as to inhibit rather than foster ethical behavior. I would cite as evidence the indignation expressed by very many officers over debased standards, as described in the Army War College Study on Military Professionalism and as expressed in the symposia on officer responsibility conducted in 1974 and 1975 at the Command and General Staff College.

One thing derived from these latter dialogues is that the ethical concern and perhaps in some cases the ethical sense of young officers exceeds that of their seniors, a not surprising condition if we accept the view that the system contains elements that corrupt; the more senior officer has been exposed to the influence of that system for a longer time, and has prospered within it, raising almost a presumption of corruption according to this outlook. I believe many would agree with this proposition: where the system does not corrupt, the individual usually performs creditably; where the system corrupts, most individuals give in. This accords with what we ought to know by now about most people; they need a supportive environment to be the best they can be, not one which undermines their integrity and routinely penalizes honesty and straightforwardness.

It seems to me self-defeating to argue, as some have done, that the uncompromising standards of duty, honor, country ought not to be taught to aspirant officers on the grounds that they do not sufficiently reflect reality, and therefore do not prepare the student for the "real world" atmosphere in which he or she will have to operate. I think this argument misses the point badly. There is inherent in the teaching of such high standards the recognition that they do not represent the norm. On the contrary, the point in their being taught is to send out officers who will then help to affect that norm, by example and by persuasion, and thereby reduce the shortfall of practice as compared to precept.

Unless we can conclude that the gap is so great as to destroy the creative tension, which in my view it is not at present, then scaling down the ideal would make it less useful rather than more so. Few would argue that those schooled in the precepts of duty, honor, country are able to fully transmit them as an institutional norm for the army, or indeed to fully adhere to this ideal themselves as a personal standard of conduct. But to recognize that is very far from arguing that the standards therefore have no utility, or ought to be modified to bring them more in line with what may more easily be attained.

It is an intensely dynamic, rather than static, thing, this idea of institutional (and personal) standards of ethical conduct, and every success or failure by every individual or unit or staff or headquarters enhances or diminishes the persuasiveness and the supportiveness of the precept. Thus all of our judgments are and must be provisional. I know of no way to make valid comparisons between the ethical performance of the officer corps of today and that of an earlier day. What I do feel confident of, after some two decades of service, is that the precepts of duty, honor, country are strong and meaningful influences on the ethical behavior of large numbers of professional officers, and thus are important and continuing factors in assuring the responsible, honest, and disciplined leadership of our army. We need reforms, and I think I have made that clear. But the reforms we need are not related to scaling down the standards. Rather they are policy reforms, designed to remove institutional practices which place individual integrity under unwise and unnecessary stress.

General Creighton Abrams, while Chief of Staff of the Army, is said at one point to have asked, "Doesn't anyone out there just want to do a good job?" Lots of people do, and the system should be supportive of them, rather than putting obstacles in their way. In that way, and in that way only, can we get on with the pursuit of what Drew Middleton has called "the services' great if unrealized ideals of duty, honor, country."[22]

Notes

The views expressed in this article are those of the author and do not necessarily represent those of the Department of Defense or the United States Government.

1. *Cadet Honor Code and System,* 1973 (West Point: United States Military Academy, 1973), p. 9.

2. *The Officer's Guide,* 22d ed. (Harrisburg: Military Service Publishing, 1956), p. 253.

3. *Catalogue* (West Point: United States Military Academy, 1974/1975).

4. *Officer's Guide,* p. 254.

5. Ibid.

6. *The Armed Forces Officer,* Department of Defense Pamphlet 600-2 (Washington: Government Printing Office, 1950), p. 6.

7. Ibid., p. 1.

8. *Cadet Honor Code,* p. 9.

9. Daniel P. Moynihan, *Coping: Essays on the Practice of Government* (New York: Random House, 1973), p. 257.

10. B. Barnes, "Cheating Causes End of Hopkins' Honor Code," *Washington Post,* 21 September 1975, p. B3.

11. John Kenneth Galbraith, *The New Industrial State* (Boston: Houghton Mifflin, 1971), p. 340.

12. Arnold Toynbee, "Why I Dislike Western Civilization," *New York Times Magazine,* 10 May 1964, p. 15.

13. *Cadet Honor Code,* p. 1.

14. Art Buchwald, "Art Buchwald is Bullish on America," *New York Times,* 8 June 1975, p. 17.

15. Charles J. Hitch and Roland N. McKean, *The Economics of Defense in the Nuclear Age* (New York: Atheneum, 1966).

16. Philip Geyelin, "What Do We Expect of the Military?" *Washington*

Post, 5 May 1975, p. A24.

17. Russell F. Weigley, *The American Way of War* (New York: Macmillan, 1973), p. 459.

18. David Halberstam, *The Best and the Brightest* (Greenwich, N.Y.: Fawcett, 1973), p. 229.

19. G. C. Wilson, "Midshipmen Study Morality," *Washington Post*, 1975, A4.

20. Martin Landau, "On the Concept of a Self-correcting Organization," *Public Administration Review* (1973), p. 542.

21. George Santayana, "Materialism and Idealism in American Life," in *Character and Opinion in the United States* (Garden City: Doubleday, n.d.), p. 109.

22. Drew Middleton, *Can America Win the Next War?* (New York: Scribner's, 1975), p. 3.

9

Conflicting Loyalties
and the American Military Ethic

Philip M. Flammer

Professor Flammer, a former Air Force officer, critically evaluates in this paper the status of the military ethic. He provides a standard perception of the strains produced by the assumption of power in the military hierarchy and some helpful distinctions, e.g., between "professionalism" and "careerism," between legitimate ambition and selfish concern for personal image. He catalogues a number of specific instances where compromise of integrity and stubborn unwillingness to admit error led military leaders and others to moral disasters. He highlights the dangers in a "zero defects" mind-set and the critical problems that result from unwillingness to report errors. Flammer also provides a brief analysis of the concept of loyalty and its distortions within the military structure. In general, he emphasizes great concern and support for the highest values of the military ethic and is saddened by the fact that the ethic is not sufficiently indicative of current practice among American military professionals.

—M.M.W.

After visiting the United States in 1831, Alexis de Tocqueville noted that while democracies need armies, they inherently find these "troublesome." The nation and the army, he wrote, have "opposite tendencies" which "expose democratic communities to great dangers."[1] The "opposite tendencies" between a political democracy and its armed forces are obvious. The former is oriented towards the individual with emphasis on personal freedoms. It is characterized by debate, attempted reconciliation between

Reprinted from *The American Behavioral Scientist* 19, no. 5 (May/June 1976), pp. 589-604, by permission of the publisher, Sage Publications, Inc.

conflicting freedoms, and inefficiency. The military, on the other hand, is necessarily group oriented with strong emphasis on rigid discipline and obedience. It is also unavoidably authoritarian if not totalitarian in approach, which means that it is a closed organization with its own jargon, expertise, customs, and justice system. As such, it is vulnerable to dangerous tendencies such as abuse of power, careerism, and overconcern for image.

The American military ethic, which, for the purposes of this paper, I take to be all that is implied in the West Point motto of duty, honor, country, is designed, in part at least, to bridge this chasm between the U.S. armed forces and their parent society. It does so by pledging honorable and dutiful service to the state, which includes the American way of life. In short, the U.S. military pledges strict allegiance to a loyalty higher than itself, and its internal, nondemocratic codes and practices are, in theory at least, designed to enhance the means of meeting the resultant obligations in the most efficient manner.

That the U.S. military has had trouble maintaining its ethic at the best possible level is not surprising. Soldiers are, after all, not supermen, and the system has certain inherent weaknesses and tendencies that work against its own ethic. To speak about these weaknesses and deficiencies is sometimes considered trespassing on "sacred ground."[2]

Many in the military, in fact, seem to operate under the dubious assumption that criticism, even internal criticism of the highest order, is a form of disloyalty.[3] Nevertheless, most genuine conflict of loyalties involving the military ethic often initially stems from the system itself. William Mitchell, for example, gave the army considerable provocation before eliciting anything but a slap on the wrist; Hyman Rickover eventually won over his opposition on the matter of the nuclear submarine; Admiral Zumwalt, while encouraging some unhealthy opposition, still used his top position to reconcile the often conflicting goals of permitting initiative and preventing costly mistakes.

Power does tend to corrupt, and throughout history military men have had no special immunity to what Will Durant aptly calls the "poison of power."[4] Power is essential to the military ethic, but its possession does not necessarily enhance allegiance to that ethic. Indeed, the military commander rarely tolerates adverse comments from any subordinate source. It is no accident, therefore, that the military has its own public relations and justice systems, and that it clings tenaciously to a system whereby a sterling career may be ruined by the single adverse rating by a superior.[5] Moreover, the system instinctively protects itself by strongly discouraging admission of error, particularly serious error. The powerful, in other words, not only make mistakes but can dictate cover-up mistakes.

A recent and serious example of such cover-up occurred in Vietnam when General Bill Dupuy, a bright young officer recently named commander of the crack First Infantry Division, "made a fetish of firing his battallion and company commanders" and replacing them with men of his own choosing. Public relief of command is a serious detriment to an officer's career, but Dupuy's abuse of power was not counteracted even though Army Chief of Staff Harold Johnson thought the behavior "criminal."[6] Later, when some of the usually wise and seasoned veterans of the Indo-China conflict tried to warn Dupuy of potential error, he rejected their advice outright. "Dupuy," wrote David Halberstam, "was not interested; no one who had been associated with the past, flawed as it was, could teach him anything. He told the old-timers, in effect, 'Just stay out of my way and I will show you how it is done!' "[7]

The Dupuy story is not foreign to my own experience. While serving with the air force in Vietnam, I questioned a Seventh Air Force intelligence officer about a stunning discrepancy between very optimistic air force estimates of air interdiction along the Ho Chi Minh trail and the pessimistic reports of "road watch teams" that physically counted troop and truck movements along the network. "The general knows what he wants before he sees the data," the captain told me with some bitterness. "He writes the words. We are to provide the music."[8]

The abuse of power so prevalent in the armed forces is not always the responsibility of the commander. In the military, as in all hierarchies, there are subtle tendencies at work which enlarge the power and in so doing, encourage its abuse. One of these is the inherent relationship that exists between an individual commander with real or potential power and those who are part of or are trying to become part of the "inner ring" that surrounds him. It is a maxim that "authority comes to the leader from those who consent to do what he asks." Unfortunately, there has never been a shortage of followers, even if what is asked is obviously wrong. This stems partly from fear, partly from ambition and partly because of man's well-recognized affinity for a person-to-person type loyalty. For the timid, it may range from applause for what the person in power says and does, to strict adherence to social protocol.

A recent example from a state Air National Guard aptly demonstrates this moral myopia. In March 1970, the commanding general of the Air Guard told a group of his officers, "Gents, I know that what I am about to do is illegal as hell, but I've got to have political contributions; I've got to have one hundred dollars from each of you." Major John Calhoun refused; his loyalty to the ethic would not permit this moral wrong. As a consequence, he suffered severe personal abuse, including deliberate mistreatment by fellow officers who accepted favors from the general in return for whipping Calhoun into line.[9] Calhoun took the case to civil court, and won legal vindication. But his action was neither understood nor forgiven by many responsible leaders. Sometime after the scandal broke, for example, my position as editor of an air force journal allowed me to attend a national meeting of Air Guard commanders. Three generals sitting in front of me were talking about the case and I did my best to listen in. "It is a damn shame," one of them said. "He is ruining the guard." The others vigorously agreed. Sad to say, it was Calhoun and not the general they were talking about.

The abuse and courting of power combine to set up conflicts of loyalty. These conflicts exist not only between the commander and the ethic he claims to support, but between the subordinate who finds his loyalty to this commander in conflict with the higher loyalty theoretically common to both. Basil Liddell Hart offers two rather profound observations about the use and abuse of high level military power. The first, given to him, he said, by "his beloved old chief" was, "You'll find that generals are as sensitive as prima donnas." To this Liddell Hart added, "Royalty is also a state of mind."[10]

Another area of conflict involving the military ethic is ambition. Like loyalty, ambition does not take its value from the objective it seeks. Thus, an officer who wants to win a battle to preserve his nation has a worthy and lofty ambition, while one who seeks the same victory to get another star or build a foundation for political or material gain violates his ethic. Similarly, one maintains the integrity of his ambition by not doing that which is unethical, despite the fact that his action may be unpopular with those who write his efficiency ratings.

The striking personal excellence of men like George C. Marshall and Omar Bradley certifies what ambition has achieved for the armed forces. Our concern, however, is with cases that clearly conflict with the military ethic. But the conflict is largely generated by the military system itself. Rank is, after all, the basic hallmark of success for the professional military man. It determines not only pay and status, but has much to do with an individual's self-esteem. Also, the hierarchical system wherein men with power can hinder or hurry rank according to their desires carries within it opportunities for the overly ambitious that the ethically well-anchored do not have. It is not difficult, in other words, to make the subtle but terribly critical transition from professional to "careerist." "Careerism" inherently involves conflicting loyalties in relation to any idealistic ethic, and particularly the military ethic.

There is no way of knowing how much careerism has infected each of the U.S. armed forces. Despite many examples of dedicated professionalism, including whole units of men, I have seen too many instances of careerism. General Max von Hoffman, one of the ablest and most sensible generals in World War I, confided in his reminiscenses that among his fellow officers, "The race for power and personal positions seems to destroy all men's character."[11] Liddell Hart also lamented what he saw as "the growing obsession with personal career ambition": "As a young officer I had cherished a deep respect for the Higher Command, but I was sadly disillusioned about many of them when I came to see them more closely from the angle of a military correspondent. It was saddening to discover how many apparently honorable men would stoop to almost anything to help advance their careers."[12]

If one can debate the quantity of careerism in the armed forces, one can hardly debate its negative effects. The change from "professionalism" to "careerism" has the same effect that the change from the "public servant" to the "public official" has for some politicians. It automatically signals a change in emphasis from service to others to self-interest, from the responsibilities of trust to self-defined "rights" of position. It is a subtle and often unnoticed transition, but the true professional and the genuine careerist are poles apart when it comes to the viability of the military ethic.

One important factor which links the powerful who want to strengthen their positions and the ambitious who want to achieve positions of power is concern for image. Concern for image can have significant positive effects on any group. The U.S. marines, special forces, and rangers have demonstrated the strong relationship between morale and the self-image that stems from rigorous training, personal accomplishment, and belonging to an "elite" group. But concern for image can also have the unintended consequence of suppressing anything that might tarnish it.

Official military histories offer numerous illustrations. During World War I, one of the top French generals officially ordered troops in a particular area to stand firm during the night and begin a counterattack the next morning. When a perplexed corps commander reminded the general that the line in question was "behind the German front. You lost it yesterday," the commander smiled and said, "c'est pour l'histoire."[13] Jean de Pierrefeu, who helped edit the official French dispatches of World War I, was so stunned by the discrepancies he found that he later wrote his disturbing book, *Plutarch Lied*, in which he charged that "history itself is made the auxiliary of legend," and that "our historians [have] dressed the Staff in a cloth embroidered with gold palms, woven in its own factories."[14]

My own experience with official military history confirmed these experiences. While in Vietnam, where I worked on the official, top secret Military Assistance Command Vietnam (MACV) history, I often found shocking discrepancies about such important items as body count, number of sorties flown, effectiveness of interdiction, and so on. But it was the "official" and often demonstrably false figures that found their way into the MACV account, which we jokingly referred to as the "official progess report." In several instances I ran across official high level *forecasts* of operations for periods several days hence which were written in the *past* tense and gave detailed statistics on engagements, body count, and weapons captured. Also, the history always went through command channels for review, where unfavorable events and even "discouraging" words were altered or deleted. Indeed, my experience paralleled that of Sir Colin Coote who attempted to write a history of the British Eighth Army in World War II. "Productions of that kind," he wrote, "had to pass through so many 'vets' that by the time they had finished, an original Cruft's prize winner had become a toothless mongrel." Sir Colin attempted to salvage his honor as a historian by short-circuiting some of the censors "without full regard for protocol." This, he records, "was very nearly lethal."[15]

But the concern for image goes far beyond the official histories. Liddell Hart writes that not only does the military have many things "too sacred to write about," but that armies tend to be "temples of ancestor worship."[16] As a result, the services tend to regard as inherently "dishonorable" or "disloyal" any suggestion that important errors were made or that leadership, at least at the top levels, was ever less than sterling. This is true even of in-house documents. As editor of a military journal, I once attempted to authorize the publication of a remarkable article about a potential disaster apparently set up by unusually stringent "rules of engagement." It seemed an ideal chance to confirm a basic military lesson, i.e., if the mission is important enough, both politically and militarily, then the rules of engagement ought to foster its accomplishment. If not, then the mission itself should be questioned. I dutifully took the manuscript up the chain of command, only to be told by the commandant of the War College that the subject was "not important." At my request the general passed the manuscript on to his superior who, it turned out, had been in charge of the official investigation. He too felt the subject was "unimportant." Several months later, however, an aviator who flew the mission in question informed me that the discrepancy in the rules of engagement, which prevented adequate protection of the bomber force, had been recognized by air crews for months. The fliers had repeatedly reported it to superiors; the latter just as often discounted the warnings. The implications are obvious and it is incidents such as this that leave one wondering why the air force has been so silent about its role in the Mayaguez incident.

The fact that the military has been overconcerned with image is not surprising. As indicated earlier, it represents a basic weakness characteristic of "closed societies." Still, concern for image to the point where truth is covered up or distorted is fundamental to the viability of our military ethic and the credibility of the military establishment. A false image, like camouflaged history, "not only conceals faults and deficiencies that could otherwise be remedied," it fosters "false confidence—and false confidence underlies most of the failures that military history records. It is the dry rot of armies. But its effects go wider and are felt earlier. For the false confidence of military leaders has been a spur to war."[17] Moreover, maintaining an image of expertise and infallibility helps explain why, in the words of one critic, "Soldiers are so supersensitive to criticism that they feel it even when it does not exist. This tendency corresponds to the well-known medical condition of a nervous rash."[18]

Concern for image, however, inherently carries with it a subsidiary failing that runs directly counter to the military ethic and hence calls the viability of that ethic into question. This is the unwillingness of men in authority to admit error. Because the military service involves the "management of violence," human lives are in the balance and unwillingness to admit error, which in the long run may be more serious than the original error, potentially carries with it the unnecessary loss of life. A graphic example of this failing was the doctrine of élan with which the French entered World War I. This doctrine, which stemmed from Clausewitz's conclusion that an army is not beaten until it thinks it is, together with the triumphal vigor of the Prussian armies in 1870, suggested that will and determination were the keys to success. But this doctrine soon hardened into dogma that automatically transformed reasoned doubt into a form of heresy and hence effectively neutralized the few who dared to question it. The initial test of this doctrine was catastrophic. The number of casualties suffered by the French in 1914, when this doctrine ran headlong into quickfiring artillery, machine guns, and entrenched positions, is still classified. But the French clung to the doctrine long after the virtue of perseverance had become the vice of stubbornness. General Foch, one of those responsible for this doctrine, later called it an "infantile notion," but not until France had paid a fearful price. "The French came into World War I the slaves of an abstract military concept which was totally invalid," Sir John Hackett told his audience at Cambridge in 1962, "but from which they only painfully struggled free."[19]

A recent and striking example of the twin failings of unwillingness to admit error and the hardening of doctrine into dogma involved the U.S. Air Force's adoption of the so-called Zero Defect System. Taken from industry, this program sought professional and personal excellence to the point of minimum error. But interpreted literally, as some image-conscious and ambitious commanders were inclined to do, it automatically moved from the realm of the plausible and desirable to the impossible and impractical. In many instances, the program evolved into a "zero error mentality," that is, the commander felt that his command had to be error free. Since these men did not generally distinguish between mistake and misfortune, the inevitable result was not so much a positive objective of excellence but a passive, even negative, approach to the mission, one that precluded risk. Yet outlawing risk precludes initiative, which is a basic requisite for modern combat effectiveness. In the end, many errors were made and consequently covered up, for the zero error mentality is automatically wedded to the grotesque philosophy that it is worse to report a mistake than it is to make one. Such a philosophy has had severe reverberations throughout the entire military system and, unavoidably, runs into headlong conflict with the military ethic itself.

The nature of the military system, particularly as reinforced by the assumption of infallibility, concern for image, and unwillingness to admit error, demands that no military force be immune to the real possibility of dogmatic adherence to what ought to be flexible if not questionable doctrine. In World War II, the Germans suffered grave effects for their belief in Aryan supremacy and the personal infallibility of Hitler. The French lost the war, in large part, because of the "Maginot Line mentality." The British suffered from the doctrine of "limited liability" and the "indirect approach," while the Americans initially clung to the belief that their eagerness could not fail—a view that was severely undermined at Kasserine Pass—and that the bomber would always get through. In Vietnam, the "heroic infallibility" of certain political-military leaders caused serious errors, forced extensive cover-up, and effectively created a disastrous credibility gap between the politicians and military, and with the American public. Surely it was not surprising that a 1972 survey showed that, among twenty occupations, U.S. Army generals ranked fourteenth in credibility (well below the mean), while politicians ranked only above used car salesmen.[20]

Unwillingness to admit error is so common that one is tempted to call it a simple failing rather than a malignancy. But it is inherently no less critical than the error it is trying to hide, and because of a cumulative effect, it has often proven to be enormously costly. The Dreyfuss case and now Watergate should serve as constant reminders of what desperate men will and will not do when their images are threatened.

Primarily because of the tendencies and weaknesses noted above, the U.S. armed forces are much more distant from the military ethic than they claim to be. Most of this inadequacy is inherent to the system and could not be rooted out without radically changing the system itself. But these changes must certainly come. Errors, corruption, and wrong attitudes are generally more critical than in some other professions, since in battle these errors are paid for in lives loaned to the commanders in the sacred trust that unnecessary sacrifices will be kept to a minimum. The implications of this assertion are, of course, quite uncomfortable to military leaders.

Granted that in wartime there is little time to consider the kinds of problems we are discussing in this paper, there is little excuse for not doing so in time of peace.

In short, the military ethic calls for ultimate loyalty to cause and principles higher than self or branch of service. For that ethic to be truly viable, therefore, loyalty inherently demands emphasis on such fundamentals as integrity, a firm will to justice, and to truth, per se. But since "loyalty" is so often regarded as a virtue in and of itself, Liddell Hart's warning is salutary—that loyalty is a "noble quality, so long as it does not blind and does not exclude the high loyalty to truth and decency."[21]

Much like their civilian counterparts, the vast majority of U.S. servicemen simply close their minds to the dichotomy posed by serious conflict in loyalty. By reducing almost any crisis to its simplest form, they pass off the dilemma as "something no one can do anything about." If a true critic has spoken out, one can easily avoid a moral decision by automatically reducing the issue to a personality conflict between the critic and those suppressing him. For some, the natural reaction is to follow Nicodemus of Messina's response to charges of inconsistency. He saw "no contradiction in this," he said, "since it was always wise to be on the side of conquerers."[22] For the "simplifiers," the dilemma generates a form of moral blindness. As Joachim Fest writes in his monumental *Face of the Third Reich*, "Heroes are rare and in bad times weakness and blindness are for many a technique of survival."[23]

More enlightened or courageous soldiers may recognize the dangers and ardently wish for someone to do something about it. They themselves would stand firm, but not in the first line. Their problem is a basic lack of moral courage, a virtue so rare that, in Theodor Fontane's words, it "is always bound up with insults and contempt."[24] At the far extreme stand the *true* critics—men like Mitchell, Mahan, Lonnie Franks, or John Vann, who spoke out when the occasion demanded, and paid the price. The initial charges inevitably brought against these disturbers of complacency were disloyalty, ambition, and/or bitterness.

Perhaps the overall process of resolving the disharmonies between a military ethic and concrete problems inherent in the military system can best be illustrated by what happened to the German officer corps under Hitler. The German ethic put duty and honor at levels equal to the American and, in theory at least, the state remained supreme even after Hitler extracted the famous oath of obedience. But when he began overtly and covertly to undermine the officer corps with its remarkable reputation for solidarity and professionalism, the ethic disintegrated. When Hitler fired his minister of war, Von Blomberg, for marrying his secretary, who had a questionable reputation, and framed the chief of staff of the army, General Fritsch, a bachelor, on the charge of homosexuality using a perjured and pressured witness, conflict in loyalty became inevitable. The frameup of Fritsch became widely known, especially throughout the army: but in this crisis, blindness quickly set in for those who chose to see it as a personality conflict and opted for the obvious conquerer. The most enlightened saw that the removal of Fritsch and Blomberg were only stepping stones to Hitler's real target, the officer corps. But they did nothing. In thus eliminating the two officers without the resistance that was demanded by the ethic, Hitler, Fest writes:

> had eliminated the last power center of any significance and, along with the whole civilian power, now held the military in his hand. Contemptuously he commented that he now knew all generals were cowards. His contempt was reinforced by the unhesitating readiness of numerous generals to move into the positions which had become free, even before Fritsch's rehabilitation. This process also demonstrated that the inner unity of the officer corps was finally broken and that the solidarity of the caste, which had already failed to vindicate itself in the case of the murder of Schleicher and Bredow, no longer existed.[25]

It is significant that one man, Chief of General Staff General Ludwig Beck, had the vision to see what the ultimate loss of the military ethic would mean. "What are at stake here, are decisions which in the last analysis affect the existence of the nation."

If the German ethic, like the American, "repudiated disobedience, it nonetheless left room for the refusal of obedience."[26] Those, like Beck, who eventually were involved in the plot on Hitler's life, did so because they saw an unavoidable conflict between personal loyalty to a constituted authority who was leading a nation to ruin and their higher duty to the nation itself. "We are purifying ourselves," General Stieff replied when asked the reason for the attempt. But others, who lacked both perspective and moral courage, showed themselves unwilling or unable to understand the necessity of recapturing the lost ethic. When asked at Nuremberg whether he ever thought of getting rid of Hitler, former Field Marshall von Rundstedt replied without hesitation that he was a soldier not a traitor.[27] For his part, Field Marshall Keitel, Hitler's military aide and a toad of a man, had so far lost his grip on the military ethic that he could see nothing in the attempt on Hitler's life other than "injured pride, frustrated ambition and office-seeking."

Keitel, like the crack SS, sought refuge from moral decisions in clinging to an abstract loyalty that was "isolated from all reason and hence from all meaning."[28] In thus maintaining a personal ethic that separates loyalty from the object one is supposed to be loyal to, the latter helped write the most sordid and bloody chapter in German history. Not all German officers, of course, were Nazis, and one is left with Fest's melancholy conclusion that "It was not solely the Nationalist Socialist party officer who damaged the reputation and prestige of the army. It was no less the obsequiousness of so many, the total lack of moral courage in so many, that dulled the lustre of undoubtedly real soldierly and professional virtues and did more to dishonor the image of the officer corps than all the reproaches of its bitterest opponents."[29]

The U.S. military ethic is designed to put principle above self-interest. Personal integrity and moral courage are the keys to viability of that ethic. Yet Liddell Hart found moral courage "was quite as rare in the top levels of the services as among politicians."[30] And the "inherent isolation" that he says awaits the true critic is possible only because of the weakness on the part of the army. Indeed, I know of no single instance where moral courage on the part of more that a few of the military professionals played a significant part in correcting a major defect in the system or corrected a major injustice, despite the fact that moral courage is, in theory, encouraged in the military. An army ROTC manual, for example, currently used throughout the country contains the following statement: "There probably comes a time in every military leader's career when a fundamental disagreement with a superior exists. Here the institution expects the subordinate to have the moral courage (an example of a trait in action) to make his objection known to his superior. Adjusting to personality differences is a normal human reaction and does not imply compromise of principles."[31]

Yet, to my personal knowledge, a very bright young ROTC cadet who applied this principle at a major academic institution by questioning what happened to John Vann was denied a regular commission. That the reason was largely due to the moral courage of this student in honestly questioning some things his superiors said, is evident from the fact that the major who broke the news to him did so without rancor, telling him, in effect, that "your kind are not appreciated in the military"; "we are doing you a favor by keeping you from making the service a career."

As for the U.S. military, I know many honest, upright servicemen who cling to the most scrupulous integrity that does not discount moral courage. But, in the aggregate, they are much more rare than we have a right to expect. In the final analysis, integrity is the only thing that can certify any idealistic ethic. "Integrity is the glue that ties us all together," Air Force Chief of Staff General John Ryan told a class at the Air War College in May, 1973. *"Fierce adherence to one's personal integrity is the greatest strength that any soldier or statesman could have."*[32] T. K. Finletter's remark that character is the "first requirement" of leadership goes well in hand with the sensible observation that occasional virtue simply does not imply any long-range values. Or we have Charles W. Ackley's conviction "that the problem of military power especially in America cannot be comprehended in less than moral terms."[33]

I do not consider myself an alarmist although that charge is inevitably brought against anyone who complains aloud about the conditions of society. But the unfortunate conditions revealed in the Watergate mess, in books such as Halberstam's *The Best and the Brightest,* and David Wise's *The Politics of Lying,* and in examples of selfishness, indifference, unethical or dishonorable conduct on a massive scale is worrisome. And it deepens my concern for the U.S. armed forces for which I retain a strong affinity. As understandable as errors are in such a massive bureaucracy, as easy as it is to comprehend that the military can hardly avoid reflecting its parent society, recognizing, as Arnold Toynbee put it, that military virtues are not a class apart but "are virtues in every walk of life . . . nonetheless, virtues for being jewels set in blood and iron,"[34] one basic conclusion remains. Unlike politics or business, where individual failings are rarely lethal, military errors inherently involve the potential loss of life. The stakes are too high for anyone in or out of the armed forces to excuse military failings on the basis that everyone else is doing them.

Put another way, loyalty to the American ethic requires a dedicated effort on the part of commanders and officers to develop the art of leadership rather than fall back on raw "drivership," which is merely the offshoot of power. Perhaps the basic problem of conflicting loyalties and the American military ethic, including its relationship to the American ethic, can be summed up in a question posed by Walter Karp, one which he said "has never been precisely formulated, and we are in danger of answering it without even knowing what has been asked."

The question is this: do men, as a matter of ascertainable fact, want serious demands made upon their courage, loyalty, generosity and understanding? Do men, in other words, care to be moral beings, and do we prefer a life that might penalize us somehow for being craven, faithless and ungenerous? If we do not, then there is nothing radically wrong with the world. It is being fashioned in every way to suit us. If we do, then there is a great deal wrong with the world, and it is getting worse.[35]

Notes

1. A. de Tocqueville, *Democracy in America*, 2 vols. (New York: Colonial Press, 1899), Vol. 2, pp. 227-229.

2. Brigadier General R. W. Williams, "Commanders and Intelligence," *Army Magazine*, 1972, p. 11.

3. R. F. Weigley, "Review of *The Patton Papers*," *Military Review*, 1972, p. 103.

4. W. Durant, *Caesar and Christ* (New York: Simon & Schuster, 1944), p. 266.

5. In the January 1962 issue of *Military Review*, a journal associated with the Army Command and Staff College, an article appeared containing the following statement: "It is common knowledge, moreover, that for every bad efficiency report that is justified on the grounds of incompetence, another is the product of a vindictive rater meting vengeance on a junior who has crossed him. The way to get promoted is to keep a clean nose—a little brown will not hurt, though, and not step on any toes." Quoted in Anthony J. Daniel, "Evaluations and Systems and Superior-Subordinate Relationships," *Military Review*, January 1972, pp. 5-6.

6. D. Halberstam, *The Best and the Brightest* (Greenwich, Conn.: Fawcett, 1972), p. 657.

7. Ibid.

8. Personal interview with Captain P. W., Tan Son Nhut AB, Republic of South Vietnam, 16 February 1969.

9. *Montgomery Advertiser*, 28 November 1971. By this time, of course, the suit had been filed and the *Montgomery Advertiser* ran a lengthy series on the scandal. In December 1971, Harold Martin, the editor, confessed to this writer that he was under considerable pressure to cease his "crusade." I also had a chance to talk with Major Calhoun about the matter and to read a portion of the trial transcript. Harold Martin did not overstate the case.

10. B. H. Liddell Hart, *Thoughts on War* (London: Faber & Faber, 1944), p. 66.

11. B. H. Liddell Hart, *Why Don't We Learn From History* (New York: Hawthorne, 1971), p. 62.

12. Ibid., pp. 25-29.

13. Ibid., p. 21.

14. J. de Pierrefeu, *Plutarch Lied* (London: Grant Richards, 1924), pp. 12-13.

15. Sir J. Masterman, "The YY Papers," *Yale Alumni Magazine*, 1972, p. 9.

16. Liddell Hart, *Thoughts on War*, p. 131.

17. Liddell Hart, *Why Don't We Learn From History*, p. 27.

18. Liddell Hart, *Thoughts on War*, p. 138.

19. Lieutenant General Sir J. Hackett, *The Profession of Arms* (London: Times Publishing, 1962), p. 50. (This small booklet is based on a series of lectures given at Cambridge University.)

20. The survey enjoyed wide distribution. Most newspapers which carried the survey published the results in the first week of July 1972.

21. Liddell Hart, *Why Don't We Learn From History*, pp. 30-31.

22. Plutarch, *Plutarch's Lives*, Dryden translation, revised by A. H. Clough (New York: A. L. Burt, n.d.), p. 375.

23. J. C. Fest, *The Face of the Third Reich* (New York: Pantheon, 1970), p. 208.

24. Ibid., p. 235.

25. Ibid., p. 242.

26. Ibid., p. 245.

27. Ibid., p. 244.

28. Ibid., p. 186.

29. Ibid., p. 248.

30. Liddell Hart, *Why Don't We Learn From History*, pp. 29-30.

31. Colonel S. A. Hays and Lieutenant Colonel W. N. Thomas, *Taking Command* (Harrisburg, Pa.: Stackpole, 1967), p. 34.

32. Secretary of the Air Force, 1973. Parts of the speech were quoted in "AF Policy Letter for Commanders."

33. C. W. Ackley, *The Modern Military in American Society* (Philadelphia, Pa.: Westminster, 1972), p. 16.

34. Hackett, p. 52.

35. W. Karp, "What's Wrong With the World?" *Interplay*, 1969, p. 35.

10

Loyalty, Honor, and the Modern Military

Michael O. Wheeler

In this article, Michael Wheeler focuses on the concept of loyalty, particularly as it is relevant to the military profession. He analyzes the standard perception of military obedience, opting for "reflective" rather than "unquestioning" obedience in the military and pointing up the role that loyalty must play in military discipline. He suggests that loyalty, to be effective in the long term, must be inspired by trust rather than fear, and that trust is given to the person who possesses a clearly consistent moral integrity.

—M.M.W.

Like many other abstractions, loyalty is an often confusing, much abused concept. It has been employed by different people in different ages to mean a host of different things. For instance, author Hannah Arendt has written in her highly acclaimed work *The Origins of Totalitarianism* that "Himmler's ingenious watchword for his SS men [was] 'My honor is my loyalty.' "[1] Himmler's use of "loyalty" was intended to convey a certain idea to his listeners. Unfortunately, one finds much the same distorted idea in contemporary U.S. society—the notion of the dedicated military professional as one who gives his unthinking consent to all orders issued to him, whose very honor is a function of his unquestioning obedience.

Upon examination, it becomes apparent that this view of the military man is troubling to professional military officers as well as to civilian critics of the stereotyped "military mind." To quote Colonel Malham M. Wakin of the United States Air Force

Reprinted from *Air University Review*, vol. 24, no. 4 (May-June 1973).

Academy faculty: "We are concerned, all of us, about a picture of a profession that leaves us feeling that a man must give up his rationality, his very creativeness, the source of his dignity as a man, in order to play his role as a soldier."[2] What should especially concern the contemporary American in this view of the man of loyalty is, I would suggest, a twofold sort of thing. First, when soldiers have in fact wrapped themselves up in their jobs and obeyed orders unthinkingly, they have aided in perpetrating some of the gravest crimes in human history. An example that comes to mind is that of the German officer insuring the timely arrival of trainloads of Jews bound for concentration camps.[3] Surely this and any similar instance of aiding in the commission of a clearly immoral act would be vigorously condemned by the U.S. military tradition, the tradition of a Robert E. Lee, a 'Hap' Arnold, or a George Marshall. But second, even given the evils that unquestioning obedience has helped produce, there is still a certain reluctance on the part of any thoughtful man to condemn a soldier *categorically* for sincerely following orders and remaining loyal to his superiors. In the military environment, a set of related virtues— such as loyalty, obedience, and discipline—is necessary for the successful employment of military forces in the pursuit of politico-military goals. If wars are to be with us for the forseeable future, as most students of human behavior reluctantly agree is the case, then how are we to strike a balance between the necessary virtue of loyalty in the military, on the one hand, and on the other the democratic social goal of having every citizen become a morally sensitive human being? That is the question to which my article is addressed.

Giving and Obeying Orders

To get into this question, let us first examine the sorts of situations in which a soldier gives or obeys an order. In combat situations, orders are frequently given where life or death depends on instant obedience. For example, the infantry platoon leader upon seeing a suspicious movement out of the corner of his eye yells, "Hit the dirt!" Or the flight leader, spotting a missile rising through the clouds to meet his flight of aircraft, shouts "Break left!" or "Break right!" These are instances where unthinking, instant obedience is necessary to preserve lives.

I would suggest that these sorts of instances are often taken as the paradigm when one sets out to defend the thesis of unthinking obedience to orders, despite the fact that the instances cited are themselves the exception and not the rule where the activities of the modern military are concerned. Most orders are given in peacetime, not in combat. And even in combat environments, there is usually some reasonable delay between the giving and the carrying out of an order. This interval allows time for reflection upon the order, and reflection may produce a concern for the rationale of the order. Why was the order given? What purpose does the order seek to obtain?

Those operating under the suggested paradigm tend to question whether such reflection ever has any place at all in the military. Is it not true, they might point out, that the military runs on discipline, and is not discipline acquired by strict compliance with orders? The mistake in their reasoning is that they tend to reduce all instances of "discipline" to the model of the life-and-death combat situation, either consciously or unconsciously. If they are conscious of what they are doing, they may employ the Aristotelian argument that the soldier acquires the habit of instant obedience in combat by practicing instant obedience in peacetime. But even with this seemingly sound argument before him, one might still raise a question as to which is the proper goal of the military, blind obedience or reflective obedience. That is the question to which I shall now turn.

It is interesting first to note that some of the most effective military leaders in modern history have been sympathetic to the combat needs of the soldier and have nevertheless stressed training the military in intelligent rather than blind obedience. General George C. Marshall provides an excellent example. I shall frequently be citing him in this article, but let us first turn to Dr. Forrest C. Pogue, Marshall's respected official biographer, to find Marshall's views on the matter. In the Tenth Harmon Memorial Lecture in Military History at the United States Air Force Academy in 1968, Dr. Pogue said of Marshall:

> While he would not coddle soldiers, he would not attempt to kill their spirit. "Theirs not to reason why—theirs but to do or die" did not fit a citizen army, he said. He believed in a discipline based on respect rather than fear; "on the effect of good example given by

officers: on the intelligent comprehension by all ranks of why an
order has to be and why it must be carried out; on a sense of duty, on
esprit de corps."[4]

In the first volume of his biography of Marshall, Pogue writes
that "it had always been Marshall's style to lead by commanding
assent rather than mere formal obedience."[5] One can note that this
style of leadership is certainly not unique to Marshall. Intelligent
commanders have recognized the effectiveness of such leadership
for centuries. But what makes Marshall important for our purpose
is that he is close to the temper of our times. The problems that
Marshall faced—in raising and equipping an army in a time of
austerity, in maintaining the morale of the military in a society that
was largely antimilitary, in developing discipline in men from all
walks of life, in coordinating national military aims with the aims
of allies—are not far different from the problems faced by the U.S.
military today.[6] Perhaps, then, Marshall's approach to these kinds
of matters has lessons for the present.

Three recurring aspects of Marshall's military experience are
especially valuable here. First, Marshall valued loyalty. Second,
he was recognized by friend and foe alike as a man of imposing
moral integrity. And third, in the major war of this century,
Marshall passed the ultimate military test of the commander: he
brought his nation victory. These three things are important, and I
shall spend much of the remainder of this article arguing that,
given the proper view of loyalty, there need be no incompatibility
between loyalty, honor (in the sense of preserving one's moral
integrity), and military success, even in today's world.

A Perspective on Loyalty

Whenever we speak of loyalty, we are speaking of a two-object
context: a context in which one gives loyalty and another receives
loyalty. Now, given this rather simple conceptual picture, what we
might focus our attention on is neither the giving nor the receiving
of loyalty but instead the *inspiring* of loyalty. That is to say, put
yourself in a commander's position and ask, "What inspires men to
be loyal to me?" Once the semantical issues are sifted through,

there will remain, I would suggest, a single theme which forms the answer to that question. The theme is "trust." If a commander can inspire trust, he will at the same time inspire loyalty. Without trust, he may be able momentarily to *compel* compliance with his orders, but this compliance will not be the same as loyalty. Loyalty is not compelled; it is inspired. Where loyalty exists, obedience to orders is characterized by a certain kind of superior-subordinate relationship. Colonel Truman Smith, one of Marshall's subordinates at the Infantry School, Fort Benning, Georgia, before World War II, put this in words: "He would tell you what he wanted and then you would do it. There was something about him that made you do it, and of course you wanted to do it the way he wanted—which is the trait of a commanding officer."[7]

Now why, one might ask, did men respond to Marshall in this way? What was it about Marshall that inspired trust? This is a complex question, but of all Marshall's character traits, there is one that shines through and perhaps suggests the main part of the answer to that question. Marshall's acquaintances, in commenting on the man, invariably come around to a discussion of his personal integrity. For example, General Omar N. Bradley, in his foreword to the first volume of Pogue's biography of Marshall, immediately stresses the integrity of the man.[8] Pogue himself in writing of Marshall says, "Born in an era which spoke often of responsibility, duty, character, integrity, he was marked by these so-called 'Victorian' virtues."[9] Dean Acheson, who served with Marshall in the postwar period, speaks of "the immensity of his integrity, the loftiness and beauty of his character."[10] And Sir Winston Churchill, in a tribute paid Marshall shortly before his death, said: "During my long and close association with successive American administrators, there are few men whose qualities of mind and character have impressed me so deeply as those of General Marshall."[11]

Integrity, I would suggest, was the crucial factor in inspiring men to trust George C. Marshall. Marshall was a competent man, but competence did not account for the trust he received. Many other competent men of his era were unable to inspire the same sense of trust. Marshall was a powerful man, a man in a position of authority, but the authority alone did not explain the sense in which he was trusted, for he had inspired trust long before he attained the heights of power. It was, quite simply, the moral integrity of the man, an unmistakable hallmark, that inspired the trust and—in turn—the loyalty which characterized Marshall's public service.

The thesis which I have proposed is that loyalty is primarily a function of trust, and that trust is usually given if integrity is perceived in the object of one's trust. To evaluate this thesis, let us consider it in two parts. The first part concerns loyalty, with ancient lineage in the Western tradition. In his classic treatise on leadership in the sixteenth century, Machiavelli advised the prince that he need not be loved by his subordinates in order to lead them. He need only be feared, Machiavelli suggested.[12] But Machiavelli's analysis of leadership was defective, as Rousseau was to demonstrate two and a half centuries later. A man may obey you if he is afraid of you, but his obedience is a weak and fleeting thing. Remove the immediate grounds of his fear and you have removed his sole reason for obeying. But if that same man is *loyal* to you, his obedience will have been insured in a much more lasting way, for the attitude of loyalty is a stronger stimulus than the attitude of fear. Rousseau wrote: "The strongest is never strong enough to be always the master unless he transforms strength into right, and obedience into duty."[13]

Now, a danger still lurks in this kind of loyalty, inasmuch as the demagogue can inspire blind, unthinking loyalty to himself and his programs simply through his personal charisma. The danger is precisely that this view of loyalty is compatible with Himmler's dictate to his troops, that their honor was their loyalty. What I now shall turn to, however, is a different view of how loyalty can be inspired, in a manner such that the military goal of discipline can be achieved along with the social goal of having soldiers who are also reflective, morally sensitive men. This conception of loyalty is one of loyalty inspired by trust, where that trust resides in the moral integrity of the commander.

Trust and Personal Integrity

The *Oxford English Dictionary* defines trust as "confidence in or reliance on some quality or attribute or thing." The attribute that we shall focus on is moral integrity. Now, the minimum content of moral integrity is being a morally sensitive person, and to see what this means, we shall turn to the respected British social philosopher H.L.A. Hart. Professor Hart writes:

> In moral relationships with others the individual sees questions of conduct from an impersonal point of view and applies general rules impartially to himself and to others; he is made aware of and takes account of the wants, expectations, and reactions of others; he exerts self-discipline and control in adapting his conduct to a system of reciprocal claims. These are universal virtues and indeed constitute the specifically moral attitude to conduct.[14]

Hart's important points are three: an impartial point of view, an active concern for others, and a disciplined attempt to meet the claims made on one's behavior. These are the marks of the morally sensitive man, and they constitute a large part of what we ordinarily mean when we speak of personal integrity. These qualities are found in great leaders in any age, and they are exemplified by George C. Marshall. He paid strict attention to the notion of impartial behavior, so as not to use his position to benefit himself or his friends unfairly. For example, Pogue writes, "Marshall applied the same rigid standards to himself that he set for others. During the war, he told his Secretary, General Staff, that if he received any decorations, honorary degrees, or had a book written about him, he would transfer out of the Pentagon. Only at the president's personal direction did he waive the first prohibition."[15] Even when he agreed, at the President's insistence, to accept personal decorations, he held them to a minimum, saying: "I thought for me to be receiving any decorations while our men were in the jungles of New Guinea or the islands of the Pacific especially or anywhere else there was heavy fighting . . . would not appear at all well."[16] This statement was made with an attitude of humility, indicating the strict command Marshall had over his own ambitions as well as his true concern for his soldiers.

This concern for his soldiers had characterized his entire career. While he was assigned to the Infantry School, for instance, he was responsible for training several groups of Air Corps National Guardsmen and reservists. In one group were two black officers. Given the prejudice of the times and the location of the training base (Fort Benning, Georgia), it was not surprising when some of the students circulated a petition demanding that the blacks withdraw from the school. When Marshall learned of the petition, he exercised his moral leadership and defeated it. One of the two blacks involved was to write Marshall many years later: "Your quiet and courageous firmness, in this case, has served to hold my belief in the eventual solution of problems which have beset my people in their ofttimes pathetic attempts to be Americans."[17]

Marshall could fire subordinates, but he never became hardened to the needs and concerns of his men. He had, one must conclude, a notable moral attitude toward his military duty, and this attitude merely reflected his integrity as a man. He directed one of the most difficult wars in history, without surrendering that integrity to the needs of the moment. He was, in the highest sense, the truly moral military leader.

Loyalty and the Needs of a Democracy

Thus, in George C. Marshall a reasonable blend of loyalty, honor, and military success was achieved. The question remaining is whether the perspective on loyalty that I have proposed is the proper perspective for today's military.

In the United States today, the young officer or enlisted man who is beginning his military service comes from a society whose values do not support the rigidly conceived notion of discipline. That is to say, discipline is not valued for discipline's sake. The young American is attuned to questions concerning morality and war. He expects to be given a reason when told to do something. He does not always accept established traditions without question. He is often suspicious of bureaucracy and its ways.[18] He is, in short, the type of person who leads respected military writers to say that "the gap between the values held by a large percentage of American youth and those required for effective military service is probably larger today than ever before."[19]

There remains, however, at least one thing that such a young man or woman responds to, today as in the past. He or she recognizes a man of integrity and can be inspired to trust such a man. This trust can serve to close the gap between the values of the soldier and his commander, for trust creates a sympathetic attitude and a propensity to obey. If you trust someone, you give him the benefit of the doubt when it comes to doing what he tells you to. Thus, the soldier of a democracy can remain a moral agent, ultimately responsible for his actions, and can at the same time obey the orders of a person he trusts, on the presumption that the orders are legally and morally correct. This is a presumption that all Americans would like to be able to make about the military commander, and it is one which they are justified in making if the commander is a man of integrity.

This picture of the military places a heavy responsibility (some would say burden) on all those in positions of command, commissioned and noncommissioned officers alike. But this is no more than ought to be expected of those in such positions in the military service of a democracy. The military life has long been considered a life of sacrifice, not a life of personal gain. It is essential that the emphasis remain on the former in developing a professional soldier. Given this perspective, and with the humility and wisdom characteristic of the soldier-scholar of Plato's *Republic*, the modern American soldier can revise Himmler's phrase and write his own epitaph: "My loyalty is my honor"—my loyalty resides in a man of integrity, to whom I give my trust.

Notes

1. Hannah Arendt, *Totalitarianism*, Part 3 of *The Origins of Totalitarianism* (New York: Harcourt, Brace & World, Inc., 1966), p. 22.

2. Colonel Malham M. Wakin, "The American Military—Theirs to Reason Why," *Air Force Magazine* 54 (March 1971):54.

3. This example was suggested by a *Denver Post* article of 12 April 1972 entitled "Ex-Nazi Given Life in Prison," which concerned the conviction of Friedrich Bosshammer, an SS officer on Eichmann's staff, who had been responsible for transporting four trainloads of Italian Jews from Italy to Auschwitz in 1944.

4. Forrest C. Pogue, *George C. Marshall, Global Commander*, The Harmon Memorial Lectures in Military History, Number Ten, United States Air Force Academy, Colorado, 1968, p. 18.

5. Forrest C. Pogue, *George C. Marshall*, Vol. 1: *Education of a General* (New York: Viking Press, 1963), p. 249.

6. The many excellent articles dealing with contemporary problems of the military include Colonel Robert G. Gard, Jr., "The Military and American Society," *Foreign Affairs* 49 (July 1971):698-710; Haynes Johnson et al., *The Washington Post National Report: Army in Anguish* (New York: Pocket Books, 1972); Morris Janowitz, "Volunteer Armed Forces and Military Purpose," *Foreign Affairs* 50 (April 1972):427-43; and Herman S. Wolk, "Antimilitarism in America," *Air University Review* 23 (May-June 1972):20-25.

7. Pogue, Vol. 1, pp. 259-60.

8. Ibid., p. ix.

9. Ibid., p. xv.

10. Pogue, Harmon Memorial Lecture, p. 13.

11. Ibid., p. 20.

12. Machiavelli, *The Prince* (1513).

13. Jean Jacques Rousseau, *The Social Contract,* Book 1, Chapter 3 (1762).

14. H.L.A. Hart, *Law, Liberty and Morality* (New York: Vintage Books, 1963), p. 71.

15. Pogue, Harmon Memorial Lecture, p. 16.

16. Ibid.

17. Pogue, Vol. 1, p. 260.

18. The many studies available on American youth include Paul Goodman, *Growing Up Absurd: Problems of Youth in the Organized System* (New York: 1956); Theodore Roszak, *The Making of a Counter Culture: Reflections on the Technocratic Society and its Youthful Opposition* (New York: 1968); Charles A. Reich, *The Greening of America* (New York: 1970).

19. Gard, "Military and American Society," p. 705.

11

Integrity

John D. Ryan

This brief statement concerning the importance of integrity to the military leadership function was issued by General John D. Ryan, Air Force Chief of Staff, as a policy letter for commanders on November 1, 1972. General Ryan disseminated this policy in the wake of revelations of false reporting in Vietnam, some instances at very high levels of command.

—M.M.W.

Integrity—which includes full and accurate disclosure—is the keystone of military service. Integrity in reporting, for example, is the link that connects each flight crew, each specialist and each administrator to the commander in chief. In any crisis, decisions and risks taken by the highest national authorities depend, in large part, on reported military capabilities and achievements. In the same way, every commander depends on accurate reporting from his forces. Unless he is positive of the integrity of his people, a commander cannot have confidence in his forces. Without integrity, the commander in chief cannot have confidence in us.

Therefore, we may not compromise our integrity—our truthfulness. To do so is not only unlawful but also degrading. False reporting is a clear example of a failure of integrity. Any order to compromise integrity is not a lawful order.

Integrity is the most important responsibility of command. Commanders are dependent on the integrity of those reporting to them in every decision they make. Integrity can be ordered but it can only be achieved by encouragement and example.

12

Truthfulness and Uprightness

Nicolai Hartmann

This brief excerpt from Nicolai Hartmann's Ethics *provides a meaningful distinction between truth as an objective value and truthfulness as a moral value. His explication of the concept of truthfulness relates it to trust, love, integrity, shame, courage, and objective truth. He further casts some light on circumstances in which the moral duty to be truthful may conflict with other moral duties, concluding that even the permissible lie must carry with it unavoidable guilt.*

—M.M.W.

Truth and truthfulness are not the same. Both are of value, but only the latter is a moral value. Truth is the objective agreement of thought, or conviction, with the existing situation. The agreement is not in the least dependent upon the free will of man. Hence it has no moral value.

Truthfulness, on the other hand, is agreement of one's word with one's thought or conviction. It is in the power of man to establish this agreement; he bears the responsibility of doing so. Truthfulness is a moral value. One's word, the object of which is to be a witness to one's real opinion, conviction, and attitude, ought to achieve this end solely. For as this is its object, everyone assumes involuntarily that one's word is truthful—unless there exists some special ground for distrust. The thing said is taken as really meant. Nothing is presupposed, but that the sense peculiar to the words will be fulfilled. Herein consists the natural and good trust of anyone who is not morally corrupted, the faith he puts in the words he hears. The lie is the misuse of this good trust. It is not simply a

Reprinted with permission of George Allen and Unwin Ltd., from *Ethics* by Nicolai Hartmann, trans. Stanton Coit, 1932, Vol. 2, pp. 281-285.

violation of the sense of the words, but at the same time a deception of another person, based upon his trustfulness.

Inasmuch as words are not the only form of expressing one's actual attitude of mind, there is together with truthfulness of word also truthfulness of act, of allowing oneself to appear to be such and such, indeed of conduct in general. One can tell a lie by means of a deed, by one's bearing, one's pose. Straightforwardness, or uprightness, is related to pretence not otherwise than truthfulness to a lie. Still, mere silence can be a lie. One who pretends and conceals is a liar in the wider sense of the word.

A lie injures the deceived person in his life; it leads him astray. Sincere expression is a good for the other person, since he can depend upon it; and under these circumstances it is a high and inestimable good. One might accordingly think that the dispositional value of truthfulness is only a special instance of brotherly love. A lie is, in fact, loveless. This connection may exist; and a trace of it must always be at hand. But it is not the distinguishing mark of truthfulness as such. There is something here besides. The unloving man, for instance, is merely less worthy from the moral point of view, but he is not reprehensible, not despicable. But the untruthful man is indeed so. He heaps upon himself an odium of an entirely different kind. He is "branded" as a liar, as one in whom we can have no confidence, as an untrustworthy person. Trustworthiness is a quite distinctive moral value; it inheres as a constituent element in what gives a man "integrity." The liar is precisely the man who cannot be regarded as an "integer," his worth as a witness is damaged.

In truthfulness and uprightness there is an element of purity. A lie is a kind of stain—which one cannot say of a failure to love; it is a degradation of one's own personality, something to be ashamed of. In it there is always a certain breach of trust. And there is also in it an element of cowardice. For in truthfulness there inheres "the courage of truth." All this distinguishes it from neighborly love. A truthful man may in some other respects be immoral; likewise one who loves may be untruthful. For there are lies which do not at all injure the person who is deceived; indeed, there are some which one commits out of genuine love. And conversely, there is a truthfulness which is highly unloving.

But despite everything, the essential connection between truth and truthfulness is by no means broken. Objective truth is still the value which is intended and striven for by the truthful person. It is the goods value upon which truthfulness is based. The situation that the truth-speaker aims to bring about is that the other person shall experience the truth. Upon this reference to objective truth—in which the general connection between the intended value and the value of the intention reappears—depends the high situational value of truthfulness in private as well as in public life. There is also a public truthfulness, just as there is a fraudulent and falsified public opinion. Freedom of speech, of conviction, of instruction, of confession, is a fundamental moral requirement of a healthy communal life. In the ethos of nations the struggle for such freedom is a special chapter on truthfulness; likewise the official lie, the deliberate misleading of the masses to attain particular ends, even down to the practice of official calumniation and instigation to hatred, constitute another special chapter. Truthfulness as a community value is a permanent ideal of the moral life, which in history forever meets with new obstacles.

Valuational Conflicts Between Truthfulness and the So-called "Necessary Lie"

Truthfulness as a value, with its specific moral claim, admits of no exception at all. What is called the necessary lie is always an anti-value—at least from the point of view of truthfulness as a value. No end can justify deliberate deception as a means—certainly not in the sense of causing it to cease to be a moral wrong.

Still we are confronted here with a very serious moral problem, which is by no means solved by the simple rejection of each and every lie. There are situations which place before a man the unescapable alternative either of sinning against truthfulness or against some other equally high, or even some higher, value. A physician violates his professional duty if he tells a patient who is dangerously ill the critical state of his health; the imprisoned soldier who, when questioned by the enemy, allows the truth about his country's tactics to be extorted from him, is guilty of high treason; a friend who does not try to conceal information given to him in strictest personal confidence is guilty of breach of confidence. In all such cases the mere virtue of silence is not adequate. Where suspicions are aroused, mere silence may be extremely eloquent. If the physician, the prisoner, the possessor of confidential information will do their duty of warding off a calamity that threatens, they must resort to a lie. But if they do so, they make themselves guilty on the side of truthfulness.

It is a portentous error to believe that such questions may be solved theoretically. Every attempt of the kind leads either to a one-sided and inflexible rigorism concerning one value at the expense of the rest, or to a fruitless casuistry devoid of all significance—not to mention the danger of opportunism. Both rigorism and casuistry are offences against the intention of genuine moral feeling. The examples cited are so chosen that truthfulness always seems to be inferior to the other value which is placed in opposition to it. It is the morally mature and seriously minded person who is here inclined to decide in favor of the other value and take upon himself the responsibility for the lie. But such situations do not permit of being universalized. They are extreme cases in which the conflict of conscience is heavy enough and in which a different solution is required according to the peculiar ethos of the man. For it is inherent in the essence of such moral conflicts that in them value stands against value and that it is not possible to escape from them without being guilty. Here it is not the values as such in their pure ideality that are in conflict; between the claim of truthfulness as such and the duty of the soldier or friend there exists no antinomy at all. The conflict arises from the structure of the situation. This makes it impossible to satisfy both at the same time. But if from this one should think to make out a universal justification of the necessary lie, one would err, as much as if one were to attempt a universal justification for violating one's duty to one's country or the duty of keeping one's promise.

Nevertheless a man who is in such a situation cannot avoid making a decision. Every attempt to remain neutral only makes the difficulty worse, in that he thereby violates both values; the attempt not to commit oneself is at bottom moral cowardice, a lack of the sense of responsibility and of the willingness to assume it; and often enough it is also due to moral immaturity, if not to the fear of others. What a man ought to do, when he is confronted with a serious conflict that is fraught with responsibility, is this: to decide according to his best conscience; that is, according to his own living sense of the relative height of the respective values, and to take upon himself the consequences, external as well as inward, ultimately the guilt involved in the violation of the one value. He ought to carry the guilt and in so doing become stronger, so that he can carry it with pride.

Real moral life is not such that one can stand guiltless in it. And that each person must step by step in life settle conflicts, insoluble theoretically, by his own free sense of values and his own creative energy, should be regarded as a feature of the highest spiritual significance in complete humanity and genuine freedom. Yet one must not make of this a comfortable theory, as the vulgar mind makes of the permissible lie, imagining that one brings upon oneself no guilt in offending against clearly discerned values. It is only unavoidable guilt that can preserve a man from moral decay.

13

The Ethics of Leadership

Malham M. Wakin

Colonel Wakin here reviews some well-known positions on the military ethic and comes to grips with the task of discerning the specific role that certain ethical values (integrity, loyalty, subordination of the individual to the group) play in the military function. He advises caution concerning the use of specific ethical codes, pointing up the natural tendency to treat such codes as exhaustive when they can only serve to highlight a limited number of moral precepts. He argues that integrity is the fundamental root trait of leadership. He points out that institutional demands for perfection often generate false reports from those who are afraid to appear inadequate and fail to appreciate the crucial need for functional integrity. In an attempt to clarify confused characterizations of the "absolutist" military leader, the "pragmatist," and the "relativist," Colonel Wakin analyzes briefly the status of moral principles, suggesting that the alternatives are not restricted to merely the absolute or the relative.

—M.M.W.

Western world literature is replete with references to the normal qualities supposedly inherent in or at least inextricably associated with the profession of arms. From Thucydides and Plato to writings associated with Nuremberg and the My Lai and Lavelle affairs, emphasis has been placed on discerning the moral responsibilities of individuals within the constraints of bureaucratic disciplinary structures. Fixing responsibility in these circumstances is not simple because the relationship between

Reprinted from the *American Behavioral Scientist* 19, no. 5 (May/June 1976). Reprinted by permission of the publisher, Sage Publications, Inc.

human values and the military function is so intricate and complex. It will be my purpose in this paper to examine that complexity with two major concerns in mind: an attempt, first, to understand the relationship between ethics and military leadership, and second, to venture some normative proposals concerning that relationship.

Ethos, Ethics, and Military Honor

Considerable confusion concerning ethics and military leadership is generated by the varying employment of terms like "military honor," "the military ethos," "the military ethic," "the military mind," "professionalism," "the military way," and so on. When Alfred Vagts provided his definition of "the military way" he seemed to have in mind a prescription of the "true" military function which would clearly distinguish the military role from the abuses of militarism. His definition appears devoid of value terms: "The military way is marked by a primary concentration of men and materials on winning specific objectives of power with the utmost efficiency, that is, with the least expenditure of blood and treasure. It is limited in scope, confined to one function, and scientific in its essential qualities."[1] However, as soon as Vagts begins to discuss the distinction between militarism and the military way, he finds himself involved immediately in a number of value questions, e.g., "humane use of materials and forces," misuse of power, self-perpetuation, placing the military above the interest of the nation-state, and so on. It is important to point out that while it is possible to discuss meaningfully the "scientific" character of the military function per se, that characterization does not remove the essential moral tone of the military function. This point needs critical examination since there are many who would argue that the military function and hence the military leadership charged with carrying out that function, when viewed from the point of view of professional competence, must be considered morally neutral.

Perhaps one of the most extremely expressed opposing views is that voiced by Dean Acheson in a speech bearing on the use of military force. Acheson said:

Those involved in the Cuban crisis of October, 1962, will remember the irrelevance of the supposed moral considerations brought out in the discussions. Judgment centered about the appraisal of dangers and risks, the weighing of the need for decisive and effective action against considerations of prudence; the need to do enough, against the consequences of doing too much. Moral talk did not bear on the problem. Nor did it bear upon the decision of those called upon to advise the president in 1949 whether and with what degree of urgency to press the attempt to produce a thermonuclear weapon. A respected colleague advised me that it would be better that our nation and people should perish rather than be party to a course so evil as producing that weapon. I told him that on the Day of Judgment his view might be confirmed and that he was free to go forth and preach the necessity for salvation. It was not, however, a view which I could entertain as a public servant.[2]

One plausible interpretation of Acheson's statement is that those military leaders providing advice to civilian policy makers need not concern themselves with ethical issues since the only relevant considerations are practical, not moral. Lieutenant General Sir John Winthrop Hackett provides a definition of the military function which might well fit Acheson's view, yet Hackett draws a profoundly opposite conclusion regarding the relationship of the moral to the military. Hackett suggests that the legitimate military function is "to furnish to a constituted authority . . . in situations where force is, or might be, used the greatest possible number of options." But those options are not devoid of moral considerations. Hackett affirms several times in different lectures that the principal task of the military today may well be to avoid war, the military function evolving to "the containment of violence" and not merely "the management of violence."[3] He says, "War in the sense of general unrestricted war, however, can no longer be regarded as a normal continuation of foreign policy or an alternative to peace."[4] Again he states, "War, total war, we have to avoid."[5]

Hackett, perhaps more than most other writers on this topic, emphasizes the intimate relationship between the moral and the functional aspects of the "military virtues." Hackett holds the eminently sound view that while loyalty, courage, and fortitude may well be and are desirable virtues in other walks of life, they are critically indispensable to the military function.[6] He further states that "the major service of the military institution to the community of men it serves may well lie neither within the political sphere nor the functional. It could easily lie within the moral."[7] We shall find occasion to return to this notion as we pursue in more detail the role of ethical considerations in military leadership. At this point we may wish to admit that an extension of the Acheson view previously cited is a possible description of the relationship between moral considerations and military advice (namely, that moral values are irrelevant); nevertheless, I shall attempt to show that such a strong involvement between the moral and the military exists and/or ought to exist from a normative point of view that the moral neutrality position must become untenable.

Those who use terms like "the military ethos" or "the military ethic" may have a slightly broader interpretation in mind than does Vagts when he refers to "the military way." I take "ethos" and "ethic" to be relatively synonomous collective references to the way of life and perspectives of the professional military leader. In modeling "the professional military ethic," Samuel Huntington attempts to characterize a relatively timeless view of "(1) basic values and perspectives, (2) national military policy, and (3) the relation of the military to the state." His justification for including any elements as part of this idealized ethic is "relevance to the performance of the military function."[8] Thus the function of the military profession implies a Hobbesian view of human nature that is weak, egoistic, savage, permanent, and prone to conflict. Further, success in war depends critically on subordination of the individual to the group. The military ethic is "fundamentally anti-individualistic"; in this realm we may find the strongest difference between the military value system and that of a liberal civilian society which stresses the importance and rights of the individual.

With respect to national military policy, Huntington's version of the military ethic is that it must view the nation-state as primary; it stresses the external threats to military security; it emphasizes the magnitude and the immediacy of the threats; it must favor strong, diverse, and ready military forces; it opposes international commitments and entry into war unless victory is assured. In discussing the relationship of the military and the state, Huntington holds that the professional ethic must view war as an instrument of politics and the military as the instrument of the state. The supremacy of civilian control is critical to the ethic. This leads to consideration of loyalty and obedience which Huntington calls the highest of the military virtues. Because of their importance, I shall postpone consideration of these virtues to a subsequent section of this paper and continue this section with some reflections on the concept of "military honor."[9]

The notion of military honor seems considerably more narrow than that of the professional military ethos or ethic. As Janowitz (1960) has pointed out, the belief system of all but the very elite military leaders may be more directly associated with the narrower notion of professional honor than with concern for political ideologies or more comprehensive views of a military ethic as depicted by Huntington.[10] My concern is that too narrow a view of honor has led to peculiar behavior patterns by military professionals in the past, and, in some ways, this narrow view continues to generate confusion and distortion. In the Western world we can find roots of the contemporary view of military honor in the aristocratic traditions of early European armies. Alfred Vagts relates the story of those peasants of southern Germany who fought for their emperor in 1078 against knights of the feudal armies who, upon defeating the peasants, castrated them for daring to bear arms, a privilege reserved for the aristocratic knights. Military honor, as characterized by Vagts, involved the practices of chivalry, including duels, but extended only to aristocratic peers.[11] Janowitz suggests that the "code" of military honor in the military was inherited from the British and contained the following four components: (1) officers are gentlemen, (2) personal loyalty is owed to the commander, (3) officers are members of one big brotherhood, and (4) officers fight for traditional glory.[12]

Modification of this code in the contemporary U.S. military is obvious. While we find American officers still concerned about being "gentlemen," that term refers today to standards of behavior and officer responsibilities rather than to aristocratic birth. Chivalry has generally survived only in attempts to provide appropriate treatment for prisoners of war. It is no longer the case that extreme value is placed on personal loyalty to a commander; that aspect of military honor is transferred to the oath of office which requires allegiance to the Constitution and to the position rather than the person of the president as commander in chief. The notion of brotherhood remains a strong component of the concept of military honor. It is still a matter of pride for many professionals to point out that "an officer's word is his bond," and it is a continual source of annoyance to many that they should be required to supply identification cards or driver's licenses or any references other than the fact that they are military officers if they should wish to cash a check or require credit. But the notion of group unity and brotherhood is most emphatically felt in what Janowitz calls "a single overriding directive": the professional soldier always fights. To refuse a combat assignment is to commit the most serious offense against one's military honor and to break faith with one's peers. As for the fourth component of military honor, we must agree with Janowitz that "contemporary military honor repudiates the glory of war." Perhaps we have substituted for the pursuit of glory the perception that the military life is a rugged and strenuous life of service to the state demanding personal sacrifice.

But discussion of "military honor" in its classical setting does not do justice to the complex uses of the concept of "honor" as it relates to military leadership. Many military leaders first associated honor with military life through their exposure to honor codes at the service academies. Certainly there has been sufficient publicity in recent years to generate curiosity about, opposition to, defense of, and emotional responses to the employment of these codes. Such codes have been characterized as too stringent when compared to the value standards of the present society from which the service academy students come (this criticism seems to have been ameliorated considerably since the Watergate affair and the alleged false reporting associated with the highly publicized case of General Lavelle). Administration of the codes has been criticized, particularly as regards the maturity of the student honor committees and the legal protection afforded those who are accused of honor violations. But a more important issue to examine should be the question of the lasting perception of honor that experience with an honor code provides to military leaders.

Codes of conduct, whether they be framed as honor codes for service academies, moral commandments for religious groups, prescriptions for medical or legal practitioners, and so on, all seem subject to the same sort of narrow interpretation which may cause distortions in our general view of moral behavior. The immature or unsophisticated frequently narrow their ethical sights to the behavior specifically delineated in the code so that what may have originally been intended as a minimum listing becomes treated as an exhaustive guide for ethical action. We forget all too easily the wisdom concerning these matters given us by almost every moral philosopher dating back at least as far as Socrates, Plato, or Aristotle. The classical Greek conception of the just or honorable man encompassed all of one's human acts. Moral prescriptions are given in broad terms, e.g., "seek the golden mean of moderation between the extremes of too much and too little," or "act in accordance with right reason." Aristotle would advise us not to seek more precision than our subject matter permits; moral philosophy cannot provide the specific conclusions of a mathematical system. We can identify general classes of good and bad human actions, e.g., promise-keeping, truth-telling, lying, cheating, stealing, and so on; but the crucial step to right behavior is not following a rule because it is a rule. Rather one becomes a good man through performing good actions. The critical thing is what kind of person one becomes in the long run, throughout a lifetime. Perhaps as far back as the sixth century B.C., Lao Tzu, the alleged founder of ancient Taoism, expressed this view of mankind's moral goal in the saying, "The way to do is to be."

The honor codes at the service academies single out lying, cheating, stealing (and tolerating these actions by peers) as act-types which are strictly proscribed with severe penalties (usually dismissal) for those who engage in these actions. In a real sense, this suggests a very Aristotelian approach to character development. If one practices telling the truth all the time—if one refrains from cheating and stealing all of the time—then these actions may well become part of the habitual human response to one's environmental circumstances. Such a person's character may be described as truthful and honest. But the avoidance of lying, cheating, and stealing does not by itself encompass all that we mean when we judge a person to be honorable.

At least one of the academies (the Air Force Academy) has a separate committee called an ethics committee which is concerned with cadet behavior not specifically included in the honor code. The existence of separate committees may lead the immature into an erroneous separation of "honorable" behavior from "ethical" behavior. Further, this same unsophisticated perception has yet to account for "moral" behavior, which some view as the very narrow "personal" area of sexual conduct which is somehow outside the realm of honor or ethics. Perhaps I have pursued this extreme distortion of views of honor, ethics, and morality much further than warranted by existing perceptions. However, we have occasionally had placed before us images of military leaders (often fictional heroes) whose private conduct (sexual, social, and so on) seems to function on a totally different level from their public conduct or their functioning in their areas of "professional competence." One thinks of the parallel with the age of chivalry in which the courtesies involved in the "rules" of chivalric conduct were extended only to one's peers but did not apply to behavior in other contexts or with other persons. It would seem rather ironic if the extreme separation of human acts into these artificially distinguished categories—the honorable, the ethical, and the moral—were to find some beginnings for military leaders in the very institutions which place profound stress on the development of the "whole man." And how would such category distinctions affect the advice of a Plato or an Aristotle who would recommend to the young who might aspire to military and moral leadership to "find a good man and imitate him"? The strange notion that honor is public but morality is private will receive further attention.

Obedience

As was noted previously, Huntington tells us that "loyalty and obedience are the highest military virtues," and Hackett pointed out that these virtues are absolutely critical to the military function. Huntington quotes Alfred T. Mahan on this point: "The rule of obedience is simply the expression of that one among the military virtues upon which all the others depend."[13] Huntington places before us such a strict view of military obedience that it is worth reproducing here for commentary.

When the military man receives a legal order from an authorized superior, he does not argue, he does not hesitate, he does not substitute his own views; he obeys instantly. He is judged not by the policies he implements, but rather by the promptness and efficiency with which he carries them out. His goal is to perfect an instrument of obedience; the uses to which that instrument is put are beyond his responsibility. His highest virtue is instrumental not ultimate. Like Shakespeare's soldier in *Henry V* he believes that the justice of the cause is more than he should "know" or "seek after." For if the king's "cause be wrong, our obedience to the King wipes the crime of it out of us."[14]

This statement of the military ideal is slightly softened by noting that it begins with reference to legal orders from authorized superiors. Huntington himself goes on to discuss the limits of military obedience. But the latter part of the quotation above presents us with an issue concerning military leadership that requires much consideration. Telford Taylor has performed an excellent service in summarizing American and international law and court decisions regarding lawful orders and the responsibilities of military subordinates and superiors.[15] He directs our attention to *The Law of Land Warfare* where the following statement of American law is found: "The fact that the law of war has been violated pursuant to an order of a superior authority, whether military or civil, does not deprive the act in question of its character as a war crime, nor does it constitute a defense in the trial of an accused individual, unless he did not know and *could not reasonably have been expected to know* that the act ordered was unlawful."[16]

The emphasis on instant obedience and total loyalty to the military ideal of subordination to military superiors and civilian leaders is critical and appropriate. An enlisted man in a battle context may well be unable to examine battle orders for legality. But the military professional, the officer leader, ought in fact "to seek after" the "justice of the cause." Obedience to orders is not in itself either a legal or a moral claim of right action although it is certainly a mitigating circumstance. Military leaders cannot be *merely* instrumental to the state. They are instrumental, yes; but they must at the same time accept a portion of the responsibility for the uses of the military instrument. How else, without investigating the issues involved, could any military leader ever make a decision concerning the legality or morality of his orders? Our current laws say that if he could reasonably be expected to know that his orders were not lawful, then "obedience to the King" could not remove the crime from his own responsibility.

It is clear from the behavior of some military officers as well as from some of their public statements that it is possible to divorce oneself from moral considerations altogether and insist that the contractual nature of service to the state is *merely* legal. It is at the same time clear that this position fails to recognize that a freely given commitment generates one of the strongest moral claims against the person who gives it whether that commitment be to private individuals or to a larger segment of society. That commitments voluntarily given involve obligations to fulfill them is not easily proven although it is easily seen. On utilitarian grounds alone one can establish that fulfillment of commitments made must lead to a better ordered universe and provide for the greater good of society than nonfulfillment. On Kantian grounds one easily sees that promise-keeping is the kind of human act that can be universalized and that keeping one's word involves treating other human beings as ends-in-themselves, beings with dignity whose worth is recognized when our commitments to them are honored. The military leader who does not accept this funda-mental approach to the moral relevance of his oath of office may do many things well but he will not command the respect or loyalty of his subordinates.

Even Thomas Hobbes (1651) observed that once one enters into a contractual agreement with others (the state), one has accepted the fulfillment of his part of the agreement as a moral obligation; indeed, Hobbes defines injustice as the breaking of one's contractual agreements.[17] If one is morally bound to keep his promises, then he takes on a *moral* commitment to obey the orders of his superiors when he takes the military oath of office just as the marriage promise constitutes a moral commitment even though it too takes the form of a legal contract. Thus obedience to orders is not merely a functional expedient for military men; it involves at the same time a moral commitment. The ground rules for violating this moral commitment are subject to the same considerations as are relevant to other moral contexts: we are justified in violating one of our moral obligations just when that obligation is in conflict with another, higher obligation and the circumstances are such that we cannot fulfill both. This principle, of course, involves critical normative considerations to which we will return.

That there are limits to military obedience can be readily granted; what these limits are is not so easily determined precisely because obedience is so critical to the military function. Huntington's discussion of these limits is excellent. He points out that military obedience can conflict with the aims of professional competence when a subordinate perceives that the orders received will not accomplish the superior's objectives or when rigid adherence to past ways of doing things does not permit new ideas to develop. Huntington expresses these conflicts between military obedience and professional competence as issues of an officer's moral virtue versus his intellectual virtue. He further notes that there arc at least four kinds of conflict which can arise between military obedience and nonmilitary values.[18] Military obedience may conflict with political wisdom as in the case of General MacArthur, who disagreed with the policies laid down by his civilian political superiors for prosecuting the Korean War. Military obedience may conflict also when civilian leaders dictate military strategy which supposedly rests within the professional competence of the military leaders. Further conflicts with military obedience include the obvious cases of legality and morality. The case of Lieutenant Calley and My Lai certainly involved the intertwined questions of obedience to orders versus both the legality and the morality of these orders concerning the treatment of prisoners.

Much attention has been given recently to the ethical responsibilities of military officers on this complex issue of conflict with the military ideal of obedience. In the *Congressional Record— Senate* some interesting commentary on this subject is made, principally by Senator Hughes of Iowa.[19] His remarks were made in the context of Senate hearings regarding the nominations for promotion of general officers, two of whom were air force officers who had previously been in General John D. LaVelle's chain of command in Southeast Asia during the period that General Lavelle was accused of ordering falsified reports of bombing strikes which violated the written rules of agreement. Senator Hughes opposed the promotion of these two officers on the grounds that they should have questioned General Lavelle's orders but did not.

His view is that military leaders remain responsible for insuring that the law of the land is carried out and are not permitted merely to accept the orders of an immediate superior when that order is known to conflict with national policy and written directives from the Joint Chiefs of Staff. Some of Senator Hughes' remarks that bear relevance for our consideration of the complex role of obedience follow:

> I could not rest easy if I thought that one of these men who knowingly participated in this false reporting might one day become chairman of the Joint Chiefs of Staff.
>
> The integrity of our command and control structure, both within the military and under civilian authority, depends upon men of the highest character, whose obedience to our laws and the Constitution is unquestioned. . . . If we choose to reward these men with promotions, what will the consequences be? . . . Will the officers down the line conclude that loyalty and obedience within one's service are more important than adherence to the higher principles of law and civilian control of the military?[20]

General John D. Ryan, former Air Force Chief of Staff, issued a policy letter to his commanders, subsequent to the Lavelle incident, regarding the relationship between integrity and command. It is clear that the ideal which General Ryan proposes places the value of integrity above unquestioning obedience of commands; indeed, he makes integrity the *sine qua non* of the military command structure.

> Integrity—which includes full and accurate disclosure—is the keystone of military service. . . . In any crisis decisions and risks taken by the highest national authorities depend, in large part, on reported military capabilities and achievements. In the same way every commander depends on accurate reporting from his forces. . . . Therefore, we may not compromise our integrity—our truthfulness. To do so is not only unlawful but degrading. False reporting is a clear example of a failure of integrity. Any order to compromise integrity is not a lawful order.
>
> Integrity is the most important responsibility of command. Commanders are dependent on the integrity of those reporting to them in every decision they make. Integrity can be ordered but it can only be achieved by encouragement and example.[21]

We are reminded of Hackett's view that while some moral qualities are merely desirable in other walks of life, they may be absolutely imperative for the military function. Integrity would appear to be one of those critical moral qualities which makes loyalty and obedience possible. In this sense Mahan may need to be corrected: integrity rather than obedience may well be "that one among the military virtues upon which all of the others depend."

There have been a plethora of stories concerning false body counts reported in Vietnam. Lieutenant Colonel M. T. Smith details further inaccurate reporting in such areas as aircraft equipment status reports, aircraft accident reports, and general military training requirements.[22] Smith attributes much of the inaccurate (euphemism for "false") reporting to two major aspects of current institutional reality: our stated goals are so high as to appear unrealistic, and some leaders give bad examples. There are high-ranking officers who do not take bad news well, so members of their staffs frequently tell their bosses just what they want to hear. "It is difficult to expect integrity from the rank and file if the rank and file do not see that same quality in those who lead them."[23] According to Smith, our stated goals for such things as aircraft operationally ready rates and repair cycle rates have on occasion been unrealistic; and out of fear, competent people have simply not reported truthfully that those rates were not being met. Smith's suggested solutions to inaccurate reporting involve total emphasis on integrity for every leader and adjustment of management systems to provide more realistic, achievable goals which are mission oriented. A recent empirical "Study on Military Professionalism" requested by General Westmoreland and produced by the Army War College verifies that in the army, as well as in the air force, management systems have sometimes emphasized the development of statistical results at the high cost of diluting the quality of moral leadership. Indeed a summary description from the U.S. Army War College study strikes a remarkable parallel with the situation described by Smith.

A scenario that was repeatedly described in seminar sessions and narrative responses includes an ambitious, transitory comman-der—marginally skilled in the complexities of his duties—engulfed in producing statistical results, fearful of personal failure, too busy to talk with or listen to his subordinates, and determined to submit acceptably optimistic reports which reflect faultless completion of a variety of tasks at the expense of the sweat and frustration of his subordinates.[24]

The Army War College study is well done. It utilizes a data base generated from questionnaires administered to 420 relatively elite officers from six different service schools (69 percent of them were lieutenant colonels and colonels) and 25 seminar discussions with a total of 250 officers including a much larger percentage of captains and majors. One general finding was the large number of strong perceptions of a marked "disharmony between traditional, accepted ideals and the prevailing institutional pressures." The traditional ideals are briefly summed up in the phrase "duty, honor, country." The study concludes that there has been little change in officers' perceptions of the professional ethical ideals but that the current institutional climate (*not* changes in civil society at large) is largely responsible for the perceived failure of many officers to live up to those ideals. High on the list of possible institutional causal factors for unethical behavior is the demand for perfection: "Faultless performance may be a suitable immediate goal for production line workers who have routine tasks or for skilled technicians who have nearly infinite time. For those who deal with complex organizations, changing missions, and people of various aptitudes, perfection or "zero defects" is an impossibility."[25]

In exploring the relationship between "ethical behavior" and "military competence" as viewed by the officers in their sample, the Army War College study found the two concepts to be so closely intertwined that "inadequate performance in one area contributes to inadequate performance in the other."[26] In general, the War College study confirms the view already expressed in various ways in this paper that ethical values are absolutely critical to the function of military leadership. If the present climate in the services can itself be viewed as generating a deterioration of those moral values, then it must also be viewed as hindering rather than facilitating the prosecution of the military function. The study suggested the following consequences of the army's present (1970) climate:

It is conducive to self-deception because it fosters the production of inaccurate information; it impacts on the long-term ability of the army to fight and win because it frustrates young, idealistic, energetic officers who leave the service and are replaced by those who will tolerate if not condone ethical imperfection; it is corrosive of the army's image because it falls short of the traditional idealistic code of the soldier—a code which is the key to the soldier's acceptance by a modern free society; it lowers the credibility of our top military leaders because it often shields them from essential bad news; it stifles initiative, innovation, and humility because it demands perfection or the pose of perfection at every turn; it downgrades technical competence by rewarding instead trivial, measurable, quota-filling accomplishments; and it eventually squeezes much of the inner satisfaction and personal enjoyment out of being an officer.[27]

It is certainly a tenable thesis that the structure of an institution that depends critically on the acceptance of obedience as one of its highest values may place a strain on the moral integrity of its members. But structures are ultimately molded by individuals; and those individuals charged with the responsibility of guiding the institution can, if they have the wisdom and will to do so, revise institutional pressures so that they become supportive of a healthy relationship between integrity and obedience and minimize possible conflicts which could arise between these essential attributes of the military leadership function.

Some Normative Considerations

In *The Professional Soldier,* Janowitz distinguished between "absolutists" and "pragmatists" regarding orientations of military leaders toward international relations. Janowitz did not interpret these conceptions in terms of personal moral values per se but restricted his discussion to the differing perceptions of the role of war; e.g., the absolute school, which was viewed as growing out of the punitive expedition tradition, views war as the basis of international relations and generally accepts no substitute for victory. The pragmatic school on the other hand views war as only one component of international relations and is more likely to think of furthering political objectives by the "right amount" of military force.[28] The absolutists are more likely to believe in major atomic warfare than the pragmatists. Because "absolutism" and "pragmatism" are more commonly used in their broader applications to human values and are frequently used to characterize the personal value systems of military leaders, I should like to enter into some fundamental considerations of these conceptions.

Those military officers who are viewed as moral absolutists are often called "men of high principle" and "uncompromising." Those viewed as pragmatists are often associated with "expediency" or "flexibility." Either of these characterizations is viewed as praiseworthy or pejorative depending upon the context and the persons employing them. To be flexible is sometimes to be mature and sophisticated; to be accused of expediency is sometimes equivalent to being accused of being unethical. Analogously, to be uncompromising is sometimes to be narrow and stubborn and unsophisticated; on the other hand, a leader who is unwilling to compromise his absolute principles is sometimes viewed as noble. I maintain that most of us are very fuzzy in our thinking about moral absolutes and their alternatives in a fashion parallel to the confusion mentioned earlier regarding honor, ethics, and personal morality.

In making the distinction between absolutism and pragmatism we seem to imply that the two conceptions represent exhaustive opposing categories, that one holds either one of these positions or the other. Further, because of our general predilections for simplicity, we often rest with the notion that the only alternative to absolutism is relativism; and hence pragmatism and relativism in ethics must be identical.[29] It is a very easy step from these popular conceptions to conclude that a military officer who subscribes to absolute moral principles may well be so inflexible as to demand and give unquestioning obedience in every context. Analogously, those who do not subscribe to the absolute character of moral principles are easily viewed as relativists, either in the cultural or the subjective sense. That this simple bifurcation is inaccurate is easily seen if we attempt to define carefully what is meant by an absolute moral principle or an absolute obligation. If we maintain that an absolute obligation is one that holds with no exceptions for all human beings and in all possible sets of circumstances, then many will argue that there are no such obligations which could be morally binding. But there are. For example, "One ought always to seek to do good and avoid evil" is an absolute obligation in the sense defined. So is: "One ought always to act in accordance with right reason." Immediately we see something very important to notice about absolutes characterized in this fashion: the more human actions we attempt to incorporate under a single principle, the less specific the principle can be; absolute moral principles are necessarily vague. Further we should note that if principles really are absolute in the sense defined above, they could never be in conflict with each other since each must be obeyed in *all* possible circumstances.

Clearly, those moral obligations dealing with human act-types, like truth-telling, promise-keeping, preservation of life, respect for the property of others, and so on, are not absolute obligations. Does that mean that they are relative obligations to be observed only when we find it expedient to do so? Certainly not. Rather it is the case that we could best refer to these types of moral obligations by use of another term; for the moment, let us call them "universal" obligations. How are they different from either absolute or relative principles? Ought they always to be observed? No. Then they cannot be absolutes. Can they conflict? Yes. Then they cannot be absolutes. Are they sufficiently arbitrary to be ignored whenever one is in a different society or whenever it is convenient or expedient to do so? No. Then they cannot be relative principles in either the cultural or most subjective sense. Universal obligations of this sort hold for all human beings (they are not subjectively or culturally relative) but not in all possible circumstances (they are not absolute). They hold in analogous sets of circumstances and they may conflict with each other.

An easy example may help clarify the nature and status of universal obligations. Suppose we agree that we have a universal obligation to keep our promises and also a universal obligation to preserve human life whenever it is in our power to do so. Suppose further we have promised to meet our commanding officer for lunch at the officers' club and we depart in sufficient time to keep our commitment but en route we encounter an automobile accident with a victim screaming for help. Shall we stop? Of course we will stop even though to do so will mean breaking our promise. In this particular case, simple as it is, we see immediately that the obligation to attempt to preserve life is higher than the obligation to keep a promise in these particular circumstances. Other circumstances might demand a different moral judgment. The role that circumstances or "situations" play is an important one when obligations conflict. Please note that the fact that we judged it morally permissible to break the promise in this case does not mean that we have given up the universal obligation to keep our promises. We still accept that obligation as strongly as ever. Our rule of action is that we are justified in violating our universal moral obligations only when they conflict with a higher obligation and we cannot fulfill both at once. Thus if one is torn between obedience to an order and fulfillment of another moral obligation, he or she must judge which is the higher obligation in those circumstances. Universal obligations are neither absolute nor relative. They bind all human beings in analogous sets of circumstances, but they may conflict. The larger question dealing with the source of these obligations must be dealt with on a philosophical level beyond the scope of this paper.

"The Way to Do is to Be"

Loyalty and obedience, integrity and courage, subordination of the self to the good of the military unit and the nation-state—these are among the moral virtues critical to the military function, and they take the form of universal obligations. Seen in this context, the moral tone must be pervasive for both public and private actions of the ideal military leader. These qualities are essential to the effective and appropriate functioning of all military people, but those who lead are most responsible for exemplifying them and inculcating them in others. Only a narrowly faulty view of the moral life could sustain the view that one must be honorable in his public duties but that one's private moral code might operate on some other level. Consider the inconsistency in a leader who might insist on truthful reporting but falsifies his personal income tax return. Consider also the leader who asks for trust and loyalty from his subordinates but is unfaithful to his wife on temporary duty trips. Narrow views of ethics will not do for one who aspires to effective military leadership. One's character is what counts and evaluations of character are all-encompassing.

Because the military function is so directly related to our highest human values, those charged with the leadership of that function must be sensitive to those values and must exhibit some understanding of them. The values of American society are said by many to be "liberal," yet the military services responsible for defending those liberal values are said themselves to be "conservative," for those who would defend the status quo are so labeled. Concern for the individual dignity of each person suggests a liberal orientation while those who would fight to preserve individual dignity must be asked to sublimate in many ways their own individualism for the sake of the group. It is in this sense that contemporary commentators are wont to point out a paradoxical discrepancy between supposed civilian values and the military virtues. Yet, most acknowledge that without the conservative values of loyalty, obedience, and self-restraint, the military function would disintegrate. Hackett suggests that it is the responsibility of the military leader to bridge this seeming paradox when he reminds us that "the young officer . . . has to be made to remember that only a person of liberal mind is entitled to exercise coercion over others in a society of free men."[30] The authority of military superiors over their subordinates is stronger and more complete than that of almost any other human relationship in our societal structure. With that authority goes the frightening responsibility to respect the dignity of individual subordinates at the same time that military order and discipline are preserved. It is precisely in the person of the military leader that the liberal and the conservative values must be brought together in a daily attempt at fragile balance. It is not an easy thing that we ask of these leaders, but it is necessary.

In this context, how does a military leader inspire loyalty, the loyalty which leads one to accept enlightened obedience in an understanding way as a moral obligation in a military structure? In his excellent treatment of this topic, Captain Michael Wheeler suggests that loyalty is best engendered in subordinates when they can reside their full trust in their leaders and that trust itself is readily given only to those superiors who are perceived to be persons of high moral integrity.[31] How often we are driven back to this critical point! We must ask as much of our leaders as Tennyson attributed to the Duke of Wellington when he referred to him as "The statesman-warrior, moderate, resolute / Whole in himself, a common good."

Where military leadership has been less than ideal, it has faltered because of a faulty view of the whole man; it has seen the role of morality in military leadership too narrowly or from a relativistic framework. We ask of today's leader that he be neither absolutist nor relativist but retain a balanced perspective that understands the full complexity which characterizes the interweaving of moral value with military function. We ask him to be that good man, that wise man, that the Greek philosopher could advise subordinates to find and imitate. Fully accepting the Aristotelian wisdom that moral character develops out of repeating good actions, that it cannot be ordered but can be exemplified and imitated, our advice to those who aspire to become worthy military leaders can be none other than that of the ancient Chinese sage: "The way to do is to be."

Notes

1. Alfred Vagts, *A History of Militarism* (New York: Free Press, 1959), p. 13.

2. Dean Acheson, "Ethics in International Relations Today," in M. Raskin and B. Fall, eds., *The Vietnam Reader* (New York: Random House, 1965), p. 13. See R. Wasserstrom's analysis on p. 300 ff., this volume.

3. Sir John Winthrop Hackett (General), "The Military in the Service of the State" (Harmon Memorial Lecture, U.S. Air Force Academy, Colorado, 1970), Chap. 6.

4. Ibid.

5. Ibid.

6. Sir John Winthrop Hackett (General), *The Profession of Arms* (London: Times Publishing, 1962), p. 45.

7. Hackett, "Military in the Service of the State."

8. Samuel P. Huntington, *The Soldier and the State* (New York: Random House, 1957), p. 62. Further delineation of Huntington's view of the professional military ethic is taken essentially from Chapter 3, which is descriptively entitled "The Military Mind: Conservative Realism of the Professional Military Ethic."

9. Huntington, pp. 64-65.

10. Morris Janowitz, *The Professional Soldier* (New York: Free Press, 1960).

11. Vagts, "History of Militarism," p. 42.

12. Janowitz, *Professional Soldier*, p. 217.

13. Huntington, *Soldier and the State*, p. 73.

14. Ibid.

15. Telford Taylor, *Nuremberg and Vietnam: An American Tragedy* (New York: Bantam, 1971).

16. U.S. Army, *The Law of Land Warfare*, U.S. Army Field Manual, Department of the Army, 1956, p. 182.

17. Thomas Hobbes, *The Leviathan*, 1651.

18. Huntington, *Soldier and the State*, pp. 74-78.

19. *Congressional Record—Senate*, 1974, pp. 56257-56262.

20. Ibid., p. 56258.

21. John D. Ryan (General), "Air Force Policy Letter for Commanders," Washington, D.C., 1 November 1972. General Ryan's view of integrity versus obedience starkly contrasts with that of Murray Kempton, who stated, "The good soldier will lie under orders as bravely as he will die under them." ("Review of Eisenhower's *Mandate for Change*, *New Republic* [30 November 1963].)

22. M. T. Smith (Lieutenant Colonel), "Reporting Inaccuracies—a Rose by Another Name," *Air University Review*, 1974.

23. Ibid., p. 85.

24. U.S. Army War College, *Study on Military Professionalism* (Carlisle Barracks, Pa.: U.S. Army War College, 1970), pp. 13-14.

25. Ibid., p. 24.

26. Ibid., pp. 30-31.

27. Ibid., p. 29.

28. Janowitz, *Professional Soldier*, pp. 272ff.

29. Chaplain Kermit D. Johnson (Colonel), "Ethical Issues of Military Leadership," *Parameters* 4 (1974), pp. 35-39. Chaplain Johnson makes an interesting comment on the relationship between "what works" and ethical relativism, suggesting that the pragmatic outlook is in fact a "subtle and disguised form of ethical relativism practiced frequently in the military setting." Johnson identifies ethical relativism as one of four pressing issues concerning military leadership. The other three are the exaggerated loyalty syndrome, the obsession with image, and the drive for success.

30. Hackett, "Military in the Service of the State."

31. Michael O. Wheeler, "Loyalty, Honor, and the Modern Military," *Air University Review* (1973), pp. 50-55.

14

From Institution to Occupation: Trends in Military Organization

Charles C. Moskos, Jr.

Professor Moskos proposes two models for analyzing the military profession: the institutional model and the occupational model. The institutional model incorporates traditional characteristics of the military profession that permit it to be viewed as a unique calling. The occupational model takes its cue from the marketplace, viewing military life as a job and concentrating on monetary incentives rather than the more traditional ethical values of loyalty, obedience, service, etc. The first model essentially subordinates the individual to the interest of the whole (unit, service branch, country); the second is based on self-interest. Moskos details events which lead him to believe that the traditional institutional model of the military calling is changing to the occupational model carrying with it very serious implications for the carrying out of the military function and the ultimate dissolution of military professionalism. One of the alarming signs of the onset of the occupational model is increased military pay within the structure of an all-volunteer force; another is the increasing use of civilian technicians to perform military functions. Possible consequences of these trends are the unionization of the military and the ultimate loss of military legitimacy.

—M.M.W.

The military can be understood as a social organization which maintains levels of autonomy while refracting broader societal trends. It is from this perspective that we apply a developmental analysis to the emergent structure of the armed forces.

Developmental analysis entails historical reconstruction, trend specification, and, most especially, a model of a future state of affairs toward which actual events are heading.[1] Developmental

This article originally appeared in *Armed Forces and Society*, Vol. 4, No. 1, pp. 41-50 (November 1977). Published with permission.

analysis, that is, emphasizes the "from here to there" sequence of present and hypothetical events. Stated in a slightly different way, a developmental construct is a "pure type" placed at some future point by which we may ascertain and order the emergent reality of contemporary social phenomena. Models derived from developmental analysis bridge the empirical world of today with the social forms of the future. Put plainly, what is the likely shape of the military in the foreseeable future?

Initially, two models—institution versus occupation—will be presented to describe alternative conceptions of military social organization. These models are evaluated as to which best fits current empirical indicators. The basic hypothesis is that the American military is moving from an institutional format to one more and more resembling that of an occupation. Second, there will be specification of some expected organizational outcomes in the military system resulting from the shift to an occupational model.

Institution or Occupation

Terms like institution and occupation have obvious limitations in both popular and scholarly discussion.[2] Nevertheless, they contain core connotations which serve to distinguish each from the other. For present purposes these distinctions can be described as follows.

An *institution* is legitimated in terms of values and norms, i.e., a purpose transcending individual self-interest in favor of a presumed higher good. Members of an institution are often viewed as following a calling; they generally regard themselves as being different or apart from the broader society and are so regarded by others. To the degree one's institutional membership is congruent with notions of self-sacrifice and dedication, it will usually enjoy esteem from the larger community. Although remuneration may not be compatible to what one might expect in the economy of the marketplace, this is often compensated for by an array of social benefits associated with an institutional format as well as psychic income. When grievances are felt, members of an institution do not organize themselves into interest groups. Rather, if redress is sought it takes the form of one-to-one recourse to superiors, with its implications of trust in the paternalism of the institution to take care of its own.

Military service traditionally has had many institutional features. One thinks of the extended tours abroad, the fixed terms of enlistment, liability for twenty-four-hour service availability, frequent movements of self and family, subjection to military discipline and law, and inability to resign, strike, or negotiate over working conditions. All this is above and beyond the dangers inherent in military maneuvers and actual combat operations. It is also significant that a paternalistic remuneration system has evolved in the military corresponding to the institutional model: compensation received in noncash form (e.g., food, housing, uniforms), subsidized consumer facilities on the base, payments to service members partly determined by family status, and a large proportion of compensation received as deferred pay in the form of retirement benefits.

The military variant of professionalism historically has been consistent with the institutional model.[3] The traditional milieu of the service academies has been likened to that of a seminary.[4] Certainly the multitiered military educational system for career officers—as typified by the command schools and the war colleges—is as much institutional reinforcement as it is narrow professional training. Moreover, unlike civilian professionals for whom compensation is heavily determined by individual expertise and can even be in the form of fee for service, the compensation received by the military professional is a function of rank, seniority, and need—not, strictly speaking, professional expertise. (The exception to this occurs, interestingly enough, when the military organization takes into account—via the mechanism of off-scale compensation—certain professionals whose skills are intrinsically nonmilitary, the notable example being physicians). To compound matters, there are societal forces eroding the institutional features of the professions within and outside the military.[5]

An *occupation* is legitimated in terms of the marketplace, i.e., prevailing monetary rewards for equivalent competencies. In a modern industrial society employees usually enjoy some voice in the determination of appropriate salary and work conditions. Such rights are counterbalanced by responsibilities to meet contractual obligations. The occupational model implies priority of self-interest rather than that of the employing organization. A common form of interest articulation in industrial—and increasingly governmental—occupations is the trade union.

Traditionally, the military has sought to avoid the organizational outcomes of the occupational model. This in the face of repeated recommendations of governmental commissions that the armed services adopt a salary system which would incorporate all basic pay, allowances, and tax benefits into one cash payment, and which would eliminate compensation differences between married and single personnel, thus conforming to the equal-pay-for-equal-work principle of civilian occupations. Such a salary system would set up an employer-employee relationship quite at variance with military traditions. Nevertheless, even in the conventional military system there has been some accommodation to occupational imperatives. Special supplements and proficiency pay have long been found necessary to recruit and retain highly skilled personnel.

The distinction between institution and occupation can be overdrawn. Reality, moreover, is complicated by the fact that the armed forces have had and will continue to have elements of both the institutional and occupational types.[6] There are also important differences between the various services, the most obvious being faster-paced technological development in the air force and navy compared to the army and marine corps. But the heuristic value of the typology is deemed valid. It allows for a conceptual grasp of the basic hypothesis that the overarching trend within the contemporary military is the erosion of the institutional format and the ascendancy of the occupational model.

Although antecedents predated the appearance of the all-volunteer force in early 1973, the end of the draft served as the major thrust to move the military toward the occupational model. In contrast to the all-volunteer force, the selective service system was premised on the notion of the citizen's obligation—and the ideal of a broadly representative enlisted force (though this ideal was not always realized in practice). The occupational model clearly underpinned the philosophic rationale of the 1970 report of the President's Commission on an All-Volunteer Force (Gates Commission Report).[7] Instead of a military system anchored in the normative values of an institution, captured in words like "duty, honor, country," the Gates Commission explicitly argued that primary reliance in recruiting an armed force should be on monetary inducements guided by marketplace standards.

Actually, the move toward making military remuneration competitive with the civilian sector preceded the advent of the all-volunteer force. Since 1967, military pay has been formally linked to the civil service and thus, indirectly, to the civilian labor market. From 1964 to 1974, average earnings in the private economy rose 52 percent while regular military compensation—basic pay, allowances, tax advantages—rose 76 percent for representative grade levels, such as lieutenant colonels and master sergeants.[8] Even more dramatic, recruit pay from 1964 to 1976 increased 193 percent in constant dollars compared to 10 percent for the average unskilled laborer.[9]

It is important to stress that although the army was the only service to rely directly on large numbers of draftees for its manpower needs, all the services were beneficiaries of the selective service system. It is estimated that close to half of all voluntary accession into the military in the peacetime years between the wars in Korea and Vietnam were draft-motivated. The draft was also the major impetus for recruitment into the ROTC and the reserve/guard units.

Termination of the draft and the rise in military pay have been two of the most visible changes in the contemporary military system, but other indicators of the trend away from the institutional format can also be noted: (1) proposals to eliminate or reduce a host of military benefits, e.g., subsidies for commissaries, health care for dependents, and major restructuring of the retirement system; (2) the increasing overrepresentation of certain class and racial groups in the ground combat forces; (3) the separation of work and residence locales accompanying the growing numbers of single enlisted men living off base; (4) the burgeoning resistance of many military wives, at officer and noncom levels, to participating in customary social functions; (5) the high rate of attrition and desertion among enlisted personnel in the post-Vietnam military; and (6) the increasing tendency of active-duty personnel to bring grievances into litigation. The sum of these and related developments is to confirm the ascendancy of the occupational model in the emergent military.

Consequences of the Occupational Model

A shift in the rationale of the military toward the occupational model implies organizational consequences in the structure and perhaps the function of the armed forces. This discussion should not be construed as advocacy of such organizational consequences or even of their inevitability. But it does suggest that certain outcomes can be anticipated if the military becomes even more like an occupation. Two changes, in particular, are presently apparent in military social organization: the growing likelihood of unionization and the increasing reliance on contract civilians to perform military tasks. Although seemingly unrelated, both such organizational changes derive from the ascendant occupational model.

Trade Unionism

The possibility that trade unionism might link with the armed forces of the United States was barely more than a remote thought just a few years ago. Today, there are signs that such an eventuality could come to pass. The growing militancy of previously quiescent public employees at municipal, state, and federal levels may be a precursor of similar activity within the military system.[10] Many western European countries, including several members of NATO, have long-standing military trade unions.[11] It has been the advent of the all-volunteer force that has made unionization of the U.S. armed forces a strong possibility. Reliance on monetary incentives to recruit military members is quite consistent with the notion of trade unionism.

In 1975, the National Maritime Union (NMU), a union affiliated with the AFL-CIO, reported that it was considering organizing sailors in the U.S. Navy. For some time, the independent Association of Civilian Technicians (ACT) has been a union for civilians who work full-time for the reserve and National Guard (almost all of whom are also members of the units employing them). Of the various possibilities for military trade unionism, the most substantial initiatives, by far, are those of the American Federation of Government Employees (AFGE), affiliated with the AFL-CIO. In its 1976 annual convention, the AFGE amended its constitution to extend membership eligibility to military personnel serving on active duty. The majority of the

AFGE's 325,000 members are civilian employees working on military installations. In mid-1977, the AFGE was conducting a referendum to decide whether the union should proceed toward a full-fledged drive to organize military personnel.[12]

Such groups as the AFGE, NMU, and ACT are staunchly patriotic, conservative in their approach to social change, and professed bread-and-butter unions. There is no connection between these unions and the radical, self-styled servicemen's unions that appeared in the late years of the Vietnam war. But there is a potentially disquieting implication if these established unions succeed in organizing the military: the politicization of the armed forces arising from the usually close working relationship between the AFL-CIO and the Democratic party at national and local levels.[13]

Military unions face a number of legal obstacles. Current defense department directives allow service members to join unions, but forbid commanders from negotiating with them. Additionally, legislation has been introduced in recent congressional sessions to prohibit unionization of the armed forces. Even if Congress passed a law prohibiting military unions and the president signed the law, its constitutionality certainly would be tested in the courts. Military commanders already are permitted to negotiate with unionized civilian employees on military installations, and, since 1975, they have also been delegated explicit authority to sign local labor agreements with civilian personnel.

Even though military unions are anathema to the service associations, most senior officials, and many civilians, there is a widespread view among all ranks of military personnel that the institutional qualities of military life are being undermined. Much of this dissatisfaction focuses on the perceived erosion of military benefits and the job insecurities resulting from periodic reductions in force. Not so well understood is that the institutional features of the military system may have been traded off for the relatively good salaries enjoyed by military personnel in the all-volunteer force. The potential for unionization is great precisely because military social organization has moved in the direction of the occupational model, while much of its membership harkens to the social supports of the older institutional format. It is also possible that a unionized military would not be accorded the favor that it

presently enjoys from the public (which is prone to view the
military as the embodiment of a calling).[14] Indeed, society might
view a military union in more crass terms than would be
anticipated because of a reaction against public employee unions
in general.

Civilian Technicians

Trends toward military unionization are organizational developments that could be incorporated, albeit with some strain, into
the structure of the armed forces, but another consequence of the
ascendant occupational model departs entirely from formal military organization. This is the use of civilians to perform tasks
which, by any conventional measure, would be seen as military in
content. The private armies of the Central Intelligence Agency
have long been an object of concern within the regular military
command. But what is anomalous in the emerging order is that,
rather than assigning its own military personnel, the U.S.
government increasingly gives contracts directly to civilian
firms—with salary levels much higher than comparable military
rates—to perform difficult military tasks. In other words, the very
structure of the military system no longer encompasses the full
range of military functions.

One finds it difficult to overstate the extent to which the
operational side of the military system now relies on civilian
technicians. The large warships of the U.S. Navy are combat
ineffective without the technical skills of contract civilians, the so-
called "tech reps," who serve permanently aboard these ships.
Major army ordnance centers, including those in combat theaters,
require contract civilians to perform necessary maintenance and
assembly. Missile warning systems in Greenland are, in effect,
civilian-manned military installations operated by firms responsible to the U.S. Air Force. In Southeast Asia and Saudi Arabia,
the U.S. government gave contracts to private companies, such as
Air America and Vinnel Corporation, to recruit civilians who
performed military activities. In Isfahan, Iran, the Bell Helicopter
and Grumman companies established a quasi-military base staffed
by former U.S. military personnel who trained Iranian pilots.[15]
During the collapse of South Vietnam in 1975, chartered civilian
aircraft were used to rescue American nationals under virtual

combat conditions. The U.S. monitoring force in the Sinai was contracted out to private industry, with the government retaining only policy control.

External political considerations obviously impinge on decisions to use civilian contracts for certain military tasks. It may be that the employment of civilian technicians overseas does not symbolize a national commitment to the same extent as would the deployment of uniformed personnel. Apparently, in certain roles requiring high levels of technical sophistication, civilians are simply more cost effective than military personnel. Nevertheless, if task efficiency is the issue, a more nagging implication is that military personnel cannot or will not perform long-term arduous duty with the efficacy of contract civilians. If this were to become the norm, beliefs conducive to organizational integrity and societal respect—the whole notion of military legitimacy—become untenable. The trend toward the employment of contract civilians to perform military tasks could be the culmination of occupational ascendancy in the military purpose.

Conclusion

The hypothesis of the ascendant occupational model in the armed forces alerts one to, and makes sense out of, current organizational trends in the social structure of the military. If there is concern with current developments—the possibility of trade unionism, excessive reliance on contract civilians, service morale, and the like—then attention ought to be focused on the root cause and not just on the overt symptoms. To describe observable trends in military organization is not to mean they are inevitable.[16] But developmental analysis reveals the impetus and probable outcomes of present trends in the emergent military.

Notes

Support from the U.S. Army Research Institute for the Behavioral and Social Sciences during the preparation of this article is gratefully acknowledged. The usual caveat that all findings and interpretations are the sole responsibility of the author is especially stressed.

1. Heinz Eulau, "H. D. Lasswell's Developmental Analysis,"

Western Political Quarterly 2 (1958), pp. 229-242.

2. Robert Dubin, ed., *Handbook of Work, Organization, and Society* (Chicago: Rand McNally, 1976).

3. Samuel P. Huntington, *The Soldier and the State* (Cambridge, Mass.: Harvard University Press, 1957); Morris Janowitz, *The Professional Soldier* (New York: Free Press, 1960).

4. John P. Lovell, "The Service Academies in Transition," in Lawrence J. Korb, ed., *The System of Educating Military Officers in the U.S.* (Pittsburgh, Pa.: International Studies Association, 1976), pp. 35-50.

5. Elliott A. Krause, *The Sociology of Occupations* (Boston: Little, Brown, 1971), pp. 84-108.

6. Although the conceptual referent differs from the hypothesis of the ascendant occupational model presented here, there are certain parallels to be found in Jacques van Doorn, "The Decline of the Mass Army in the West," *Armed Forces and Society* 1 (1975), pp. 147-158.

7. *The Report of the President's Commission on an All-Volunteer Force* (Washington, D.C.: Government Printing Office, 1970).

8. Steven L. Canby and Robert A. Butler, "The Military Manpower Question," in William Schneider, Jr., and Francis P. Hoeber, eds., *Arms, Men, and Military Budgets* (New York: Crane, Russak, 1976), pp. 186-187.

9. Tulay Demirles, "Adjusted Consumer Price Index for Military Personnel and a Comparison of Real Civilian and Military Earnings, 1964-1973," *Technical Memorandum, TM-1200* (Washington, D.C.: George Washington University, 1974), p. 9.

10. An overview of the precedents and potentialities for military unionization is Ezra S. Krendal and Bernard Samhoff, *Unionizing the Armed Forces* (Philadelphia: University of Pennsylvania Press, 1977).

11. On Western Europe, see the "Special Symposium of Trade Unionism in the Military," *Armed Forces and Society* 2 (1976), pp. 477-522; also Gwyn Garries-Jenkins, "Trade Unions in the Armed Forces," paper presented at the Conference of the British Inter-University Seminar on Armed Forces and Society, April 1976.

12. "Organizing the Military," *The Government Standard* [the official organ of the American Federation of Government Employees] (May 1977), pp. 11-14.

13. In June 1977, Congress was considering repeal of the Hatch Act which since 1939 has banned federal employees from participating in political activities. One consequence of repeal of the Hatch Act would be removal of restrictions on the use of government employee union funds for political purposes. *Washington Post* (June 9, 1977), p. 1.

14. David R. Segal, "Civil-Military Relations in the Mass Public," *Armed Forces and Society* 1 (1975), pp. 215-230; David R. Segal and John D.

Blair, "Public Confidence in the U.S. Military," *Armed Forces and Society* 3 (1976), pp. 3-12; John D. Blair and Jerald G. Bachman, "The Public View of the Military," in Nancy L. Goldman and David R. Segal, eds., *The Social Psychology of Military Service* (Beverly Hills, Calif.: Sage, 1976), pp. 215-236.

15. U.S. Congress, Senate. Staff Report to the Subcommittee on Foreign Assistance of the Committee on Foreign Relations, *U.S. Military Sales to Iran*, 94th Congress, 2nd Session (Washington, D.C.: Government Printing Office, 1976).

16. To phrase discussion of the emergent military solely in terms of factors internal to the military organization is to beg the larger question. Ultimately, the organizational direction of the armed forces is connected with more general values of citizen participation and obligation. Even though there is renewed talk of reinstituting conscription in the wake of recruitment inadequacies of the all-volunteer force, this possibility is viewed as unlikely in the current political climate. More salient, a return to the draft might well result in troop morale and discipline problems exceeding what the military system could accommodate.

Perhaps this is the opportune time to consider a voluntary national service program—in which military service is one of several options—that would be a prerequisite for future federal employment. Such a program would be philosophically defensible by linking future employment by the taxpayer to prior commitment to national service. It would meet pressing national needs in both the civilian and military spheres and make public service an essential part of growing up in America. Most important, it would clarify the military's role by reinvigorating the ethic of national service.

15

From Institutional to Occupational: The Need for Conceptual Continuity

Morris Janowitz

In this brief article, Professor Morris Janowitz, contemporary dean of U.S. military sociologists, criticizes the conceptual models developed by Charles Moskos ("From Institutional to Occupational"). Janowitz reaffirms the legitimacy of the current military professionalism, stressing the elevated skill level, self-regulation, and corporate cohesion. He refers to his 1960 thesis concerning the civilianization of the military, suggesting that this process is continuing but without reducing the "profession" to an "occupation." The process may be better described as one of adaptation rather than a shift away from professionalism.

—M.M.W.

Language and concepts are important in guiding social analysis; therefore, some minimum continuity in the usage of the concept must be required in order to chart social and organizational change. To suddenly give new meaning to old concepts weakens the development of social research. It is better to fashion new concepts, if existing concepts are no longer useful or relevant.

Language and concepts are particularly important when the social scientist is dealing with politically and emotionally charged topics. Such is the case with contemporary civil-military relations. And let there be no misunderstanding, political and emotional tensions are considerable and are growing. There are elements of the officer corps that are discontented and unclear about their personal and professional future; likewise, there are persistent concerns among elected officials about the cost and effectiveness of the all-volunteer force.

This article originally appeared in *Armed Forces and Society*, Vol. 4, No. 1, pp. 51-54 (November 1977). Published with permission.

Overnight, Charles Moskos, one of the most careful students of
military institutions, attracted nationwide attention with his
conceptual reformulation. The initial presentation was at a
Regional Conference of the Inter-University Seminar in Alabama
in October 1976. Extensive mass media publicity was given to the
core of his presentation even before it was entered into the
academic literature.

Moskos argued that the U.S. military was moving from a
profession (or institution in this version of his paper) to an
occupation. A variety of military officers and elected officials and
administrators concerned with defense management and the
impact of the all-volunteer forces immediately made use of this
formulation. It resonated with their deep concerns that an effective
transition to the all-volunteer force has not yet been accomplished.
Social science language was being used to direct the attention of
the American society to pressing problems of public policy.

From the point of view of a critical organization analysis, I
believe that there is no basis—analytic or empirical—to apply such
a formulation, for either the short-term or long-term trends in
military organization and military profession in the United States.
Moskos is changing the rules of the game of social analysis without
clearly signaling the changes he has introduced. The result could
be to disrupt the all-too-fragile language of social research.

The concept of profession (and of professionalism) continues, in
the current setting, to apply to the military because it implies (1) a
high level of skills (higher than for an occupation); (2) an important
degree of self-regulation; and (3) a strong element of corporate
cohesion. To shift from a profession to an occupation, the officer
corps would have to undergo a number of changes which are most
unlikely (the shift from an institutional to an occupational format is
more difficult to clarify). (1) The skill level would have to decline
markedly, and this is not the case; if anything the skill level
continues to rise. (2) The officer corps would have to lose significant
areas of self-management. In effect, the officer corps maintains
effective control for areas such as promotion and decision making
about military organization. The Supreme Court continues to
reaffirm particular elements of these procedures. (3) The officer
corps would have to be decisively weakened in its corporate
identity. There already are powerful strains and even signs of

decisive cleavages in the military officer corps. Some are of long standing; others are more recent and of a new variety. And as mentioned earlier, there is considerable discontent in particular quarters. But to be discontented does not automatically mean a loss of professionalism; some of the discontent may well be legitimate and require political solutions. Even if cohesion has been strained, it has hardly been weakened to the point of undermining professional identity. It might be more accurate to stress that the cohesion and sense of solidarity in the officer corps now contain a strong defensive element, and that is "unhealthy."

Contrary to Moskos' formulation, it is necessary to recognize that to demonstrate the presence of particular professional characteristics in a group does not mean that the group will necessarily operate with high degrees of effectiveness and responsibility. There are varying degrees and levels of professionalism, and it is obvious that measures of skill, self-regulation, and corporate cohesion do not automatically guarantee high levels of performance. These characteristics must be present in sufficient degree and in effective combinations to achieve particular tasks. It is also the case that some characteristics may be overconcentrated in a particular group. Organizational analysis is designed to facilitate the assessment of effective professionalism and not to substitute for such assessments. Moreover, in the final analysis, all professionals are subject to political and social control—and the character of such control is decisive.

The military profession is undergoing long-term transformation which involves increased penetration by other professions and institutions. In 1960, I described these trends as those of the civilianization of the military, as they converged more and more with civilian professions. The end of this convergence is being reached, but we are not there yet. One of the essential characteristics of this convergence is the introduction of more and more contractual relations between the officer and the state.

However, it must be recognized that we are not dealing with a "zero sum" game. The military can and must participate in the larger society and at the same time maintain its relative autonomy, specialized competence, and crucial element of group cohesion. In particular, the contractual element in the officer's position in a democratic society is designed to insure equity and guarantee his rights. Therefore, there is reason to believe that contractual relations will be strengthened in the years ahead. But such contracts need not undermine professional affiliations and group cohesion. They can serve as positive elements and assist in performing the required and redefined mission of the military.

It may have been the case that in the past some officers fought effectively without clear recognition of purpose. But the contemporary officers cannot serve in a military dedicated to deterrence without stronger understanding of professional purpose. The need to understand professional purpose reflects the increased interdependence of contemporary society; each new doctor, lawyer, and school teacher is also struggling in an advanced industrial society to achieve a clearer sense of purpose. The movement is toward higher levels of professionalism and its requirements. Of course, I am fully aware that progress is frighteningly slow at best and often in the reverse direction.

The formulation of the shift from institution to occupation sounds to me to have overtones of an ideological appeal to return to the "good old days." But there is no return, although there is much to be learned about the transmission of the viable aspects of tradition and the record of adaptation.

Part 2
War and Morality

Introduction to Part 2

Malham M. Wakin

The selections in Part 1 of this text generally provide a
normative view of the military profession; given the importance of
the function the profession of arms fulfills for its society, we are told
by the authors what our military leadership ought to be like and
are reminded of the critical ethical issues associated with the
carrying out of the military function. That function has been
variously characterized as involving the management of violence
or the containment of violence in the defense or preservation of a
way of life. However else the military function might be described,
it seems clear that the profession derives whatever positive or noble
attributes it may have from its dedication to providing for its
nation's security—its defensive role is most frequently viewed as
morally sound. As we turn to considerations of war itself, we may
note immediately that those who seek to provide moral justification for the use of war as an instrument of national policy find their
task easiest when they restrict the category of just wars to those
which are strictly defensive.

Several of the selections in Part 2 analyze the morally justifiable
purposes of war. The pacifist obviously argues that even wars that
are strictly fought in defense of one's home territory against
aggressive invasion are not morally permissible (see Donald Wells,
"How Much Can the 'Just War' Justify?"). Others (Taylor,
Anscombe, Wasserstrom) consider the possibility that defense
against active attack is not the only moral justification for engaging
in war. Robert Tucker, in summarizing the public statements of
U.S. spokesmen during the middle portion of this century, suggests
that the general "American" position has been that "the just war

is the war fought either in self-defense or in collective defense against an armed attack."[1] Each of these views carries with it a complexity not reflected in its brief statement; some of these complexities are analyzed in the works included here.

Moral reflections on warfare can be separated into two major categories roughly referred to as considerations concerning the morality *of* war and those concerning morality *in* war. When we ask about the morality of war, we want to know whether or not engaging in war is ever morally permitted or justified. If nations may legitimately use war as an instrument of national policy, then we wish to know when and what the conditions are that would provide acceptable moral reasons for waging war. Once war has begun, we must ask whether there are any moral restrictions on the way in which it may be fought. Is all fair in war? Are there rules which must be observed and, if so, where are they to be found?

Morality of War

In the opening selection of Part 2, Telford Taylor reviews what has come to be known as classical just war theory. This theory derives from European Christian thinkers, notably Augustine, Aquinas, Suarez, Bellarmine, Vitoria, and Grotius. The theory holds generally that a war can be judged to be just or unjust depending upon whether it satisfies or does not conform to a certain set of conditions. If the war is declared by legitimate authority (those entrusted with the governance of the nation-state), is embarked upon for a just cause, is waged with the right intention, and employs just means, then that war may be morally justified. The issue of just cause has been the subject of much concern; over the centuries much has been included in the concept of just cause. If the cause is just, then the nation will be responding to some prior wrong with the intention of righting that wrong, and the use of violent force must be the last resort after all other nonviolent methods of righting the wrong have been attempted without success. The use of force in war must have some fair chance of success; that is, it would be irrational to engage in war if there were absolutely no possibility of winning. A nation wages war justly only if conditions for that nation or the wronged nation it is supporting have a decent chance of being better after the fighting ends: the object of war is to provide a better peace. Similarly, nations must concern themselves with proportionality; the damage already endured must be weighed against the damage likely to be caused by a war initiated to repress the injustice.

In the twentieth century, just cause seems to have been narrowed down by many philosophers, statesmen, and moral theologians to almost a single circumstance: response to aggression. For example, John Courtney Murray holds that: (1) All wars of aggression, whether just or unjust, fall under the ban of moral prescription; and (2) a defensive war against unjust aggression is morally admissible both in principle and in fact.[2] As several of the authors of our selections point out, wars of aggression have been condemned in a number of international agreements, including, for example, the Kellogg-Briand Pact of 1928. Richard Wasserstrom in his article, "On the Morality of War: A Preliminary Inquiry," points out that at the Nuremberg trials aggression seemed to be treated as identical with initiation of war. He quotes Mr. Justice Jackson as saying, "The wrong for which their [the German] fallen leaders are on trial is not that they lost the war, but that they started it." Wasserstrom as well as Elizabeth Anscombe ("War and Murder") seem more nearly correct when they point out that the act of initiating the fighting may be morally justified as a response to grave moral evil and every initiation of the fighting is not automatically to be identified with unjust aggression. Their discussions are well worth examining. The critical question is not simply answered by determining who has initiated the fighting; there may be other forms of aggression against fundamental human rights to which the legitimate response might include the use of force. In his recent work entitled *Just and Unjust Wars*, Michael Walzer constructs an amended legal paradigm which suggests that just cause includes defense of a nation's territorial integrity and political sovereignty plus special cases of intervention on behalf of states unable to protect themselves when these essential societal rights are violated.[3]

With respect to the condition of right intention, it seems clear that just war theorists have been concerned to insure that rulers intend good and not evil in authorizing the use of force against an enemy. Fighting in order to right a wrong, to assure a just peace, and to see justice done all may constitute having a morally acceptable intention. Seeking revenge, more power, the destruction of an entire race or national population can never be morally acceptable intentions. Analysis of intentions obviously is difficult and is closely related to the choice of means in waging war. If a nation's war aims are simply to seek redress for violations of territorial integrity or political sovereignty, those aims will govern the means employed and the duration of the fighting. If a nation intends to "fight a war that will end all wars" or to "make the world safe for democracy," then certainly the duration of the fighting and means employed will be affected.

Discussion of the right use of means takes us immediately into the considerations relevant to morality *in* war. We should note that a war which otherwise might meet the just war theorists' conditions (legitimate authority, just cause, right intention, etc.) could become an unjust war if a nation, even acting defensively, employs evil means. The issues generated by evaluations of the means to be employed in waging war are complex and, in the nuclear age, almost overwhelming.

Morality in War

In evaluating possible modern applications of the conditions of the just war, Donald Wells ("How Much Can the 'Just War' Justify?") argues that the means available for waging modern wars make it impossible to avoid killing the innocent and hence no war at this point in human history could be morally justified. Any nuclear war, in his view, must inevitably violate the principles of right intention and proper proportion. Many modern writers have held that certain means must always violate the condition of "right intention" for essentially the reasons that Wells gives. Anscombe, Wasserstrom, and Murphy, to mention only a few whose selections are included here, all argue that direct attacks on the "innocent" must always be immoral; but they do not conclude from their discussions of this issue that all wars must therefore be declared unjust. The issue of who is innocent in war is itself complex and receives considerable attention from these writers.

If we define a "total war" as a war in which no distinction is made between combatant and noncombatant, or as general war at the highest level of escalation possible today, then perhaps General

Harkett's position makes considerable sense. In his lecture "Today and Tomorrow," included in Part 1, he maintained that total war must be avoided and that the future task of the profession of arms may be better described as the "containment of violence" and "by timely warfare to lessen the risk of general war." If we combine our evaluations of classical just war theory with considerations of international law as it relates to warfare, we can readily discern a common purpose underlying the reflections of all serious proposals: to limit the human suffering caused by war and to protect those who are not implicated in the struggle. Since total war as described above carries with it the possibility of the annihilation of human life as we know it, total war could never be the aim of rational policy. If nations are morally permitted to wage war in response to unjust aggression, then the means employed must be judiciously selected in order to contain violence at the lowest level possible consistent with the purpose of arresting the unjust aggression. Conditions of peace at the conclusion of a total war could not be visualized as better in any sense than before such a war was initiated.

Any cursory examination of the pronouncements of our representatives at the Nuremberg tribunal after World War II, of the agreements reached at the various Hague and Geneva Conventions, of the Kellogg-Briand Treaty, and of the court martial trials of military men accused of war crimes should clearly and unambiguously conclude that we do *not* believe that all is fair in war. Civilized nations provide strong guidance to their military forces regarding conduct in war. In the United States, armed forces are bound by the provisions of *The Law of Land Warfare*, which is published as an army field manual (latest edition, 1956) and which summarizes the various treaty provisions governing the waging of war that the United States has agreed to observe. In 1976 the United States Air Force published a similar manual (pamphlet) entitled *International Law—The Conduct of Armed Conflict and Air Operations*. The variety of "rules" of war deal with treatment of prisoners, outlawing certain weapons, identifying and protecting noncombatants, superior orders, treatment of the sick and wounded, private property, hospitals, neutrality, espionage, aerial bombardment, etc.

In confirming the death sentence for the Japanese General

Tomayuki Yamashita after World War II, General MacArthur said, "The soldier, be he friend or foe, is charged with the protection of the weak and unarmed. It is the very essence and reason for his being. When he violates this sacred trust, he not only profanes his entire cult but threatens the fabric of international society."[4] Yamashita's conviction was based on his failure to control the men under his command who committed vicious atrocities against both civilians and prisoners. He was convicted in spite of the fact that it was not demonstrated that he ordered any of the atrocities or was aware of many of them. War is a physical evil, but the reasoning process which permits its use in the name of justice is bound by consistency to insist on making moral judgments concerning the means used in the pursuit of justice. In "The Laws of War" article, Richard Wasserstrom questions whether or not our laws of war satisfactorily accomplish their purposes in safeguarding noncombatants and guaranteeing the humane conduct of war.

The problems that modern weapons pose for our consideration of the "right use of means" are enormous. In "On the Morality of Chemical/Biological War," Richard Krickus suggests an important distinction and raises the possibility that nonlethal chemical warfare might satisfy moral demands for the right use of means. In "Some Paradoxes of Deterrence," Gregory Kavka provides some insights into the moral dilemma posed by contemporary "counter-value" strategies. The insights he provides are not likely to leave morally sensitive persons very comfortable, but they highlight what may well reveal an endemic ambiguity in moral judgments of "intentions" as distinguished from moral judgments of "acts." But the moral issues associated with modern wars are not restricted merely to concern for the mass destructiveness of available weapons systems. The conduct of guerrilla warfare or wars of insurgency raises analogous difficulties in distinguishing who is innocent. How does one distinguish an act of terrorism (ordinary criminality) from an act of war? How may one identify legitimate combatants where no one wears a distinctive uniform? These and other issues already mentioned have caused many contemporary thinkers to turn away from questions involving morality in war, some to become moral nihilists on this issue (moral rules are impossible to apply in war so anything goes), others to become extreme pacifists (all uses of force are morally forbidden in all circumstances).

Wars happen. It is not *necessary* that war will continue to be viewed as an instrument of national policy, but it is likely to be the case for a very long time. Those who believe in the progress and perfectability of man's nature may continue to hope that at some future point reason will prevail and all international disputes will be resolved by nonviolent means, perhaps ultimately through the agency of an international structure beyond the level of the nation-state. Unless and until that occurs, our best thinkers must continue to pursue the moral issues related to war. Those who romanticize war do not do mankind a service; those who ignore it abdicate responsibility for the future of mankind, a responsibility we all share even if we do not choose to do so. The articles which follow are representative of the concerned thinking being done on the hard issues regarding morality of war and morality in war. These issues must be pondered by statesmen charged with the responsibility of conducting foreign policy; they must occupy a high priority in the minds of those who negotiate international treaties, especially, for example, the principals at the Strategic Arms Limitation Talks; and they must be studied by those entrusted to develop, manage, and use the modern weapons of war.

Notes

1. Robert W. Tucker, *The Just War*, Johns Hopkins, 1960.
2. John Courtney Murray, *Morality and Modern War*, The Council on Religion and International Affairs, 1959, pp. 9-10.
3. Michael Walzer, *Just and Unjust Wars*, Basic Books, 1977, see especially Chapters 4-6.
4. Quoted on the frontispiece of Telford Taylor's *Nuremberg and Vietnam: An American Tragedy*, Bantam Books, 1970.

16

Just and Unjust Wars

Telford Taylor

This brief review of the evolution of just war theory appeared as Chapter 3 of Telford Taylor's Nuremberg and Vietnam: An American Tragedy, *published in 1970. Taylor, a brigadier general at the end of World War II, served as U.S. Chief Counsel at Nuremberg. In this passage of his book he distinguishes between the specific laws of war and the more general theories of "just and unjust wars," tracing the latter from the time of Christ up through the considerations that led to the Nuremberg trials. He indicates in passing that the very early Christians numbered many pacifists, but credits St. Augustine with formulating a basic Christian position on just wars that received elaboration in the thirteenth century from St. Thomas Aquinas. Later theorists include Vitoria, Suarez, and Hugo Grotius (d. 1645), after whom little is added to just war theory until after World War I. Taylor indicates that the 1928 Kellogg-Briand Pact changed the general conception and terminology from "just and unjust wars" to "aggressive and defensive wars." He details the processes which led to the decision to bring charges against Axis leaders for the crime of initiating a war of aggression—charges never attempted previously.*

—M.M.W.

Over the centuries of recorded history, warfare has shown a remarkable and, to most of us, distressing vitality as a staple ingredient of intercourse among families and tribes at first, and then peoples, religions, and nations. No doubt a continuing pessimism about the likelihood that war can be abolished has lent force to men's efforts to confine wars and limit their methods and effects, as described in the previous chapters.

Throughout these same centuries, however, war has been practiced against a counterpoint of belief that as a destroyer of man and men's works, war is evil—an insult to human dignity and a peril to humanity's capacity to develop or, indeed, to survive. Since the early civilizations men have speculated about ways of eliminating war, and since the Middle Ages one of those ways has been the enunciation of rules of conduct, which gradually assumed the characteristics of law.

The laws of war have been developed largely by men who fought in them—military men. The principles concerning the moral or legal legitimacy of war itself, on the other hand, have been the work of theologians, jurists, and in more recent years, of diplomats. It was St. Augustine of Hippo (A.D. 354-430) who first enunciated the doctrine of "just and unjust wars," and the names of two ministers for foreign affairs, Frank B. Kellogg of the United States and Aristide Briand of France, are attached to the 1928 Pact of Paris, which condemned "recourse to war for the solution of international controversies."

Jesus Christ, as far as we know, had little to say about war or international relations; he was not a nationalist ("My Kingdom is not of this world") nor a political revolutionary ("Render to Caesar the things that are Caesar's"). But in the Gospels there is much emphasis on nonresistance and forgiveness of enemies, and during the first three centuries after Christ there grew up among his followers a strong school of religious pacifism. Furthermore, the early Christians were a religious minority in a pagan state, and the higher ranks of the Roman military service were required to offer sacrifice to the emperor—an act of idolatry that was anathema to Christians. For these reasons Tertullian, Origen, and other fathers of the Church condemned all military service as incompatible with the Christian life.

But there were those who thought otherwise, and in fact there were many Christians in the Roman soldiery. The Emperor Constantine's official toleration of Christianity (A.D. 312) and deathbed conversion (A.D. 337) foreshadowed a great change in the Christian attitude toward war: "A Christian empire and a Christian army defending the nucleus of the civilized world against heretics and vandals created an atmosphere more favorable to the conception of a holy war waged by a Chosen People than did a pagan empire persecuting a Christian minority." In this state of doctrinal flux, St. Augustine emerged as "the great coordinator of Christian doctrine upon peace and war."[1]

He accomplished this by drawing a distinction between "just and unjust wars," a vocabulary that was not new, but that the saint applied by reference to general ethical standards rather than the ambitions of rulers. The Roman wars of conquest he did not hesitate to condemn: "To make war on your neighbors, and thence to proceed to others and through mere lust of dominion to crush and subdue people who do you no harm, what else is this to be called than robbery on a grand scale?" He praised as "elegant and excellent" the pirate's reply to Alexander the Great, who had asked how he dared molest the seas: "Because I do it with a little ship only, I am called a thief; thou, doing it with a great navy, art called an emperor." On the other hand, it was wholly possible "to please God while engaged in military service." Just wars, according to Augustine, "are usually defined as those which avenge injuries, when the nation or city against which warlike action is to be directed has neglected to punish wrongs committed by its own citizens, or to restore what has been unjustly taken by it." Indeed, the true aim of a just war is peace, so that "after the resisting nations have been conquered, provision may more easily be made for enjoying in peace the mutual bond of piety and justice."

Augustine's tenets were approved and elaborated by the medieval theologians, most notably by St. Thomas Aquinas (1225-1274) in his *Summa Theologiae*. "In order that a war may be just," he wrote, "three things are necessary":

> In the first place, the authority of the prince, by whose order the war is undertaken; for it does not belong to a private individual to make war, because, in order to obtain justice he can have recourse to the judgment of his superior. . . . But, since the care of the State is confided to princes . . . it is to them that it belongs to bear the sword in combats for the defense of the State against external enemies. . . .
>
> In the second place, there must be a just cause; that is to say, those attacked must, by a fault, deserve to be attacked. . . .
>
> In the third place, it is necessary that the intention of those who

fight should be right; that is to say, that they propose to themselves a good to be effected or an evil to be avoided . . . those who wage wars justly have peace as the object of their intention.

The Augustinian and Thomist teachings have remained the core of Catholic doctrine on the rightfulness of war. It is really a matter of necessity; if there were a higher mundane power to order disputes among nations, as there is for individuals, there would be no basis for war. Lacking any other arbitration, war may be resorted to if the cause is just. On what constitutes a just war, Aquinas added little to Augustine, but stressed the importance of a pure motive; one who has been injured may not exploit his just grievance as an opportunity to gratify a lust for revenge.

How the "justness" of a war should be determined was examined more closely in the sixteenth and seventeenth centuries by the great Spanish theologians Francisco de Vitoria (1480-1546), a Dominican, and Francisco Suarez (1548-1617), a Jesuit. Vitoria became concerned about the application of the "just war" principles to the Spanish conquests in the New World. Very much an "establishment" figure, Vitoria vindicated the Spanish government's policies, but the strength of the Indians' right of self-defense must have impressed him, for his works lay great emphasis on the care that rulers should exercise before judging a prospective war to be "just." A mistake "would bring great evil and ruin to multitudes"; therefore "the reasons of those who on grounds of equity oppose the war ought to be listened to," and the final decision made only on the judgment "of many, and they wise and upright men."

Suarez's approach to these questions is much more legal and remarkably modern. The right of Christian rulers to make war, he declares, must have "at least some relation to the natural law"; that being so, it is not solely a Christian prerogative, and must also "suffice in some manner for non-Christian rulers." Defensive war is always legitimate, and may be a duty; this is as true between nations as between private individuals, for "the right of self-defense is a natural and necessary one." This sort of analogy he used as the basis for a triad of situations that would justify war: defense of life, defense of property, and aid to a third party who is unjustly attacked. Thus the parallel between domestic and international

criminal principles was articulated by a Spanish cleric three
centuries before the efforts of recent years to define "aggressive
war."

But the long reign of theological jurisprudence was at an end,
and the next great name in the history of international law is that of
a Dutch lay scholar and diplomat. Hugo Grotius (1583-1645)
hardly deserves the sobriquet "father of international law"
commonly bestowed on him, for his criteria of "just and unjust
wars" are largely derived from the writings of his Catholic
predecessors. Perhaps because he was a Protestant invoking the
individual conscience rather than churchly authority, and wrote as
a jurist (his work is entitled "Concerning the Law of War and
Peace"[2]) rather than a churchman, it is to Grotius that most
lawyers refer today when describing the foundations of international law.

Concerning "just and unjust wars" as a legal concept, however,
Grotius is not the beginning but nearly the end of the story. He had
a few followers—the Germans Pufendorf and Wolff and the Swiss
Emmerich de Vattel—who treated the doctrine seriously, but by
the end of the eighteenth century it was generally disregarded or
discredited by governments and writers alike. The principle causes
of its decline and virtual disappearance were the Reformation and
the growth of nationalism, bringing changes in the structure of
European civilization that the concept was ill-equipped to survive.

Until the end of the sixteenth century, the pope and other
princes of the Church often settled disputes among the temporal
rulers, either by their own force or upon request as arbitrators. St.
Thomas and his successors were not engaging in mere academic
disputation when they pondered the justness of wars, for the
Church was deeply and powerfully involved in wars and their
consequences. But with the Reformation and the ensuing decline
in the pope's temporal power, the Church's arbitraments were less
frequent or significant. The stream of theological jurisprudence
soon ran dry, and the seventeenth century Spaniards had no
notable successors.

At the same time the western nation-states, with a nationalist-
minded population and nationally organized armed forces, was
coming into full flower. Wars played a large part in this process,
and a nation's record of victories and defeats began to be regarded

as the major theme of its history. In these wars, who was to say on which side justice lay? On such matters the pope's voice, should he raise it, would no longer be heeded, and since there was no other source of supranational judgment it was left to each nation to make its own decision. The only way that international injustice could be rectified was by war or its threat. Furthermore, with the growth of international trade the concept of neutrality was increasingly important, and the development and observance of "neutral rights" was impossible unless the neutral nations forebore to pass judgment as between the belligerents.

In the course of the nineteenth century, as Germany and Italy coalesced into nation-states born of wars and new nations sprouted in the wake of the Turkish retreat from Europe, the temper of international law grew increasingly pragmatic. The "just and unjust war" concept was scorned as sentimental rubbish, hopelessly vague in content and impossible to enforce for lack of a tribunal competent to pass judgment. War, in short, was a fact of life that the law must accept.

To be sure, governments would still give reasons for resorting to war that stressed the justice of their cause, and individuals might legitimately entertain beliefs about the morality of a particular war. But none of this was of any *legal* significance. All belligerents started out in identical legal positions and possessed of equal rights. Lieber, progressive and humane as he was with regard to the manners and methods of warfare, had no doubts about its intrinsic validity. "Ever since the foundation of the modern nations, and ever since wars have become great national wars," he wrote, "war has come to be acknowledged not to be its own end, but the means to obtain great ends of state." Consequently: "The law of nations allows every sovereign government to make war upon another sovereign state."

And so when in 1914 the lights went out in Europe, although there were lamentations for the death and destruction that loomed and accusations and counter-accusations of blame for bringing on the war, no one said that those responsible (whoever they might be) had committed a crime under international law. After the war had ended, despite the hatreds aroused by four years of carnage, the view still prevailed that launching the war had been a moral outrage but not a crime.[3]

This conclusion was reached and recommended to the Paris Peace Conference by a fifteen-member "Commission on Responsibilities," charged with investigating the "responsibility of the authors of the war" as well as violations of the laws of war, and proposing appropriate machinery for the trial of those accused. On the matter of responsibility for the war itself, the commission had no difficulty in finding that the Central Powers (the German and Austro-Hungarian Empires) had "premediated" the war, acted deliberately "in order to make it unavoidable," and violated the neutrality of Belgium and Luxembourg despite treaty guarantees to which they were parties. These findings certainly met the Augustinian criteria of an "unjust war," and the commission found the Central Powers guilty of "conduct which the public conscience reproves and history will condemn." But as a legal matter, the commission declared that "a war of aggression may not be considered as an act directly contrary to positive law, or one which can be successfully brought before a tribunal." Except for confused and bungling efforts to try the ex-Kaiser "for a supreme offence against international morality and the sanctity of treaties,"[4] the views of the commission prevailed at the peace conference, and the criminal provisions of the Versailles treaty were confined to violations of the laws of war.

These events sufficiently demonstrate an international consensus in 1919 that to initiate a war—even an aggressive war—was not a crime under international law. But that year may also be taken to mark the beginning of the trend that led to Nuremberg, for the Commission on Responsibilities viewed its own conclusion as revealing a grave shortcoming in the scope of international law, and recommended "that for the future penal sanctions should be provided for such gross outrages." This proposal was not implemented in the Versailles treaty, and not until the end of the Second World War were any "penal sanctions" authorized. The commission's recommendation, nonetheless, was the signal of a new international view of the legality of war, the first fruits of which appeared at once in the covenant of the League of Nations.

The new approach was, unquestionably, the product of the unprecedented scope and destructiveness of the First World War, and especially the greatly increased risks to civilian life stemming from the advent of military air power. The only possible justification for the highly organized slaughter was that it had been a "war to end war," and that aim was the League's chief purpose.

No explicit statement that aggressive war is criminal was made in the covenant. Its most significant contribution was the establishment of a procedure for international resolution of disputes among its members, and the application of international force against any who, in defiance of the decision, resorted to war. It was a necessary inference from such a determination that the offending *government* was guilty of a crime, though the covenant left untouched any question of the criminal liability of the individuals, few or many, responsible for their government's unlawful act. Furthermore, the covenent procedure met what had been the fatal flaw of the "unjust war" concept, by providing for international rather than unilateral determinations of "justness." This precisely fitted the Thomist test, for now there was a higher power to order disputes among nations. That being so, resort to war by individual nations would henceforth be as "unjust" as it had always been for a private person; under the covenant the only just war would be the use of international force in order to subdue the recalcitrant nation.[5]

The First World War, unlike the Second, was followed by a dozen years of general peace and, toward the end of the twenties, of prosperity and contentment in the western world. On a number of occasions the League peace-keeping machinery was successfully used to forestall or terminate small wars—between Yugoslavia and Albania in 1921, Italy and Greece in 1923, Greece and Bulgaria in 1925, Bolivia and Paraguay in 1928, and Colombia and Peru in 1933. The Locarno and other regional or bilateral nonaggression treaties testified to the pacific temper of western statesmen and peoples.

Outstanding among these between-war efforts to abolish war was the treaty officially entitled "International Treaty for the Renunciation of War as an Instrument of National Policy." On April 6, 1927, the tenth anniversary of the United States' entry into the First World War, the French foreign minister, Aristide Briand, suggested that the occasion be celebrated by a Franco-American agreement to outlaw war between the two countries. The U.S. secretary of state, Frank B. Kellogg, proposed that the pact be multilateral, and impetus was given to the project by a resolution of the League Assembly unanimously adopted in September, 1927, which described "a war of aggression" as "an international crime" and declared that "all wars of aggression are and shall always be prohibited." The treaty itself—commonly known as the "Pact of Paris" or "Kellogg-Briand Pact," and eventually accepted by the United States, France, and forty-two other nations—was signed in August, 1928. Its two substantive articles were:

> Article 1. The High Contracting Parties solemnly declare . . . that they condemn recourse to war for the solution of international controversies, and renounce it as an instrument of national policy in their relations with one another.
> Article 2. The High Contracting Parties agree that the settlement or solution of all disputes or conflicts, of whatever nature or whatever origin they may be, which may arise among them, shall never be sought except by pacific means.

The Kellogg-Briand treaty was the high-water mark of the peaceful tide.[6] With the 1930s came economic depression, Adolf Hitler, and a surge of militant nationalism in the nations— Germany, Italy, and Japan—that later comprised the "Axis powers." The league's peace-keeping procedures were dependent for their effectiveness on the will of its members, especially the major European powers, and the will proved insufficient to check Japan's invasion of China or Italy's conquest of Ethiopia. After 1936 the League's prestige dwindled rapidly, and European crises in Spain, Austria, Czechoslovakia, Lithuania, and Albania were resolved, one after another, by unilateral military action on the part of Nazi Germany and Fascist Italy. By 1939, when war came, the League was little more than a relic of better times.

The Second World War raised anew the question pondered by the Commission on Responsibilities and answered in the negative at the end of the First World War. Had the Kellogg-Briand treaty or any other event between the wars sufficiently altered the controlling considerations so that individuals could now be charged with crime under international law on grounds of responsibility for aggressive war?

The problem reemerged in March, 1944, at meetings of the legal committee of the United Nations War Crimes Commission in London.[7] The Czechoslovak member of the committee, Dr.

Bohuslav Ečer, submitted a report on the permissible scope of "retributive action," the thrust of which was that the war was of such terrible and unprecedented dimensions that its initiators should be held criminally responsible. The committee was persuaded, and in May it recommended to the commission that the "war crimes" with which it was concerned should be deemed to include: "The crimes committed for the purpose of preparing or launching the war, irrespective of the territory where these crimes have been committed."

But the commission members were cautious, and doubted that their governments would move so far into unfamiliar legal and political territory. The matter was referred back to the legal committee, and in turn to a four-member subcommittee. The American and Dutch members approved the recommendations of the British member, Sir Arnold McNair, and the majority report of the subcommittee concluded that the Kellogg-Briand treaty had not significantly altered the circumstances that had been thought decisive in 1919. Just as in 1919, the majority proposed to recommend that the "outrages" of the Axis leaders be "the subject of formal condemnation," and that penal sanctions should be provided "for the future."

The fourth member of the subcommittee was Dr. Ečer, who submitted a minority report reiterating his earlier views, and suggesting that the commission need not take a position on the legality of aggressive war in general, but should declare that the aims and methods of the Axis leaders, and the "total" character of the war they had launched, made them criminally liable.

When the two reports came before the commission in October, 1944, the Australian representative (and future chairman of the commission), Lord Wright of Durley, was the principal spokesman for the Czechoslovakian view. As a common law lawyer, Lord Wright was accustomed to finding law in developing customs and practices, and for him the Kellogg-Briand pact and other agreements and pronouncements since the First World War were sufficient evidence of a "general consensus of authoritative opinion."[8]

Opinion in the commission was sharply divided, with the representatives of Britain, France, Greece, the Netherlands and the United States supporting the majority report, and Australia,

China, Czechoslovakia, New Zealand, Poland, and Yugoslavia on the other side. The division was too even to warrant action either way, and the members decided to consult their respective governments. In the upshot, the commission never came to a decision on the issue, and after 1944 it ceased to be the principal forum for its determination.

Between the theologians and Grotians of past centuries, and the diplomats of the between-war years of the present one, there is a difference in the concept of justifiable war that is of great significance today. From St. Augustine to Vattel the test was stated in terms of "just" and "unjust wars," whereas after the First World War the issue was drawn between "aggressive wars" and "defensive wars."

Despite the imprecision and generality of both "just" and "aggressive," there is a substantive and describable difference between the meanings intended by their users. It is true that warfare undertaken to repel an attack was generally regarded by theologians as "just," for if one country had a "just" claim or grievance against another, it could "justly" resort to war to enforce its rights. Thus if Prince A had been wronged by Prince B, Prince A's attack would be aggressive yet just, and Prince B's defensive fighting would be unjust, for he should have yielded voluntarily to a righteous claim.

The difficulty with all this, which especially troubled the later scholiasts like Vitoria and Suarez, was that "just" was too open-ended a test, and unilateral determinations of what was "just" were too subjective to constitute anything resembling law. Granted that there is plenty of room for argument about the meaning and application of "aggression," its ambiguities are of narrower range. Furthermore, its specificity was measurably sharpened by the Kellogg-Briand pact's condemnation of war "as an instrument of national policy" or "for the solution of international controversies," for that said pretty plainly that Nation A could *not* use war to enforce a claim, no matter how just, against Nation B. Under the "aggression" test, self-defense is practically the only basis on which it is legitimate to engage in warfare.[9] On its face at least, this is a much more objective test, more readily satisfied by evidentiary proof, and analogous to legal standards long established in domestic criminal law. And unquestionably it was this circumstance, coupled with the nature of the Hitler wars, that enabled the victorious governments, led by the United States, to take the leap in 1945 that they had shied from in 1918. Presumably according to his own standards, Hitler believed his own wars to be "just." But whatever the historians might ultimately say about the root causes of the Second World War, it was indisputable that neither Poland, Denmark, Norway, Holland, Belgium, Yugoslavia, Greece, nor the Soviet Union had attacked Germany. If aggression was the test of criminality, it seemed clear where the blame lay.

The reason that the United Nations War Crimes Commission was crowded off the stage, and that the Nuremberg trials took place, was that legally trained men in the seats of power in Washington concluded that German aggression could be judicially proved, that the future peace of the world would be promoted by an international determination that aggressive warfare is a crime under international law, and that those responsible may be punished. Chief among the architects of Nuremberg was Henry L. Stimson, who had been secretary of war under President William Howard Taft, secretary of state under Herbert Hoover, and was again secretary of war under Franklin D. Roosevelt; others closely involved included Attorney General Francis Biddle, Judge Samuel Rosenman of the White House staff and, after Roosevelt's death, Justice Robert H. Jackson, who took leave from the Supreme Court of the United States to take charge of U.S. interests in the war crimes field and serve as chief prosecutor.

The purpose of charging the Axis leaders with criminal responsibility for launching wars of aggression, and trying them before an internationally constituted tribunal, was part of the "Nuremberg project"[10] from its inception in the late fall of 1944. It was a design more readily accomplished by a high-level political decision than by committees of international lawyers for, as we have seen, in professional circles there still was sharp disagreement. The laws of war had been considered, compiled, and codified in the Hague and Geneva conventions, and enforced by courts-martial and military commissions for many years past; there was no substantial disagreement about their judicial enforceability. But the crime of engaging in aggressive warfare—the "crime against peace" as it was called at Nuremberg—had never before been the basis of a charge or proceeding of any description.

Unprecedented as it was, the inclusion of the aggressive war charge was bound to enmesh the Nuremberg proceedings in lasting controversy, although in the upshot no man suffered death and few any lesser penalty on that basis. Opinions still differ on whether Stimson, Jackson, and their colleagues were well-advised to press the proposition as they did. We need not wrestle here with might-have-beens. Indisputably it was a cardinal part of the postwar policy of the United States government to establish the criminality under international law of aggressive warfare, and the Nuremberg and Tokyo trials were the vehicles by which that purpose was accomplished. And if one seeks the reasons for that policy, they are nowhere better stated than in Jackson's progress report to President Truman in June, 1945, a few months before the trials began:

> In untroubled times, progress toward an effective rule of law in the international community is slow indeed. Inertia rests more heavily upon the society of nations than upon any other society. Now we stand at one of those rare moments when the thought and institutions and habits of the world have been shaken by the impact of world war on the lives of countless millions. Such occasions rarely come and quickly pass. We are put under a heavy responsibility to see that our behavior during this unsettled period will direct the world's thought toward a firmer enforcement of the laws of international conduct, so as to make war less attractive to those who have governments and the destinies of peoples in their power.

Notes

1. The quotations are from Eppstein, *The Catholic Tradition of the Law of Nations* (London, 1935), p. 65. Other useful works on the relation between war and Christian doctrine include Nussbaum, "Just War—A legal Concept?" *Michigan Law Review* 42 (1943):453; Von Elbe, "The Evolution of the Concept of the Just War in International Law," *American Journal of International Law* 33 (1939):665; Regout, *La Doctrine de Guerre Juste* (1934).

2. Grotius, *De Jure Belli ac Pacis* (1625).

3. The course of events with respect to war crimes charges of all descriptions following the First World War is set forth comprehensively and clearly in *History of the United Nations War Crimes Commission* (London, HMSO 1948).

4. This language was part of Article 227 of the Treaty of Versailles, which provided that a "special tribunal" would be established to try "William II of Hohenzollern, formerly German Emperor." The government of the Netherlands, where the ex-Kaiser had sought refuge, refused to turn him over to the Allies, on the ground that the offense charged was unknown in Dutch law and appeared to be of a political rather than a criminal character.

5. There was, however, a significant gap in the procedure, in that the decision of the superior body (the Council of the League of Nations) had to be unanimous, except for the parties to the dispute themselves. If unanimity was unattainable, then all members were free "to take such action as they shall consider necessary for the maintenance of right and justice." The action might be war, thus legitimized by the League's inaction.

6. There were other agreements and international resolutions to which the United States was a party that renounced war. Perhaps the most important was the resolution of the Sixth Pan-American Conference at Havana in 1928, which characterized "war of aggression" as "an international crime against the human species" and declared it "illicit" and "prohibited."

7. The discussion in the United Nations War Crimes Commission and in its legal committee is set forth in the commission's "History," *supra* note 3.

8. Lord Wright's views on the nature of international law, it is interesting to note, were in line with those of the Roman Catholic theologians. Suarez had written: "The Precepts of the Law of Nations differ in this from those of civil law, that they are not in writing, but in customs . . . of all or almost all nations . . . if it is introduced by the customs of all nations and binds all, we believe this to be the Law of Nations properly speaking."

9. This appears now to approximate the position of the Roman Catholic Church as stated in the "Pastoral Constitution on the Church in the Modern World, December 7, 1965," adopted at the Second Vatican Council: "As long as the danger of war remains and there is no competent and sufficiently powerful authority at the international level, governments cannot be denied the right to legitimate defense once every means of peaceful settlement has been exhausted." "Just War and Vatican Council II: A Critique" (Council on Religion and Industrial Affairs, 1966), p. 40.

10. At the outset, of course, it was not known where the trials would be held. It was not until August, 1945, that Nuremberg was definitely selected as the site.

17

How Much
Can the "Just War" Justify?

Donald A. Wells

Donald A. Wells, who teaches philosophy at the University of Hawaii and is the author of The War Myth *(1967), here argues that the general principles of the medieval theory of just war surely have no application today—if they ever did. Taking up one by one a contemporary list of conditions which must be met if a war is to be morally evaluated as just, he finds that in the context of the presuppositions underlying theories of just war (such as the right of a nation to survive at no matter what cost) the "just war" justifies too much.*
—R. C.

Justification, as is well known, is not an unambiguous term. Even in the context of logical justification the criteria are debatable, but at least in this milieu justification is assumed to be a function of a set of given rules in an agreed-upon system. Within a context of a set of truth claims consistency is a necessary and almost sufficient criterion. In normative discourse, however, justification takes on an honorific and emotion-laden aura. Adequacy here entails notions of "rightness" or "goodness" in addition to putative truth claims. The problem of "the just war" is, in this latter sense, more than a matter of the occurrence of matters of fact, more than a matter of consistency within a system of given axioms, more than a matter of demonstrating what is permissible legally, and more than an exercise in casuistry.

In a very ordinary sense of the term 'justify' we may merely seek an explanation of why war is waged in the sense of showing the

Reprinted with permission of the author and *The Journal of Philosophy*. From *The Journal of Philosophy*, vol. 66, no. 23 (4 December 1969), pp. 819-829.

premises that prompted us to the conclusion to wage war. When asked, "Why did you wage this war?" we could reply, "I did it because x, y, and z had occurred," and we might now conclude that the war in question had now been justified. If, on the other hand, we justify war the way an appellant defends himself before the judge, we would then need to show that what we did was consistent with the laws under which we have agreed to operate. But suppose that the justification of war is like the famous "justification of induction" and that its resolution involves us in a metalinguistic search. In fact, the attempts to justify war, or to identify what a just war would be like, share common properties with all these interpretations. In addition, however, there is an implicit contradiction which discussants of war and justice ordinarily recognize. Since the havoc of war is normally classed with immoral actions and evil consequences, what the notion of "the just war" attempts to do is to show that under some circumstances it would be "just" to perform immoral acts and to contribute to evil consequences. Some justifications of war aim to show that actions deemed normally forbidden by moral mandates are now permissible when performed under the aegis of war.

Since the history of ethical speculation has virtually no other instance of the defense of immoral acts under the extenuating circumstance of prudential risk, the "just war" concept needs special attention. It constitutes an anomalous instance in moral discourse, namely, a glaring exception to an otherwise accepted prohibition of acts of human brutality.

Traditionally the doctrine of "the just war" intended to curb excessively inhumane war practices, reduce the likelihood of war, identify who may properly declare war, ensure that the means of war bore a relation of proportion to the ends of war, and generally to promote a conscience on the practice. Incidently, the concept functioned as a defense of national sovereignty and of the "right" of nations to defend themselves in a basically lawless world. It made national survival feasible, while making international organization unlikely.

Since the notion of "the just war" has been revived after nearly two centuries of silence on the issue, it seems appropriate to look again at the medieval claims to see whether, if they had a defense then, they have any rationale now. The entire discussion for the medievalist rested, of course, on a concession which itself needs reassessment; namely, that war has a place in the moral scheme. The traditional questions about war were prudential, and the discussion centered around such questions as the time, place, and cause for war. Wars were presented to be neutral means which could be given moral properties under the appropriate conditions. Wars were criticized, if at all, in practice rather than in principle. In this, medieval war discussion shared a common starting point with medieval speculation on capital punishment. It wasn't the fact of killing that was the determinant; rather the reasons given for the acts of killing were decisive.

The Criteria of Saint Thomas

In order for a war to be just, three conditions had to be met: (1) an authoritative sovereign must declare the war; (2) there must be a just cause; and (3) the men who wage the war must have just intentions, so that good actually results from the war. In application of these criteria, the criticisms that did emerge of particular wars were so few as to suggest that princes were basically moral men or that the criteria were too vague to be useful. In addition, the critics were commonly persons not officially in government, so that their protests were a kind of baying at the moon. George Fox, for example, challenged the wars of Cromwell, but then Fox rejected the war method utterly. Franciscus de Vitoria, a theological professor at the University of Salamanca in the sixteenth century, chastised his Spanish superiors for the wars against the Indians[1]—but the remarks of university professors, then as now, were rarely influential in the determination of foreign policy, particularly when such remarks were critical of decisions of state already made.

More recently, Joseph McKenna[2] has revived the "just war" doctrine with an expanded list of seven conditions. They are: (1) the war must be declared by the duly constituted authority; (2) the seriousness of the injury inflicted on the enemy must be proportional to the damage suffered by the virtuous; (3) the injury to the aggressor must be real and immediate; (4) there must be a reasonable chance of winning the war; (5) the use of war must be a last resort; (6) the participants must have right intentions; and (7) the means used must be moral. Our question is: "Can such criteria be made applicable to modern war?" Let us consider this in terms of some general "just war" claims.

A Just War is One Declared by the Duly Constituted Authority

For a theologian like Saint Augustine or Saint Thomas, who presumed some pervading and ameliorating power from Christian prelates, such a criterion could be considered to be a limitation on careless scoundrels, as well as a limitation on the number of wars that would actually be waged. By the sixteenth century, however, with the proliferation of princes and the fading away of the influence of Christian prelates, a radically new situation had emerged. By this time, the "reasons of state," as Machiavelli elaborated them, permitted every prince to wage war whenever he saw fit. Since by the eighteenth century war had become the sport of kings, it was clear that authorities were not very reliable nor sensitive.

The rise of nationalism made this first criterion undifferentiating. It became increasingly obvious that to grant to any prince the privilege of judging his neighboring prelates was an odd situation. It was this anomaly that led Grotius and Vitoria to insist that, although only one side of a war could properly be considered just, in fact persons on both sides could, in good conscience, presume that they had justice on their side. In the absence of any international judge, who could determine the justice of the various national claims? What this criterion did do was to make clear that revolution was not to be allowed. What it could not do was to persuade or compel some prince to forego a war.

If rulers were saints and scholars there might be some reason to suppose that their judgments on war were adequate. Actually, there are no plausible reasons to suppose that secular leaders have intentions that will meet even minimal standards of humaneness. It is not necessary to have in mind Hitler, Tojo, DeGaulle, or Thieu to see that this is so. There is nothing in the nature of the process by which leaders are selected to give assurance that Johnson, Trudeau, or Wilson have moral insights that are even as good as the average, let alone sufficiently discerning to be used as the criterion for a just war. These leaders are not presumed by their loyal opposition to be especially gifted in domestic policy. Why imagine that they are so for foreign policy?

Even clerics have a rather poor reputation for moral insight or sound judgment. Witness, for example, the stand of Archbishop Groeber of Freiburg-im-Breisgau, who rejected Christian pacifism for German Catholics on the grounds that Hitler was the duly constituted authority. Pope Pius XII showed no better insight when he rejected the right of conscientious objection for German Catholics at the time of the formation of NATO. This first criterion, therefore, seems to serve no helpful purpose at all. In Vietnam, for example, it would rule out Thieu, since he is warring against his own people, while granting that President Johnson might be right and Ho Chi Minh just in killing American troops but not so for killing Vietnamese from the South.

A Just War Uses Means Proportional to the Ends

Franciscus de Vitoria had observed that if to retake a piece of territory would expose a people to "intolerable ills and heavy woes" then it would not be just to retake it. We must be sure, he continued, that the evils we commit in war do not exceed the evils we claim to be averting. But how do we measure the relative ills? This is the problem of a hedonic calculus on which Mill's system foundered. Since Vitoria granted princes the right to despoil innocent children if military necessity required it, it ceased to be clear what proportionality meant or whether any limit at all was being proposed.

In a recent paper on this issue Father John A. Connery[3] stated that the morality of the violence depends on the proportionality to the aggression. What is required is some calculus to make this measurement. The latitude with which conscientious persons have interpreted this suggests (what was clear enough to Mill) that we possess neither the quantitative nor the qualitative yardstick for this decision. Pope Pius XII thought the annihilation of vast numbers of persons would be impermissible. John Courtney Murray[4] thought this prohibition was too restrictive. Herbert Hoover thought in 1939 that the aerial bombing of cities should be banned, although he did urge the United States to build bombing

planes to perform this banned action. Jacques Maritain put
bombing from the air in the category of an absolutely proscribed
act.[5] In the early period of World War II "saturation bombing"
was considered to be too inhumane for citizens to accept. We then
practiced what was euphemistically called "precision bombing."
That the terms were empty became obvious when the air force
announced, at the time of the first test shot of the Atlas missile, that
a bomb that lands within fifty miles of its target is considered
accurate. Does the notion of proportionality have any discrimi-
natory meaning? During World War II the English writer Vera
Brittain attacked both Britain and the United States in her book
Massacre by Bombing. The Christian Century urged in editorials that its
subscribers should read the book, while taking the position that the
bombing of civilians is a necessary part of a just war. The American
Bar Association defeated a resolution calling for a condemnation of
the bombing of civilians.[6] The *Saturday Evening Post* maintained
that anyone who questioned the bombing of civilians was
"unstable."[7] McKinlay Kantor said the book was "soft-hearted."
The Reverend Carl McIntyre called the position of the sensitive
Mrs. Brittain "un-American and pro-Fascist," and the conservative Boston clergyman, H. J. Ockenga, called the view "un-
American" and said it gave aid and comfort to the enemy. Not only
do Christian prelates seem a fairly callous lot, but the notion of
proportionality has lost sense.

Where should we draw the line? Pope Piux XII decided that
communism was such a cosmic threat that atomic, chemical, and
biological bombs could all be justifiably used. But where then is the
proportion? The dilemma is not aided by the clerical dictum that
"there are greater evils than the physical death and destruction
wrought in war." What civilian would be impressed by this amid
the rain of bombs? Like "better dead than Red," this is a fiction,
enthusiasm for which is directly proportional to the square of the
distance from the potential havoc. In any case, there is simply too
much horror to be subsumed under the medieval notion of
proportionality. Indeed, our State Department's White Paper,
which was intended to explain the ends that justified our means in
Vietnam, is a monstrously casuistic document. It seems to make no
proportional sense to do what we are doing against the Vietnamese
if the only reward is American-style elections or freedom from the

threat of creeping communism.

The medieval thinkers rejected religion as a proper cause of a just war, and it is not egregious to point out that politics is in the same general class as religion. After all, is there really any doubt that men can live well under a variety of systems: capitalistic, communistic, monarchic, or democratic? It is equally obvious, I assume, that men may live poorly under any of these systems. Witness the blacks in Georgia, Mississippi, or Washington, D.C. Would any theologian wish to make a case for the bomb on Selma or Chicago? Surely the crimes against men are great there, and if there is any proportion in Hanoi, it would seem to follow that similar acts could be justified in Little Rock.

If there is any reasonable doubt left that the criterion calling for "just means" is simply a verbal genuflection, a brief look at what is currently called "rational nuclear armament" will banish it. A contemporary recommendation by proponents of "rationality" here is to limit bombs to the one-half megaton class. This is fifty times greater than the bomb dropped on Hiroshima. Limitation, proportion, or rationality do not seem to apply to the language of megakill. Once a bomb is big enough to kill every person in the area, it is not an expansion of war to use a bomb big enough to kill everyone twice, any more than it can be considered a reduction to reduce from a bomb twice as large as is needed to one the precise size that is needed to decimate the population. And, in addition, to call such a consideration "rational" may be proper to military tacticians, but alien to a concept that aimed at a moral distinction.

War May be Justly Taken Only as a Last Resort

In conventional language the notion of "last resort" presupposes a notion of "first resorts." Thus, unless a nation could show that it indeed exhausted first resorts, it would make no sense to claim the right of last resort. Presumably, first resorts would be such alternatives as economic, social, or political boycott, negotiations either through unilateral or multilateral means, or through such an agency as the United Nations, or even the contemplation of some kind of compromise. After these had been exhausted and there appeared to be no further nonviolent alternatives, we would still need to show that the last resort ought, in this case, to be taken.

It is always possible that the final resort that can be defended morally is the first resort taken. Too much of the discussion about the "justice" of war as a last resort presumes war to be proper in any case, so that the only genuine questions have to do with timing. With this kind of concession, in the first place, imagine what would happen to discussion of the war crimes trials after World War II. The problem facing the German Nazis was simply: "After having exhausted every resort, may we now as a last resort exterminate the Jews?"

The problem facing contemporary theorists of the "just war" is whether modern war is a means that may "justly" be granted as any resort at all. When we begin to speak of "massive retaliation" then perhaps it is time to question war itself. Is there any end at all of sufficient value that the sacrifice of persons on such a scale as is now possible could become "justified?" Something has happened to the medieval notion of last resort when our leaders destroy a city to save it. But the horror of war has never functioned as much of an intellectual deterrent to the justice of war. Thus it is antecedently unlikely that the ability to "overkill" or "megakill" makes any rational difference to the medieval concept. If war is a just resort at all, it makes no sense to deny nations its use as a last resort. Once the killing has been sanctioned in the first place, moral discussion, such as the medieval man carried out, takes on the aura of Pentagon calculations.

We find, in this vein, Paul Ramsey, a Protestant advocate of the "just war," endorsing the use of thermonuclear weapons, provided that an important *military target* could not otherwise be eliminated. While Ramsey deplored the death of so many civilians, he assured the survivors that this is not too great a price to pay for civilization. The possibility that surrender would be more moral than war is not even conceded a probability, making it clear that the discussants are speaking only for nations that win wars. The demand for "unconditional surrender" which American statesmen have regularly made, makes it clear that last resorts are the only ones they have in mind. For example, in August, 1958, the U.S. Senate voted 82 to 2 to deny government funds to any person or institution that proposes or actually conducts any study regarding the possible results of the surrender of the United States as an alternative to war. The sheer presence of the doctrine of "last resort" makes the compromise contingent on negotiations inadmissible.

What does our "just war" theory say to the American Indians back in the seventeenth century when they were confronted with the white man's power? Was war justified for the Indian as a last resort? It was surely a case of defense, and even white historians grant that the Indians tried many resorts short of war. Since nations with arms are loath to succumb to similar national neighbors, and more especially to do so over concern with whether war is a last resort or whether first resorts still remain, about all the theory tells us is that the "last resort" is bound to be a resort that we actually take.

A Just War Must be Waged by Men with Right Intentions

The medieval hub of this argument was the doctrine of the "double effect." A just belligerent intended only as much death as would be proportional to the threat or the offense, and he would intend to kill only combatants. It was presumed that we ought not to kill noncombatants. In the Middle Ages the weapons made such concern practical. Although the archer might shoot his arrow into the air and not be too clear about where it landed, he was not in doubt about whether he was shooting it at combatant enemies. He might miss a small barn, but he hit the right city. Modern weapons make such sensitivity about the recipients of our missiles inoperable and unfeasible. Not only this, but the number of noncombatants killed in modern war usually far exceeds that of soldiers. Whereas medieval man might pardonably weep for the accidentally slain civilians, modern man intends the death of every civilian slain when he drops his bombs from the air.

In every age, however, the problem of unintended death proved a harassing one, and the pattern of resolution seems to have been to deplete the scope of the class of the noncombatant, until in the present this is a null class. Modern war is total at least in the sense that there are no innocents. We could never have dropped the bombs on Dresden, Nagasaki, Hiroshima, or Tokyo if the class of innocents had had members. But quite apart from whether one could or did intend the death of noncombatants, there would still remain the question whether the end justified the means at all. It was this sheer inapplicability of the doctrine of the "double effect" that prompted John Bennett to reject the notion completely.[8] There is, also, another procedural problem here. The doctrine of the double effect is one that does not trouble military or political strategists. Their interest is to win the war, and not to make theological calculations. Indeed, the only concern the military appears to have had over such niceties as intentionality is whether there would be a moral response from the public. We did not, initially, practice saturation bombing in Europe, and we were told later that the military feared a public outcry against it. Once we had practiced it on the Japanese and once military necessity demanded it, Americans lost most of their sensitivity on the problem.

No defense of the intentions of a belligerent could be satisfactorily made unless it could also be shown that the means used were also moral, and this would be so even for the combatants considered to be fair game. Nowhere has the ability of man to tolerate increasing doses of violence and brutality been more evident than in his history of attempts to humanize the weapons. Richard J. Krickus[9] believed that chemical bombs were moral, whereas biological bombs were not, and this because of the difficulty of control in the case of the latter. On the other hand, napalm, anti-personnel shrapnel, and thermonuclear bombs were all "just" in their intended uses. To speak of the just use of the bayonet is difficult enough for mere mortals to grasp, but to use the same approbation for megaweapons makes the terms 'just' and 'moral' lose their conventional distinguishing function. Modern man has had long practice in handling these theoretically difficult problems. Since we use gas chambers in the United States for our domestic offenders, it must not have been their method that led to the war crimes trials against the Nazis, but simply that they gassed and cremated the wrong persons. Although there may be no way to calculate the relative horror of gas chambers in the two countries or the hedonic ratios of the death of twenty Japanese as compared with the death of twenty Americans, it is precisely this kind of question that the "just war" theorists must answer.

The discussion of "intention" in the thirteenth century, when the weapons were relatively limited in scope so that a king could implement his wish not to harm noncombatants and could practice some kind of proportionality, is something that modern man can no longer carry out. All we can consider is whether to set the projectiles in motion. From that moment on, it makes no sense to speak of proportionality, intentionality, or limitation. But here, men have attempted to think the "unthinkable." What seemed too brutal in one age becomes militarily necessary and, hence, just in the next age. As recently as twenty years ago the arms agencies deleted mention of their chemical-biological research from the public agendas for fear of a public outcry. Now there is no need for secrecy, and everyone can witness on television the operations of our nerve gas plant in Newport, Indiana, our disease bomb research at Fort Detrick, Maryland, and the bubonic plague research of the Hartford Travellers Research Corporation to discover the most efficient means to spread the disease by airplane or on foot. The history of prudential calculation reveals that every weapon sooner or later is added to the list of morally approved ones.

There may be a credible case for claiming that the medieval discussions of the just war added to man's moral insights and implemented his humane concerns. Perhaps without such discussions, the history of war would be even worse than it now is. Such counterfactual conditions are, however, technically incapable of being assigned weights or probability as to truth or falsity. But what can be determined is that the use of the terms 'just,' 'limited,' 'humane,' 'proportional,' or 'intention' in the context of modern war robs those terms of most of their traditional moral flavor. If it was poor military strategy to assert "thou shalt not kill," it was even worse ethics to claim, "thou mayest napalm thine enemy if thy country is threatened."

One could have hoped that as the scope of weapons increased there would have been an escalation of sensitivity as to their use. But all that happened was that there was an escalation of insensitivity, until today it is hard to imagine what an unjustly fought war would look like that is not already exhibited in the just variety. Conceivably some medieval sword thrusts might have been made justly, and some fortified cities justly sacked. The entire discussion vanishes, however, once we admit weapons that shoot further than the eye can see. And clearly this distinction has been lost once we use megaweapons, and even what are called "conventional" weapons like fragmentation bombs and napalm. Since we no longer admit the combatant-noncombatant distinction, what have we left to adjudicate? If the just war ever had moral significance in the past it is clear today that it justifies too much. In the Middle Ages the just war was less tragic than the alternatives. Today the just war justifies Armageddon if our hearts be pure, and this is to justify too much.

Let me close with an analogy. Suppose that, instead of national war, we were discussing the battles of Aryans against Jews. Suppose we approached this subject with medieval language and modern skill. We would, of course, consistent with the position taken on war, grant to Aryans the right to wage the war of extermination of the Jews, provided of course that the pogrom be declared by the duly constituted authority, be carried out with due decorum proportional to the threat, and with a just end in view. With this much granted, citizens would then see that they must kill Jews if their prince commanded it in the name of national defense (not unlike the Aryan concern with racial defense). Citizens would then implement the state department plan of containment of Judaism (not unlike containment of communism) and seek by every means to rid the world of the threat of creeping Judaism. With no more effort than our war leaders now exert, we would carry out essentially what the Nazis did carry out, and do it according to the laws of pogroms (not unlike the much advertised "laws of wars"). Our means would naturally be humane gas chambers and sanitary ovens. If we put it this way, then the doctrine of the "just war"—like that of the "just pogrom"—would justify too much.

Notes

1. Franciscus de Vitoria, *On the Law of War* (Washington, D.C.: The Carnegie Institute, 1917), sec. 22.

2. Joseph McKenna, "Ethics and War: A Catholic View," *American Political Science Review* (September 1960):647-658.

3. The Reverend John A. Connery, "Morality and Nuclear Armament," in William J. Nagle, ed., *Morality and Modern Warfare* (Baltimore: Helicon, 1960), p. 92.

4. John Courtney Murray, "War and the Bombardment of Cities," *Commonweal* (September 2, 1938).

5. In Nagle, ed., *Morality and Modern Warfare*, p. 107

6. *New York Times* (July 15, 1939), p. 3.

7. *Saturday Evening Post* (November 21, 1942):128.

8. Cf. Paul Ramsey, *War and the Christian Conscience* (Durham, North Carolina: Duke University Press, 1961), p. 148.

9. Richard J. Krickus, "On the Morality of Chemical/Biological War," Chapter 30 in this volume.

18

The "Just War" and the Right of Self-Defense

Frederick R. Struckmeyer

Struckmeyer takes issue with the contention of Donald Wells ("How Much Can the 'Just War' Justify?") that the moral distinctions putatively defined by the concept of a "just war" have been obliterated by the indiscriminately lethal character of modern warfare. Struckmeyer contends that the widespread destruction made possible by modern weaponry, which often makes it technically impossible to observe the "combatant-noncombatant" distinction in warfare, does not by itself render the concept of a 'just war" nugatory. He maintains that Wells' justifiable concern with the horrors of war does not resolve the crucial philosophical issue of whether war, under some circumstances, can ever be justified. Struckmeyer observes that where negotiation or compromise is impossible due to an enemy's belligerence the alternatives are capitulation or resistance. In those cases in which capitulation entails extermination of a nation or a nation's cultural values (he cites as an example the likely destruction of Israel as a nation were she to capitulate to the Arabs) the moral problem of nonresistance takes on the greatest significance. Struckmeyer asks the question whether a nation can be asked on moral grounds to sacrifice itself rather than engage in defensive hostilities. He readily acknowledges that less evil (casualties, etc.) might result from capitulation rather than resistance. He also argues that a nation may consider surrendering rather than resisting (a nation has the right to self-defense but it does not have a duty to resist). But he challenges Wells' pacifist assumption that capitulation is morally indicated as a general policy. To suggest that a nation ought never to resist, even in the face of extermination, is irrational. Struckmeyer maintains that a nation's motivation in fighting a war is morally relevant and it is this factor that Wells ignores in failing to distinguish

© 1978 by the University of Chicago. The article first appeared in *Ethics*, vol. 82, no. 1 (October 1971) pp. 48-55. Reproduced with permission.

between offensive wars, which must be considered immoral, and defensive wars, which may be morally justified.

—J. B.

Donald A. Wells has recently argued[1] that the medieval concept of the "just war" has lost whatever category it may have once possessed and has become, in the modern world, a virtually useless notion for purposes of making moral distinctions. Professor Wells almost seems to feel, in fact, that the "just war" concept *never* had any basis, but that it has taken modern warfare, with its sophisticated weaponry and immense powers of "overkill," to make this fact evident.

While I strongly concur with much of what Wells has to say, it seems to me that some of the issues he raises and some of the assumptions he makes require further elucidation. His personal antipathy to war is so strong that he apparently feels no need to defend many of his assertions. Yet there are those of us who are no less opposed than he to war and its carnage who nonetheless may feel that not all wars are immoral, or not equally immoral. Dr. Wells, as a pacifist, rejects this alternative. He tries instead to show that *no* wars can any longer be considered morally justifiable. Yet he docs not convincingly establish this conclusion, aside from pointing out, in graphic terms, those horrors of contemporary warfare which an advanced technology has made possible.

An example of the kind of unsupported assertion Wells makes is the following: "Conceivably some medieval sword thrusts might have been made justly, and some fortified cities justly sacked. The entire distinction [between just and unjust wars] vanishes, however, once we admit weapons that shoot farther than the eye can see. And clearly this distinction has been lost once we use megaweapons, and even what are called 'conventional weapons' like fragmentation bombs and napalm."[2] I must confess that I fail to grasp Wells's logic here. Does he mean that a modern soldier's frequent inability to see the enemy face to face, or in hand-to-hand combat, really distinguishes the modern military situation from that of the more distant past? If so, I cannot agree. The introduction of cannon hundreds of years ago made it possible to kill men at a distance, and the far more ancient longbow, to a lesser degree, did the same thing. The chief question, and one which Wells never explicitly raises, is nevertheless this: can a technological advance as such constitute the basis for rendering the "just war" concept, despite its moral ambiguities, obsolete?

What Wells is mainly disturbed about, it seems clear, is not so much the kind of suffering that modern weaponry makes possible, but its extent. Specifically, it is now the case that we cannot restrict most of the suffering to actual combatants only. We now have the capacity to wipe out entire nations, if we choose, and possibly the entire race. This fact does, quite clearly, constitute a historically new and frightening situation. Yet we should not forget that many "conventional" wars of the twentieth century have entailed casualties, both military and civilian, which are dwarfed by some wars of the past. China's population, during and immediately after the Mongol invasions, dropped from 100 million to about 60 million. Even if this estimate is in error by a fraction of two or three (which it probably is not), it is noteworthy that numerous times in China's history alone wars and revolutions have taken tens of millions of lives. It is superfluous to add that most of these casualties involved noncombatants. War has always involved large-scale suffering and destruction. In other words, the sheer magnitude of destruction which can be wrought by contemporary warfare does not by itself warrant a contrast between past and present. It is true that we now have more efficient ways of killing people than we have ever had before. But the key philosophical issue is still whether we should ever be prepared, under some circumstances, to go to war. In short, the question is: are wars ever justified? This issue is not resolved simply by pointing out the destructiveness or brutal efficiency of today's weapons. Nor, I think, is it resolved by insisting—as Wells does—that when modern nations go to war there are no "accidental" civilian deaths. "Whereas medieval man might pardonably weep for the accidentally slain civilians," he says, "modern man intends the death of every civilian slain when he drops his bombs from the air."[3] This statement is very questionable, for several reasons. In the first place I am not sure that medieval man always did weep for accidentally slain civilians (unless they were his own kin), partly because their deaths were not always strictly accidental. I think Wells is falsely attributing to the premoderns better intentions than they actually had (most of the time). We are not necessarily more callous about war and killing than our forebears were. But, then, neither are we demonstrably less callous. Thus I cannot agree with Wells when he says, in the statement quoted above, that "modern man intends the death of every civilian slain when he drops his bombs from the air." If this simply means that we know, in advance of the bombing, that there will certainly be "unintended" civilian casualties, and that knowledge of this fact does not deter us from dropping the bombs, then he is certainly right (if misleading). For his point then is that we can never excuse these deaths on the grounds that they were not intended, since we know what weapons of this sort can do. I rather think, however, that Wells means to say more than this, and really does wish to give military decision makers of the present day worse motives than those of other ages. This I think is unfair, for the reasons given above. It is true, especially in the case of nuclear projectiles, that we can only decide whether to use certain kinds of weapons, and not what the human cost—even approximately— will be. But this "whether" is also governed by our decision to fight or not to fight, especially given a situation in which negotiations have done their utmost, and the choice is either to capitulate or to resist. It is in this kind of situation, where capitulation (i.e., nonresistance) may in fact mean extermination—as in the Arab-Israeli conflict, looked at from the Israeli side—that the moral problem becomes most acute. To kill, or at least resist, someone who has demonstrated his intention to kill us is usually considered a necessity. But is it really a necessity, or should we prefer to be killed rather than to kill?

To these disturbing questions Wells speaks only briefly, and even then he gives only the darkest of hints as to his own view. Can a nation be asked, on moral grounds, to sacrifice itself—or one of its allies—rather than engage in hostilities which will produce an unpredictable (though certainly great) amount of bloodshed on both sides? "The possibility that surrender would be *more moral* than war is not even conceded a probability,"[4] Wells says, speaking of the common viewpoint, that the "survival of civilization" might regrettably demand, in some wartime situations, a high civilian casualty toll (most of it, of course, on the other side). Wells's allusions to the possibility of surrender as an alternative to armed resistance is interesting, because it certainly is the case that the

United States, like most other nations, has traditionally regarded surrender, whether by an individual soldier or by the nation, as ignominious and unthinkable. The recent *Pueblo* incident, in which a naval commander surrendered his ship to the North Koreans, well illustrates the usual military attitude toward surrender: namely, that to "go down fighting" is part of a soldier's duty. Thus Wells's suggestion that, in some instances at least, "surrender would be more moral than war," can scarcely be expected to appeal to the military mind. But this does not mean the suggestion has no merit. If we make a distinction between national policy and individual policy on this issue, then the question becomes: can it ever be morally right for an individual to be killed—if necessary—rather than to kill (or resist)? I assume, to be sure, that the policy of "turning the other cheek" is, in fact, morally right. The ethic of Jesus concurs with that of Socrates in the view that it is better to suffer injustice than to act unjustly. While utilitarian theories of morality have generally opposed self-sacrifice,[5] there can be no doubt that many individuals have found such self-sacrifice the only course of action morally open to them. Perhaps genuine self-sacrifice is beyond most of us; in any case, we are rarely if ever put in a position where the options are limited to "my life or yours." Killing in self-defense is legally regarded as justifiable homicide. But what is legally justifiable may be morally unjustifiable. It may, in short, really be better—though not, as already noted, on utilitarian grounds—to let the other fellow kill me, if the only alternative is to kill him. Of course there may well be other alternatives, such as convincing him (rationally) that he ought not to desire my death, or that eventually those who take the sword must perish by the sword. But failing such efforts at rational persuasion, it may really come down to the forced option of "kill or be killed."

Now the question that is of prime interest from the standpoint of international relations is this: should a nation ever surrender (or even disarm), realizing that surrender may possibly lead to collective suicide? Can surrender in the face of a belligerent who will not negotiate (although what Wells calls a "compromise contingent on negotiation"[6] is surely never to be given up as a possibility) be the *right,* even if not the most expedient, policy?

The Cambridge historian Herbert Butterfield points out that

Christian tradition justifies the resort to war "if he [the individual] fights in self-defense, and *a fortiori* if he fights to defend the weak."[7] But Butterfield points out that this traditional viewpoint (of which Wells is extremely critical, contending that Christianity and war are strictly incompatible) does *not* mean that "a man or any body of men need regard it as a *duty* to resort to self-defense when they prefer to submit."[8] In other words, while self-defense is, on this view, a right, it is hardly an obligation. In fact, a "higher morality," as Butterfield shows, may demand the forfeiture of our "rights" in the interest of an ethical standard which does not place supreme value on merely staying alive.

The question, then, is this: can we really expect a nation, and not merely an occasional rare individual, to put such a "higher morality" into practice? Psychologically it would appear that we cannot, and even from the moral point of view the question is not unambiguous. For inevitably military and political decisions are made by a handful of men, and are hardly likely, especially in wartime situations, to reflect the participation of all or most of the people. Can a head of state rationally will his own nation's capitulation and possible destruction, so long as there is some alternative (i.e., some capacity to resist)? Hitler did in fact will the utter destruction of Germany when once he realized, near the end of World War II, that the Reich had been completely crushed. Germany's defeat, he said, proved that it was not "fit" to survive. His efforts at collective suicide were fortunately thwarted by those who were less eager than he to die rather than endure postwar humiliation. But can we not conceive of a situation where collective suicide, whether actual or merely threatened—as when Ghandi would all but starve himself to death, in order to dramatize certain demands for reform—might really be the most moral policy to follow? I am not now speaking of suicide (or, at least, surrender) prompted by the impossibility or uselessness of resistance, but of surrender motivated simply by a refusal to fight.

Looking at the question from the standpoint of individual policy, it would seem that, while I clearly have the prerogative of taking my own life, or of allowing someone else to take it, I do not have the same prerogative where the lives of others are concerned. I cannot compel another man to sacrifice himself if he wishes to defend his life, property, etc. Oddly enough, soldiers are sometimes placed in military situations where it is a virtual certainty that they will be killed, yet they are obliged, as soldiers, to go down fighting—taking as many of the enemy with them as they can. This presumably is because of the reasoning (if any is involved) that, even if they die, they will have shortened the war somewhat. Thus at least some, and perhaps many, lives will in the long run have been saved. But sometimes the insistence that the soldier go down fighting is motivated more by pure vindictiveness than by utilitarian or strategic considerations: we are to kill or to try to kill as many of the enemy as we can because he is the enemy (thus being, by definition, wicked), and because he is determined to kill us. We may therefore feel, quite self-righteously, that the enemy *deserves* to be killed. (It is precisely this kind of twisted reasoning that Professor Butterfield so effectively undermines in the aforementioned book.) And if we do feel this way, we will doubtlessly feel it right, if not obligatory, to kill him. This kind of punitive psychology, Butterfield argues, has animated many a "war for righteousness." However, I agree with him and with Wells that the "war for righteousness" concept has been thoroughly discredited. It is not our place as men to punish the sins or "mistaken" ideologies of other men. We have a general right, even if not a duty, to defend ourselves as a nation. But we manifestly do not have the right to wage unlimited war, and to seek the destruction of the enemy because we think him deserving of death. To fight in self-defense and to fight for this latter reason are two vastly different things, a point Wells overlooks.

Wells does not clearly distinguish between offensive and defensive wars, possibly because the Vietnam conflict has blurred this distinction so much. He implies that *no* wars can any longer be morally justifiable, but he does not give us compelling reasons for accepting this conclusion—aside from the a priori premise that the taking of human life is always wrong. Yet the distinction between offensive and defensive warfare cannot, I think, be dispensed with—not even after Vietnam, and not even in view of the horrors which may occur during the course of what is truly a defensive war. (I assume there are such, even in the twentieth century.) Mo Tzu, the ancient Chinese thinker who condemned offensive warfare in the strongest terms, nevertheless fathered a movement of philosophers and social activists who later developed sophisticated techniques of defensive warfare (e.g., regarding the fortification of cities). This ought not to surprise us, unless we take the position that all armed resistance is evil, and that anything is preferable to taking another man's life (or attempting to). It still seems possible to wage some purely defensive wars, wars which are limited in scope and which do not have the effect of destroying what they originally intended to save. (I leave out of account the problem of a confrontation between nuclear powers, for I concede that to speak of a defensive war in this context does introduce a radically new factor, namely the possibility of worldwide destruction, which does not arise in conventional warfare.) The Arab-Israeli conflict, again seen from the standpoint of the Israelis, strikes me as one such instance. It must be admitted, of course, that the Arab states do not officially view Israel as pursuing a purely defensive policy; they claim that the 1967 war demonstrated Israel's real aggressiveness. So the question of what constitutes a defensive war is far from obvious. But the fact remains that the distinction is still useful: to resist when one's life or country is threatened is not the same as to kill out of personal (or collective) hatred or vindictiveness. Wells only confuses this important distinction when he says that "if it was poor military strategy to assert 'thou shalt not kill,' it was even worse ethics to claim, 'thou maycst napalm thine enemy if thy country is threatened'."[9]

Why is this bad ethics? If napalm should never be used in the defense of one's country, then which weapons *are* permissible? From a pacifistic standpoint, of course, the only possible answer is "none." This is simply because the pacifist is committed to a refusal to fight no matter what the provocation or likely consequences.

In his book, *The War Myth,* Wells suggests that the "likely consequences" of a refusal to go to war, when threatened with attack or invasion, might often entail less evil than would a determination to resist to the limits of one's power.[10] This is no doubt true, and one may agree with him that a nation threatened with invasion, and not just one already overrun after having attempted resistance, might give serious consideration to the possibility of surrendering without a fight. But can it be urged upon nations as a general policy that they should be prepared to surrender rather than fight, given a belligerent who refuses to negotiate or compromise in any way? If, in the ultimate case, surrender will mean extermination of the nation or of its primary cultural values, can nonresistance rationally be urged? Would it really be better if the Israelis were to lay down their arms or accede to the Arab demands, even if this meant the eventual destruction of Israel as a nation? If "better" here is taken to mean "productive of less evil than any alternative action," then it is not at all clear that surrender would—in the case of Israel, at least—actually be better. But even if we grant that surrender would under some circumstances entail less evil (fewer casualties, above all) than would armed resistance, it still does not follow that a nation should never resist—unless, again, our reasoning is strictly utilitarian. I find it interesting, in this connection, that Wells constantly impugns the motives which lead nations to resort to war. He evidently feels that motives finally count for nothing where the threat or actual use of military force is concerned. "Today the just war justifies Armageddon," he asserts, "if only our hearts be pure."[11] I do not wish to be construed as welcoming Armageddon, but one must ask: do "pure hearts" count for nothing? More specifically, is it the case that a nation's (or individual's) intentions are irrelevant to the moral worth of the actions stemming from those intentions? It is unfortunate that Wells fails to deal with these questions, and nowhere attempts a defense, or even a delineation, of his major ethical assumptions. What he does do is beg the question in favor of a quasi utilitarianism, evidently because a utilitarian approach to war supports his pacifistic premises.[12] As noted earlier, he ascribes worse motives to modern militarists than to premodern man, though for implausible reasons. I grant that no one's heart is completely pure and no nation's hands free of some other nation's blood. I further grant that to defend war on the grounds that it is our "duty" to fight, when threatened, is usually to argue speciously. But I do not grant that the reasons *why* a nation goes to war are irrelevant to an evaluation of its moral position. In short, I refuse to accept Wells's dictum that the very willingness to consider war as an alternative, no matter what the provocation, is grounds for condemnation. I must hasten to add that I agree with his view that nations are generally too willing to resort to war, as evidenced by the weapons and armies they keep in readiness. I further admit that the very existence of those weapons and armies invites, if it does not many times ensure, eventual war. But I cannot go so far as to say that our major international problems would be solved if nations such as Israel would, when threatened with attack, capitulate rather than fight. Obviously, if all nations disarmed and followed a policy of nonresistance there would be no full-scale wars. I do not rule out such a possibility as hopelessly utopian, but given the proclivities of human nature as we know it one can hardly expect individual nations to find nonresistance an attractive alternative to self-defense. Even Ghandi's India has found it impossible (or impractical) to make nonviolence, the traditional virtue of *ahimsa,* a national policy.

I regret that I have put myself in the position of appearing to favor war as a way of solving international problems, for I am as convinced of the futility of war, especially aggressive wars, as is Wells. I differ from him in refusing to concede that there is no third position between the extremes of pacifism and jingoistic militarism. It is simply not the case that one is either for war or against it. Surely one can work for disarmament among nations while recognizing the need for some kind of defense budget (though not necessarily, of course, the one the United States presently has). To adopt such a position is not necessarily to be a moral coward. The pacifist is to be admired for his conscientious refusal to bear arms, and his fervent wish that nations generally would forgo the use of military power. But we are not all pacifists, temperamentally, and it is not even clear that we all should be—so long as there are nations and individuals (including possibly ourselves) who are determined to commit aggression. Just what constitutes aggression in a given situation is of course a thorny issue, as I indirectly admitted while pleading for a retention of the offensive-defensive war distinction. Nations, like individuals, can easily deceive themselves into believing that someone else is an aggressor, and they the loyal patriots or defenders of the oppressed. In other words the moral ambiguities surrounding international relations, especially when ideological differences add fuel to the fire, are quite obvious. This is all the more reason why a blanket appeal to a policy of nonresistance, while in many ways attractive, has its flaws. (I say this while recognizing that men like Ghandi and Martin Luther King have shown just what such a policy can accomplish in the way of social and legal reform.)

Wells is to be thanked for having reminded us that there is an alternative to war. It is an alternative which nations presently tend to ignore, but whose moral sanctions and reasoned hopefulness may make it the *only* alternative within the foreseeable future.

Notes

1. Donald A. Wells, "How Much Can the 'Just War' Justify." Chapter 17 in this volume.

2. Ibid.

3. Ibid.

4. Ibid. (italics mine). By "more moral," in this context, he evidently means "less productive of suffering, death, etc." In *The War Myth* (New York: Pegasus, 1967), Wells argues cogently that "if nations had foresight, and knew when they were going to lose before the fact, they would doubtless be able to do a more credible job of showing when and whether military protection was the lesser of two evils" (p. 190).

5. "The utilitarian morality does recognize in human beings the power of sacrificing their own greatest good for the good of others. It only refuses to admit that the sacrifice is itself a good. A sacrifice which does not increase or tend to increase the sum total of happiness, it considers as wasted" (J. S. Mill, *Utilitarianism* [New York: Dutton & Co., 1951], chapter 2, p. 20).

6. Wells, "'Just War.'"

7. Herbert Butterfield, *Christianity, Diplomacy, and War*, 3d ed. (London: Epworth Press, Wyvern Books, 1962), p. 27.

8. Ibid., pp. 27-28 (italics mine).

9. Wells, "Just War."

10. Wells, *The War Myth*, pp. 189-91. This is precisely the view that Bertrand Russell advocated during his last years, especially in the course of his well-known debate with Sidney Hook in the pages of the *New Leader* in 1958. (The most significant of these exchanges are reprinted in Raziel Abelson, ed., *Ethics and Metaethics* [New York: St. Martin's Press, 1963], pp. 158-79). Hook and Russell were of course debating the issue of whether it would be better to be "Red than dead," in the event a United States–Soviet nuclear confrontation came down to the alternatives of surrender or death. Professor Hook felt that death was preferable to life under communism, while Russell argued that almost any kind of political or military regime could be tolerated if the alternative was the end of the human race or a large segment of it. Wells, quite clearly, would take sides with Russell in this debate. This is shown in his assertions that slogans like "better dead than Red" are fictions, and that enthusiasm for them "is directly proportional to the square of the distance from the potential

havoc" ("Just War").

11. Wells, "Just War."

12. Of course, a dictum like "thou shalt not kill" sounds much more deontological than it does utilitarian, and I am not sure that Wells would attempt to defend it on utilitarian grounds.

19

War and Murder

Elizabeth Anscombe

Elizabeth Anscombe argues that pacifism is an indefensible position: it simply does not take account of the simple fact that society without coercive power is generally impossible. This is not to say that war is not generally a great evil, principally because it tends to lead to the morally indefensible killing of the innocent. (The principle of double effect offers help in distinguishing when killing the innocent is, and when it is not, murder.) Pacifism, she adds, tends to have a morally pernicious effect: by ignoring the distinction between shedding any blood and shedding innocent blood, it tends to lead to an "anything goes" position once war is initiated. One is, furthermore, misguided if one believes that Christianity entails pacifism; such a position sees Christianity not, as in truth it is, a severe and practicable religion, but rather as a beautifully ideal and impracticable one.

—R.C.

The Use of Violence by Rulers

Since there are always thieves and frauds and men who commit violent attacks on their neighbours and murderers, and since without law backed by adequate force there are usually gangs of bandits; and since there are in most places laws administered by people who command violence to enforce the laws against lawbreakers; the question arises: what is a just attitude to this exercise of violent coercive power on the part of rulers and their subordinate officers?

Two attitudes are possible: one, that the world is an absolute

From *Nuclear Weapons: A Catholic Response*, edited by Walter Stein, pp. 45-62. Copyright © 1961 by the Merlin Press Ltd. Reprinted with the permission of the author.

jungle and that the exercise of coercive power by rulers is only a manifestation of this; and the other, that it is both necessary and right that there should be this exercise of power, that through it the world is much less of a jungle than it could possibly be without it, so that one should in principle be glad of the existence of such power, and only take exception to its unjust exercise.

It is so clear that the world is less of a jungle because of rulers and laws, and that the exercise of coercive power is essential to these institutions as they are now—all this is so obvious, that probably only Tennysonian conceptions of progress enable people who do not wish to separate themselves from the world to think that nevertheless such violence is objectionable, that some day, in this present dispensation, we shall do without it, and that the pacifist is the man who sees and tries to follow the ideal course, which future civilization must one day pursue. It is an illusion which would be fantastic if it were not so familiar.

In a peaceful and law abiding country such as England, it may not be immediately obvious that the rulers need to command violence to the point of fighting to the death those that would oppose it; but brief reflection shows that this is so. For those who oppose the force that backs law will not always stop short of fighting to the death and cannot always be put down short of fighting to the death.

Then only if it is in itself evil to violently coerce resistant wills, can the exercise of coercive power by rulers be bad as such. Against such a conception, if it were true, the necessity and advantage of the exercise of such power would indeed by a useless plea. But that conception is one that makes no sense unless it is accompanied by a theory of withdrawal from the world as man's only salvation; and it is in any case a false one. We are taught that God retains the evil will of the devil within limits by violence: we are not given a picture of God permitting to the devil all that he is capable of. There is current a conception of Christianity as having revealed that the defeat of evil must always be by pure love without coercion; this at least is shown to be false by the foregoing consideration. And without the alleged revelation there could be no reason to believe such a thing.

To think that society's coercive authority is evil is akin to thinking the flesh evil and family life evil. These things belong to the present constitution of mankind; and if the exercise of coercive power is a manifestation of evil, and not the just means of restraining it, then human nature is totally depraved in a manner never taught by Christianity. For society is essential to human good; and society without coercive power is generally impossible.

The same authority which puts down internal dissension, which promulgates laws and restrains those who break them if it can, must equally oppose external enemies. These do not merely comprise those who attack the borders of the people ruled by the authority; but also, for example, pirates and desert bandits, and, generally, those beyond the confines of the country ruled whose activities are viciously harmful to it. The Romans, once their rule in Gaul was established, were eminently justified in attacking Britain, where were nurtured the Druids whose pupils infested northern Gaul and whose practices struck the Romans themselves as "dira immanitas." Further, there being such a thing as the common good of mankind, and visible criminality against it, how can we doubt the excellence of such a proceeding as that violent suppression of the man-stealing business[1] which the British government took it into its head to engage in under Palmerston? The present-day conception of "aggression," like so many strongly influential conceptions, is a bad one. Why *must* it be wrong to strike the first blow in a struggle? The only question is, who is in the right?

Here, however, human pride, malice and cruelty are so usual that it is true to say that wars have mostly been mere wickedness on both sides. Just as an individual will constantly think himself in the right, whatever he does, and yet there is still such a thing as being in the right, so nations will constantly wrongly think themselves to be in the right—and yet there is still such a thing as their being in the right. Palmerston doubtless had no doubts in prosecuting the opium war against China, which was diabolical, just as he exulted in putting down the slavers. But there is no question but that he was a monster in the one thing, and a just man in the other.

The probability is that warfare is injustice, that a life of military service is a bad life, "militia or rather malitia," as St. Anselm called it. This probability is greater than the probability (which also exists) that membership of a police force will involve malice, because of the character of warfare: the extraordinary occasions it offers for viciously unjust proceedings on the part of military commanders and warring governments, which at the time attract praise and not blame from their people. It is equally the case that the life of a ruler is usually a vicious life: but that does not show that ruling is as such a vicious activity.

The principal wickedness which is a temptation to those engaged in warfare is the killing of the innocent, which may often be done with impunity and even to the glory of those who do it. In many places and times it has been taken for granted as a natural part of waging war: the commander, and especially the conqueror, massacres people by the thousand, either because this is part of his glory, or as a terrorizing measure, or as part of his tactics.

Innocence and the Right to Kill Intentionally

It is necessary to dwell on the notion of non-innocence here employed. Innocence is a legal notion; but here, the accused is not pronounced guilty under an existing code of law, under which he has been tried by an impartial judge, and therefore made the target of attack. There is hardly a possibility of this; for the administration of justice is something that takes place under the aegis of a sovereign authority; but in warfare—or the putting down by violence of civil disturbance—the sovereign authority is itself engaged as a party to the dispute and is not subject to a further earthly and temporal authority which can judge the issue and pronounce against the accused. The stabler the society, the rarer it will be for the sovereign authority to have to do anything but apprehend its internal enemy and have him tried: but even in the stablest society there are occasions when the authority has to fight its internal enemy to the point of killing, as happens in the struggle with external belligerent forces in international warfare; and then the characterization of its enemy as non-innocent has not been ratified by legal process.

This, however, does not mean that the notion of innocence fails in this situation. What is required for the people attacked to be non-innocent in the relevant sense, is that they should themselves be engaged in an objectively unjust proceeding which the attacker has the right to make his concern; or—the commonest case— should be unjustly attacking him. Then he can attack them with a view to stopping them, and also their supply lines and armament factories. But people whose mere existence and activity supporting existence by growing crops, making clothes, etc. constitute an impediment to him—such people are innocent and it is murderous to attack them, or make them a target for an attack which he judges will help him towards victory. For murder is the deliberate killing of the innocent, whether for its own sake or as a means to some further end.

The right to attack with a view to killing is something that belongs only to rulers and those whom they command to do it. I have argued that it does belong to rulers precisely because of that threat of violent coercion exercised by those in authority which is essential to the existence of human societies. It ought not to be pretended that rulers and their subordinates do not choose[2] the killing of their enemies as a means, when it has come to fighting in which they are determined to win and their enemies resist to the point of killing: this holds even in internal disturbances.

When a private man struggles with an enemy he has no right to kill him, unless in the circumstances of the attack on him he can be considered as endowed with the authority of the law and the struggle comes to that point. By a "private" man, I mean a man in a society; I am not speaking of men on their own, without government, in remote places; for such men are neither public servants nor "private." The plea of self-defense (or the defense of someone else) made by a private man who has killed someone else must in conscience—even if not in law—be a plea that the death of the other was not intended, but was a side effect of the measures taken to ward off the attack. To shoot to kill, to set lethal man traps, or, say, to lay poison for someone from whom one's life is in danger, are forbidden. The deliberate choice of inflicting death in a struggle is the right only of ruling authorities and their subordinates.

In saying that a private man may not choose to kill, we are touching on the principle of "double effect." The denial of this has been the corruption of non-Catholic thought, and its abuse the corruption of Catholic thought. Both have disastrous consequences which we shall see. This principle is not accepted in English law: the law is said to allow no distinction between the foreseen and the intended consequences of an action. Thus, if I push a man over a cliff when he is menacing my life, his death is considered as intended by me, but the intention to be justifiable for the sake of self-defense. Yet the lawyers would hardly find the laying of poison to be tolerable as an act of self-defense, but only killing by a violent action in a moment of violence. Christian moral theologians have taught that even here one may not seek the death of the assailant, but may in default of other ways of self-defense use such violence as will in fact result in his death. The distinction is evidently a fine one in some cases: what, it may be asked, can the intention be, if it can be said to be absent in this case, except a mere wish or desire?

And yet in other cases the distinction is very clear. If I go to prison rather than perform some action, no reasonable person will call the incidental consequences of my refusal—the loss of my job, for example—intentional just because I knew they must happen. And in the case of the administration of a pain-relieving drug in mortal illness, where the doctor knows the drug may very well kill the patient if the illness does not do so first, the distinction is evident; the lack of it has led an English judge to talk nonsense about the administration of the drug's not having *really* been the cause of death in such a case, even though a post mortem shows it was. For everyone understands that it is a very different thing so to administer a drug, and to administer it with the intention of killing. However, the principle of double effect has more important applications in warfare, and I shall return to it later.

The Influence of Pacifism

Pacifism has existed as a considerable movement in English speaking countries ever since the first world war. I take the doctrine of pacifism to be that it is *eo ipso* wrong to fight in wars, not the doctrine that it is wrong to be compelled to, or that any man, or some men, may refuse; and I think it false for the reasons that I have given. But I now want to consider the very remarkable effects it has had: for I believe its influence to have been enormous, far exceeding its influence on its own adherents.

We should note first that pacifism has as its background conscription and enforced military service for all men. Without conscription, pacifism is a private opinion that will keep those who hold it out of armies, which they are in any case not obliged to join. Now universal conscription, except for the most extraordinary reasons, i.e. as a regular habit among most nations, is such a horrid evil that the refusal of it automatically commands a certain amount of respect and sympathy.

We are not here concerned with the pacifism of some peculiar sect which in any case draws apart from the world to a certain extent, but with a pacifism of people in the world, who do not want to be withdrawn from it. For some of these, pacifism is prevented from being a merely theoretical attitude because they are liable to, and so are prepared to resist, conscription; or are able directly to affect the attitude of some who are so liable.

A powerful ingredient in this pacifism is the prevailing image of Christianity. This image commands a sentimental respect among people who have no belief in Christianity, that is to say, in Christian dogmas, yet do have a certain belief in an ideal which they conceive to be part of "true Christianity." It is therefore important to understand this image of Christianity and to know how false it is. Such understanding is relevant, not merely to those who wish to believe Christianity, but to all who, without the least wish to believe, are yet profoundly influenced by this image of it.

According to this image, Christianity is an ideal and beautiful religion, impracticable except for a few rare characters. It preaches a God of love whom there is no reason to fear; it marks an escape from the conception presented in the Old Testament, of a vindictive and jealous God who will terribly punish his enemies. The "Christian" God is a *roi fainéant*, whose only triumph is in the Cross; his appeal is to goodness and unselfishness, and to follow him is to act according to the Sermon on the Mount—to turn the other cheek and to offer no resistance to evil. In this account some of the evangelical counsels are chosen as containing the whole of Christian ethics: that is, they are made into precepts. (Only some of them; it is not likely that someone who deduces the *duty* of pacifism from the Sermon on the Mount and the rebuke to Peter, will agree to take "Give to him that asks of you" equally as a universally binding precept.)

The turning of counsels into precepts results in high-sounding principles. Principles that are mistakenly high and strict are a trap; they may easily lead in the end directly or indirectly to the justification of monstrous things. Thus if the evangelical counsel about poverty were turned into a precept forbidding property owning, people would pay lip service to it as the ideal, while in practice they went in for swindling. "Absolute honesty!" it would be said: "I can respect that—but of course that means having no property; and while I respect those who follow that course, I have to compromise with the sordid world itself." If then one must "compromise with evil" by owning property and engaging in trade, then the amount of swindling one does will depend on convenience. This imaginary case is paralleled by what is so commonly said: absolute pacifism is an ideal; unable to follow that, and committed to "compromise with evil," one must go the whole hog and wage war *à outrance*.

The truth about Christianity is that it is a severe and practicable religion, not a beautifully ideal but impracticable one. Its moral precepts, (except for the stricter laws about marriage that Christ enacted, abrogating some of the permissions of the Old Law) are those of the Old Testament; and its God is the God of Israel.

It is ignorance of the New Testament that hides this from people. It is characteristic of pacifism to denigrate the Old Testament and exalt the New: something quite contrary to the teaching of the New Testament itself, which always looks back to and leans upon the Old. How typical it is that the words of Christ, "You have heard it said, an eye for an eye and a tooth for a tooth, but I say to you," are taken as a repudiation of the Old Testament! People seldom look up the occurrence of this phrase in the juridical code of the Old Testament, where it belongs, and is the admirable principle of law for the punishment of certain crimes, such as procuring the wrongful punishment of another by perjury. People often enough *now* cite the phrase to justify private revenge; no doubt this was as often "heard said" when Christ spoke of it. But no justification for this exists in the personal ethic taught by the Old Testament. On the contrary. What do we find? "Seek no revenge," (Lev. 19:18), and "If you find your enemy's ox or ass going astray, take it back to him; if you see the ass of someone who hates you lying under his burden, and would forbear to help him; you must help him" (Exod. 23:4-5). And "If your enemy is hungry, give him food, if thirsty, give him drink" (Prov. 25:21).

This is only one example; given space, it would be easy to show how false is the conception of Christ's teaching as *correcting* the religion of the ancient Israelites, and substituting a higher and more "spiritual" religion for theirs. Now the false picture I have described plays an important part in the pacifist ethic and in the ethic of the many people who are not pacifists but are influenced by pacifism.

To extract a pacifist doctrine—i.e., a condemnation of the use of force by the ruling authorities, and of soldiering as a profession—from the evangelical counsels and the rebuke to Peter, is to disregard what else is in the New Testament. It is to forget St. John's direction to soldiers: "do not blackmail people; be content with your pay"; and Christ's commendation of the centurion, who compared his authority over his men to Christ's. On a pacifist view, this must be much as if a madam in a brothel had said: "I know what authority is, I tell this girl to do this, and she does it" and Christ had commended her faith. A centurion was the first Gentile to be baptized; there is no suggestion in the New Testament that soldiering was regarded as incompatible with Christianity. The martyrology contains many names of soldiers whose occasion for martyrdom was not any objection to soldiering, but a refusal to perform idolatrous acts.

Now, it is one of the most vehement and repeated teachings of the Judaeo-Christian tradition that the shedding of innocent blood is forbidden by the divine law. No man may be punished except for his own crime, and those "whose feet are swift to shed innocent blood" are always represented as God's enemies.

For a long time the main outlines of this teaching have seemed to be merely obvious morality: hence, for example, I have read a passage by Ronald Knox complaining of the "endless moralizing," interspersed in records of meanness, cowardice, spite, cruelty, treachery and murder, which forms so much of the Old Testament. And indeed, that it is terrible to kill the innocent is very obvious; the morality that so stringently forbids it must make a great appeal to mankind, especially to the poor threatened victims. Why should it need the thunder of Sinai and the suffering and preaching of the prophets to promulgate such a law? But human pride and malice are everywhere so strong that now, with the fading of Christianity from the mind of the West, this morality once more stands out as a demand which strikes pride- and fear-ridden people as too intransigent. For Knox, it seemed so obvious as to be dull; and he failed to recognize the bloody and beastly records that it accompanies for the dry truthfulness about human beings that so characterizes the Old Testament.[3]

Now pacifism teaches people to make no distinction between the shedding of innocent blood and the shedding of any human blood. And in this way pacifism has corrupted enormous numbers of people who will not act according to its tenets. They become convinced that a number of things are wicked which are not; hence, seeing no way of avoiding "wickedness," they set no limits to it. How endlessly pacifists argue that all war must be *à outrance!* that those who wage war must go as far as technological advance permits in the destruction of the enemy's people. As if the Napoleonic wars were perforce fuller of massacres than the French war of Henry V of England. It is not true: the reverse took place. Nor is technological advance particularly relevant; it is mere squeamishness that deters people who would consent to area bombing from the enormous massacres *by hand* that used once to be committed.

The policy of obliterating cities was adopted by the Allies in the last war; they need not have taken that step, and it was taken largely out of a villainous hatred, and as corollary to the policy, now universally denigrated, of seeking "unconditional surrender." (That policy itself was visibly wicked, and could be and was judged so at the time; it is not surprising that it led to disastrous consequences, even if no one was clever and detached enough to foresee this at the time.)

Pacifism and the respect for pacifism is not the only thing that has led to a universal forgetfulness of the law against killing the innocent; but it has had a great share in it.

The Principle of Double Effect

Catholics, however, can hardly avoid paying at least lip service to that law. So we must ask: how is it that there has been so comparatively little conscience exercised on the subject among them? The answer is: double-think about double effect.

The distinction between the intended, and the merely foreseen, effects of a voluntary action is indeed absolutely essential to Christian ethics. For Christianity forbids a number of things as being bad in themselves. But if I am answerable for the foreseen consequences of an action or refusal, as much as for the action itself, then these prohibitions will break down. If someone innocent will die unless I do a wicked thing, then on this view I am his murderer in refusing: so all that is left to me is to weigh up evils. Here the theologian steps in with the principle of double effect and says: "No, you are no murderer, if the man's death was neither your aim nor your chosen means, and if you had to act in the way that led to it or else do something absolutely forbidden." Without understanding of this principle, anything can be—and is wont to be—justified, and the Christian teaching that in no circumstances may one commit murder, adultery, apostasy (to give a few examples) goes by the board. These absolute prohibitions of Christianity by no means exhaust its ethic; there is a large area where what is just is determined partly by a prudent weighing up of consequences. But the prohibitions are bedrock, and without them the Christian ethic goes to pieces. Hence the necessity of the notion of double effect.

At the same time, the principle has been repeatedly abused from the seventeenth century up till now. The causes lie in the history of philosophy. From the seventeenth century till now what may be called Cartesian psychology has dominated the thought of philosophers and theologians. According to this psychology, an intention was an interior act of the mind which could be produced at will. Now if intention is all important—as it is—in determining the goodness or badness of an action, then, on this theory of what intention is, a marvellous way offered itself of making any action lawful. You only had to "direct your intention" in a suitable way. In practice, this means making a little speech to yourself: "What I mean to be doing is . . ."

This perverse doctrine has occasioned repeated condemnations by the Holy See from the seventeenth century to the present day. Some examples will suffice to show how the thing goes. Typical doctrines from the seventeenth century were that it is all right for a servant to hold the ladder for his criminous master so long as he is merely avoiding the sack by doing so; or that a man might wish for and rejoice at his parent's death so long as what he had in mind was the gain to himself; or that it is not simony to offer money, not *as a price* for the spiritual benefit, but only *as an inducement* to give it. A condemned doctrine from the present day is that the practice of *coitus reservatus* is permissible: such a doctrine could only arise in connection with that "direction of intention" which sets everything right no matter what one does. A man makes a practice of withdrawing, telling himself that he *intends* not to ejaculate; of course (if that is his practice) he usually does so, but then the event is "accidental" and *praeter intentionem:* it is, in short, a case of "double effect."

This same doctrine is used to prevent any doubts about the obliteration bombing of a city. The devout Catholic bomber secures by a "direction of intention" that any shedding of innocent blood that occurs is "accidental." I know a Catholic boy who was puzzled at being told by his schoolmaster that it was an *accident* that the people of Hiroshima and Nagasaki were there to be killed; in fact, however absurd it seems, such thoughts are common among priests who know that they are forbidden by the divine law to justify the direct killing of the innocent.

It is nonsense to pretend that you do not intend to do what is the means you take to your chosen end. Otherwise there is absolutely no substance to the Pauline teaching that we may not do evil that good may come.

Some Commonly Heard Arguments

There are a number of sophistical arguments, often or sometimes used on these topics, which need answering.

Where do you draw the line? As Dr. Johnson said, the fact of twilight does not mean you cannot tell day from night. There are borderline cases, where it is difficult to distinguish, in what is done, between means and what is incidental to, yet in the circumstances inseparable from, those means. The obliteration bombing of a city is not a borderline case.

The old "conditions for a just war" are irrelevant to the conditions of modern warfare, so that must be condemned out of hand. People who say this always envisage only major wars between the great powers, which powers are indeed now "in blood stepp'd in so far" that it is unimaginable for there to be a war between them which is not a set of enormous massacres of civil populations. But these are not the only wars. Why is Finland so far free? At least partly because of the "posture of military preparedness" which, considering the character of the country, would have made subjugating the Finns a difficult and unrewarding task. The offensive of the Israelis against the Egyptians in 1956 involved no plan of making civil populations the target of military attack.

In a modern war the distinction between combatant and non-combatants is meaningless, so an attack on anyone on the enemy side is justified. This is pure nonsense; even in war, a very large number of the enemy population are just engaged in maintaining the life of the country, or are sick, or aged, or children.

It must be legitimate to maintain an opinion—viz., that the destruction of cities by bombing is lawful—if this is argued by competent theologians and the Holy See has not pronounced. The argument from the silence of the Holy See has itself been condemned by the Holy See. How could this be a sane doctrine in view of the endless twistiness of the human mind?

Whether a war is just or not is not for the private man to judge: he must obey his government. Sometimes, this may be, especially as far as concerns causes of war. But the individual who joins in destroying a city, like a Nazi massacring the inhabitants of a village, is too obviously marked out as an enemy of the human race, to shelter behind such a plea.

Finally, horrible as it is to have to notice this, we must notice that even the arguments about double effect—which at least show that a man is not willing openly to justify the killing of the innocent—are now beginning to look old-fashioned. Some Catholics are not scrupling to say that *anything* is justified in defense of the continued existence and liberty of the Church in the West. A terrible fear of communism drives people to say this sort of thing. "Our Lord told us to fear those who can destroy body and soul, not to fear the destruction of the body" was blasphemously said to a friend of mine; meaning: "so, we must fear Russian domination more than the destruction of people's bodies by obliteration bombing."

But whom did Our Lord tell us to fear, when he said: "I will tell you whom you shall fear" and "Fear not them that can destroy the body, but fear him who can destroy body and soul in hell"? He told us to fear God the Father, who can and will destroy the unrepentant disobedient, body and soul, in hell.

A Catholic who is tempted to think on the lines I have described should remember that the Church is the spiritual Israel: that is, that Catholics are what the ancient Jews were, salt for the earth and the people of God—and that what was true of some devout Jews of ancient times can equally well be true of us now: "You compass land and sea to make a convert, and when you have done so, you make him twice as much a child of hell as yourselves." Do Catholics sometimes think that they are immune from such a possibility? That the Pharisees—who sat in the seat of Moses and who were so zealous for the true religion—were bad in ways in which we cannot be bad if we are zealous? I believe they do. But our faith teaches no such immunity, it teaches the opposite. "We are in danger all our lives long." So we have to fear God and keep his commandments, and calculate what is for the best only within the limits of that obedience, knowing that the future is in God's power and that no one can snatch away those whom the Father has given to Christ.

It is not a vague faith in the triumph of "the spirit" over force (there is little enough warrant for that), but a definite faith in the divine promises, that makes us believe that the Church cannot fail. Those, therefore, who think they must be prepared to wage a war with Russia involving the deliberate massacre of cities, must be prepared to say to God: "We had to break your law, lest your Church fail. We could not obey your commandments, for we did not believe your promises."

Notes

1. It is ignorance to suppose that it takes modern liberalism to hate and condemn this. It is cursed and subject to the death penalty in the Mosaic law. Under that code, too, runaway slaves of all nations had asylum in Israel.

2. The idea that they may lawfully do what they do, but should not *intend* the death of those they attack, has been put forward and, when suitably expressed, may seem high-minded. But someone who can fool himself into this twist of thought will fool himself into justifying anything, however atrocious, by means of it.

3. It is perhaps necessary to remark that I am not here adverting to the total extermination of certain named tribes of Canaan that is said by the Old Testament to have been commanded by God. That is something quite outside the provisions of the Mosaic Law for dealings in war.

20

On The Morality of War:
A Preliminary Inquiry

Richard Wasserstrom

Among the positions people hold about the relation between war and morality is one which asserts that wars, unlike other human enterprises, cannot be subject to moral assessment: wars simply cannot be evaluated morally. In this article, Richard Wasserstrom analyzes and finds such a view wanting, though attempting to explore the reasons which incline many to adopt such a stance. He then goes on to suggest plausible criteria for evaluating war morally, and responds to a line of argument which would insist that unilateral pacifism is the only moral, because effective, response to international conflict. He proceeds to an analysis of the "strongest argument against war": that which sees modern war as causing the death of "innocent" persons, and concludes with some reasons for believing that an absolute ban on the intentional killing of innocent persons (a view he attributes to a number of moralists, including Elizabeth Anscombe) is an extreme and finally indefensible view.

—R.C.

Before we examine the moral criteria for assessing war, we must examine the claim that it is not possible to assess war in moral terms. Proponents of this position assert that moral predicates either cannot meaningfully or should not be applied to wars. For want of a better name for this general view, I shall call it moral nihilism in respect to war. If it is correct, there is, of course, no point in going further.

It is apparent that anyone who believes that all moral predicates are meaningless, or that all morality (and not just conventional morality) is a sham and a fraud, will regard the case of the morality of war as an *a fortiori* case. This is not the position I am interested in considering. Rather the view I call moral nihilism in respect to war is, I think, more interesting in the sense that it is restricted to the case of war. What I have in mind is this: During the controversy over the rightness of the Vietnam War there have been any number of persons, including a large number in the university, who have claimed that in matters of war (but not in other matters) morality has no place. The war in Vietnam may, they readily concede, be stupid, unwise, or against the best interests of the United States, but it is neither immoral nor unjust—not because it is moral or right, but because these descriptions are *in this context* either naive or meaningless or inapplicable.

Nor is this view limited to the Vietnam War. Consider, for instance, the following passage from a speech given only a few years ago by Dean Acheson:

> Those involved in the Cuban crisis of October, 1962, will remember the irrelevance of the supposed moral considerations brought out in the discussions. Judgment centered about the appraisal of dangers and risks, the weighing of the need for decisive and effective action against considerations of prudence; the need to do enough, against the consequences of doing too much. Moral talk did not bear on the problem. Nor did it bear upon the decision of those called upon to advise the President in 1949 whether and with what degree of urgency to press the attempt to produce a thermonuclear weapon. A respected colleague advised me that it would be better that our nation and people should perish rather than be party to a course so evil as producing that weapon. I told him that on the Day of Judgment his view might be confirmed and that he was free to go forth and preach the necessity for salvation. It was not, however, a view which I would entertain as a public servant.[1]

Admittedly, the passage just reproduced is susceptible of different interpretations. Acheson may be putting forward the view that even if moral evaluation is relevant to the "ends" pursued by any country (including our own) it is not relevant to the policies adopted in furtherance of these ends. But at times, at least, he appears to expound a quite different view, namely, that in the realm of foreign affairs, moral judgments, as opposed to strategic or prudential ones, are simply misplaced and any attempts at moral assessment misdirected.

Whatever may be the correct exegesis of this text, I want to treat it as illustrative of the position that morality has no place in the assessment of war.[2] There are several things worth considering in respect to such a view. In the first place, the claim that in matters of war morality has no place is ambiguous. To put it somewhat loosely, the claim may be descriptive, or it may be analytic, or it may be prescriptive. Thus it would be descriptive if it were merely the factual claim that matters relating to war uniformly turn out to be decided on grounds of national interest or expediency rather than by appeal to what is moral.[3] This claim I will not consider further; it is an empirical one better answered by students of U.S. (and foreign) diplomatic relations.

It would be a prescriptive claim were it taken to assert that matters relating to war ought always be decided by appeal to, say, national interest rather than an appeal to the moral point of view. For reasons which have yet to be elucidated, on this view the moral criteria are capable of being employed but it is undesirable to do so. I shall say something more about this view in a moment.[4]

The analytic point is not that morality ought not be used, but rather that it cannot. On this view the statement "The United States is behaving immorally in the way it is waging war in Vietnam" (or, "in waging war in Vietnam") is not wrong but meaningless.

What are we to make of the analytic view? As I have indicated, it could, of course, be advanced simply as an instance of a more sweeping position concerning the general meaninglessness of the moral point of view. What I find particularly interesting, though, is the degree to which this thesis is advanced as a special view about war and not as a part of a more general claim that all morality is meaningless.[5]

I think that there are at least four reasons why this special view may be held. First, the accusation that one's own country is involved in an immoral war is personally very threatening. For one thing, if the accusation is well-founded it may be thought to imply that certain types of socially cooperative behavior are forbidden to the citizen and that other kinds of socially deviant behavior are obligatory upon him. Yet, in a time of war it is following just this sort of dictate that will be treated most harshly by the actor's own government. Hence the morally responsible citizen is put in a most troublesome moral dilemma. If his country is engaged in an immoral war then he may have a duty to oppose and resist; yet opposition and resistance will typically carry extraordinarily severe penalties.

The pressure is, I suspect, simply too great for many of us. We are unwilling to pay the fantastically high personal price that goes with the moral point of view, and we are equally unwilling to plead guilty to this most serious charge of immorality. So we solve the problem by denying the possibility that war can be immoral. The relief is immediate; the moral "heat" is off. If war cannot be immoral, then one's country cannot be engaged in an immoral war, but only a stupid or unwise one. And whatever one's obligations to keep one's country from behaving stupidly or improvidently, they are vastly less stringent and troublesome than obligations imposed by the specter of complicity in an immoral war. We may, however, pay a price for such relief since we obliterate the moral distinctions between the Axis and the Allies in World War II at the same time as the distinctions between the conduct of the United States in 1941-45 and the conduct of the United States in 1967-68 in Vietnam.

Second, I think that moral judgments are meaningless sometimes seems plausible because of the differences between personal behavior and the behavior of states. There are not laws governing the behavior of states in the same way in which there are positive laws governing the behavior of citizens. International law is a troublesome notion just because it is both like and unlike our concept of positive law.

Now, how does skepticism about the lawlike quality of international law lead to the claim that it is impossible for war to be either moral or immoral? It is far from obvious. Perhaps it is because there is at least one sense of justice that is intimately bound up with the notion of rule violation; namely, that which relates justice to the following of rules and to the condemnation and punishment of those who break rules. In the absence of positive laws governing the behavior of states, it may be inferred (although I think mistakenly) that it is impossible for states to behave either justly or unjustly.[6] But even if justice can be said to be analyzable solely in terms of following rules, morality certainly cannot. Hence the absence of international laws cannot serve to make the moral appraisal of war impossible.

Third, there is the substantially more plausible view that, in the absence of positive laws *and* in the absence of any machinery by which to punish even the grossest kinds of immorality, an adequate excuse will always exist for behaving immorally. This is one way to take Hobbes' assertion that in the state of nature the natural laws bind in conscience but not in action. Even this view, however, would not render the moral assessment of the behavior of states meaningless; it would only excuse immorality in the absence of effective international law. More importantly, though, it, too, misstates the general understanding of morality in its insistence that morality depends for its *meaning* on the existence of guarantees of moral conformity by others.

Fourth, and still more plausible, is the view that says there can be no moral assessment of war just because there is, by definition, no morality in war. If war is an activity in which anything goes, moral judgments on war are just not possible.

To this there are two responses. To begin with, it is not, as our definitional discussion indicates, a necessary feature of war that it be an activity in which everything is morally permissible. There is a difference between the view that war is unique because killing and violence are morally permissible in contexts and circumstances where they otherwise would not be and the view that war is unique because everything is morally permissible.

A less absolutist argument for the absurdity of discussing the morality of war might be that at least today the prevailing (although not necessary) conception of war is one that as a practical matter rules out no behavior on moral grounds. After all, if flamethrowers are deemed perfectly permissible, if the bombing of cities is applauded and not condemned, and if thermonuclear weapons are part of the arsenal of each of the major powers, then the remaining moral prohibitions on the conduct of war are sufficiently insignificant to be ignored.

The answer to this kind of an argument requires, I believe, that we distinguish the question of what is moral in war from that of the morality of war or of war generally. I return to this distinction later,[7] but for the present it is sufficient to observe that the argument presented only goes to the question of whether moral judgments can meaningfully be made concerning the *way* in which war is conducted. Paradoxically, the more convincing the argument from war's conduct, the stronger is the moral argument *against* engaging in war at all. For the more it can be shown that engaging in war will inevitably lead to despicable behavior to which no moral predicates are deemed applicable, the more this also constitutes an argument against bringing such a state of affairs into being.[8]

There is still another way to take the claim that in matters of war morality has no place. That is what I have called the prescriptive view: that national interest ought to determine policies in respect to war, not morality. This is surely one way to interpret the remarks of Dean Acheson reproduced earlier. It is also, perhaps, involved in President Truman's defense of the dropping of the atomic bomb on Hiroshima. What he said was, "Having found the bomb, we have to use it. We have used it against those who attacked us without warning at Pearl Harbor, against those who have starved and beaten and executed American prisoners of war, against those who have abandoned all pretense of obeying international laws of warfare. We have used it in order to shorten the agony of war, in order to save the lives of thousands and thousands of young Americans."[9] Although this passage has many interesting features, I am concerned only with President Truman's insistence that the dropping of the bomb was justified because it saved the lives "of thousands and thousands of young Americans."

Conceivably, this is merely an elliptical way of saying that on balance fewer lives were lost through the dropping of the bomb and the accelerated cessation of hostilities than through any alternative course of conduct. Suppose, though, that this were not the argument. Suppose, instead, that the justification were regarded as adequate provided only that it was reasonably clear that fewer *American* lives would be lost than through any alternative course of conduct. Thus, to quantify the example, we can imagine someone maintaining that Hiroshima was justified because 20,000 fewer Americans died in the Pacific theater than would have died if the bomb had not been dropped. And this is justified even though 30,000 more Japanese died than would have been killed had the war been fought to an end with conventional means. Thus, even though 10,000 more people died than would otherwise have been the case, the bombing was justified because of the greater number of American lives saved.

On this interpretation the argument depends upon valuing the lives of Americans higher than the lives of persons from other countries. As such, is there anything to be said for the argument? Its strongest statement, and the only one that I shall consider, might go like this: Truman was the president of the United States and as such had an obligation always to choose that course of conduct that appeared to offer the greatest chance of maximizing the interests of the United States.[10] As president, he was obligated to prefer the lives of American soldiers over those from any other country, and he was obligated to prefer them just because they were Americans and he was their president.

Some might prove such a point by drawing an analogy to the situation of a lawyer, a parent, or a corporation executive. A lawyer has a duty to present his client's case in the fashion most calculated to ensure his client's victory; and he has this obligation irrespective of the objective merits of his client's case. Similarly, we are neither surprised nor dismayed when a parent prefers the interests of *his* child over those of other children. A parent *qua* parent is certainly not behaving immorally when he acts so as to secure satisfactions for his child, again irrespective of the objective merits of the child's needs or wants. And, *mutatis mutandis,* a corporate executive has a duty to maximize profits for his company. Thus, as public servants, Dean Acheson and Harry Truman had no moral choice but to pursue those policies that appeared to them to be in the best interest of the United States. And to a lesser degree, all persons *qua* citizens of the United States have a similar, if slightly more attenuated, obligation. Therefore morality has no real place in war.

The analogy, however, must not stop halfway. It is certainly both correct and important to observe that public officials, like parents, lawyers, and corporate executives, do have special moral obligations that are imposed by virtue of the position or role they fill. A lawyer does have a duty to prefer his client's interests in a way that would be improper were the person anyone other than a client. And the same sort of duty, I think, holds for a parent, an executive, a president, and a citizen in their respective roles. The point becomes distorted, however, when it is supposed that such an obligation always, under all circumstances, overrides any and all other obligations that the person might have. The case of the lawyer is instructive. While he has an obligation to attend to his client's interests in very special ways, there are many other things that it is impermissible for the lawyer to do in furtherance of his client's interest—irrespective, this time, of how significantly they might advance that interest.

The case for the president, or for public servants generally, is similar. While the president may indeed have an obligation to prefer and pursue the national interests, this obligation could only be justifiable—could only be a moral obligation—if it were enmeshed in a comparable range of limiting and competing obligations. If we concede that the president has certain obligations to prefer the national interest that no one else has, we must be equally sensitive to the fact that the president also has some of the same obligations to other persons that all other men have—if for no other reason than that all persons have the right to be treated or not treated in certain ways. So, whatever special obligations the president may have cannot by themselves support the view that in war morality ought have no place.

In addition, the idea that one can separate a man's personality from the duties of his office is theoretically questionable and practically unbelievable. Experience teaches that a man cannot personally be guided by moral dictates while abjuring them in public life even if he wants to.

It is also unlikely that a man on becoming president will try to adopt such an approach unless there is something about the office that compels a dual personality. Common sense indicates there is not. If there were, it would mean that the electorate could not purposely choose someone to follow a course not dictated by the "national interest" since, whatever his preelection promises, the office would reform him.

But the major problem with the national interest argument is its assumption that the national interest not only is something immutable and knowable but also that it limits national interest to narrowly national concerns. It is parochial to suppose that the American national interest really rules out solicitude for other states in order to encourage international stability.

Finally, national interest as a goal must itself be justified. The United States' position of international importance may have imposed on it a duty of more than national concern. The fact that such a statement has become hackneyed by constant use to justify U.S. interference abroad should not blind us to the fact that it may be viable as an argument for a less aggressive international responsibility.[11]

If we turn now to confront more directly the question of the morality of wars, it is evident that there is a variety of different perspectives from which, or criteria in terms of which, particular wars may be assessed. First, to the extent to which the model of war as a game continues to have a place, wars can be evaluated in terms of the degree to which the laws of war—the rules for initiating and conducting war—are adhered to by the opposing countries. Second, the rightness or wrongness of wars is often thought to depend very much upon the *cause* for which a war is fought. And third, there is the independent justification for a war that is founded upon an appeal of some kind to a principle of self-defense.

In discussing the degree to which the laws of war are followed or disregarded there are two points that should be stressed. First, a skepticism as to the meaningfulness of any morality *within* war is extremely common. The gnomic statement is Sherman's: "War is hell." The fuller argument depends upon a rejection of the notion of war as a game. It goes something like this. War is the antithesis of law or rules. It is violence, killing, and all of the horror they imply. Even if moral distinctions can be made in respect to such things as the initiation and purposes of a war, it is absurd to suppose that moral distinctions can be drawn once a war has begun. All killing is bad, all destruction equally wanton.[12]

Now, there does seem to me to be a fairly simple argument of sorts that can be made in response. Given the awfulness of war, it nonetheless appears plausible to discriminate among degrees of awfulness. A war in which a large number of innocent persons are killed is, all other things being equal, worse than one in which only a few die. A war in which few combatants are killed is, *ceteris paribus,* less immoral than one in which many are killed. And more to the point, perhaps, any unnecessary harm to others is surely unjustifiable. To some degree, at least, the "laws of war" can be construed as attempts to formalize these general notions and to define instances of unnecessary harm to others.[13]

The second criterion, the notion of the cause that can be invoked to justify a war, may involve two quite different inquiries. On the one hand, we may intend the sense in which cause refers to the consequences of waging war, to the forward-looking criteria of assessment. Thus, when a war is justified as a means by which to make the world safe for democracy, or on the grounds that a failure to fight now will lead to a loss of confidence on the part of one's allies, or as necessary to avoid fighting a larger, more destructive war later, when these sorts of appeals are made, the justification is primarily consequential or forward-looking in character. Here the distinction between morality and prudence—never a very easy one to maintain in international relations—is always on the verge of collapse. On the other hand, a war may be evaluated through recourse to what may be termed backward-looking criteria. Just as in the case of punishment or blame where what happened in the past is relevant to the justice of punishing or blaming someone, so in the case of war, what has already happened is, on this view, relevant to the justice or rightness of the war that is subsequently waged. The two backward-looking criteria that are most frequently invoked in respect to war are the question of whether the war was an instance of aggression and the question of whether the war involved a violation of some prior promise, typically expressed in the form of a treaty or concord.

Two sorts of assertions are often made concerning the role of the treaty in justifying resort to war. First, if a country has entered into a treaty not to go to war and if it violates that treaty, it is to be condemned for, in effect, having broken its promise. And second, if a country has entered into a treaty in which it has agreed to go to war under certain circumstances and if those circumstances come to pass, then the country is at least justified in going to war—although it is not in fact obligated to do so.

Once again, even if we pass over the difficult analytic questions that might be asked about whether countries can promise to do anything and, if they can, what the nature and duration of such promises are, it is clear that treaties can be relevant but not decisive factors. This is so just because it is sometimes right to break our promises and sometimes wrong to keep them. The fact that a treaty is violated at best tends to make a war unjust or immoral in some degree, but it does not necessarily render the war unjustified.[14]

The other backward-looking question, that of aggression, is often resolved by concluding that under no circumstances is the initiation of a war of aggression justified. This is a view that Americans and the United States have often embraced. Such a view was expounded at Nuremberg by Mr. Justice Jackson when he said: "The wrong for which their [the German] fallen leaders are on trial is not that they lost the war, but that they started it. And we must not allow ourselves to be drawn into a trial of the causes of war, for our position is that no grievances or policies will justify resort to aggressive war. . . . Our position is that whatever grievances a nation may have, however objectionable it finds that *status quo,* aggressive warfare is an illegal means for settling those grievances or for altering those conditions."[15] A position such as this is typically thought to imply two things: (1) the initiation of war is never justifiable; (2) the warlike response to aggressive war is justifiable. Both views are troublesome.

To begin with, it is hard to see how the two propositions go together very comfortably. Conceivably, there are powerful arguments against the waging of aggressive war. Almost surely, though, the more persuasive of these will depend, at least in part, on the character of war itself—on such things as the supreme importance of human life, or the inevitable injustices committed in every war. If so, then the justifiability of meeting war with war will to that degree be called into question.

To take the first proposition alone, absent general arguments about the unjustifiability of all war, it is hard to see how aggressive war can be ruled out in a wholly a priori fashion. Even if we assume that no problems are presented in determining what is and is not aggression, it is doubtful that the quality of aggression could always be morally decisive in condemning the war. Would a war undertaken to free innocent persons from concentration camps or from slavery always be unjustifiable just because *it was aggressive?* Surely this is to rest too much upon only one of a number of relevant considerations.[16]

From a backward-looking point of view, the claim that a warring response to aggressive war is always justified is even more perplexing. One way to take this claim is to regard it as plain retributivism. A country is justified in fighting back because the aggressor hit first. Since aggression is wrong, it deserves to be thwarted and punished. The difficulty with this position is, in part, that retributivism generally is more plausible as a statement of necessary rather than of sufficient conditions. Thus, it would be one thing to claim that a war was justified *only* if undertaken in response to aggression, but it is quite another thing to assert that a war is justified *provided* it is undertaken in response to aggression. For reasons already stated, I think even this would be unsatisfactory, but it would surely come closer to being right than a view that finds aggression to be a sufficient justification for making war. A number of these issues reappear in the related problem of self-defense as a justification.

In order to understand the force of the doctrine of self-defense when invoked in respect to war, and to assess its degree of legitimate applicability, it is necessary that we look briefly at self-defense as it functions as a doctrine of municipal criminal law. The first thing to notice is that the doctrine of self-defense does not depend upon either typically retributive or typically consequential considerations. Instead, it rests upon the prevention by the intended victim of quite immediate future harm to himself. To be sure, the doctrine is backward-looking in its insistence that an "attack" of some sort be already under way. But the fact that it is not retributive can be seen most clearly from the fact that self-defense cannot be invoked in response to an attack that is over. In the same fashion, the doctrine is forward-looking in its insistence upon the prevention of future harm.

Second, it is by no means clear whether the doctrine can be understood better as a justification or as an excuse. It can be understood to rest upon the notion that one is *entitled* to defend oneself from a serious and imminent attack upon life and limb. Concomitantly, the doctrine can be interpreted to depend upon the proposition that it is a natural, almost unavoidable—and hence excusable—reaction to defend oneself when attacked.

In either case what is important is that we keep in mind two of the respects in which the law qualifies resort to the claim of self-defense. On one hand, the doctrine cannot be invoked successfully if the intended victim could have avoided the encounter through a reasonable escape or retreat unless the attack takes place on one's own property. And on the other hand, the doctrine requires that no more force be employed than is reasonably necessary to prevent the infliction of comparable harm.

Now how does all of this apply to self-defense as a justification for engaging in war? In the first place, to the extent to which the basic doctrine serves as an excuse, the applicability to war seems doubtful. While it may make sense to regard self-defense of one's person as a natural, instinctive response to an attack, it is only a very anthropomorphic view of countries that would lead us to elaborate a comparable explanation here.[17]

In the second place, it is not even clear that self-defense can function very persuasively as a justification. For it to do so it might be necessary, for example, to be able to make out a case that countries die in the same way in which persons do, or that a country can be harmed in the same way in which a person can be. Of course, persons in the country can be harmed and killed by war, and I shall return to this point in a moment, but we can also imagine an attack in which none of the inhabitants of the country will be killed or even physically harmed unless they fight back. But the country, as a separate political entity, might nonetheless disappear. Would we say that this should be regarded as the equivalent of human death? That it is less harmful? More harmful? These are issues to which those who readily invoke the doctrine of self-defense seldom address themselves.

Even if we were to decide, however, that there is no question but that a country is justified in relying upon a doctrine of self-defense that is essentially similar to that which obtains in the criminal law, it would be essential to observe the constraints that follow. Given even the unprovoked aggressive waging of war by one country against another, the doctrine of self-defense could not be invoked by the country so attacked to justify waging unlimited defensive war or insisting upon unconditional surrender. Each or both of the these responses might be justifiable, but not simply because a country was wrongly attacked. It would, instead, have to be made out that something analogous to retreat was neither possible nor appropriate, and, even more, that no more force was used than was reasonably necessary to terminate the attack.

There is, to be sure, an answer to this. The restrictions that the criminal law puts upon self-defense are defensible, it could be maintained, chiefly because we have a municipal police force, municipal laws, and courts. If we use no more than reasonable force to repel attacks, we can at least be confident that the attacker will be apprehended and punished and, further, that we live in a society in which this sort of aggressive behavior is deterred by a variety of means. It is the absence of such a context that renders restrictions on an international doctrine of self-defense inappropriate.

I do not think this answer is convincing. It is relevant to the question of what sorts of constraints will be operative on the behavior of persons and countries, but it is not persuasive as to the invocation of *self*-defense as a justification for war. To use more force than is reasonably necessary to defend oneself is, in short, to do more than defend oneself. If such non-self-defensive behavior is to be justified, it must appeal to some different principle or set of principles.

There are, therefore, clearly cases in which a principle of self-defense does appear to justify engaging in a war: at a minimum, those cases in which one's country is attacked in such a way that the inhabitants are threatened with deadly force and in which no more force than is reasonably necessary is employed to terminate the attack.

One might argue, of course, for some of the reasons discussed above, that this is too restrictive a range for the legitimate application of the principle. More specifically, it might be observed that I have provided an unduly restricted account of the cases in which the use of deadly force is permissible in our legal system; namely, to defend certain classes of third parties from attacks threatening serious bodily harm or death, and to prevent the commission of certain felonies. These, clearly, would also have ostensibly important applications to the justifiable use of deadly force in the international setting. I shall return to this point when I discuss the problem of war and the death of innocent persons. At present, however, I want to consider an argument for refusing to accord any legitimacy whatsoever to an appeal to self-defense. The argument is a version of what can appropriately be called the pacifist position. The formulation I have in mind is found in the writings of the nineteenth-century pacifist, Adin Ballou, and it merits reproduction at some length. What Ballou says is this:

If it [self-defense] be the true method, it must on the whole work well. It must preserve human life and secure mankind against injury, more certainly and effectually than any other possible method. Has it done this? I do not admit it. How happens it that, according to the lowest probable estimate, some fourteen thousand millions of human beings have been slain by human means, in war and otherwise? Here are enough to people eighteen planets like the earth with its present population. What inconceivable miseries must have been endured by these worlds of people and their friends, in the process of those murderous conflicts which extinguished their earthly existence! ... If this long-trusted method of self-preservation be indeed the best which nature affords to her children, their lot is most deplorable. To preserve what life has been preserved at such a cost, renders life itself a thing of doubtful value. If only a few thousands, or even a few millions, had perished by the two edged sword; if innocence and justice and right had uniformly triumphed; if aggression, injustice, violence, injury and insult, after a few dreadful experiences, had been overawed; if gradually the world had come into wholesome order—a stage of truthfulness, justice and peace; if the sword of self-defense had frightened the sword of aggression into its scabbard, there to consume in its rust; then might we admit that the common method of self-preservation was the true one. But now we have ample demonstration that *they who take the sword, perish with the sword.* Is it supposable that if no injured person or party, since the days of Abel, had lifted up a deadly weapon, or threatened an injury against an offending party, there would have been a thousandth part of the murders and miseries which have actually taken place on our earth? Take the worst possible view; resolve all the assailed and injured into the most passive non-resistants imaginable, and let the offenders have unlimited scope to commit all the robberies, cruelties and murders they pleased; would as many lives have been sacrificed, or as much real misery have been experienced by the human race, as have actually resulted from the general method of self-preservation, by personal conflict and resistance of injury with injury? He must be a bold man who affirms it.[18]

What is most interesting about Ballou's argument is that it is, in essence, an empirical one. His claim is not the more typical pacifist claim that there is some principle that directly forbids the use of force even in cases of self-defense. His assertion is rather that the consequences of regarding the use of force as appropriate in self-defensive situations have been disastrous—or, more exactly, worse precisely in terms of the preservation of human life than would have been the case if the use of force even in such circumstances were always deemed impermissible.

It is very difficult to know what to make of such an argument. In particular, it is more difficult than it may appear at first to state the argument coherently. What precisely is Ballou's thesis? Perhaps he is saying something like this: The principle that force may justifiably be used in cases of self-defense tends to be misapplied in practice. Persons almost inevitably tend to overestimate the imminence and severity of a threat of violence to themselves. They use force prematurely and in excess under an invocation of the doctrine of self-defense. And if this is true of persons generally, it is probably even truer of countries in their relations with other countries. The answer, therefore, is to induce persons and countries to forgo the resort to force even in cases of self-defense.

This argument is something of a paradox. If everyone were to accept and consistently to act upon the principle that force ought never to be used, even in cases of self-defense, then there would be nothing to worry about. No one would ever use force at all, and we really would not have to worry about misapplications of the principle of self-defense.

But Ballou's appeal is to persons to give up the principle of self-defense even if others have not renounced even the aggressive resort to force. In other words, Ballou's argument is one for unilateral rather than bilateral pacifism, and that is precisely what makes it so hard to accept. As I have said, Ballou's thesis appears to be an empirical one. He appears to concede that if only some persons renounce the doctrine of self-defense they certainly do not thereby guarantee their own safety from attack. Innocent persons in this position may very well be killed by those who use force freely. Ballou seems to be saying that while this is so, the consequences have been still worse where self-defense has not been abandoned. But there is just no reason to suppose that unilateral pacifism if practiced by an unspecified group of persons would have resulted in fewer rather than more deaths.[19]

Perhaps, though, this is not what Ballou really has in mind. Perhaps instead the main thrust of his argument is as follows:

People generally agree that force should not be used except in self-defense. But the evidence indicates that this principle is usually misapplied. Hence, a partial pacifism, restricted to the use of force only in cases of self-defense, is illusory and unsound. Even if all countries agreed never to use force except in self-defense, they would still be so prone to construe the behavior of other countries as imminently threatening that wars would be prevalent and the consequences horrendous. This is the reason why even self-defense cannot be permitted as an exception to pacifism. Everyone and every country should, therefore, renounce self-defense as the one remaining exception to pacifism.

Again there is an element of paradox to the argument. Suppose it looks to country Y as though country X is about to attack it. Ballou would say country Y should not, under the principle of self-defense, prepare to fight back. Of course, if all countries do follow the principle of never using force except in self-defense, this makes good sense because country Y can rely on the fact that country X will not attack first. So there is no need to eliminate the defense of self-defense. But what if country X should in fact attack? Here Ballou's advice is that country Y should still not respond because of the likelihood of misapplying the doctrine of self-defense. Once again the case is simply not convincing. In any particular case it just might be that the doctrine would not be misapplied and that the consequences of not defending oneself would in fact be less desirable than those of resorting to self-defensive force.

In short, the case against a limited doctrine of self-defense cannot, I think, be plausibly made out on grounds such as those urged by Ballou. Although a world without war would doubtless be a better one, it is by no means clear that unilateral abandonment of the doctrine of self-defense would have such beneficial consequences. If there is an argument against war, it must rest on something other than the harms inherent in the doctrine of self-defense.

The strongest argument against war is that which rests upon the connection between the morality of war and the death of innocent persons. The specter of thermonuclear warfare makes examination of this point essential; yet the problem was both a genuine and an urgent one in the preatomic days of air warfare, particularly during the Second World War.

The argument based upon the death of innocent persons goes something like this: Even in war innocent persons have a right to life and limb that should be respected. It is no less wrong and no more justifiable to kill innocent persons in war than at any other time. Therefore, if innocent persons are killed in a war, that war is to be condemned.

The argument can quite readily be converted into an attack upon all modern war. Imagine a thoroughly unprovoked attack upon another country—an attack committed, moreover, from the worst of motives and for the most despicable of ends. Assume too, for the moment, that under such circumstances there is nothing immoral about fighting back and even killing those who are attacking. Nonetheless, if in fighting back innocent persons will be killed, the defenders will be acting immorally. However, given any war fought today, innocent persons will inevitably be killed. Therefore, any war fought today will be immoral.

There are a variety of matters that require clarification before the strength of this argument can be adequately assessed. In particular, there are four questions that must be examined: (1) What is meant by "innocence" in this context? (2) Is it plausible to suppose that there are any innocents? (3) Under what circumstances is the death of innocent persons immoral? (4) What is the nature of the connection between the immorality of the killing of innocent persons and the immorality of the war in which this killing occurs?

It is anything but clear what precisely is meant by "innocence" or "the innocent" in an argument such as this. One possibility would be that all noncombatants are innocent. But then, of course, we would have to decide what was meant by "noncombatants." Here we might be tempted to claim that noncombatants are all of those persons who are not in the army—not actually doing the fighting; the combatants are those who are. There are, however, serious problems with this position. For it appears that persons can be noncombatants in this sense and yet indistinguishable in any apparently relevant sense from persons in the army. Thus, civilians may be manufacturing munitions, devising new weapons, writing propaganda, or doing any number of other things that make them indistinguishable from many combatants vis-à-vis their relationship to the war effort.

A second possibility would be to focus upon an individual's causal connection with the attempt to win the war rather than on his status as soldier or civilian. On this view only some noncombatants would be innocent and virtually no combatants would be. If the causal connection is what is relevant, meaningful distinctions might be made among civilians. One might distinguish between those whose activities or vocations help the war effort only indirectly, if at all, and those whose activities are more plausibly described as directly beneficial. Thus the distinctions would be between a typical grocer or a tailor on the one hand, and a worker in an armaments plant on the other. Similarly, children, the aged, and the infirm would normally not be in a position to play a role causally connected in this way with the waging of war.[20]

There are, of course, other kinds of possible connections. In particular, someone might urge that attention should also be devoted to the existence of a causal connection between the individual's civic behavior and the war effort. Thus, for example, a person's voting behavior, or the degree of his political opposition to the government, or his financial contributions to the war effort might all be deemed to be equally relevant to his status as an innocent.

Still a fourth possibility, closely related to those already discussed, would be that interpretation of innocence concerned with culpability rather than causality per se. On this view a person would properly be regarded as innocent if he could not fairly be held responsible for the war's initiation or conduct. Clearly, the notion of culpability is linked in important ways with that of causal connection, but they are by no means identical. So it is quite conceivable, for example, that under some principles of culpability many combatants might not be culpable and some noncombatants might be extremely culpable, particularly if culpability were to be defined largely in terms of state of mind and enthusiasm for the war. Thus, an aged or infirm person who cannot do very much to help the war effort but is an ardent proponent of its aims and objectives might be more culpable (and less innocent in this sense) than a conscriptee who is firing a machine gun only because the penalty for disobeying the command to do so is death.[21]

But we need not propose an airtight definition of "innocence" in order to answer the question of whether, in any war, there will be a substantial number of innocent persons involved. For irrespective of which sense or senses of innocence are ultimately deemed most instructive or important, it does seem clear that there will be a number of persons in any country (children are probably the clearest example) who will meet any test of innocence that is proposed.

The third question enumerated earlier is: Under what circumstances is the death of innocent persons immoral? One possible view is that which asserts simply that it is unimportant which circumstances bring about the death of innocent persons. As long as we know that innocent persons will be killed as a result of war, we know all we need to know to condemn any such war.

Another, and perhaps more plausible, view is that which regards the death of innocent persons as increasingly unjustifiable if it was negligently, recklessly, knowingly, or intentionally brought about. Thus, if a country engages in acts of war with the intention of bringing about the death of children, perhaps to weaken the will of the enemy, it would be more immoral than if it were to engage in acts of war aimed at killing combatants but which through error also kill children.[22]

A different sort of problem arises if someone asks how we are to differentiate the deaths of children in war from, for example, the deaths of children that accompany the use of highways or airplanes in times of peace. Someone might, that is, argue that we permit children to ride in cars on highways and to fly in airplanes even though we *know* that there will be accidents and that as a result of these accidents innocent children will die. And since we know this to be the case, the situation appears to be indistinguishable from that of engaging in acts of war where it is known that the death of children will be a direct, although not intended, consequence.

I think that there are three sorts of responses that can be made to an objection of this sort. In the first place, in a quite straightforward sense the highway does not, typically, cause the death of the innocent passenger; the careless driver or the defective tire does. But it is the intentional bombing of the heavily populated city that does cause the death of the children who live in the city.

In the second place, it is one thing to act where one knows that certain more or less identifiable persons will be killed (say, bombing a troop camp when one knows that those children who live in the vicinity of the camp will also be killed), and quite another thing to engage in conduct in which all one can say is that it can be predicted with a high degree of confidence that over a given period of time a certain number of persons (including children) will be killed. The difference seems to lie partly in the lack of specificity concerning the identity of the persons and partly in the kind of causal connection involved.

In the third place, there is certainly a difference in the two cases in respect to the possibility of deriving benefits from the conduct. That is to say, when a highway is used, one is participating in a system or set of arrangements in which benefits are derived from that use (even though risks, and hence costs, are also involved). It is not easy to see how a similar sort of analysis can as plausibly be proposed in connection with typical acts of war.

The final and most important issue that is raised by the argument concerning the killing of the innocent in time of war is that of the connection between the immorality of the killing of innocent persons and the immorality of the war in which this killing occurs. Writers in the area often fail to discuss the connection.

Miss Anscombe put the point this way: "It is murderous to attack [the innocent] or make them a target for an attack which [the attacker] judges will help him toward victory. For murder is the deliberate killing of the innocent, whether for its own sake or as a means to some further end."[23] And Father John Ford, in a piece that certainly deserves to be more widely known outside of theological circles, puts the point several different ways: At one place he asserts that noncombatants have a right to live, even in wartime;[24] and at another place he says that "to take the life of an innocent person is always intrinsically wrong";[25] and at still a third place: "Every Catholic theologian would condemn as intrinsically immoral the direct killing of innocent noncombatants."[26]

Now, leaving aside the question of whether Miss Anscombe has defined murder correctly and leaving aside the question of whether Father Ford's three assertions are equivalent expressions, the serious question that does remain is what precisely they mean to assert about the intentional killing of innocent persons in time of war.

There are two very different ambiguities in their statements that have to be worked out. In the first place, we have to determine whether the immorality in question is in their view "absolute" or in some sense "prima facie." And in the second place, we should ask whether the immorality in question is in their view to be predicated of the particular act of intentional killing or of the entire war. To elaborate briefly in turn on each of these two ambiguities: Suppose someone were to claim that it is immoral or wrong to lie. He might mean any one of at least three different things: (1) He might mean that it is *absolutely* immoral to lie. That is to say, he might be claiming that there are no circumstances under which one would be justified in telling a lie and that there are no circumstances under which it would, morally speaking, be better to lie than to tell the truth. (2) Or he might mean that it is prima facie immoral to lie. That is to say, he might be claiming that, absent special, overriding circumstances, it is immoral to lie. On this view, even when these special, overriding circumstances do obtain so that an act of lying is justifiable, it still involves some quantum of immorality. (3) The third possibility is that he might mean that, typically, lying is wrong. As a rule it is immoral to lie, but sometimes it is not. And when it is not, there is nothing whatsoever wrong or immoral about telling a lie.

For the purposes of the present inquiry the differences between (2) and (3) are irrelevant;[27] the differences between a position of absolute immorality and either (2) or (3) are not. The question of the killing of the innocents should similarly fit into the foregoing categories and identical conclusions should obtain, although to some degree the differences among these views and the plausibility of each are affected by the type of activity under consideration. Thus, the absolutist view, (1), may seem very strange and unconvincing when applied to lying or promise-keeping; it may seem less so, though, when applied to murder or torture. Similarly (3) may seem quite sensible when predicated of lying or promise-keeping but patently defective when applied to murder or torture.

In any event the case at hand is that of murder. It is likely that Father Ford and Miss Anscombe mean to assert an absolutist view here—that there are no circumstances under which the intentional killing of innocent persons, even in time of war, can be justified. It is always immoral to do so.[28] At least their arguments are phrased in absolutist terms. If this is the view that they intend to defend, it is, I think, a hard one to accept. This is so just because it ultimately depends upon too complete a rejection of the relevance of consequences to the moral character of action. It also requires too rigid a dichotomy between acts and omissions. It seems to misunderstand the character of our moral life to claim that, no matter what the consequences, the intentional killing of an innocent person could never be justifiable—even, for example, if a failure to do so would bring about the death of many more innocent persons.

This does not, of course, mean that the argument from the death of the innocent is either irrelevant or unconvincing. It can be understood to be the very convincing claim that the intentional or knowing killing of an innocent person is always prima facie (in sense (2)) wrong. A serious evil is done every time it occurs. Moreover, the severity of the evil is such that there is a strong presumption against its justifiability. The burden, and it is a heavy one, rests upon anyone who would seek to justify behavior that has as a consequence the death of innocent persons.

The second question concerns what we might call the "range" of the predication of immorality. Even if we were to adopt the absolutist view in respect to the killing of the innocent, it would still remain unclear precisely what it was that was immoral. The narrowest view would be that which holds that the particular action—for instance, the intentional killing of a child—is immoral and unjustified. A broader view would be one that holds that the side that engages in such killing is conducting the war immorally. But this too could mean one of two different things.

A moderate view would be that if one is helpless to prevent the death of the innocent, it is appropriate to weigh such a result against such things as the rightness of the cause for which the war is being fought, the offensive or defensive character of the war, and so on. While there is nothing that can justify or excuse the killing of a particular innocent, this does not necessarily mean that, on balance, the total participation in the war by the side in question is to be deemed absolutely immoral or unjustifiable.

A more extreme view would hold that the occurrence of even a single instance of immorality makes the entire act of fighting the war unjustifiable. Thus, the murder of innocent persons is absolutely immoral in not one but two quite different senses.

My own view is that as a theoretical matter an absolutist position is even less convincing here. Given the number of criteria that are relevant to the moral assessment of any war and given the great number of persons involved in and the extended duration of most wars, it would be false to the complexity of the issues to suppose that so immediately simple a solution were possible.

But having said all of this, the practical, as opposed to the theoretical, thrust of the argument is virtually unabated. If wars were conducted, or were likely to be conducted, so as to produce only the occasional intentional killing of the innocent, that would be one thing. We could then say with some confidence that on this ground at least wars can hardly be condemned out of hand. Unfortunately, though, mankind no longer lives in such a world and, as a result, the argument from the death of the innocent has become increasingly more convincing. The intentional, or at least knowing, killing of the innocent on a large scale became a practically necessary feature of war with the advent of air warfare. And the genuinely indiscriminate killing of very great numbers of innocent persons is the dominant legacy of the birth of thermo-nuclear weapons. At this stage the argument from the death of the innocent moves appreciably closer to becoming a decisive objection to war. For even if we reject, as I have argued we should, both absolutist interpretations of the argument, the core of truth that remains is the insistence that in war, no less than elsewhere, the knowing killing of the innocent is an evil that throws up the heaviest of justificatory burdens. My own view is that in any major war that can or will be fought today, none of those considerations that can sometimes justify engaging in war will in fact come close to meeting this burden. But even if I am wrong, the argument from the death of the innocent does, I believe, make it clear both where the burden is and how unlikely it is today to suppose that it can be honestly discharged.

Notes

This article appeared in the *Stanford Law Review* 21, no. 6 (June 1969): 1627-1656. Copyright 1969 by the Board of Trustees of the Leland Stanford Junior University. The portion included here is from pp. 1636-1656 and comprises Parts II, III, and IV of the article.

1. Acheson, "Ethics in International Relations Today," in M. Raskin and B. Fall (eds.), *The Vietnam Reader* (1965), p. 13.

2. Acheson's view is admittedly somewhat broader than this since it appears to encompass all foreign relations.

3. Such a view could also hold, although it need not, that it would be desirable for matters relating to war to be determined on moral grounds, even though they are not.

4. See notes 9-11 below and accompanying text.

5. Much of this analysis applies with equal force to what I call the prescriptive view, which is discussed more fully in notes 9-11 and and accompanying text. Although I refer only to the analytic view, I mean to include them both where appropriate.

6. It is a mistake just because justice is not analyzable solely in terms of rule-following and rule-violating behavior.

One of the genuine puzzles in this whole area is why there is so much talk about *just* and *unjust* wars. Except in this very limited context of the relationship of justice to rules, it appears that the predicates "just" and "unjust" when applied to wars are so synonymous with "moral" and "immoral."

7. See notes 12-19 below and accompanying text.

8. But suppose someone should argue that the same argument applies to the question of *when* and *under what circumstances* to wage war, and that here, too, the only relevant criteria of assessment are prudential or strategic ones. Again, my answer would be that this also constitutes a perfectly defensible and relevant reason for making a moral judgment about the desirability of war as a social phenomenon.

9. Address to the Nation by President Harry S Truman, August 9, 1945, quoted in R. Tucker, *The Just War* (1960), pp. 21-22, n. 14.

10. Other arguments that might be offered—such as that the president was justified because Japan was the aggressor, or that he was justified because this was essentially an attack on combatants—are discussed at notes 12-19 below and accompanying text.

11. It is probably a reaction to the parochial view of national interest that makes plausible movements that seek to develop a single world government and a notion of world rather than national citizenship.

12. This may be what Paul Henri Spaak had in mind when he said: "I must . . . say that the proposal to humanize war has always struck me as hypocrisy. I have difficulty in seeing the difference from a moral and humane point of view between the use of a guided missile of great power which can kill tens and even hundreds of people without regard for age or sex, and which if used repeatedly will kill millions, and the use of an atomic bomb which achieves the same result at the first stroke. Does crime

against humanity begin only at the moment when a certain number of innocent people are killed or at the moment when the first one is killed?" Quoted in R. Tucker, *The Just War*, pp. 78-79, n. 71.

13. This is the view put forward by Michael Walzer in his piece "Moral Judgment in Time of War," *Dissent*, May-June 1967, p. 284.

I purposely say "to some degree" because there are powerful objections to taking the "laws of war" too seriously, particularly if they are to be construed as laws or even binding rules. More generally, there are at least four respects in which their character as laws seems suspect: (1) There is no authoritative body to make or declare them. (2) The distinctions made by the rules are specious and unconvincing; for example, the use of irregular-shaped bullets and projectiles filled with glass violates our standards of land warfare—see U.S. Department of the Army, *The Law of Land Warfare*, article 34 (Basic Field Manual 27-10, 1956)—but the use of an atomic bomb does not. (3) The sanctions are typically applied only to the losing side. (4) The countries involved tend to regard their own behavior as lawful because falling under some exception or other.

14. I discuss this distinction between injustice and unjustifiability at notes 23-28 below and accompanying text.

15. Quoted in R. Tucker, *The Just War*, p. 12.

16. G.E.M. Anscombe makes the same point in her article "War and Murder," Chapter 19: "The present-day conception of 'aggression,' like so many strongly influential conceptions, is a bad one. Why *must* it be wrong to strike the first blow in a struggle? The only question is, who is in the right."

17. Such a view certainly exists, however; we talk, for instance, about national pride and honor, insults to a country, etc. One real question is whether this way of thinking ought to be exorcised. In any event, however, countries do not respond "instinctively" in the way in which persons sometimes do, and, hence, the excuse rationale is just not appropriate.

18. Ballou, "Christian Non-Resistance," in S. Lynd, ed., *Nonviolence in America: A Documentary History* (1966), pp. 31, 38-39.

19. Still another argument against unilateral pacifism is, of course, that there are evils other than the destruction of lives. Suppose, for example, that unilateral pacifism would result in fewer deaths but in substantially greater human slavery. It is by no means clear that such would be a morally preferable state of affairs.

20. For a fuller development of this point see Ford, "The Morality of Obliteration Bombing," *Theological Studies* 5 (1944):261, 280-86.

21. This discussion hardly exhausts the possible problems involved in making clear the appropriate notion of innocence. I have not, for example, discussed at all the view that culpability is linked with the *cause*

for which a war is fought. On this view, innocence might turn much more on the question of which side a person was on than on his connection with or responsibility for waging the war. I do not think this sense of innocence is intended by those who condemn wars that involve the deaths of innocent persons.

Similarly, I have avoided completely a number of difficulties inherent in the problem of culpability for the behavior of one's country. To what degree does the denial of access to adequate information about the war excuse one from culpability in supporting it? Are children who are taught that their country is always right to be regarded as innocents even though they act on this instruction and assiduously do what they can to aid the war effort? To what degree does the existence of severe penalties for political opposition render ostensibly culpable behavior in fact innocent?

All of these questions arise more directly in connection with the issue of individual responsibility for the behavior of one's country and oneself in time of war. This issue is, as I have indicated, beyond the scope of this article. As is apparent, however, a number of the relevant considerations are presented once the problem of the death of innocent persons is raised.

22. There is a substantial body of literature on the problem of the intentionality of conduct in time of war. Discussion has focused chiefly on the plausibility of the Catholic doctrine of "double" or "indirect" effect. See, e.g., P. Ramsey, *War and the Christian Conscience* (1961), pp. 46-59; Anscombe, pp. 57-59; Ford, pp. 289, 290-98.

23. Anscombe, p. 49.

24. Ford, p. 269.

25. Ibid., p. 272.

26. Ibid., p. 273.

27. For discussion of the differences between these two positions in other contexts, see Wasserstrom, "The Obligation to Obey the Law," *U.C.L.A. Law Review* 10 (1963):780, 783-85.

28. I offer this interpretation because the language typically used seems to support it. For example, Miss Anscombe says: "Without understanding of this principle [of double effect] anything can be—and is wont to be—justified, and the Christian teaching *that in no circumstances may one commit murder, adultery, apostasy (to give a few examples) goes by the board.* These absolute prohibitions of Christianity by no means exhaust its ethic; there is a large area where what is just is determined partly by a prudent weighing up of consequences. But the prohibitions are bedrock, and without them the Christian ethic goes to pieces." Anscombe, "War and Morality" (emphasis added). And it is also consistent with what I take to be the more general Catholic doctrine on the intentional taking of "innocent" life—the absolute prohibition against abortion on just this ground.

21

Conventions and the Morality of War

George I. Mavrodes

Professor George Mavrodes's concern in his paper is to criticize "immunity theorists," those who claim that the noncombatant segment of the population have a moral immunity from being killed (unless permitted by the principle of double effect). He finds no way to defend the position that the "innocence" of noncombatants is a morally relevant property. But, Mavrodes asserts, there is something in the combatant/noncombatant distinction that deserves moral consideration: the obligation to spare noncombatants is a "convention" which has the effect of limiting the death and destruction of total war and imposes moral obligations on the warring parties (much as driving conventions impose moral obligations on drivers to drive on the right, say). Mavrodes's view has the practical consequences that, so to speak, "it takes two to make a convention" and that oftentimes there is no obligation to observe a convention unilaterally, giving due weight, to be sure, to considerations of justice and proportionality.

—R. C.

The point of this paper is to introduce a distinction into our thinking about warfare, and to explore the moral implications of this distinction. I shall make two major assumptions. First, I shall assume without discussion that under some circumstances and for some ends warfare is morally justified. These conditions I shall lump together under such terms as "justice" and "just cause," and say no more about them. I shall also assume that in warfare some means, including some killing, are morally justified. I sometimes

From *Philosophy and Public Affairs* 4, no. 2 (Winter 1975). Copyright © 1975 by Princeton University Press. Reproduced by permission.

call such means "proportionate," and in general I say rather little about them. These assumptions, incidentally, are common to all of the philosophers whom I criticize here.

The distinction which I introduce can be thought of either as dividing wars into two classes, or else as distinguishing wars from certain other international combats. I have no great preference for one of these ways of speaking over the other, but I shall generally adopt the latter alternative. I am particularly interested in the moral significance of this distinction, and I shall explore in some detail its bearing on one moral question associated with warfare, that of the intentional killing of noncombatants.

My paper has two main parts. In the first I examine three closely related treatments of this moral question: the arguments of Elizabeth Anscombe, John C. Ford, and Paul Ramsey. These treatments seem to ignore the distinction that I will propose. I argue that on their own terms, and without reference to that distinction, they must be counted as unsatisfactory.

In the second part of the paper I propose and explain my distinction. I then explore what I take to be some of its moral implications, especially with reference to the alleged immunity of noncombatants, and I argue that it supplies what was missing or defective in the treatments previously criticized.

The Immunity Theorists

A number of philosophers have held that a large portion of the population of warring nations have a special moral status. This is the *noncombatant* segment of the population, and they have a moral immunity from being intentionally killed. This view seems to have been especially congenial to philosophers who have tried to apply Christian ethics to the problems of warfare. Among the philosophers who have held this view are Elizabeth Anscombe, John C. Ford, and Paul Ramsey. I shall refer to this trio of thinkers as the *immunity theorists*.

Perhaps we should indicate a little more in detail just what the immunity theorists appear to hold, specifying just what segment of the population is being discussed and just what their immunity consists in. The immunity theorists commonly admit that there is some difficulty in specifying exactly who are the noncombatants.[1]

Roughly, they are those people who are not engaged in military operations and whose activity is not immediately and directly related to the war effort. Perhaps we should say that if a person is engaged only in the sort of activities which would be carried on even if the nation were not at war (or preparing for war) then that person is a noncombatant. So generally farmers, teachers, nurses, firemen, sales people, housewives, poets, children, etc. are noncombatants.[2] There are, of course, difficult cases, ranging from the high civilian official of the government to the truck driver (either military or civilian) who hauls vegetables toward the front lines. But despite the hard cases it is held that warring nations contain large numbers of readily identifiable people who are clearly noncombatants.

What of their immunity? The writers whom I consider here make use of the "principle of double effect."[3] This involves dividing the consequences of an act (at least the foreseeable consequences) into two classes. Into the first class go those consequences which constitute the goal or purpose of the act, what the act is done for, and also those consequences which are means to those ends. Into the other class go those consequences which are neither the sought-after ends nor the means to those ends. So, for example, the bombing of a rail yard may have among its many consequences the following: the flow of supplies toward the front is disrupted, several locomotives are damaged, and a lot of smoke, dust, etc. is discharged into the air. The disruption of transport may well be the end sought by this action, and perhaps the damage to locomotives is sought as a means of disrupting transport. If so, these consequences belong in the first class, a class which I shall generally mark by using the words "intentional" or "intended." The smoke, on the other hand, though as surely foreseeable as the other effects, may be neither means nor end in this situation. It is a side effect, and belongs in the second class (which I shall sometimes call "unintentional" or "unintended").

Now, the moral immunity of noncombatants consists, according to these writers, in the fact that their death can never, morally, be made the intended consequence of a military operation. Or to put it another way, any military operation which seeks the death of noncombatants either as an end or a means is immoral, regardless of the total good which it might accomplish.

The *unintended* death of noncombatants, on the other hand, is not absolutely forbidden. A military operation which will foreseeably result in such deaths, neither as means nor ends but as side effects, may be morally acceptable according to these writers. It will be morally acceptable if the good end which it may be expected to attain is of sufficient weight to overbalance the evil of these noncombatant deaths (as well as any other evils involved in it). This principle, sometimes called the principle of proportionality, apparently applies to foreseen but unintended noncombatant deaths in just the same way as it applies to the intended death of combatants, the destruction of resources, and so on. In all of these cases it is held to be immoral to cause many deaths, much pain, etc., in order to achieve minor goals. Here combatant and noncombatant stand on the same moral ground, and their deaths are weighed in the same balances. But when the slaying of noncombatants is envisioned as an end or, more commonly, as a means—perhaps in order to reduce the production of foodstuffs or to damage the morale of troops—then there is an unqualified judgment that the projected operation is flatly immoral. The intentional slaying of combatants, on the other hand, faces no such prohibition. This, then, is the place where the moral status of combatant and noncombatant differ sharply.

Now, if a scheme such as this is not to appear simply arbitrary it looks as though we must find some morally relevant basis for the distinction. It is perhaps worthwhile to notice that in this context the immunity of noncombatants cannot be supported by reference to the sanctity or value of human life, nor by reference to a duty not to kill our brothers, etc. For these authors recognize the moral permissibility, even perhaps the duty, of killing under certain circumstances. What must be sought is the ground of a distinction, and not merely a consideration against killing.

Such a ground, however, seems very hard to find, perhaps unexpectedly so. The crucial argument proposed by the immunity theorists turns on the notions of guilt and innocence. Anscombe, for example, says, "Now, it is one of the most vehement and repeated teachings of the Judaeo-Christian tradition that the shedding of innocent blood is forbidden by the divine law. No man may be punished except for his own crime, and those 'whose feet are swift to shed innocent blood' are always represented as God's enemies."[4]

Earlier on she says, "The principal wickedness which is a temptation to those engaged in warfare is the killing of the innocent,"[5] and she has titled one of the sections of her paper, "Innocence and the Right to Kill Intentionally." Clearly enough the notion of innocence plays a large role in her thinking on this topic. Just what that role is, or should be, will be considered shortly.

Ford, in the article cited earlier, repeatedly couples the word "innocent" with "civilian" and "noncombatant." His clearest statement, however, is in another essay. There he says, "Catholic teaching has been unanimous for long centuries in declaring that it is never permitted to kill directly noncombatants in wartime. Why? Because they are innocent. That is, they are innocent of the violent and destructive action of war, or of any close participation in the violent and destructive action of war. It is such participation *alone* that would make them legitimate targets of violent repression themselves."[6] Here we have explicitly a promising candidate for the basis of the moral distinction between combatants and noncombatants. It is promising because innocence itself seems to be a moral property. Hence, if we could see that noncombatants were innocent while combatants were not it would be plausible to suppose that this fact made it morally proper to treat them in different ways.

If we are to succeed along this line of thought, then we must meet at least two conditions. First, we must find some one sense of "innocence" such that all noncombatants are innocent and all combatants are guilty. Second, this sense must be morally relevant, a point of the greatest importance. We are seeking to ground a moral distinction, and the facts to which we refer must therefore be morally relevant. The use of a morally tinged word, such as "innocent," does not of itself guarantee such relevance.

Well, is there a suitable sense for "innocent"? Ford said that noncombatants "are innocent of the violent and destructive action of war." Anscombe, writing of the people who can properly be attacked with deadly force, says, "What is required, for the people attacked to be noninnocent in the relevant sense, is that they themselves be engaged in an objectively unjust proceeding which the attacker has the right to make his concern; or—the commonest case—should be unjustly attacking him." On the other hand, she speaks of "people whose mere existence and activity supporting existence by growing crops, making clothes, etc.," might contribute to the war effort, and she says, "such people are innocent and it is murderous to attack them, or make them a target for an attack which he judges will help him towards victory."[7] These passages contain, I think, the best clues we have as to the sense of "innocent" in these authors.

It is probably evident enough that this sense of "innocent" is vague in a way parallel to the vagueness of "noncombatant." It will leave us with troublesome borderline cases. In itself, that does not seem to me a crucial defect. But perhaps it is a clue to an important failing. For I suspect that there is this parallel vagueness because "innocent" here is just a synonym for "noncombatant."

What can Ford mean by saying that some people are "innocent of the violent and destructive action of war" except that those people are not engaged in the violence of war? Must not Anscombe mean essentially the same thing when she says that the noninnocent are themselves "engaged in an objectively unjust proceeding"? But we need not rely wholly on these rhetorical questions. Ramsey makes this point explicitly. He first distinguishes between close and remote cooperation in military operations, and then he alludes to the distinction between the "guilty" and the "innocent." Of this distinction he says, "These are very misleading terms, since their meaning is exhaustively stated under the first contrast, and is reducible to degrees of actual participation in hostile force."[8] In this judgment Ramsey certainly seems to me to be right.

Now, we should notice carefully that a person may be an enthusiastic supporter of the unjust war and its unjust aims, he may give to it his voice and his vote, he may have done everything in his power to procure it when it was yet but a prospect, now that it is in progress he may contribute to it both his savings and the work which he knows best how to do, and he may avidly hope to share in the unjust gains which will follow if the war is successful. But such a person may clearly be a noncombatant, and (in the sense of the immunity theorists) unquestionably "innocent" of the war. On the other hand, a young man of limited mental ability and almost no education may be drafted, put into uniform, trained for a few weeks, and sent to the front as a replacement in a low-grade unit.

He may have no understanding of what the war is about, and no heart for it. He might want nothing more than to go back to his town and the life he led before. But he is "engaged," carrying ammunition, perhaps, or stringing telephone wire or even banging away ineffectually with his rifle. He is without doubt a combatant, and "guilty," a fit subject for intentional slaughter. Is it not clear that "innocence," as used here, leaves out entirely all of the relevant moral considerations—that it has no moral content at all? Anscombe suggests that intentional killing during warfare should be construed on the model of punishing people for their crimes, and we must see to it, if we are to be moral, that we punish someone only for his own crime and not for someone else's. But if we construe the criminality involved in an unjust war in any reasonable moral sense then it must either be the case that many noncombatants are guilty of that criminality or else many combatants are innocent. In fact, it will probably be the case that *both* of these things are true. Only if we were to divest "crime" of its moral bearings could we make it fit the combatant/noncombatant distinction in modern wars.

The fact that both Anscombe and Ramsey[9] use the analogy of the criminal in discussing this topic suggests that there is an important fact about warfare which is easily overlooked. And that is that warfare, unlike ordinary criminal activity, is not an activity in which individuals engage *qua* individuals or as members of voluntary associations. They enter into war as members of nations. It is more proper to say that the nation is at war than that its soldiers are at war. This does not, of course, entail that individuals have no moral responsibility for their acts in war. But it does suggest that moral responsibility may not be distributed between combatant and noncombatant in the same way as between a criminal and his children. Many of the men who are soldiers, perhaps most of them, would not be engaged in military operations at all if they did not happen to be citizens of a warring nation. But noncombatants are citizens of warring nations in exactly the same sense as are soldiers. However these facts are to be analyzed they should warn us not to rely too heavily on the analogy with ordinary criminality.

We seem, then, to be caught in a dilemma. We can perhaps find some sense for notions such as *innocence* and *criminality* which will make them fit the distinction in which we are interested. But the price of doing so seems to be that of divesting these notions of the moral significance which they require if they are to justify the moral import of the distinction itself. In the ordinary senses, on the other hand, these notions do have the required moral bearings. But in their ordinary senses they do not fit the desired distinction. In neither way, therefore, can the argument from innocence be made to work, and the alleged moral immunity of noncombatants seems to be left as an arbitrary claim.

Convention-Dependent Morality

Despite the failure of these arguments I have recently come to think that there may be something of importance in this distinction after all, and even that it may have an important moral bearing. How might this be?

Imagine a statesman reflecting on the costliness of war, its cost in human life and human suffering. He observes that these costs are normally very high, sometimes staggering. Furthermore, he accepts the principle of proportionality. A consequence of this is that he sometimes envisions a just war for a just cause, but nevertheless decides not to prosecute that war even though he believes it could be won. For the cost of winning would be so high as to outweigh the good which would be attained. So he must sometimes let oppression flourish and injustice hold sway. And even in those wars which can be prosecuted the costs eat very seriously into the benefits.

Then he has an idea. Suppose—just suppose—that one could replace warfare with a less costly substitute. Suppose, for example, that one could introduce a convention—and actually get it accepted and followed by the nations—a convention which replaced warfare with single combat. Under this convention, when two nations arrived at an impasse which would otherwise have resulted in war they would instead choose, each of them, a single champion (doubtless a volunteer). These two men would then meet in mortal combat, and whoever won, killing his opponent or driving him from the field, would win for his nation. To that nation would then be ceded whatever territory, influence, or other prize would have been sought in the war, and the nation whose champion was defeated would lose correspondingly.

Suppose, too, that the statesman believes that if such a convention were to come into force his own nation could expect to win and lose such combats in about the same proportion as it could now expect to win and lose ordinary wars. The same types of questions would be settled by such combats as would otherwise be settled by war (though perhaps more questions would be submitted to combat than would be submitted to war), and approximately the same resolutions would be arrived at. The costs, however— human death and suffering—would be reduced by several orders of magnitude. Would that not be an attractive prospect? I think it would.

While the prospect may seem attractive it may also strike us as hopelessly utopian, hardly to be given a serious thought. There seems to be some evidence that exactly this substitution was actually attempted in ancient times. Ancient literature contains at least two references to such attempts. One is in the Bible, I Samuel 17, in the combat between David and Goliath. The other is in the *Iliad*, book 3, where it is proposed to settle the siege of Troy in the very beginning by single combat between Menelaus and Paris. It may be significant that neither of these attempts appears to have been successful. The single combats were followed by bloodier and more general fighting. Perhaps this substitute for warfare is too cheap; it cannot be made practical, and nations just will not consent in the end to abide by this convention. But consider, on the one hand, warfare which is limited only by the moral requirements that the ends sought should be just and that the means used should be proportionate, and, on the other hand, the convention of single combat as a substitute for warfare. Between these extremes there lie a vast number of other possible conventions which might be canvassed in the search for a less costly substitute for war. I suggest that the long struggle, in the western world at least, to limit military operations to "counter-forces" strategies, thus sparing civilian populations, is just such an attempt.

If I am right about this, then the moral aspects of the matter must be approached in a way rather different from that of the immunity theorists. Some, but not all, of their conclusions can be accepted, and somewhat different grounds must be given for them. These thinkers have construed the immunity of noncombatants as though it were a moral fact which was independent of any actual or envisioned convention or practice. And they have consequently sought to support this immunity by argument which makes no reference to convention. I have already argued that their attempts were failures. What I suggest now is that all such attempts *must* be failures, for they mistake the sort of moral requirement which is under consideration. Let me try to make this clearer.

I find it plausible to suppose that I have a moral obligation to refrain from wantonly murdering my neighbors. And it also seems plausible to discuss this, perhaps in utilitarian terms, or in terms of the will of God, or of natural law, or in terms of a rock-bottom deontological requirement, but in any case without essential reference to the laws and customs of our nation. We might, indeed, easily imagine our laws and customs to be other than they are with respect to murder. But we would then judge the moral adequacy and value of such alternative laws and customs by reference to the moral obligation I have mentioned and not vice versa. On the other hand, I may also have a moral obligation to pay a property tax or to drive on the right side of the street. It does not seem plausible to suppose, however, that one can discuss these duties without immediately referring to our laws and customs. And it seems likely that different laws would have generated different moral duties, e.g. driving on the left. These latter are examples of "convention-dependent" moral obligations. More formally, I will say that a given moral obligation is convention-dependent if and only if (1) given that a certain convention, law, custom, etc., is actually in force one really does have an obligation to act in conformity with that convention, and (2) there is an alternative law, custom, etc. (or lack thereof) such that if that had been in force one would not have had the former obligation.

At this point, before developing the way in which it may apply to warfare, let me forestall some possible misunderstandings by a series of brief comments on this notion. I am not claiming, nor do I believe, that all laws, customs, etc., generate corresponding moral obligations. But some do. I am not denying that one may seek, and perhaps find, some more general moral law, perhaps independent of convention, which explains why this convention generates the more specific obligation. I claim only that one cannot account for the specific obligation apart from the convention. Finally, I am not denying that one might have an obligation, perhaps independent of convention, to try to change a convention of this sort. For I think it possible that one might simultaneously have a moral obligation to conform to a certain convention and also a moral obligation to replace that convention, and thus eliminate the first obligation.

Now the core of my suggestion with respect to the immunity of noncombatants is this. The immunity of noncombatants is best thought of as a convention-dependent obligation related to a convention which substitutes for warfare a certain form of limited combat. How does this bear on some of the questions we have been discussing?

To begin with, we might observe that the convention itself is presumably to be justified by its expectable results. (Perhaps we can refer to some moral rule to the effect that we should minimize social costs such as death and injury.) It seems plausible to suppose that the counter-forces convention, if followed, will reduce the pain and death involved in combat—will reduce it, that is, compared to unlimited warfare. There are surely other possible conventions which, if followed, would reduce those costs still more, e.g. the substitution of single combat. Single combat, however, is probably not a live contender because there is almost no chance that such a convention would actually be followed. It is possible, however, that there is some practical convention which is preferable to the present counter-forces convention. If so, the fact that it is preferable is a strong reason in favor of supposing that there is a moral obligation to promote its adoption.

It does not follow, however, that we now have a duty to act in conformity with this other possible convention. For the results of acting in conformity with a preferable convention which is not widely observed may be much worse than the results of acting in conformity with a less desirable convention which is widely observed. We might, for example, discover that a "left-hand" pattern of traffic flow would be preferable to the present system of "right-hand" rules, in that it would result in fewer accidents, etc. The difference might be so significant that we really would be morally derelict if we did not try to institute a change in our laws. We would be acquiescing in a very costly procedure when a more economical one was at hand. But it would be a disaster, and, I suspect, positively immoral, for a few of us to begin driving on the left before the convention was changed. In cases of convention dependent obligations the question of what convention is actually in force is one of considerable moral import. That one is reminded to take this question seriously is one of the important differences between this approach and that of the immunity theorists.

Perhaps the counter-forces convention is not really operative now in a substantial way. I do not know. Doubtless, it suffered a severe blow in World War II, not least from British and U.S. bombing strategies. Traffic rules are embedded in a broad, massive, comparatively stable social structure which makes their status comparatively resistant to erosion by infraction. Not so, however, for a convention of warfare. It has little status except in its actual observance, and depends greatly on the mutual trust of the belligerents; hence it is especially vulnerable to abrogation by a few contrary acts. Here arises a related difference with the immunity theorists. Taking the obligation to be convention-independent they reject argument based on the fact that "the enemy did it first," etc.[10] If the obligation were independent they would be correct in this. But for convention-dependent obligations, what one's opponent does, what "everyone is doing," etc., are facts of great moral importance. Such facts help to determine within what convention, if any, one is operating, and thus they help one to discover what his moral duties are.

If we were to decide that the counter-forces convention was dead at present, or, indeed, that no convention at all with respect to warfare was operative now, it would not follow that warfare was immoral. Nor, on the other hand, would it follow that warfare was beyond all moral rules, an area in which "anything goes." Instead, we would simply go back to warfare per se, limited only by independent moral requirements, such as those of justice and proportionality. That would, on the whole, probably be a more costly way of handling such problems. But if we live in a time when the preferable substitutes are not available, then we must either forgo the goods or bear the higher costs. If we had no traffic laws or customs, traffic would be even more dangerous and costly than it is now. Traveling, however, might still be justified, if the reason for traveling were sufficiently important.

In such a case, of course, there would be no obligation to drive on the right, or in any regular manner, nor would there be any benefit in it. Probably the best thing would be to drive in a completely ad hoc way, seeking the best maneuver in each situation as it arose. More generally, and ignoring for the moment a final consideration which will be discussed below, there is no obligation and no benefit associated with the unilateral observance of a convention. If one's cause is unjust then one ought not to kill noncombatants. But that is because of the independent moral prohibition against prosecuting such a war at all, and has nothing to do with any special immunity of noncombatants. If one's cause is just, but the slaying of noncombatants will not advance it to any marked degree, then one ought not to slay them. But this is just the requirement of proportionality, and applies equally and in the same way to combatants. If one's cause is just and the slaying of noncombatants would advance it—if, in other words, one is not prevented by considerations of justice and proportionality—this is the crucial case. If one refrains unilaterally in this situation then he seems to choose the greater of two evils (or the lesser of two goods). By hypothesis, the good achieved, i.e., the lives spared, is not as weighty as the evil that he allows in damage to the prospects for justice or in the even more costly alternative measures, e.g. the slaying of a larger number of combatants, which he must undertake. Now, if the relevant convention were operative, then his refraining from counter-population strategies here would be related to his enemy's similar restraint, and indeed it would be related to the strategies which would be used in future wars. These larger considerations might well tip the balance in the other direction. But by hypothesis we are considering the case in which there is no such convention, and so these larger considerations do not arise. One acts unilaterally. In such a situation it certainly appears that one would have chosen the worse of the two alternatives. It is hard to suppose that one is morally obligated to do so.

I said above that we were ignoring for the moment one relevant consideration. It should not be ignored forever. I have already called attention to the fact that conventions of warfare are not, like traffic rules, embedded in a more massive social structure. This makes them especially precarious, as we have noted. But it also bears on the way in which they may be adopted. One such way, perhaps a rather important way, is for one party to the hostilities to signal his willingness to abide by such a convention by undertaking some unilateral restraint on his own part. If the opponent does not reciprocate, then the offer has failed and it goes no further. If the opponent does reciprocate, however, then the area of restraint may be broadened, and a kind of mutual respect and confidence may grow up between the belligerents. Each comes to rely on the other to keep the (perhaps unspoken) agreement, and therefore each is willing to forgo the immediate advantage which might accrue to him from breaking it. If this happens, then a new convention has begun its precarious life. This may be an event well worth seeking.

Not only may it be worth seeking, it may be worth paying something for. For a significant increase in the likelihood that a worthwhile convention will be adopted it may be worth accepting an increased risk or a higher immediate cost in lives and suffering. So there may be some justification in unilateral restraint after all, even in the absence of such a convention. But this justification is prospective and finite. It envisions the possibility that such a convention may arise in the future as a result of this restraint. Consequently, the justification should be proportioned to some judgment as to the likelihood of that event, and it should be reevaluated as future events unfold.

Convention vs. Morality

I began by examining some attempts to defend a certain alleged moral rule of war, the immunity of noncombatants. These defenses have in common the fact that they construe this moral rule as independent of any human law, custom, etc. I then argued that these defenses fail because they leave a certain distinction without moral support, and yet the distinction is essential to the rule. Turning then to the task of construction rather than criticism, I suggested that the immunity of noncombatants is not an independent moral rule but rather a part of a convention which sets up a morally desirable alternative to war. I argued then that some conventions, including this one, generate special moral obligations which cannot be satisfactorily explained and defended without reference to the convention. And in the final pages I explored some of the special features of the obligation at hand and of the arguments which are relevant to it.

The distinction I have drawn is that between warfare per se on the one hand, and, on the other hand, international combats which are limited by convention and custom. But the point of the distinction is to clarify our thinking about the *morality* of such wars and combats. That is where its value must be tested.

Notes

1. Elizabeth Anscombe, "War and Murder," Chapter 19 in this volume; John C. Ford, "The Morality of Obliteration Bombing," in *War and Morality*, ed. Richard A. Wasserstrom (Belmont, Calif., 1970), pp. 19-23; Paul Ramsey, *The Just War* (New York, 1968), pp. 157, 158.

2. Ford gives a list of over 100 occupations whose practitioners he considers to be "almost without exception" noncombatants.

3. Anscombe; Ford, pp. 26-28; Ramsey, pp. 347-358.

4. Anscombe.

5. Ibid.

6. John C. Ford, "The Hydrogen Bombing of Cities," *Morality and Modern Warfare*, ed. William J. Nagle (Baltimore: Helicon Press, 1960), p. 98.

7. Anscombe.

8. Ramsey, p. 153.

9. Ibid., p. 144.

10. For example, Ford, "The Morality of Obliteration Bombing," pp. 20, 33.

22

The Killing of the Innocent

Jeffrie G. Murphy

Consider:

(1) Murder is the intentional and uncoerced killing of the innocent.

(2) Murder is by definition morally wrong.

(3) Modern war by its very nature involves the intentional killing of innocent people.

Therefore, modern war is morally wrong.

Though Professor Murphy does not take a stand on this issue (it may be false that modern war necessarily involves killing the innocents), he appeals to the Kantian moral perspective that the motive *of the agent is the preeminent moral consideration to give some sense to an absolute prohibition against killing innocent persons. His argument: I can kill in warfare, but only those who are trying to kill me. Such persons are members of a causal and logical* chain of agency. I must have reasonable evidence *that those I intend to kill are in this chain, for to kill without such evidence is to intend to kill innocent persons. Though the aging Nazi octogenarian in Dresden may in fact be in this chain, I cannot practically know this and therefore cannot kill him. In practical situations, then, a person's status as a combatant or noncombatant determines the moral character of the act of killing rather than objective guilt or innocence. In borderline cases, such as workers in factories producing goods of peripheral interest to the war effort, the burden of proof is on the agent considering the killing. Professor Murphy rejects the utilitarian justification for killing innocents or noncombatants. He considers it a moral datum that we should treat people as ends and not means for our projects, regardless of the objective good we calculate as the outcome.*

—M. B.

From *The Monist* 57, no. 4 (1973). Printed with permission.

After war has been begun, and during the whole period thereof up to the attainment of victory, it is just to visit upon the enemy all losses which may seem necessary either for obtaining satisfaction or for securing victory, provided that these losses do not involve intrinsic injury to innocent persons, which would be in itself an evil.

—Suarez, *The Three Theological Virtues*

*Fight on land and on sea
All men want to be free
If they don't, never mind
We'll abolish all mankind*

—Peter Weiss, *Marat Sade*

Introduction

Murder, some may suggest, is to be defined as the intentional and uncoerced killing of the innocent; and it is true by definition that murder is wrong. Yet wars, particularly modern wars, seem to require the killing of the innocent, e.g., through antimorale terror bombing. Therefore war (at least modern war) must be wrong.

The above line of argument has a certain plausibility and seems to lie behind much philosophical and theological discussion of such problems as the "just war" and the nature of war crimes.[1] If accepted in full, it seems to entail the immorality of war (i.e., the position of pacifism) and the moral blameworthiness of those who participate in war (i.e., warmakers and uncoerced soldiers are all murderers). To avoid these consequences, some writers will challenge some part of the argument by maintaining (a) that there are no innocents in war, or (b) that modern war does not in fact require the killing of the innocent, or (c) that war involves the suspension of moral considerations and thus stands outside the domain of moral criticism entirely, or (d) that contributing to the death of innocents is morally blameless so long as it is only foreseen but not intended by those involved in bringing it about (the Catholic principle of the double effect), or (e) that the prohibition against killing the innocent is only prima facie[2] and can be overridden by even more important moral requirements, e.g., the defense of freedom.

In this paper I want to come to terms with at least some of the important issues raised by the killing of innocents in time of war. The issues I shall focus on are the following:

1. What does it mean, in a context of war, to describe an individual as *innocent?*
2. Why is it morally wrong to kill individuals so described?
3. Is the moral wrongness merely prima facie (i.e., subject to being overridden by other, more weighty, moral considerations) or is it absolute?

I shall avoid making any final judgments on the morality of war (modern wars or otherwise) since such judgments would involve not just philosophical claims but also empirical claims, e.g. the claim that in fact modern war cannot be waged so as to avoid the killing of the innocent. However, certain answers to the questions I shall explore will, when coupled with empirical premises, clearly have moral consequences. For example: If the killing of innocents is absolutely and not just prima facie immoral (a philosophical claim), and if modern wars necessarily involve the killing of innocents (an empirical claim), then war for modern times must be absolutely condemned, i.e. pacifism is the required moral posture for the twentieth century. I shall leave it to sociologists and military historians, however, to supply the correct factual premises.

I shall, then, mainly be concerned to seek answers to the above three questions. However, before launching into my discussion, I want to make one thing clear. Just because I am focusing upon the killing of innocents, it should not be thought that I am confident that it is right to kill the guilty and thus that it is *only* the killing of the innocent that stands in need of analysis and justification. I have no such confidence. I am starting with what any man who is not a moral imbecile must admit to be, at the very least, an obvious prima facie objection to indiscriminate war. In so doing, I do not mean to suggest that there may not be strong nonobvious objections to be made against discriminate war.

The Concept of Innocence

The notions of innocence and guilt seem most at home in a legal context and, somewhat less comfortably, in a moral context. Legally, a man is innocent if he is not guilty, i.e. if he has not engaged in conduct explicitly prohibited by rules of the criminal law. A man may be regarded as morally innocent if his actions do not result from a mental state (e.g. malice) or a character defect (e.g. negligence) which we regard as morally blameworthy. In any civilized system of criminal law, of course, there will be a close connection between legal guilt and innocence and moral guilt and innocence, e.g. murder in the criminal law has as one of its material or defining elements the blameworthy mental state (*mens rea*) of "malice aforethought." But this close connection does not show that the legal and moral concepts are not different. The existence of strict liability criminal statutes is sufficient to show that they are different. Under a strict liability statute, a man can be guilty of a criminal offense without having, at the time of his action, any blameworthy mental state or character defect, not even negligence.[3] However, the notion of strict *moral* responsibility makes little sense; for an inquiry into moral responsibility for the most part is just an inquiry into such matters as the agent's motives, intentions, beliefs, etc.[4] Also, the issue of legal responsibility is much more easily determinable than that of moral responsibility. For example: It is noncontroversial that negligence can make one legally responsible. Anyone who doubts this may simply be given a reading assignment in any number of penal codes.[5] But whether or not negligence is a mental state or a character defect for which one is *morally* responsible is a matter about which reasonable men can disagree. No reading assignment or simple inquiry into "the facts" will lay this worry to rest.[6]

Now our reasonably comfortable ability to operate with these concepts of guilt and innocence leaves us when we attempt to apply them to the context of war. Of course, the legal notions will have application in a limited number of cases, i.e. with respect to those who are legally war criminals under international law. But this will by no means illuminate the majority of cases. For example: Those who have written on the topic of protecting innocents in war would not want to regard the killing of an enemy soldier engaged in an attack against a fortified position as a case of killing the innocent. He is surely, in the right sense (whatever that is), among the guilty (or, at least, among the noninnocent) and is thus a fitting object for violent death. But he is in no sense *legally* guilty. There are no rules of international law prohibiting what he is doing; and, even if such rules were created, they would surely not involve the setting up of a random collection of soldiers from the other side to act as judges and executioners of this law. Thus the legal notions of guilt and innocence do not serve us well here.

What, then, about moral guilt or innocence? Even to make this suggestion plausible in the context of war, we surely have to attempt to narrow it down to moral innocence or guilt of the war or of something within the war—not just moral innocence or guilt *simpliciter*. That is, we surely do not want to say that if a bomb falls (say) on a man with a self-deceiving morally impure heart who is a civilian behind the lines that this is not, in the relevant sense, a case of killing an innocent. Similarly, I think it would be odd for us to want to say that if a soldier with a morally admirable character is killed in action that this is a case of killing an innocent and is to be condemned on those grounds. If we take this line, it would seem that national leaders should attempt to make some investigation of the motives and characters of both soldiers and civilians and kill the unjust among both classes and spare the just. (Only babes in arms would be clearly protected.) Now this sort of judgment, typically thought to be reserved for God if for anyone, is surely a very disquieting thing if advocated for generals and other war leaders. Thus the notions of moral innocence and guilt *simpliciter* must be dropped in this context.

Suppose, then, we try to make use of the notions of moral innocence of the war or moral guilt of the war (or of something within the war). Even here we find serious problems. Consider the octogenarian civilian in Dresden who is an avid supporter of Hitler's war effort (pays taxes gladly, supports warmongering political rallies, etc.) and contrast his case with that of the poor, frightened, pacifist frontline soldier who is only where he is because of duress and who intends always to fire over the heads of the enemy. It seems reasonable to say that the former is much more morally guilty of the war than the latter; and yet most writers on the topic would regard killing the former, but not the latter, as a case of killing an innocent.

What all this suggests is that the classical worry about protecting the innocent is really a worry about protecting *noncombatants*.

And thus the distinction between combatants and noncombatants is what needs to be elucidated. Frontline soldiers are clearly combatants; babes in arms clearly are not. And we know this without judging their respective moral and legal guilt or innocence. And thus the worry, then, is the following: Under what circumstances is an individual truly a combatant? Wars may be viewed as games (terrible ones of course) between enemies or opponents. Who, then, is an enemy or opponent?

One suggestion for defining a combatant might be the following: Only soldiers engaged in fighting are combatants. But this does not seem adequate. For if killing an enemy soldier is right, then it would also seem to be right to kill the man who orders him to the frontline. If anything, the case for killing (say) a general seems better, since the soldier is presumably simply acting in some sense as his agent, i.e. the general kills through him. Perhaps the way to put the point, then, is as follows: The enemy is represented by those who are *engaged in an attempt* to destroy you.[7] And thus all frontline combat soldiers (though not prisoners, or soldiers on leave, or wounded soldiers, or chaplains, or medics) are enemies and all who issue orders for destruction are enemies. Thus we might try the following: Combatants are those anywhere within the *chain of command or responsibility*—from bottom to top. If this is correct, then a carefully planned attack on the seat of government, intended to destroy those civilians (and only those) directing the war effort, would not be a case of killing noncombatants or, in the relevant sense, innocents.

But what is a chain of command or responsibility? It would be wrong to regard it solely as a causal chain, though it is at least that. That is, the notion of responsibility has to be stronger than that expressed in the sentence "The slippery pavement was responsible for the accident." For to regard the chain here as solely causal in character would lead to the following consequence: If a combatant is understood solely as one who performs an action which is a causally necessary condition for the waging of war, then the following are going to be combatants: farmers, employees at a city water works, and anyone who pays taxes. Obviously a country cannot wage war if there is no food, no management of the basic affairs of its cities, and no money to pay for it. And of course the list of persons "responsible" for the war in this sense could be greatly extended. But if all these persons are in the class of combatants, then the rule "protect noncombatants" is going to amount to little more than "protect babies and the senile." But one would, I think, have more ambition for it than that, e.g. one would hope that such a rule would protect housewives even if it is true that they "help" the war effort by writing consoling letters to their soldier husbands and by feeding them and providing them with emotional and sexual relief when they are home on leave. Thus I think that it is wrong to regard the notion of chain here as merely causal in character.

What kind of chain, then, is it? Let us call it a *chain of agency*. What I mean by this is that the links of the chain (like the links between motives and actions) are held together logically and not merely causally, i.e. all held together, in this case, under the notion of who it is that is engaged in an attempt to destroy you. The farmer *qua* farmer is, like the general, performing actions which are causally necessary conditions for your destruction; but, unlike the general, he is not necessarily engaged in an attempt to destroy you. Perhaps the point can better be put in this way: The farmer's role bears a contingent connection to the war effort whereas the general's role bears a necessary connection to the war effort, i.e. his function, unlike the farmer's, is not logically separable from the waging of war. Or, following Thomas Nagel,[8] the point can perhaps be put in yet another way: The farmer is aiding the soldier *qua* human being whereas the general is aiding the soldier *qua* soldier or fighting man. And since your enemy is the soldier *qua* soldier, and not *qua* human being, we have grounds for letting the farmer off. If we think of a justified war as one of self-defense,[9] then we must ask the question "Who can be said to be attacking us such that we need to defend ourselves against him?" Viewed in this way, the farmer seems an unlikely candidate for combat status.

This analysis does, of course, leave us with borderline cases. But since there are borderline cases, this is a virtue of the analysis so long as it captures just the right ones. Consider workers in a munitions factory. Are they or are they not combatants? At least with certain munitions factories (making only bombs, say) it is certainly going to be odd to claim that their activities bear only a contingent connection to the war effort. What they make, unlike food, certainly supports the fighting man *qua* fighting man and not *qua* human being. Thus I should be inclined to say that they are properly to be regarded as combatants and thus properly subject to attack. But what about workers in munitions factories that only in part supply the war effort, e.g. they make rifles both for soldiers and for hunters? Or workers in nonmunitions factories that do make some war products, e.g. workers in companies like Dow Chemical, which make both Saran Wrap and Napalm? Or workers in ball bearing factories or oil refineries, some of their product going to war machines and some not? Here, I submit, we do have genuine borderline cases. And with respect to these, what should we do? I should hope that reasonable men would accept that the burden of proof lies on those claiming that a particular group of persons are combatants and properly vulnerable. I should hope that men would accept, along with the famous principle in the criminal law, the principle "noncombatant until proven otherwise" and would attempt to look at the particular facts of each case as carefully and disinterestedly as possible. I say that I hope this, not that I expect it.

Who, then, is a combatant? I shall answer this question from the point of view of one who believes that the only legitimate defense for war is self-defense.[10] It is, in this context, important to remember that one may legitimately plead self-defense even if one's belief that one's life is being threatened is false. The only requirement is that the belief be reasonable given the evidence that is available. If a man comes to my door with a toy pistol and says, pointing the pistol at me, "Prepare to meet your Maker for your time has come," I act in my self-defense if I kill him even if he was joking so long as my belief was reasonable, i.e. I had no way of knowing that the gun was a toy or that he was joking. Thus: combatants may be viewed as all those in the territory or allied territory of the enemy of whom it is reasonable to believe that they are engaged in an attempt to destroy you.

What about our Dresden octogenarian? Is he a combatant on this analysis? Since he does not act *on authority,* it is at least prima facie odd to regard him as part of a chain of command literally construed—the concept of command being most at home in a context of authority. He does not, of course, have much to do with the war effort; and so we might find his claim that he is "helping to defeat the Americans" quaint on purely factual grounds. And yet none of this prevents its being true that he can properly be said to be engaged in an attempt to destroy the enemy. For people can attempt even the impossible so long as they do not know it is impossible. Thus I am prepared to say of him that he is, in fact, engaged in an attempt to destroy the enemy. But I would still say that killing him would count as a case of killing a noncombatant for the following reason: that the concept of attempt here is to be applied, not from the agent's point of view, but from the point of view of the spectator who proposes to plead self-defense in defense of his acts of killing. Combatants are all those who may reasonably be regarded as engaged in an attempt to destroy you. This belief is reasonable (though false) in the case of the frontline soldier who plans always to shoot over the heads of the enemy and unreasonable (even if true) in the case of our octogenarian. It would be quite unreasonable to plan a bombing raid on a nonmilitary and nonindustrial city like Dresden and say, in defense of the raid, that you are just protecting yourself or your country from all those warmongering civilians who are attempting to destroy you. For making such a judgment imposes upon you a burden of proof which, given the circumstances of war, you could not satisfy. You probably could not get *any* evidence for your claim. You certainly could not get what the law calls a "preponderance of the evidence"—much less "proof beyond a reasonable doubt."

Combatants, then, are all those of whom it is reasonable to believe that they are engaged in an attempt at your destruction. Noncombatants are all those of whom it is not reasonable to believe this. Having the distinction, we must now inquire into its moral importance.

Why Is It Wrong to Kill the Innocent?

From what I have said so far, it should be obvious that this question cannot adequately be answered unless one specifies the sense of innocence that one has in mind. First, with respect to moral innocence, we can take babes in arms as paradigms. Here I should argue that no reasons can be given for why it is wrong to kill babies; neither are any reasons needed. If anything can be taken as a brute datum for moral philosophy, surely the principle "Do not kill innocent babies" is a very good candidate—much more plausible for an ethical primitive than, say, "promote your self-interest" or "maximize the general utility" (other candidates that have been offered for ethical primitives). The person who cannot just *see* that there is something evil about killing babies could not, I suspect, be made to see anything else about morality and thus could not understand any reasons that one might attempt to give. And any "ethical" theory which entailed that there is nothing wrong at all with killing babies would surely deserve to be rejected on the basis of this counterexample alone. Miss G.E.M. Anscombe puts the point in the following way: "If someone really thinks, *in advance,* that it is open to question whether such an action as procuring the judicial execution of the innocent should be quite excluded from consideration—I do not want to argue with him; he shows a corrupt mind."[11]

Consider an example from literature: If a reader of Melville's *Billy Budd* cannot see why Captain Vere is deeply troubled because he has a legal obligation to execute Billy, a morally innocent (though legally guilty) man, what would one say to him? What could one do except repeat, in a louder tone of voice perhaps, "But, don't you see, Billy is morally *innocent*"? What I am saying is that, though it is reasonable to expect ethical theories to correct some of our moral intuitions or pretheoretical convictions, we can not reasonably expect these theories to correct all of them—since there is a class of such intentions or convictions which makes ethical theory itself possible and testable.[12] Kant, I think, was perhaps one of the first to begin to see this when he argued that utilitarianism cannot be correct because it cannot account for the obvious wrongness of making slaves of people, punishing the innocent, etc.

Now with respect to legal innocence (when this does not, as it often does, overlap moral innocence) a set of reasons for not killing (or punishing) the innocent *can* be given. These reasons will be in terms of *utility* (it makes people insecure to live in a society which punishes them whether they obey the rules or not), *justice* (it is not fair to punish people who conform their conduct to the rules), and general observations about the *purposes* and *techniques* of the criminal law as a system of control through rules. As John Rawls has argued,[13] a system of criminal law can be viewed minimally as a price system for controlling conduct (i.e. the rules state a price that has to be paid for certain bits of behavior in the hope that most people will regard the price as too high to pay). And obviously this sort of system is going to work only if the price is generally charged when and only when the "commodity" (i.e. the behavior) is "purchased."

When we move to war, however, difficulties begin to present themselves. We have seen that what people have had in mind when they have argued for the protection of innocents in war was neither clearly moral innocence not clearly legal innocence. Rather it was *noncombatant* protection. But when we put the principle as "Do not kill noncombatants" we lose the background of moral and legal thinking which makes the principle seem plausible when formulated in terms of innocence.

Why, then, should we worry about killing noncombatants and think it wrong to do so—especially when we realize that among the noncombatants there will be some, at any rate, who are morally and/or legally guilty of various things and that among the combatants there will be those who are morally and/or legally innocent?

What I suggest is the following: If one believes (as I do) that the only even remotely plausible justification for war is self-defense, then one must in waging war confine one's hostility to those against whom one is defending oneself, i.e. those in the (both causal and logical) chain of command or responsibility or agency—all those who can reasonably be regarded as engaged in an attempt to destroy you. If one does not do this, then one cannot be said merely to be defending oneself. And insofar as one is not defending oneself, then one acts immorally in killing one's fellow human beings. The enemy can plausibly be expanded to include all those who are "criminal accomplices"—those who, in Judge Learned Hand's phrase, have a "stake in the venture."[14] But it cannot be expanded to include all those who, like farmers, merely perform actions causally necessary for the attack—just as in domestic law I cannot plead self-defense if I kill the one (e.g. the wife or mother) who feeds the man who is engaged in an attempt to kill me.[15]

In passing, I should note why I described my position as weakly as I did—namely, that self-defense is the only *remotely plausible* defense of war. I do this because, with respect to nations, the whole idea of self-defense is strongly in need of analysis. What, for example, is it for a state to die or to be threatened with death? Can nations, like individuals, fear death and act compulsively on the basis of that fear? And, insofar as the death of a state is not identical with the deaths of individual human beings, why is the death of a state a morally bad thing? Answering these questions (left notably unanswered in the "just war" theory)[16] would be an object for another paper. I mention them here to point up latent problems and to further explain my unwillingness, expressed earlier, to affirm that even the killing of the "guilty" (combatants) is morally justified. I am certainly inclined to suspect the just war theory's willingness to regard war as an activity giving rise to autonomous moral problems (i.e. problems solely about war and not reducible to ordinary moral problems) and thus to make moral capital out of suspect notions like "national honor" and "national interests" and "national self-defense." Though I am obviously inclined to regard the concept of self-defense as having an important application in the context of war, I am skeptical that the "self" to be legitimately defended must always be the nation or state. It is at least worth considering the possibility that the only moral problems arising in war are the oldest and most common and most important— namely, are human beings being hurt and killed, who are they, and why are they?

Is Killing the Innocent Absolutely Immoral?

That is, is killing the innocent a prima facie immorality that can be overriden by other, more weighty, moral considerations or is it absolutely immoral, i.e. incapable of being overridden by any other moral requirements? Miss Anscombe[17] holds that the prohibition against killing the innocent is absolute in this sense. And one would suspect that she would echo Kant's sentiments that we should do no injustice though the heavens fall. Unfortunately, she tends simply to assert her position rather than argue for it and so fails to come to terms with the worry that might bother anti-Kantians—namely, does it not matter upon whom the heavens fall? I agree with Miss Anscombe that no argument can be given to demonstrate that there is *something* wrong with killing babies, but it does not follow from this alone that this "something" is not capable of being overridden by another "something"—saving the lives of even more babies, perhaps.

Now in trying to come to grips with this issue, I propose to start with the case of killing babies as a clear example of killing creatures innocent in every possible sense. If a case can be made out that it is sometimes right to kill them, then I assume it will follow *a fortiori* that it is sometimes right to kill those who may be innocent in a less rich sense, e.g. merely noncombatant. Of course if it is not ever right to kill babies, this will not in itself show that it is not ever right to kill noncombatants; for it may be the special kind of innocence found in babies (but not necessarily in noncombatants) which protects them.

First of all, we need to ask ourselves the question "What is it deliberately to kill a baby?" I am certain that Miss Anscombe does not mean the following: that one deliberately kills a baby whenever one pursues a policy that one knows will result in the deaths of some babies. If anyone meant this, then that person would have to regard the construction of highways as absolutely immoral. For it is a statistical fact that on every completed highway a certain number of babies meet their death in accidents. Yet normally we do not regard this as a moral case against highways or as a moral proof that highway engineers are murderers. What is done is to weigh the social value of a highway against the knowledge that some deaths will occur and judge that the former outweighs the latter. (If we did not make this judgment, and if this judgment was not reasonable, then we *would* be acting immorally. For example: Suppose we let people blast with dynamite whenever and wherever they felt like it—conduct with little or no social value—in spite of our knowledge that this would result in many children dying.) Of course, situations comparable to the highway example arise in war. For example, consider the pinpoint bombing of a military installation in a war reasonably believed to be necessary and just coupled with the knowledge that bombs will occasionally go off target and that occasionally a wife, with baby in arms, may be visiting her husband on the base.

The natural way to interpret Miss Anscombe's view is as follows: One kills a baby deliberately either when one (a) brings about the death of a baby as one's final purpose or (b) brings about the death of a baby as a *means* to one's final purpose.[18] Since war is hardly to be regarded as motivated by fetishistic infanticide, it is (b) which is crucial. And (b) lets off the highway engineer. For the highway engineer, whom we do not want to regard as a murderer, will not be a murderer on (b). The deaths of babies in highway accidents are in no sense means to the socially useful goal of good transportation but are rather accidental products. That is, highway transportation is not furthered by these deaths but is, if anything, hindered by them. And so it is unreasonable to suppose that highway engineers desire the deaths of these babies because they want to use their deaths as a means to their goal of transportation. Similarly with the accidental deaths of babies resulting from a pinpoint bombing raid on a military institution.

But consider the following kind of case: One knows that one is fighting a war in defense of civilization itself. (It was not unreasonable to regard the war against Hitler in such terms.)[19] Suppose also that one knows that the only way (causally) to bring a power like Hitler's to a collapse is to undercut his support among the German people by achieving their total demoralization. Further suppose that one knows that the only way to do this is by the obliteration terror bombing of civilian centers (e.g. Dresden) so that, by killing many German babies among others, one can create a desire on the part of the German people to abandon the venture. I am not suggesting that we could ever in fact know these things (they might be false) or that we should ever even let ourselves believe such things.[20] But my worry here is one of principle—namely, assuming the factual situation is as described, would it be wrong *on principle* to initiate a campaign of antimorale obliteration bombing? Here I take it that Miss Anscombe will say that, even in such circumstances, those making a decision to initiate such a campaign are murderers. For they will be deliberately killing the innocent as a means to their goal and that (no matter how good the goal) is absolutely wrong.

But why? Miss Anscombe fails to bring fully into the open a latent issue that is absolutely crucial here—namely, are we as morally responsible for our omissions (e.g. failing to save lives) as for our commissions (e.g. killing people)? Of course there are differences between the two expressions, but are they morally relevant differences? If our basic value here is the sanctity of life, or the sanctity of innocents, or the sanctity of babies, then—as Jonathan Bennett has pointed out[21]—it is hard to see their moral difference. For consider the following kind of case: Suppose we know that a victory by Hitler would mean the extermination of all or a great many non-Aryan babies. And further suppose that these babies far outnumber the German babies to be killed in an obliteration bombing campaign.[22] Now, given this knowledge, what would a man who really values the lives of babies do? Is the moral case to rest upon the different descriptions "killing babies" and "letting babies die"? If so, *why?* If the argument is that by not positively killing we will at least be preserving our own moral purity, then it is important to note that this argument, in addition to being rather selfish, is question-begging. For to assume that one remains morally pure if one does nothing is to beg the question of whether we are as responsible for omissive as for commissive conduct. If moral purity means never choosing anything which one will have to regard as in some sense wrong and regret for all one's days, then moral purity may be impossible in a complex world. Albert Camus based his theory of rebellion on this kind of claim—a theory which Howard Zinn summarizes as follows: "Camus spoke in *The Rebel* of the absurdities in which we are trapped, where the very acts with which we seek to do good cannot escape the imperfections of the world we are trying to change. And so the rebel's 'only virtue will lie in never yielding to the impulse to be engulfed in the shadows that surround him, and in obstinately dragging the chains of evil, with which he is bound, toward the good.' "[23]

The issue here is not over whether we should ever allow ourselves to be persuaded by any argument that killing the innocent is in fact necessary; and I am certainly not suggesting that I find plausible such arguments as have actually been given in the past. For a practical maxim I am much in favor of the slogan "Never trade a certain evil for a possible good." However, this does not solve the issue of principle. If the good (e.g. saving the lives of scores of babies) is certain and not just possible, is it anything more than dogmatism to assert that it would never be right to bring about this good through evil means? The maxim "Never trade a certain evil for a certain good" is by no means self-evidently true and, indeed, does not even seem plausible to many people. Thus I do not think that it has yet been shown that it is always absolutely wrong, whatever the consequences, to kill innocent babies. And thus it has not yet been shown that it is absolutely wrong to kill those innocent in a less rich sense of the term, i.e. noncombatants. Of course we may *feel* differently about actually killing innocents and simply letting innocents die; but I do not think that this phenomenological evidence in itself proves anything. Bomber pilots no doubt feel differently about dropping bombs on babies from thirty thousand feet than they would about shooting a baby face to face, but surely this does not show that the acts differ in moral quality.

Feelings do not prove anything in morality; but they sometimes point to something. And it is at least possible that we have not yet captured the worry which motivates the responses of people like Kant, Miss Anscombe, and those who want to defend some version of the doctrine of the double effect. If what they really value is the lives of babies and other innocents *simpliciter*, then—as Bennett argues—it does not seem that the distinction between "killing babies" and "letting babies die" will help them to save their principle. But perhaps this is to conceive their position too teleologically. That is, we have so far (with Bennett) been assuming that the person who says "never kill babies" says this because he sees the maxim as instrumental to something else that he values—namely, the lives of babies. But it is at least possible that he does not hold this principle to be instrumentally right (in which case he would be subject to Bennett's refutation) but intrinsically right, i.e. right in itself or from its very description. The problem is to explicate this notion of intrinsic rightness in such a way that it does not involve either of the two following pitfalls noted by Bennett: "(a) *Authoritarianism*, e.g. "God commands not killing babies;" and (b) *Dogmatism*, e.g. "It is just absolutely wrong to kill babies; and, if you do not see this, you are just too corrupt to talk to."

Now the reason why (a) is a bad move is obvious—namely, it is an appeal to authority rather than reason and thus has no place in a philosophical discussion of moral questions. But (b) is more problematical. For I have said that I am willing to accept such a move if made in the name of there being *something* wrong with killing babies. Why will I not accept such a move in favor of its being *absolutely* wrong to kill babies?

Roughly, I should argue as follows: That there is something wrong with killing babies (i.e. that "*A* is a case of killing a baby" *must* count as a moral reason against *A*) explicates, in part, what may be called "the moral point of view." To be worried about moral issues is, among other things, to be worried about killing innocents. But the judgment "Never kill babies under any circumstances" does not explicate the moral point of view but is, rather, a controversial judgment—or, if you prefer, explicates *a* moral point of view rather than *the* moral point of view. And so, to build it into the moral point of view is to beg a controversial question of moral substance—something which presumably metaethics should not do. Someone who said "I see nothing at all wrong with killing babies so let's bomb Dresden" would be an amoral monster—one with whom it would be senseless to conduct a moral argument. But one who sincerely said "Of course it is terrible to kill babies but I believe, to save more lives, we must regretfully do it in this case" is not such a monster. He is one with whom, if we think him wrong (immoral), we should hope to be able to argue.[24] Since, among war supporters, there are (one would hope) few of the former sort but many of the latter sort, being able to argue with and persuade the latter has some practical importance. It will hardly do simply to say to them "But I can just see the absolute wrongness of what you contemplate and, if you do not, I refuse to discuss the matter with you." We know, alas, what will then happen.

Now I am not going to pretend that I can give anything resembling a proof that it is absolutely wrong to kill the innocent (though not to allow them to die), but I hope at least to be able to elaborate a way of thinking which (a) does give some sense to such a prohibition and (b) cannot be condemned as simple dogmatism or authoritarianism, i.e. is a way of thinking.[25]

The way of thinking I want to elaborate is one in which the notion of people's having rights plays a predominate role. (Kant's ethical theory, in broad outline, is one such way of thinking.) And an ethical outlook in which the notion of rights looms large will want to draw a distinction between the following two claims: (1) Doing *A* to Jones would be to violate one of his rights; and (2) It would be bad to do *A* to Jones.

To use Kant's own examples:[26] If I have made a promise to Jones, he has a *right* to expect me to keep it, can properly regard me as having wronged him if I do not keep it, and could properly expect that others (the state) should coerce me into keeping it. Kant's opaque way of putting this is to say that keeping a promise is a *perfect* duty. A quite different situation is the following: If Jones is in distress (assuming I have not put him there) and I could help him out without extraordinary sacrifice, he would certainly want me to help him and I would be doing something bad if I did not help him. But he does not have a *right* to expect my help, is not wronged if I fail to help him, and it would be unreasonable to expect the state or anyone else to coerce me into helping him. Helping him is beneficence and (unlike justice) is a comparatively weak moral demand. Kant's opaque way of putting this is to say that the duty to help others in distress is *imperfect*.

When a man has a right, he has a claim against interference. Simply to refuse to be beneficent to him is not an invasion of his rights because it is not to interfere with him at all. When a person uses his freedom to invade the rights of others, he forfeits certain of his own rights and renders interference by others legitimate. (Kant calls this a moral title or authorization—*Befugnis*—to place "obstacles to obstacles to freedom.")[27] Thus if I have an imperfect duty to help others, I may interfere with those trying to harm those others because, by such an attempt, they have forfeited their right against interference. Here I have the imperfect duty; and, since those attacking have by the attack forfeited certain of their rights, I violate no perfect duty in interfering with them. Thus there is no conflict here. However, if the only way I could save someone from harm would be by interfering with an innocent person (i.e. one who has not forfeited his rights by initiating attack against others) then I must not save the person, for this would be to violate a perfect duty. And, in cases of conflict, perfect duties override imperfect duties.

Suppose that Jones is being attacked by Smith. In such a case it is certainly true to say that Jones's *rights* to liberty, security, etc. are being threatened and that Smith, therefore, is acting wrongly and thereby forfeits his right to be left free from interference. Thus I would not be acting wrongly (i.e. against Smith's rights) if I attacked him to prevent his attack on Jones. Similarly, Jones would not be acting wrongly if he defended himself. However, it does not follow from any of this that I have a *duty* to help Jones or even that Jones has a *duty* to defend himself. Defense, though permissible, is not obligatory. This being so, it does not follow that Jones has a *right to be saved* by me. Thus, since it is far from obvious that Jones has a right to be saved even from an attack by the guilty, it is even more implausible to assert that he has a right to be saved if so doing would involve killing the innocent. (Consider the following: We are all, at this very moment, sitting and talking philosophy and are thus omitting to save the lives of countless people we might save throughout the world. Are we acting wrongly in so doing? If we are, is this because all these people have a *right* to be saved by us?)

Now what sort of a moral view could one hold that would make one accept the principle that perfect duties, resting on rights, override imperfect duties, not resting on rights? I think it is this: a view which makes primary the status of persons as free or choosing beings who, out of respect for that status, are to be regarded as having the right to be left alone to work out their own lives—for better or worse. This is a basic right that one has just because one is a person. Respecting it is what Kant calls respecting the dignity of humanity by not treating people as a *means* only. Part of respecting them in this sense is not to use them as a means in one's calculations of what would be good for others. It is fine (indeed admirable) for a person to sacrifice himself for others by his own choice; but it is presumptuous (because lacking in respect for his choices) if *I* choose to sacrifice him. This is his business and not mine. I may only interfere with the person who, by his own evil actions, has forfeited his right against interference. Innocent persons by definition have not done this. And therefore it is absolutely wrong to sacrifice the innocent, though not to kill aggressors. On this view there is something terribly perverse in arguing, as many do, that a defense of freedom requires a sacrifice of those who in no way give their free consent to the sacrifice.[28]

Of course babies are not yet, in the full sense, free or choosing beings who clearly have rights. They are, perhaps, only potential or dispositional persons and enjoyers of rights. But if one accepts the maxim "Innocent until proven otherwise" they may be regarded as equally protected in the above way of thinking. For they certainly cannot be described in the only way which, on this view, makes harmful interference permissible—namely, described as having, through their own deliberate acts of aggression, forfeited their right to be left in peace.

Now this view that what is central in morality involves notions like rights, dignity, freedom, and choice (rather than notions like maximizing the general utility) cannot be proven. But it is a plausible view which may lie behind the maxim "Never kill the innocent" and is a view which would be sacrificed (at least greatly compromised) by the maxim "Kill the innocent to save the innocent." I am myself deeply sympathetic to this way of thinking and would make neither the compromise nor the sacrifice. But I cannot prove that one ought not make it. Neither, of course, can my teleological opponent prove his case either. For we lie here at the boundaries of moral discourse where candidates for ultimate principles conflict; and it is part of the logical character of an ultimate principle that it cannot be assessed by some yet higher ("more ultimate"?) principle.[29] You pays your money and you takes your choice. It is simply my hope that many people, if they could see clearly what price they have to pay (i.e. the kind of moral outlook they have to give up and what they have to put in its place) would make the choice against killing the innocent.

Consider the following example: Suppose that thousands of babies could be saved from a fatal infant disease if some few babies were taken by the state and given over to a team of medical researchers for a series of experiments which, though killing the babies, would yield a cure for the disease. In what way except degree (i.e. numbers of babies killed) does this situation differ from the rationale behind antimorale obliteration bombing raids, i.e., is there not a disturbing parallel between Allied raids on Dresden and Tokyo and Nazi "medicine"? With respect to either suggestion, when we really think about it, do we not want to say with the poet James Dickey, "Holding onto another man's walls/ My hat should crawl on my head/ In streetcars, thinking of it,/ The fat on my body should pale."[30] How can any such thing be in the interest of humanity when its practice would change the very meaning of "humanity" and prevent us from unpacking from it, as we now do, notions like rights, dignity, and respect? No matter how good the consequences, is there not some point in saying that we simply do not have the *right* to do it? For there is, I think, an insight of secular value in the religious observation that men are the "children of God." For this means, among other things, that other people do not belong to me. They are not mine to be manipulated as resources in my projects. It is hard to imagine all that we might lose if we abandoned this way of thinking about ourselves and others.

My appeal here, of course, is in a sense emotive. But this in my judgment is not an objection. Emotive appeals may rightly be condemned if they are masquerading as proofs. But here I am attempting to prove nothing but only to say—"Here, look, see what you are doing and what way of thinking your doing it involves you in." If one sees all this and still goes forth to do it anyway, we have transcended the bounds of what can be said in the matter.

What about noncombatants? Though they are not necessarily innocent in all the senses in which babies are, they clearly are innocent in the sense I have elaborated above—namely, they have not performed actions which forfeit their right to be free from execution (or, better: it is not reasonable for the enemy to believe this of them). Thus, in a very tentative conclusion, I suggest the following: I have not been able to prove that we should never kill noncombatants or innocents (I do not think this could be proven in any ordinary sense of proof); but I do think that I have elaborated a way of thinking which gives sense to the acceptance of such an absolute prohibition. Thus, against Bennett, I have at least shown that one can accept the principle, "Never kill the innocent" without thereby necessarily being an authoritarian or a dogmatic moral fanatic.

Notes

Many people were kind enough to comment on this manuscript in various stages of its preparation, and I should like to take this opportunity to express my sincere appreciation for the help that they provided. In particular, I should like to thank the following: Lewis White Beck, Robert L. Holmes, Gareth Matthews, Ronald Milo, Richard Wasserstrom, Donald Wells, Peter Winch, and Anthony D. Woozley. I should also like to thank the members of my graduate seminar on war at the University of Arizona for stimulating discussion. Since I have perversely gone my own way on several points in spite of advice to the contrary, I alone am to be held responsible for any errors that remain. In setting a philosophical framework for a discussion of the problem of killing the innocent in war, I have been greatly influenced by Richard Wasserstrom's "On the Morality of War: A Preliminary Inquiry" in his useful collection of essays *War and Morality* (Belmont, Calif.: Wadsworth Publishing Co., 1970 and in this volume, Chapter 20). I am presupposing that the reader is familiar with Miss G.E.M. Anscombe's two articles

"Modern Moral Philosophy," *Philosophy* 33, no. 124 (January, 1958) and "War and Murder (in the Wasserstrom collection and in this volume, Chapter 19). I am also presupposing a familiarity with Jonathan Bennett's "Whatever the Consequences," *Analysis* 26, no. 3 (January, 1966).

1. "Murder," writes Miss Anscombe, "is the deliberate killing of the innocent, whether for its own sake or as a means to some further end" ("War and Murder," Chapter 19). Deliberate killing of the innocent (or noncombatants) is prohibited by the just war theory and is a crime in international law. A traditional account of the Catholic just war theory may be found in Chapter 35 of Austin Fagothey's *Right and Reason: Ethics in Theory and Practice* (St. Louis: C. V. Mosby Co., 1963). A useful sourcebook for inquiry into the nature of war crimes is the anthology *Crimes of War,* ed. Richard A. Falk, Gabriel Kolko, and Robert Jay Lifton (New York: Random House, 1971).

2. By "prima facie wrong" I mean "can be overridden by other moral requirements"—not, as a literal translation might suggest, "only apparently wrong."

3. For example: In the criminal offense of statutory rape, the defendant is strictly liable with respect to his knowledge of the age of a girl with whom he has had sexual relations, i.e. no matter how carefully he inquired into her age, no matter how reasonable (i.e. nonnegligent) his belief that she was of legal age of consent, he is liable if his belief is in fact mistaken. For a general discussion of such offenses, see Richard Wasserstrom's "Strict Liability in the Criminal Law," *Stanford Law Review* 12 (July 1960).

4. In discussion, Richard Wasserstrom has expressed scepticism concerning my claim that there is something unintelligible about the concept of strict moral responsibility. One could regard the Old Testament and *Oedipus Rex* as containing a strict liability conception of morality. Now I should be inclined to argue that the primitiveness of the Old Testament and of *Oedipus Rex* consists in these peoples not yet being able to draw a distinction between legality and morality. However, I am prepared to admit that it might be better to weaken my claim by maintaining simply that no *civilized* or enlightened morality would involve strict liability.

5. In California criminal law, vehicular manslaughter is defined as vehicular homocide "in the commission of an unlawful act, not amounting to felony, with gross negligence; or in the commission of a lawful act which might produce death, in an unlawful manner, and with gross negligence." (*California Penal Code,* 192, 3, a).

6. For an excellent discussion of moral and legal responsibility for negligence, see H.L.A. Hart's "Negligence, *Mens Rea* and Criminal Responsibility," in his *Punishment and Responsibility: Essays in the Philosophy of Law* (Oxford: Oxford University Press, 1963).

7. I say "engaged in an attempt" rather than "attempting" for the following reason: A mortar attack on an encampment of combat soldiers who happen to be sleeping is surely not a case of killing noncombatants even though persons who are asleep cannot be attempting anything. Sleeping persons can, however, be engaged in an attempt—just as sleeping persons can be accomplices in crime and parties to a criminal conspiracy. Being engaged in an attempt, unlike attempting, is not necessarily a full time job. I am grateful to Anthony Woozley for pointing this out to me.

8. Thomas Nagel, "War and Massacre," Chapter 23. Richard Brandt replies to Nagel in "Utilitarianism and the Rules of War," *Philosophy and Public Affairs* 2 (Winter, 1972). I am grateful to Professors Nagel and Brandt for allowing me to read their articles prior to publication.

9. For reasons of simplicity in later drawing upon important and instructive principles from the criminal law, I shall use the phrase "self-defense." (I shall later want to draw on the notion of *reasonable belief* in the law of self-defense.) However, what I really want to focus on is the concept of "defense" and not the concept of "self." For it seems to me that war can be justified, not just to defend oneself or one's nation, but also to defend others from threats that transcend nationality, e.g. genocide. If one wants to speak of self-defense even here, then it must be regarded as self-defense for the human, not just national, community. The phrase "self-defense" as it occurs in what follows should always be understood as carrying this qualification. And, of course, even clear cases of self-defense are not always necessarily justified. Given the morally debased character of Nazi Germany, it is by no means obvious that it acted rightly in trying to defend itself near the end of World War II (i.e. after it had ceased to be an aggressor).

10. Remember that this carries the qualification stated in note 9. For a survey of the law of self-defense, the reader may consult any reliable treatise on the criminal law, e.g. pp. 883 ff. of Rollin M. Perkin's *Criminal Law* (Brooklyn, N.Y.: Foundation Press, 1957). The criminal law is a highly moralized institution, and it is useful (though by no means always definitive) for the moral philosopher in that it provides an accumulated and systematized body of reflection on vital moral matters of our culture. For my purposes, I shall in what follows focus upon the *reasonable belief* condition in the law of self-defense. Other aspects of the law of self-defense

(e.g. the so-called "retreat requirement") have, I think, interesting implications for war that I cannot pursue here.

11. "Modern Moral Philosophy," p. 17. For reasons I shall note later, Miss Anscombe weakens her point by adding the word "judicial."

12. See William H. Gass, "The Case of the Obliging Stranger," *Philosophical Review* 66 (April, 1957).

13. John Rawls, "Two Concepts of Rules," *Philosophical Review* 64 (January, 1955).

14. See, for example, *United States* v. *Falcone*, United States Court of Appeals, Second Circuit, 1940, 109 F.2d 579.

15. Consider the case of the homicidal diabetic: He is chasing you through the woods of an enclosed game preserve, attempting to kill you for sport with a pistol. However, because of his medical condition, he must return to a cabin in the middle of the preserve every hour in order that his aged mother can give him an insulin shot. Without it, he will take ill or die and will thus be forced to abandon his attempt to kill you. Even if blocking that insulin shot seems your only hope, killing the mother in order to do it would be a very doubtful case of self-defense.

16. Austin Fagothey, in his well-known statement of the just war theory cited previously, allows injury to national honor to count as a ground for a war of self-defense. I cite Fagothey's book because of its influence. It was, for example, appealed to by Justice Douglas in the 1971 *Gillette* case, a case where the defendant refused induction on the grounds of his belief that the Vietnam War is unjust (*Gillette* v. *United States*, 401 U.S. 437).

17. Anscombe, "Modern Moral Philosophy."

18. Another factor, relevant both to war and to the highway example, is the following: acting with the knowledge that deaths could be prevented by taking reasonable precautions and yet not taking those precautions. Such grossly negligent or reckless behavior, while perhaps not "deliberate" in the strict sense, is surely immoral in either context.

19. See Michael Walzer, "World War II: Why Was This War Different?," *Philosophy and Public Affairs* 1, no. 1 (Fall, 1971).

20. As the citizens of London and Hanoi have illustrated, for example, terror bombing has a tendency to backfire. Rather than demoralizing the enemy, it sometimes strengthens their courage and will to resist.

21. Jonathan Bennett, "Whatever the Consequences," *Analysis* 26, no. 3 (January, 1966).

22. I take it that, from a moral point of view, their being German babies is irrelevant. As Howard Zinn has argued, we should accept the principle that "all victims are created equal" (*Disobedience and Democracy: Nine Fallacies on Law and Order* [New York: Random House, 1968], p. 50).

23. Ibid., p. 40.

24. One important metaethical inquiry that has been conducted in recent years concerns the nature of moral judgments and the moral point of view or "language game." The task here is to distinguish the moral from the nonmoral or amoral. Normative ethics, on the other hand, is concerned to distinguish the moral from the immoral. This is too large a dispute to enter here, but I can at least make my own commitments clear. Unlike the so-called "formalists" (e.g. R. M. Hare, *The Language of Morals* [Oxford: Oxford University Press, 1952]), I am inclined to believe that the moral point of view must be defined, in part, in terms of the *content of* the judgments it contains. Here I am siding, if I understand them correctly, with such writers as H.L.A. Hart (*The Concept of Law* [Oxford: Oxford University Press, 1952]), and G. J. Warnock (*The Object of Morality* [London: Methuen, 1971]). Someone who does not see that "*A* is a case of killing an innocent" is a relevant reason against doing *A*, does not understand what moral discourse is all about, what it is necessarily concerned with. And this is so no matter how much he is prepared to universalize and regard as overriding his own idiosyncratic imperatives. If this is true, then the gulf between metaethics and normative ethics is not quite as wide as many have supposed, since the relevance of certain substantive judgments is now going to be regarded as part of the meaning of morality as a point of view, language game, or form of life. There still is some gulf between metaethics and normative ethics, however, since I should argue that only the *relevance,* and not the *decisiveness,* of certain substantive judgments (e.g. do not kill the innocent) can be regarded as a defining feature of the moral point of view. Normative ethics, however, is primarily interested in which of the relevant moral considerations are, in certain circumstances, decisive. (I am grateful to Ronald Milo for discussing these matters with me. He is totally responsible for whatever clarity is to be found in my views.)

25. Though I shall not explore it here, I think that the religious acceptance of the principle could be elaborated as a way of thinking and so distinguished from the authoritarianism and dogmatism that Bennett so rightly condemns. The view I shall develop also has implications (though I shall not draw them out here) for the abortion issue. For more on this, see Philippa Foot's "Abortion and the Doctrine of the Double Effect," *Oxford Review* (1967). This has been reprinted in *Moral Problems: A Collection of Philosophical Essays,* ed. James Rachels (New York: Harper & Row, 1971) and in my *An Introduction to Moral and Social Philosophy: Basic Readings in Theory and Practice* (Belmont, Calif.: Wadsworth Publishing Co., 1973). She sees the doctrine of the double effect as groping in a confused way toward an insight of moral importance: "There is

worked into our moral system a distinction between what we owe people in the form of aid and what we owe them in the way of noninterference."

26. These well-known examples are drawn from Kant's *Foundations of the Metaphysics of Morals,* trans. Lewis White Beck (Indianapolis: Bobbs-Merrill Co., 1959), pp. 39 ff.; pp. 421 ff. of the Academy edition of Kant's works. Kant distinguishes perfect duties (duties of respect) and imperfect duties (duties of love) in many places. See, for example, *The Doctrine of Virtue,* trans. Mary J. Gregor (New York: Harper & Row, 1964), pp. 134-35; p. 463 of the Academy edition.

27. Kant, *Metaphysical Elements of Justice,* trans. John Ladd (Indianapolis: Bobbs-Merrill Co., 1965), pp. 35 ff.; pp. 230 ff. of the Academy edition. See also pp. 94 ff. and 107-9 of my *Kant: The Philosophy of Right* (New York: St. Martin's Press, 1970).

28. Someone (e.g. Jan Narveson in his "Pacifism: A Philosophical Analysis," *Ethics* 75 [1965]) might say the following: If what you value are the *rights* of people, does this not entail (as a part of what it means to say that one values something) that you would recognize an obligation to take steps to secure those rights against interference? Perhaps. But "take steps" does not have to mean "do whatever is causally necessary." Such an obligation will presumably be limited by (a) what I can reasonably be expected to do or sacrifice and (b) my moral judgment about the permissibility of the *means* employed. It does seem perverse for a person to say "I value the rights of people above all else but I do not propose to secure those rights." However, it by no means seems to me equally perverse to say the following: "I deplore interferences with human rights above all else and I will do anything in my power to prevent such interferences—everything, of course, short of being guilty of such interferences myself."

29. See Brian Barry, "Justice and the Common Good," *Analysis* 21-22 (1960-61). Though the existentialists tend to overdo this sort of claim, there is truth in their claim that there are certain moral problems that are in principle *undecidable* by any rational decision procedure. Such cases are not perhaps as numerous as the existentialists would have us believe, but they do arise, e.g. when candidates for ultimate moral principles conflict. In such cases, we find it impossible to nail down with solid arguments those principles which matter to us the most. Perhaps this even deserves to be called "absurd." In his article "The Absurd" (*Journal of Philosophy* 68, no. 20 [October 21, 1971]), Thomas Nagel suggests that absurdity in human life is found in "the collision between the seriousness with which we take our lives and the perpetual possibility of regarding everything

about which we are serious as arbitrary, or open to doubt." It is here that talk about faith or commitment seems to have some life.

30. James Dickey, "The Firebombing," in *Poems 1957-1967* Middletown, Conn.: Wesleyan University Press, 1967), p. 185. Reprinted with the permission of the publisher.

23

War and Massacre

Thomas Nagel

Thomas Nagel believes that no human being is ever, under any circumstances, justified in murdering or torturing another. In the following article, Nagel claims that this moral datum provides an objective basis for rules of war, while no conventionalist or utilitarian theory can account for morally justifiable rules of war. The limitations on war which Nagel believes justifiable are of two types: those which limit the legitimate targets of hostility and those which limit its character, even when the target is acceptable.

—J. P.

From the apathetic reaction to atrocities committed in Vietnam by the United States and its allies, one may conclude that moral restrictions on the conduct of war command almost as little sympathy among the general public as they do among those charged with the formation of U.S. military policy. Even when restrictions on the conduct of warfare are defended, it is usually on legal grounds alone: their moral basis is often poorly understood. I wish to argue that certain restrictions are neither arbitrary nor merely conventional, and that their validity does not depend simply on their usefulness. There is, in other words, a moral basis for the rules of war, even though the conventions now officially in force are far from giving it perfect expression.

From *Philosophy and Public Affairs* 1, no. 2 (copyright © 1972 by Princeton University Press). Reprinted by permission.

I

No elaborate moral theory is required to account for what is wrong in cases like the Mylai massacre, since it did not serve, and was not intended to serve, any strategic purpose. Moreover, if the participation of the United States in the Indo-Chinese war is entirely wrong to begin with, then that engagement is incapable of providing a justification for *any* measures taken in its pursuit—not only for the measures which are atrocities in every war, however just its aims.

But this war has revealed attitudes of a more general kind, that influenced the conduct of earlier wars as well. After it has ended, we shall still be faced with the problem of how warfare may be conducted, and the attitudes that have resulted in the specific conduct of this war will not have disappeared. Moreover, similar problems can arise in wars or rebellions fought for very different reasons, and against very different opponents. It is not easy to keep a firm grip on the idea of what is not permissible in warfare, because while some military actions are obvious atrocities, other cases are more difficult to assess, and the general principles underlying these judgments remain obscure. Such obscurity can lead to the abandonment of sound intuitions in favor of criteria whose rationale may be more obvious. If such a tendency is to be resisted, it will require a better understanding of the restrictions than we now have.

I propose to discuss the most general moral problem raised by the conduct of warfare: the problem of means and ends. In one view, there are limits on what may be done even in the service of an end worth pursuing—and even when adherence to the restriction may be very costly. A person who acknowledges the force of such restrictions can find himself in acute moral dilemmas. He may believe, for example, that by torturing a prisoner he can obtain information necessary to prevent a disaster, or that by obliterating one village with bombs he can halt a campaign of terrorism. If he believes that the gains from a certain measure will clearly outwiegh its costs, yet still suspects that he ought not to adopt it, then he is in a dilemma produced by the conflict between two disparate categories of moral reason: categories that may be called *utilitarian* and *absolutist*.

Utilitarianism gives primacy to a concern with what will *happen*. Absolutism gives primacy to a concern with what one is *doing*. The conflict between them arises because the alternatives we face are rarely just choices between *total outcomes:* they are also choices between alternative pathways or measures to be taken. When one of the choices is to do terrible things to another person, the problem is altered fundamentally; it is no longer merely a question of which outcome would be worse.

Few of us are completely immune to either of these types of moral intuition, though in some people, either naturally or for doctrinal reasons, one type will be dominant and the other suppressed or weak. But it is perfectly possible to feel the force of both types of reason very strongly; in that case the moral dilemma in certain situations of crisis will be acute, and it may appear that every possible course of action or inaction is unacceptable for one reason or another.

II

Although it is this dilemma that I propose to explore, most of the discussion will be devoted to its absolutist component. The utilitarian component is straightforward by comparison, and has a natural appeal to anyone who is not a complete skeptic about ethics. Utilitarianism says that one should try, either individually or through institutions, to maximize good and minimize evil (the definition of these categories need not enter into the schematic formulation of the view), and that if faced with the possibility of preventing a great evil by producing a lesser, one should choose the lesser evil. There are certainly problems about the formulation of utilitarianism, and much has been written about it, but its intent is morally transparent. Nevertheless, despite the addition of various refinements, it continues to leave large portions of ethics unaccounted for. I do not suggest that some form of absolutism can account for them all, only that an examination of absolutism will lead us to see the complexity, and perhaps the incoherence, of our moral ideas.

Utilitarianism certainly justifies *some* restrictions on the conduct of warfare. There are strong utilitarian reasons for adhering to any limitation which seems natural to most people—particularly if the limitation is widely accepted already. An exceptional measure which seems to be justified by its results in a particular conflict may create a precedent with disastrous long-term effects.[1] It may even be argued that war involves violence on such a scale that it is never justified on utilitarian grounds—the consequences of refusing to go to war will never be as bad as the war itself would be, even if atrocities were not committed. Or in a more sophisticated vein it might be claimed that a uniform policy of never resorting to military force would do less harm in the long run, if followed consistently, than a policy of deciding each case on utilitarian grounds (even though on occasion particular applications of the pacifist policy might have worse results than a specific utilitarian decision). But I shall not consider these arguments, for my concern is with reasons of a different kind, which may remain when reasons of utility and interest fail.[2]

In the final analysis, I believe that the dilemma cannot always be resolved. While not every conflict between absolutism and utilitarianism creates an insoluble dilemma, and while it is certainly right to adhere to absolutist restrictions unless the utilitarian considerations favoring violation are overpoweringly weighty and extremely certain—nevertheless, when that special condition is met, it may become impossible to adhere to an absolutist position. What I shall offer, therefore, is a somewhat qualified defense of absolutism. I believe it underlies a valid and fundamental type of moral judgment—which cannot be reduced to or overridden by other principles. And while there may be other principles just as fundamental, it is particularly important not to lose confidence in our absolutist intuitions, for they are often the only barrier before the abyss of utilitarian apologetics for large-scale murder.

III

One absolutist position that creates no problems of interpretation is pacifism: the view that one may not kill another person under any circumstances, no matter what good would be achieved or evil averted thereby. The type of absolutist position that I am going to discuss is different. Pacifism draws the conflict with utilitarian considerations very starkly. But there are other views according to which violence may be undertaken, even on a large scale, in a clearly just cause, so long as certain absolute restrictions on the character and direction of that violence are observed. The line is drawn somewhat closer to the bone, but it exists.

The philosopher who has done most to advance contemporary philosophical discussion of such a view, and to explain it to those unfamiliar with its extensive treatment in Roman Catholic moral theology, is G.E.M. Anscombe. In 1958 Miss Anscombe published a pamphlet entitled *Mr. Truman's Degree*,[3] on the occasion of the award by Oxford University of an honorary doctorate to Harry Truman. The pamphlet explained why she had opposed the decision to award that degree, recounted the story of her unsuccessful opposition, and offered some reflections on the history of Truman's decision to drop atom bombs on Hiroshima and Nagasaki, and on the difference between murder and allowable killing in warfare. She pointed out that the policy of deliberately killing large numbers of civilians either as a means or as an end in itself did not originate with Truman, and was common practice among all parties during World War II for some time before Hiroshima. The Allied area bombings of German cities by conventional explosives included raids which killed more civilians than did the atomic attacks; the same is true of certain fire-bomb raids on Japan.

The policy of attacking the civilian population in order to induce an enemy to surrender, or to damage his morale, seems to have been widely accepted in the civilized world, and seems to be accepted still, at least if the stakes are high enough. It gives evidence of a moral conviction that the deliberate killing of noncombatants—women, children, old people—is permissible if enough can be gained by it. This follows from the more general position that any means can in principle be justified if it leads to a sufficiently worthy end. Such an attitude is evident not only in the more spectacular current weapons systems but also in the day-to-day conduct of the nonglobal war in Indochina: the indiscriminate destructiveness of antipersonnel weapons, napalm, and aerial bombardment; cruelty to prisoners; massive relocation of civilians; destruction of crops, and so forth. An absolutist position opposes to this the view that certain acts cannot be justified no matter what the consequences. Among those acts is murder—the deliberate killing of the harmless: civilians, prisoners of war, and medical personnel.

In the present war such measures are sometimes said to be regrettable, but they are generally defended by reference to military necessity and the importance of the long-term consequences of success or failure in the war. I shall pass over the inadequacy of this consequentialist defense in its own terms. (That is the dominant form of moral criticism of the war, for it is part of what people mean when they ask, "Is it worth it?") I am concerned rather to account for the inappropriateness of offering any defense of that kind for such actions.

Many people feel, without being able to say much more about it, that something has gone seriously wrong when certain measures are admitted into consideration in the first place. The fundamental mistake is made there, rather than at the point where the overall benefit of some monstrous measure is judged to outweigh its advantages, and it is adopted. An account of absolutism might help us to understand this. If it is not allowable to *do* certain things, such as killing unarmed prisoners or civilians, then no argument about what will happen if one doesn't do them can show that doing them would be all right.

Absolutism does not, of course, require one to ignore the consequences of one's acts. It operates as a limitation on utilitarian reasoning, not as a substitute for it. An absolutist can be expected to try to maximize good and minimize evil, so long as this does not require him to transgress an absolute prohibition like that against murder. But when such a conflict occurs, the prohibition takes complete precedence over any consideration of consequences. Some of the results of this view are clear enough. It requires us to forgo certain potentially useful military measures, such as the slaughter of hostages and prisoners or indiscrimate attempts to reduce the enemy civilian population by starvation, epidemic infectious diseases like anthrax and bubonic plague, or mass incineration. It means that we cannot deliberate on whether such measures are justified by the fact that they will avert still greater evils, for as intentional measures they cannot be justified in terms of any consequences whatever.

Someone unfamiliar with the events of this century might imagine that utilitarian arguments, or arguments of national interest, would suffice to deter measures of this sort. But it has become evident that such considerations are insufficient to prevent the adoption and employment of enormous antipopulation weapons once their use is considered a serious moral possibility. The same is true of the piecemeal wiping out of rural civilian populations in airborne antiguerrilla warfare. Once the door is opened to calculations of utility and national interest, the usual speculations about the future of freedom, peace, and economic prosperity can be brought to bear to ease the consciences of those responsible for a certain number of charred babies.

For this reason alone it is important to decide what is wrong with the frame of mind which allows such arguments to begin. But it is also important to understand absolutism in the cases where it genuinely conflicts with utility. Despite its appeal, it is a paradoxical position, for it can require that one refrain from choosing the lesser of two evils when that is the only choice one has. And it is additionally paradoxical because, unlike pacifism, it permits one to do horrible things to people in some circumstances but not in others.

IV

Before going on to say what, if anything, lies behind the position, there remain a few relatively technical matters which are best discussed at this point.

First, it is important to specify as clearly as possible the kind of thing to which absolutist prohibitions can apply. We must take seriously the proviso that they concern what we deliberately do to people. There could not, for example, without incoherence, be an absolute prohibition against *bringing about* the death of an innocent person. For one may find oneself in a situation in which, no matter what one does, some innocent people will die as a result. I do not mean just that there are cases in which someone will die no matter what one does, because one is not in a position to affect the outcome one way or the other. That, it is to be hoped, is one's relation to the deaths of most innocent people. I have in mind, rather, a case in which someone is bound to die, but who it is will depend on what one does. Sometimes these situations have natural causes, as when too few resources (medicine, lifeboats) are available to rescue everyone threatened with a certain catastrophe. Sometimes the situations are man-made, as when the only way to control a campaign of terrorism is to employ terrorist tactics against the community from which it has arisen. Whatever one does in cases such as these, some innocent people will die as a result. If the absolutist prohibition forbade doing what would result in the deaths of innocent people, it would have the consequence that in such cases nothing one could do would be morally permissible.

The problem is avoided, however, because what absolutism forbids is *doing* certain things to people, rather than bringing about certain *results*. Not everything that happens to others as a result of what one does is something that one has done to them. Catholic moral theology seeks to make this distinction precise in a doctrine known as the law of double effect, which asserts that there is a morally relevant distinction between bringing about the death of an innocent person deliberately, either as an end in itself or as a means, and bringing it about as a side effect of something else one does deliberately. In the latter case, even if the outcome is foreseen, it is not murder, and does not fall under the absolute prohibition, though of course it may still be wrong for other reasons (reasons of utility, for example). Briefly, the principle states that one is sometimes permitted knowingly to bring about as a side effect of one's actions something which it would be absolutely impermissible to bring about deliberately as an end or as a means. In application to war or revolution, the law of double effect permits a certain amount of civilian carnage as a side effect of bombing munitions plants or attacking enemy soldiers. And even this is permissible only if the cost is not too great to be justified by one's objectives.

However, despite its importance and its usefulness in accounting for certain plausible moral judgments, I do not believe that the law of double effect is a generally applicable test for the consequences of an absolutist position. Its own application is not always clear, so that it introduces uncertainty where there need not be uncertainty.

In Indochina, for example, there is a great deal of aerial bombardment, strafing, spraying of napalm, and employment of pellet- or needle-spraying antipersonnel weapons against rural villages in which guerrillas are suspected to be hiding, or from which small arms fire has been received. The majority of those killed and wounded in these aerial attacks are reported to be women and children, even when some combatants are caught as well. However, the government regards these civilian casualties as a regrettable side effect of what is a legitimate attack against an armed enemy.

It might be thought easy to dismiss this as sophistry: if one bombs, burns, or strafes a village containing a hundred people, twenty of whom one believes to be guerrillas, so that by killing most of them one will statistically be likely to kill most of the guerrillas, then isn't one's attack on the group of one hundred a *means* of destroying the guerrillas, pure and simple? If one makes no attempt to discriminate between guerrillas and civilians, as is impossible in an aerial attack on a small village, then one cannot regard as a mere side effect the deaths of those in the group that one would not have bothered to kill if more selective means had been available.

The difficulty is that this argument depends on one particular description of the act, and the reply might be that the means used against the guerrillas is not killing everybody in the village—but rather: obliteration bombing of the *area* in which the twenty guerrillas are known to be located. If there are civilians in the area as well, they will be killed as a side effect of such action.[4]

Because of casuistical problems like this, I prefer to stay with the original, unanalyzed distinction between what one does to people and what merely happens to them as a result of what one does. The law of double effect provides an approximation to that distinction in many cases, and perhaps it can be sharpened to the point where it does better than that. Certainly the original distinction itself needs clarification, particularly since some of the things we do to people involve things happening to them as a result of other things we do. In a case like the one discussed, however, it is clear that by bombing the village one slaughters and maims the civilians in it. Whereas by giving the only available medicine to one of two sufferers from a disease, one does not kill the other, even if he dies as a result.

The second technical point to take up concerns a possible misinterpretation of this feature of the position. The absolutist focus on actions rather than outcomes does not merely introduce a new, outstanding item into the catalogue of evils. That is, it does not say that the worst thing in the world is the deliberate murder of an innocent person. For if that were all, then one could presumably justify one such murder on the ground that it would prevent a hundred thousand more. That is a familiar argument. But if this is allowable, then there is no absolute prohibition against murder after all. Absolutism requires that we *avoid* murder at all costs, not that we *prevent* it at all costs.[5]

Finally, let me remark on a frequent criticism of absolutism that depends on a misunderstanding. It is sometimes suggested that such prohibitions depend on a kind of moral self-interest, a primary obligation to preserve one's own moral purity, to keep one's hands clean no matter what happens to the rest of the world. If this were the position, it might be exposed to the charge of self-indulgence. After all, what gives one man a right to put the purity of his soul or the cleanness of his hands above the lives or welfare of large numbers of other people? It might be argued that a public servant like Truman has no right to put himself first in that way; therefore if he is convinced that the alternatives would be worse, he must give the order to drop the bombs, and take the burden of those deaths on himself, as he must do other distasteful things for the general good.

But there are two confusions behind the view that moral self-interest underlies moral absolutism. First, it is a confusion to suggest that the need to preserve one's moral purity might be the *source* of an obligation. For if by committing murder one sacrifices one's moral purity or integrity, that can only be because there is already something wrong with murder. The general reason against committing murder cannot therefore be merely that it makes one an immoral person. Secondly, the notion that one might sacrifice one's moral integrity justifiably, in the service of a sufficiently worthy end, is an incoherent notion. For if one were justified in making such a sacrifice (or even morally required to make it), then one would not be sacrificing one's moral integrity by adopting that course: one would be preserving it.

Moral absolutism is not unique among moral theories in requiring each person to do what will preserve his own moral purity in all circumstances. This is equally true of utilitarianism, or of any other theory which distinguishes between right and wrong. Any theory which defines the right course of action in various circumstances and asserts that one should adopt that course, ipso facto asserts that one should do what will preserve one's moral purity, simply because the right course of action *is* what will preserve one's moral purity in those circumstances. Of course utilitarianism does not assert that this is *why* one should adopt that course, but we have seen that the same is true of absolutism.

V

It is easier to dispose of false explanations of absolutism than to produce a true one. A positive account of the matter must begin with the observation that war, conflict, and aggression are relations between persons. The view that it can be wrong to consider merely the overall effect of one's actions on the general welfare comes into prominence when those actions involve relations with others. A man's acts usually affect more people than he deals with directly, and those effects must naturally be considered in his decisions. But if there are special principles governing the manner in which he should treat people, that will require special attention to the particular persons toward whom the act is directed, rather than just to its total effect.

Absolutist restrictions in warfare appear to be of two types: restrictions on the class of persons at whom aggression or violence may be directed and restrictions on the manner of attack, given that the object falls within that class. These can be combined, however, under the principle that hostile treatment of any person must be justified in terms of something *about that person* which makes the treatment appropriate. Hostility is a personal relation, and it must be suited to its target. One consequence of this condition will be that certain persons may not be subjected to hostile treatment in war at all, since nothing about them justifies such treatment. Others will be proper objects of hostility only in certain circumstances, or when they are engaged in certain pursuits. And the appropriate manner and extent of hostile treatment will depend on what is justified by the particular case.

A coherent view of this type will hold that extremely hostile behavior toward another is compatible with treating him as a person—even perhaps as an end in himself. This is possible only if one has not automatically stopped treating him as a person as soon as one starts to fight with him. If hostile, aggressive, or combative treatment of others always violated the condition that they be treated as human beings, it would be difficult to make further distinctions on that score *within* the class of hostile actions. That point of view, on the level of international relations, leads to the position that if complete pacifism is not accepted, no holds need be barred at all, and we may slaughter and massacre to our heart's content, if it seems advisable. Such a position is often expressed in discussions of war crimes.

But the fact is that ordinary people do not believe this about conflicts, physical or otherwise, between individuals, and there is no more reason why it should be true of conflicts between nations. There seems to be a perfectly natural conception of the distinction between fighting clean and fighting dirty. To fight dirty is to direct one's hostility or aggression not at its proper object, but at a peripheral target which may be more vulnerable, and through which the proper object can be attacked indirectly. This applies in a fist fight, an election campaign, a duel, or a philosophical argument. If the concept is general enough to apply to all these matters, it should apply to war—both to the conduct of individual soldiers and to the conduct of nations.

Suppose that you are a candidate for public office, convinced that the election of your opponent would be a disaster, that he is an unscrupulous demagogue who will serve a narrow range of interests and seriously infringe the rights of those who disagree with him; and suppose you are convinced that you cannot defeat him by conventional means. Now imagine that various unconventional means present themselves as possibilities: you possess information about his sex life which would scandalize the electorate if made public; or you learn that his wife is an alcoholic or that in his youth he was associated for a brief period with a proscribed political party, and you believe that this information could be used to blackmail him into withdrawing his candidacy; or you can have a team of your supporters flatten the tires of a crucial subset of his supporters on election day; or you are in a position to stuff the ballot boxes; or, more simply, you can have him assassinated. What is wrong with these methods, given that they will achieve an overwhelmingly desirable result?

There are, of course, many things wrong with them: some are against the law; some infringe on the procedures of an electoral process to which you are presumably committed by taking part in it, very importantly, some may backfire, and it is in the interest of all political candidates to adhere to an unspoken agreement not to allow certain personal matters to intrude into a campaign. But that is not all. We have in addition the feeling that these measures, these methods of attack are *irrelevant* to the issue between you and your opponent, that in taking them up you would not be directing yourself to that which makes him an object of your opposition. You would be directing your attack not at the true target of your hostility, but at peripheral targets that happen to be vulnerable.

The same is true of a fight or argument outside the framework of any system of regulations or law. In an altercation with a taxi driver over an excessive fare, it is inappropriate to taunt him about his accent, flatten one of his tires, or smear chewing gum on his windshield; and it remains inappropriate even if he casts aspersions on your race, politics, or religion, or dumps the contents of your suitcase into the street.[6]

The importance of such restrictions may vary with the seriousness of the case; and what is unjustifiable in one case may be justified in a more extreme one. But they all derive from a single principle: that hostility or aggression should be directed at its true object. This means both that it should be directed at the person or persons who provoke it and that it should aim more specifically at what is provocative about them. The second condition will determine what form the hostility may appropriately take.

It is evident that some idea of the relation in which one should stand to other people underlies this principle, but the idea is difficult to state. I believe it is roughly this: whatever one does to another person intentionally must be aimed at him as a subject, with the intention that he receives it as a subject. It should manifest an attitude to him rather than just to the situation, and he should be able to recognize it and identify himself as its object. The procedures by which such an attitude is manifested need not be addressed to the person directly. Surgery, for example, is not a form of personal confrontation but part of a medical treatment that can be offered to a patient face to face and received by him as a response to his needs and the natural outcome of an attitude toward him.

Hostile treatment, unlike surgery, is already addressed to a person, and does not take its interpersonal meaning from a wider context. But hostile acts can serve as the expression or implementation of only a limited range of attitudes to the person who is attacked. Those attitudes in turn have as objects certain real or presumed characteristics or activities of the person which are thought to justify them. When this background is absent, hostile or aggressive behavior can no longer be intended for the reception of the victim as a subject. Instead it takes on the character of a purely bureaucratic operation. This occurs when one attacks someone who is not the true object of one's hostility—the true object may be someone else, who can be attacked through the victim; or one may not be manifesting a hostile attitude toward anyone, but merely using the easiest available path to some desired goal. One finds oneself not facing or addressing the victim at all, but operating on him—without the larger context of personal interaction that surrounds a surgical operation.

If absolutism is to defend its claim to priority over considerations of utility, it must hold that the maintenance of a direct interpersonal response to the people one deals with is a requirement which no advantages can justify one in abandoning. The requirement is absolute only if it rules out any calculation of what would justify its violation. I have said earlier that there may be circumstances so extreme that they render an absolutist position untenable. One may find then that one has no choice but to do something terrible. Nevertheless, even in such cases absolutism retains its force in that one cannot claim *justification* for the violation. It does not become *all right*.

As a tentative effort to explain this, let me try to connect absolutist limitations with the possibility of justifying *to the victim* what is being done to him. If one abandons a person in the course of rescuing several others from a fire or a sinking ship, one *could* say to him, "You understand, I have to leave you to save the others." Similarly, if one subjects an unwilling child to a painful surgical procedure, one can say to him, "If you could understand, you would realize that I am doing this to help you." One could *even* say, as one bayonets an enemy soldier, "It's either you or me." But one cannot really say while torturing a prisoner, "You understand. I have to pull out your fingernails because it is absolutely essential that we have the names of your confederates" nor can one say to the victims of Hiroshima, "You understand, we have to incinerate you to provide the Japanese government with an incentive to surrender."

This does not take us very far, of course, since a utilitarian world would presumably be willing to offer justifications of the latter sort to his victims, in cases where he thought they were sufficient. They are really justifications to the world at large, which the victim, as a reasonable man, would be expected to appreciate. However, there seems to me something wrong with this view, for it ignores the possibility that to treat someone else horribly puts you in a special relation to him, which may have to be defended in terms of other features of your relation to him. The suggestion needs much more development; but it may help us to understand how there may be requirements which are absolute in the sense that there can be no justification for violating them. If the justification for what one did to another person had to be such that it could be offered to him specifically, rather than just to the world at large, that would be a significant source of restraint.

If the account is to be deepened, I would hope for some results along the following lines. Absolutism is associated with a view of oneself as a small being interacting with others in a large world. The justifications it requires are primarily interpersonal. Utilitarianism is associated with a view of oneself as a benevolent bureaucrat distributing such benefits as one can control to countless other beings, with whom one may have various relations or none. The justifications it requires are primarily administrative. The argument between the two moral attitudes may depend on the relative priority of these two conceptions.[7]

VI

Some of the restrictions on methods of warfare which have been adhered to from time to time are to be explained by the mutual interests of the involved parties: restrictions on weaponry, treatment of prisoners, etc. But that is not all there is to it. The conditions of directness and relevance which I have argued apply to relations of conflict and aggression apply to war as well. I have said that there are two types of absolutist restrictions on the conduct of war: those that limit the legitimate targets of hostility and those that limit its character, even when the target is acceptable. I shall say something about each of these. As will become clear, the principle I have sketched does not yield an unambiguous answer in every case.

First let us see how it implies that attacks on some people are allowed, but not attacks on others. It may seem paradoxical to assert that to fire a machine gun at someone who is throwing hand grenades at your emplacement is to treat him as a human being. Yet the relation with him is direct and straightforward.[8] The attack is aimed specifically against the threat presented by a dangerous adversary, and not against a peripheral target through which he happens to be vulnerable but which has nothing to do with that threat. For example, you might stop him by machine-gunning his wife and children, who are standing nearby, thus distracting him from his aim of blowing you up and enabling you to capture him. But if his wife and children are not threatening your life, that would be to treat them as means with a vengeance.

This, however, is just Hiroshima on a smaller scale. One objection to weapons of mass annihilation—nuclear, thermo-nuclear, biological, or chemical—is that their indiscriminateness disqualifies them as direct instruments for the expression of hostile relations. In attacking the civilian population, one treats neither the military enemy nor the civilians with that minimal respect which is owed to them as human beings. This is clearly true of the direct attack on people who present no threat at all. But it is also true of the character of the attack on those who *are* threatening you, viz., the government and military forces of the enemy. Your aggression is directed against an area of vulnerability quite distinct from any threat presented by them which you may be justified in meeting. You are taking aim at them through the mundane life and survival of their countrymen, instead of aiming at the destruction of their military capability. And of course it does not require hydrogen bombs to commit such crimes.

This way of looking at the matter also helps us to understand the importance of the distinction between combatants and non-combatants, and the irrelevance of much of the criticism offered against its intelligibility and moral significance. According to an absolutist position, deliberate killing of the innocent is murder, and in warfare the role of the innocent is filled by noncombatants. This has been thought to raise two sorts of problems: first, the widely imagined difficulty of making a division, in modern warfare, between combatants and noncombatants; second, problems deriving from the connotation of the word "innocence."

Let me take up the latter question first.[9] In the absolutist position, the operative notion of innocence is not moral innocence, and it is not opposed to moral guilt. If it were, then we would be justified in killing a wicked but noncombatant hairdresser in an enemy city who supported the evil policies of his government, and unjustified in killing a morally pure conscript who was driving a tank toward us with the profoundest regrets and nothing but love in his heart. But moral innocence has very little to do with it, for in the definition of murder "innocent" means "currently harmless," and it is opposed not to "guilty" but to "doing harm." It should be noted that such an analysis has the consequence that in war we may often be justified in killing people who do not deserve to die, and unjustified in killing people who do deserve to die, if anyone does.

So we must distinguish combatants from noncombatants on the basis of their immediate threat or harmfulness. I do not claim that the line is a sharp one, but it is not so difficult as is often supposed to place individuals on one side of it or the other. Children are not combatants even though they may join the armed forces if they are allowed to grow up. Women are not combatants just because they bear children or offer comfort to the soldiers. More problematic are the supporting personnel, whether in or out of uniform, from drivers of munitions trucks and army cooks to civilian munitions workers and farmers. I believe they can be plausibly classified by applying the condition that the prosecution of conflict must direct itself to the cause of danger, and not to what is peripheral. The threat presented by an army and its members does not consist merely in the fact that they are men, but in the fact that they are armed and are using their arms in the pursuit of certain objectives. Contributions to their arms and logistics are contributions to this threat; contributions to their mere existence as men are not. It is therefore wrong to direct an attack against those who merely serve the combatants' needs as human beings, such as farmers and food suppliers, even though survival as a human being is a necessary condition of efficient functioning as a soldier.

This brings us to the second group of restrictions: those that limit what may be done even to combatants. These limits are harder to explain clearly. Some of them may be arbitrary or conventional, and some may have to be derived from other sources; but I believe that the condition of directness and relevance in hostile relations accounts for them to a considerable extent.

Consider first a case which involves both a protected class of noncombatants and a restriction on the measures that may be used against combatants. One provision of the rules of war which is universally recognized, though it seems to be turning into a dead letter in Vietnam, is the special status of medical personnel and the wounded in warfare. It might be more efficient to shoot medical officers on sight and to let the enemy wounded die rather than be patched up to fight another day. But someone with medical insignia is supposed to be left alone and permitted to tend and retrieve the wounded. I believe this is because medical attention is a species of attention to completely general human needs, not specifically the needs of a combat soldier, and our conflict with the soldier is not with his existence as a human being.

By extending the application of this idea, one can justify prohibitions against certain particularly cruel weapons: starvation, poisoning, infectious diseases (supposing they could be inflicted on combatants only), weapons designed to maim or disfigure or torture the opponent rather than merely to stop him. It is not, I think, mere casuistry to claim that such weapons attack the men, not the soldiers. The effect of dum-dum bullets, for example, is much more extended than necesssary to cope with the combat situation in which they are used. They abandon any attempt to discriminate in their effects between the combatant and the human in all circumstances that I can imagine, whoever the target may be. Burns are both extremely painful and extremely disfiguring—far more than any other category of wound. That this well-known fact plays no (inhibiting) part in the determination of U.S. weapons policy suggests that moral sensitivity among public officials has not increased markedly since the Spanish Inquisition.[10]

Finally, the same condition of appropriateness to the true object of hostility should limit the scope of attacks on an enemy country: its economy, agriculture, transportation systems, and so forth. Even if the parties to a military conflict are considered to be not armies or governments but entire nations (which is usually a grave error), that does not justify one nation in warring against every aspect or element of another nation. That is not justified in a conflict between individuals, and nations are even more complex than individuals, so the same reasons apply. Like a human being, a nation is engaged in countless other pursuits while waging war, and it is not in those respects that it is an enemy.

The burden of the argument has been that absolutism about murder has a foundation in principles governing all one's relations to other persons, whether aggressive or amiable, and that these principles, and that absolutism, apply to warfare as well, with the result that certain measures are impermissible no matter what the consequences.[11] I do not mean to romanticize war. It is sufficiently utopian to suggest that when nations conflict they might rise to the level of limited barbarity that typically characterizes violent conflict between individuals, rather than wallowing in the moral pit where they appear to have settled, surrounded by enormous arsenals.

VII

Having described the elements of the absolutist position, we must now return to the conflict between it and utilitarianism. Even if certain types of dirty tactics become acceptable when the stakes are high enough, the most serious of the prohibited acts, like murder and torture, are not just supposed to require unusually strong justification. They are supposed *never* to be done, because no quantity of resulting benefit is thought capable of *justifying* such treatment of a person.

The fact remains that when an absolutist knows or believes that the utilitarian cost of refusing to adopt a prohibited course will be very high, he may hold to his refusal to adopt it, but he will find it difficult to feel that a moral dilemma has been satisfactorily resolved. The same may be true of someone who rejects an absolutist requirement and adopts instead the course yielding the most acceptable consequences. In either case, it is possible to feel that one has acted for reasons insufficient to justify violations of the opposing principle. In situations of deadly conflict, particularly where a weaker party is threatened with annihilation or enslavement by a stronger one, the argument for resorting to atrocities can be powerful, and the dilemma acute.

There may exist principles, not yet codified, which would enable us to resolve such dilemmas. But then again there may not. We must face the pessimistic alternative that these two forms of moral intuition are not capable of being brought together into a single, coherent moral system, and that the world can present us with situations in which there is no honorable or moral course for a man to take, no course free of guilt and responsibility for evil.

The idea of a moral blind alley is a perfectly intelligible one. It is possible to get into such a situation by one's own fault, and people do it all the time. If, for example, one makes two incompatible promises or commitments—becomes engaged to two people, for example—then there is no course one can take which is not wrong, for one must break one's promise to at least one of them. Making a clean breast of the whole thing will not be enough to remove one's reprehensibility. The existence of such cases is not morally disturbing, however, because we feel that the situation was not unavoidable: one had to do something wrong in the first place to get into it. But what if the world itself, or someone else's actions, could face a previously innocent person with a choice between morally abominable courses of action, and leave him no way to escape with his honor? Our intuitions rebel at the idea, for we feel that the constructibility of such a case must show a contradiction in our moral views. But it is not in itself a contradiction to say that someone can do X or not do X, and that for him to take either course would be wrong. It merely contradicts the supposition that *ought* implies *can*—since presumably one ought to refrain from what is wrong, and in such a case it is impossible to do so.[12] Given the limitations on human action, it is naive to suppose that there is a solution to every moral problem with which the world can face us. We have always known that the world is a bad place. It appears that it may be an evil place as well.

Notes

This paper grew out of discussions at the Society for Ethical and Legal Philosophy, and I am indebted to my fellow members for their help.

1. Straightforward considerations of national interest often tend in the same direction. the inadvisability of using nuclear weapons seems to be overdetermined in this way.

2. These reasons, moreover, have special importance in that they are available even to one who denies the appropriateness of utilitarian considerations in international matters. He may acknowledge limitations on what may be done to the soldiers and civilians of other countries in pursuit of his nation's military objectives, while denying that one country should in general consider the interests of nationals of other countries in determining its policies.

3. (Privately printed.) See also her essay "War and Murder," Chapter 19 in this volume. The present paper is much indebted to these two essays throughout. These and related subjects are extensively treated by Paul Ramsey in *The Just War* (New York, 1968). Among recent writings that bear on the moral problem are Jonathan Bennett, "Whatever the Consequences," *Analysis* 26, no. 3 (1966):83-102; and Philippa Foot, "The Problem of Abortion and the Doctrine of the Double Effect," *The Oxford Review* 5 (1967):5-15. Miss Anscombe's replies are "A Note on Mr. Bennett," *Analysis* 26, no. 3 (1966):208, and "Who is Wronged?" *The Oxford Review* 5 (1967):16-17.

4. This counterargument was suggested by Rogers Albritton.

5. Someone might of course acknowledge the *moral relevance* of the distinction between deliberate and nondeliberate killing, without being an absolutist. That is, he might believe simply that it was *worse* to bring about a death deliberately than as a secondary effect. But that would be merely a special assignment of value, and not an absolute prohibition.

6. Why, on the other hand, does it seem appropriate, rather than irrelevant, to punch someone in the mouth if he insults you? The answer is that in our culture it is an insult to punch someone in the mouth, and not just an injury. This reveals, by the way, a perfectly unobjectionable sense in which conviction may play a part in determining exactly what falls under an absolutist restriction and what does not. I am indebted to Robert Fogelin for this point.

7. Finally, I should mention a different possibility, suggested by Robert Nozick: that there is a strong general presumption against benefiting from the calamity of another, whether or not it has been deliberately inflicted for that or any other reason. This broader principle may well lend its force to the absolutist position.

8. It has been remarked that according to my view, shooting at someone establishes an I-thou relationship.

9. What I say on this subject derives from Anscombe.

10. Beyond this I feel uncertain. Ordinary bullets, after all, can cause death, and nothing is more permanent than that. I am not at all sure why we are justified in trying to kill those who are trying to kill us (rather than merely in trying to stop them with force which may also result in their deaths). It is often argued that incapacitating gases are a relatively humane weapon (when not used, as in Vietnam, merely to make people easier to shoot). Perhaps the legitimacy of restrictions against them must depend on the dangers of escalation, and the great utility of maintaining *any* conventional category of restriction so long as nations are willing to adhere to it.

Let me make clear that I do not regard my argument as a defense of the moral immutability of the Hague and Geneva Conventions. Rather, I believe that they rest partly on a moral foundation, and that modifications of them should also be assessed on moral grounds.

But even this connection with the actual laws of war is not essential to my claims about what is permissible and what is not. Since completing this paper I have read an essay by Richard Wasserstrom entitled "The Laws of War" [reprinted in this text] which argues that the existing laws and conventions do not even attempt to embody a decent moral position: that their provisions have been determined by other interests, that they are in fact immoral in substance, and that it is a grave mistake to refer to them as standards in forming moral judgments about warfare. This possibility deserves serious consideration, and I am not sure what to say about it, but it does not affect my view of the moral issues.

11. It is possible to draw a more radical conclusion, which I shall not pursue here. Perhaps the technology and organization of modern war are such as to make it impossible to wage as an acceptable form of interpersonal or even international hostility. Perhaps it is too impersonal and large-scale for that. If so, then absolutism would in practice imply pacifism, given the present state of things. On the other hand, I am skeptical about the unstated assumption that a technology dictates its own use.

12. This was first pointed out to me by Christopher Boorse.

24

Utilitarianism and the Rules of War

Richard B. Brandt

This paper was read following Thomas Nagel's "War and Massacre" (the previous reading in this anthology) at a symposium on the conduct of war. Whereas Nagel claimed that utilitarian theories cannot account for or justify rules of war, Richard Brandt attempts to show that a contractual rule utilitarian theory provides adequate justification for certain rules of war, especially those recognized by Department of the Army Field Manual PM 27-10, The Law of Land Warfare. *These rules are the ones that would maximize expected utility for the belligerents, with the restriction that each must be allowed the force necessary for victory.*

—J. P.

The topic of the present symposium is roughly the moral proscriptions and prescriptions that should govern the treatment by a belligerent, and in particular by its armed forces, of the nationals of an enemy, both combatants and noncombatants. In addressing myself to it, the central question I shall try to answer is: What, from a moral point of view, ought to be the rules of war? But this question, taken as an indication of what I shall be discussing, is both too broad and too narrow. Too broad because the rules of war include many topics like the rights and duties of neutral countries and the proprieties pertaining to an armistice. And too narrow because a full view of the topic requires me to consider, as I shall, such questions as: Is it ever morally right for a person to infringe "ideal" rules of war?

From *Philosophy and Public Affairs* 4, no. 2 (Winter 1975). Copyright © 1972 by Princeton University Press. Reproduced by permission.

I shall aim to illuminate our topic by discussing it from the point of view of a rule-utilitarianism of the "contractual" variety (to use a term employed by John Rawls in his book *A Theory of Justice*).[1] What this point of view is has of course to be explained, as do the special problems raised by the fact that the rules are to apply to nations at war. I believe it will become clear that the rule-utilitarian viewpoint is a very helpful one for thinking of rules of warfare, and I believe reflection on its implications will confirm us both in conclusions about certain normative rules and in a conviction that a contractual utilitarian view of such matters is essentially sound. Needless to say, I shall be led to express some disagreement with Professor Nagel.[2]

I shall take Nagel to be defending, first, the general view that certain kinds of action are, from a moral point of view, absolutely out of bounds, no matter what the circumstances; and second, a specific prohibition that applies this principle to the area of our interest. (His first thesis makes it proper to call his view "absolutist," in the sense that some general moral prohibitions do not have prima facie force only but are binding without exception, indefeasible.) Now Nagel is tentative in his espousal of these two theses, and sometimes contends only that we have some moral intuitions of this sort and that a study of these will show "the complexity, and perhaps the incoherence" of our moral ideas. Indeed, he says he is offering only a "somewhat qualified defense of absolutism," and concedes that in extreme circumstances there may be exceptions to his absolutist principles after all. Where Nagel is committed definitely is to a criticism of utilitarianism; he speaks scathingly of "the abyss of utilitarian apologetics for large-scale murder." In view of Nagel's tentativeness, I think it fair to disassociate him from the positive view I wish to criticize, although I am *calling* it Nagel's "absolutism." This positive view is, however, the only definite proposal he puts forward, and if I am to consider critically any positive antiutilitarian view in connection with Nagel's essay, it has to be this one. At any rate, this view is one that somebody *might* hold, and is well worth discussing.

The first point I wish to make is that a rule-utilitarian may quite well agree with Nagel that certain kinds of action are morally out of bounds absolutely and no matter what the circumstances. Take, for instance, some of the rules of warfare recognized by the

United States Army:

> It is especially forbidden . . . to declare that no quarter will be given.
> . . . It is especially forbidden . . . to kill or wound an enemy who, having laid down his arms, or having no longer means of defense, has surrendered at discretion. . . .
>
> It is especially forbidden . . . to employ arms, projectiles, or material calculated to cause unnecessary suffering. . . .
>
> The pillage of a town or place, even when taken by assault, is prohibited. . . .
>
> A commander may not put his prisoners to death because their presence retards his movements or diminishes his power of resistance by necessitating a large guard, or by reason of their consuming supplies, or because it appears certain that they will regain their liberty through the impending success of their forces. It is likewise unlawful for a commander to kill his prisoners on grounds of self-preservation, even in the case of airborne or commando operations, although the circumstances of the operation may make necessary rigorous supervision of and restraint upon the movement of prisoners of war.[3]

A rule-utilitarian is certainly in a position to say that utilitarian considerations cannot morally justify a departure from these rules; in that sense they are absolute. But he will of course also say that the moral justification of these rules lies in the fact that their acceptance and enforcement will make an important contribution to long-range utility. The rule-utilitarian, then, may take a two-level view: that in justifying the rules, utilitarian considerations are in order and nothing else is; whereas in making decisions about what to do in concrete circumstances, the rules are absolutely binding. In the rule-utilitarian view, immediate expediency is not a moral justification for infringing the rules.[4]

It is not clear that Nagel recognizes this sort of absolutism about "ideal" rules of war as a possible utilitarian view, but he seems to disagree with it when he claims that some moral prohibitions are entirely independent of utilitarian considerations.

What absolute rule, then, does Nagel propose? I shall formulate and criticize his proposal in a moment. But first we should note that his rule is intended to be restricted in scope; it applies only to what "we deliberately do to people." This is an important restriction.

Suppose bombers are dispatched to destroy a munitions
factory—surely a legitimate military target in a night raid; in fact
and predictably, and from a military point of view incidentally, the
bombs kill five thousand people. Is this a case of "deliberately
doing" something to these people? Nagel's view here seems
obscure. He rejects the law of double effect and says he prefers to
"stay with the original, unanalyzed distinction between what one
does to people and what merely happens to them as a result of what
one does." He concedes that this distinction "needs clarification."
Indeed, it does. Without more clarification, Nagel is hardly giving
an explicit theory. I note that the U.S. Army Manual appears to
reject this distinction, and in a paragraph declaring the limitations
on strategic bombing states that "loss of life and damage to
property must not be out of proportion to the military advantage to
be gained" (p. 19).

The absolutist principle that Nagel espouses as the basic
restriction on legitimate targets and weapons is this: "hostility or
aggression should be directed at its true object. This means both
that it should be directed at the person or persons who provoke it
and that it should aim more specifically at which is provocative
about them. The second condition will determine what form the
hostility may appropriately take." Now, while I find this principle
reasonably clear in its application to simple two-person cases
discussed by him, I find it difficult to apply in the identification of
morally acceptable military operations. With some trepidation I
suggest that Nagel intends it to be construed to assert something
like the following for the case of military operations: "Persons may
be attacked 'deliberately' only if their presence or their position
prevents overpowering the military forces of the enemy in some
way; and they may be attacked only in a manner that is
reasonably related to the objective of disarming or disabling
them." If this is what he has in mind it is still rather vague, since it
does not make clear whether attacks on munitions factories are
legitimate, or whether attacks on persons involved in supporting
services, say, the provisioning of the army, are acceptable.

It is worth noting that a principle resembling this one might
have a utilitarian justification of the kind alluded to above. But the
principle standing by itself does not seem to me self-evident; nor
does another principle Nagel asserts, that "the maintenance of a

direct interpersonal response to the people one deals with is a requirement which no advantages can justify one in abandoning."

Morally Justifiable Rules as Rules Impartially Preferable

I shall now proceed to a positive account of the rules of war and of their justification. We shall have to consider several distinct questions, but the central question will be: Which of the possible rules of war are morally justifiable?

But first, what do I mean by "rules of war" or by talk of the "authoritative status" of rules of war? What I have in mind is, roughly, rules with the status that the articles of the Hague and Geneva Conventions have or have had. That is, certain rules pertaining to war are stated in formal treaties. These rules are seriously taught, as being legally binding, to officers and to some extent to enlisted men; they are recognized as legally binding restrictions on the decisions of the general staff; members of the army know that actions forbidden by these rules are contrary both to international law and to their own army's manual of rules for proper conduct; these rules are enforced seriously by the courts, either military or international; and so on. Proscriptions or prescriptions with this status I call "rules of war"; and in speaking of a rule having "authoritative status" I have this kind of force in mind. The U.S. Army Manual lists such rules; and digests of international law such as those by Whiteman and Oppenheim contain information on what such rules are and have been.

I have said that I shall offer a utilitarian answer to the question which rules of war (in the above sense) are morally justifiable. But I have also said that I shall be offering what I (following Rawls) call a *contractual* utilitarian answer. What I mean by that (the term "contractual" may be a bit misleading) is this. I accept the utilitarian answer to the question which rules of war are morally justifiable because utilitarian rules of war are the ones *rational, impartial persons would choose* (the ones they would be willing to put themselves under a contract to obey). The more basic question is, then: Which rules of war would people universally prefer to have accorded authoritative status among nations if the people deciding were rational, believed they might be involved in a war at some

time, and were impartial in the sense that they were choosing
behind a veil of ignorance? (It is understood that their ignorance is
to be such as to prevent them from making a choice that would give
them or their nation a special advantage; it would, for instance,
prevent them from knowing what weaponry their country would
possess were it to be at war, and from knowing whether, were war
to occur, they would be on the front lines, in a factory, or in the
general staff office.) In other words, the more fundamental
question is: What rules would rational, impartial people, who
expected their country at some time to be at war, want to have as
the authoritative rules of war—particularly with respect to the
permitted targets and method of attack? I suggest that the rules of
war which rational, impartial persons would choose are the rules
that would maximize long-range expectable utility for nations at
war. In saying this I am offering a contractual utilitarian answer to
the question what rules of war are morally justifiable. I am saying,
then: (1) that rational, impartial persons would choose certain
rules of war; (2) that I take as a basic premise ("analytic" in some
sense, if you like) that a rule of war is morally justified if and only if
it would be chosen by rational, impartial persons; and (3) that the
rules rational, impartial persons would choose are ones which will
maximize expectable long-range utility for nations at war.[5]

Nagel objects to utilitarianism and hence presumably would
object to (3), but he might be agreeable to both (1) and (2). At least
he seems close to these principles, since he seems to hold that an
action is justified if one can justifiy to its victim what is being done
to him. For instance, he implies that if you were to say to a prisoner,
"You understand, I have to pull out your fingernails because it is
absolutely essential that we have the name of your confederates"
and the prisoner agreed to this as following from principles he
accepts, then the torture would be justified. Nagel rather assumes
that the prisoner would not agree, in an appropriate sense. In this
connection we must be clearly aware of an important distinction. A
judge who sentences a criminal might also be unable to persuade
the criminal to want the sentence to be carried out; and if
persuading him to want this were necessary for a moral
justification of the criminal law, then the system of criminal justice
would also be morally objectionable. We must distinguish between
persuading a person to whom something horrible is about to be

done to want this thing to happen or to consent to its happening at that very time and something quite different—getting him to accept, when he is rational and choosing in ignorance of his own future prospects, some general principles from which it would follow that this horrible thing should or might be done to a person in his present circumstances. I think Nagel must mean, or ought to mean, that a set of rules of war must be such as to command the assent of rational people choosing behind a veil of ignorance, *not* that a person must be got to assent at the time to his fingernails being pulled out in order to get information, if that act is to be justified. It may be, however, that Nagel does not agree with this distinction, since he hints at the end of his discussion that something more may be required for moral justification than I have suggested, without indicating what the addition might be.

We should notice that the question which rules of war would be preferred by rational persons choosing behind a veil of ignorance is roughly the question that bodies like the Hague Conventions tried to answer. For there were the representatives of various nations, gathered together, say, in 1907, many or all of them making the assumption that their nations would at some time be at war. And, presumably in the light of calculated national self-interest and the principles of common humanity, they decided which rules they were prepared to commit themselves to follow, in advance of knowing how the fortunes for war might strike them in particular. The questions the signatories to the Hague Conventions actually did ask themselves are at least very close to the questions I think we must answer in order to know which rules of war are morally justified.

The Rational, Impartial Choice: Utilitarian Rules

I wish now to explain in a few words why I think rational, impartial persons would choose rules of war that would maximize expectable utility. Then—and this will occupy almost all of the present section—I shall classify the rules of war into several types, and try to show that representative rules of each type would be utility-maximizing and therefore chosen. I shall hope (although I shall not say anything explicitly about this) that the ideal rules of war, identified in this way, will coincide with the reflective intuitions of the reader. If so, I assume that this fact will commend to him the whole of what I am arguing.

I have suggested that rational persons, choosing behind a veil of ignorance but believing that their country may well be involved in a war at some time, would prefer rules of war that would maximize expectable utility, *in the circumstance that two nations are at war.* Why would they prefer such rules? About this I shall say only that if they are self-interested they will choose rules which will maximize expectable utility generally, for then their chance of coming out best will be greatest (and they do not know how especially to favor themselves); and that if they are altruistic they will again choose that set of rules, for they will want to choose rules which will maximize expectable utility generally. The rules of war, then, subject to the restriction that the rules of war may not prevent a belligerent from using all the power necessary to overcome the enemy, will be ones whose authorization will serve to maximize welfare.

It is worth noting that a preamble to the U.S. Army Manual offers an at least partially utilitarian theory of the rules of war (I say "at least partially" because of doubts about the interpretation of clause *b*). This preamble states that the law of land warfare "is inspired by the desire to diminish the evils of war by: *a.* Protecting both combatants and noncombatants from unnecessary suffering; *b.* Safeguarding certain fundamental human rights of persons who fall into the hands of the enemy, particularly prisoners of war, the wounded and sick, and civilians; and *c.* Facilitating the restoration of peace" (p. 3).

Which rules, then, would maximize expectable utility for nations at war? (I shall later discuss briefly whether the ideal rules would altogether forbid war as an instrument of national policy.)

First, however, we must understand why the above-mentioned restriction, guaranteeing that the rules of war will not prevent a belligerent from using all the force necessary to overcome the enemy, must be placed on the utility-maximizing rules of war. The reason for this restriction is to be found in the nature of a serious war. There are, of course, many different kinds of war. Wars differ in magnitude, in the technologies they employ, in the degree to which they mobilize resources, in the type of issue the belligerents believe to be at stake, and in many other ways as well. The difference between the Trojan War and World War II is obviously enormous. The former was a simple, small-scale affair, and the issues at stake might well have been settled by a duel between Paris and Menelaus, or Hector and Achilles, and the belligerents might not have been seriously dissatisfied with the outcome. In the case of World War II, the British thought that Hitler's Germany and its policies threatened the very basis of civilized society. The destruction of Hitler's power seemed so important to the British that they were willing to stake their existence as a nation on bringing it about. Wars have been fought for many lesser reasons: to spread a political or religious creed, to acquire territory or wealth, to obtain an outlet to the sea, or to become established as a world power. Wars may be fought with mercenaries, or primarily by the contribution of equipment and munitions; such wars make relatively little difference to the domestic life of a belligerent.

It is possible that the rules which would maximize expectable utility might vary from one type of war to another. I shall ignore this possibility for the most part, and merely note that practical difficulties are involved in equipping military handbooks with different sets of rules and establishing judicial bodies to identify the proper classification of a given war. I shall take the position of Britain in World War II as typical of that of a belligerent in a serious war.

The position of a nation in a serious war is such, then, that it considers overpowering the enemy to be absolutely vital to its interests (and possibly to those of civilized society generally)—so vital, indeed, that it is willing to risk its very existence to that end. It is doubtful that both sides can be well justified in such an appraisal of the state of affairs. But we may assume that in fact they do make this appraisal. In this situation, we must simply take as a fact that neither side will consent to or follow rules of war which seriously impair the possibility of bringing the war to a victorious conclusion. This fact accounts for the restriction within which I suggested a choice of the rules of war must take place. We may notice that the recognized rules of war do observe this limitation: they are framed in such a way as not to place any serious obstacle in the way of a nation's using any available force, if necessary, to destroy the ability of another to resist. As Oppenheim has observed, one of the assumptions underlying the recognized rules of war is that "a belligerent is justified in applying any amount and any kind of force which is necessary for . . . the overpowering of the the opponent."[6] This limitation, however, leaves a good deal of room for rules of war which will maximize expectable long range utility for all parties.

This restriction, incidentally, itself manifests utilitarian considerations, for a nation is limited to the use of means *necessary* to overcome an opponent. Clearly it is contrary to the general utility that any amount or manner of force be employed when it is *not* necessary for victory.

It will be convenient to divide the rules restricting military operation, especially the targets and weapons of attack, into three types. (I do not claim that these are exhaustive.)

1. *Humanitarian Restrictions of No Cost to Military Operation.* There are some things that troops may be tempted to do which are at best of negligible utility to their nation but which cause serious loss to enemy civilians, although not affecting the enemy's power to win the war. Such behavior will naturally be forbidden by rules designed to maximize expectable utility within the understood restriction. Consider, for example, rules against the murder or ill-treatment of prisoners of war. A rule forbidding wanton murder of prisoners hardly needs discussion. Such murder does not advance the war effort of the captors: indeed, news of its occurrence only stiffens resistance and invites retaliation. Moreover, there is an advantage in returning troops having been encouraged to respect the lives of others. A strict prohibition of wanton murder of prisoners therefore has the clear support of utilitarian considerations. Much the same may be said for a rule forbidding ill-treatment of prisoners. There can, of course, be disagreement about what constitutes ill-treatment—for instance, whether a prisoner is entitled to a diet of the quality to which he is accustomed if it is more expensive than that available to troops of the captor army. It is clear, however, that in a war between affluent nations prisoners can generally be well-housed and well-fed and receive adequate medical care without cost to the war effort of the captors. And if they receive such treatment, of course the captives gain. Thus a policy of good treatment of prisoners may be expected to make many nationals of both sides better off, and at a cost which in

no way impairs the ability of either to wage the war.

Again, much the same may be said of the treatment of civilians and of civilian property in occupied territories. There is no military advantage, at least for an affluent nation, in the plunder of private or public property. And the rape of women or the ill-treatment of populations of occupied countries serves no military purpose. On the contrary, such behavior arouses hatred and resentment and constitutes a military liability. So utility is maximized, within our indicated basic limitations, by a strict rule calling for good treatment of the civilian population of an occupied territory. And the same can be said more generally for the condemnation of the wanton destruction of cities, towns, or villages, or devastation not justified by military necessity, set forth in the charter of the Nuremburg tribunal.

Obviously these rules, which the maximization of expectable utility calls for, are rules that command our intuitive assent.

2. *Humanitarian Restrictions Possibly Costly to Military Victory.* Let us turn now to rules pertaining to actions in somewhat more complex situations. There are some actions which fall into neither of the classes so far discussed. They are not actions which must be permitted because they are judged necessary or sufficient for victory, and hence actions on which no party to a major war would accept restrictions. Nor are they actions which morally justified rules of war definitely prohibit, as being actions which cause injury to enemy nations but serve no military purpose. It is this large class of actions neither clearly permitted nor definitely prohibited, for reasons already discussed, that I now wish to consider. I want to ask which rules of war are morally justified, because utility-maximizing, for actions of this kind. In what follows I shall be distinguishing several kinds of actions and suggesting appropriate rules for them. The first type is this: doing something which will result in widespread destruction of civilian life and property and at the same time will add (possibly by that very destruction) to the *probability* of victory but will not definitely decide the war. Some uses of atomic weapons, and area bombing of the kind practiced at Hamburg, illustrate this sort of case.

A proper (not ideally precise) rule for such operations might be: substantial destruction of lives and property of enemy civilians is permissible only when there is good evidence that it will significantly enhance the prospect of victory. Application of the terms "good evidence" and "significantly enhance" requires judgment, but the rule could be a useful guideline all the same. For instance, we now know that the destruction of Hamburg did not significantly enhance the prospect of victory; in fact, it worked in the wrong direction, since it both outraged the population and freed workers formerly in non-war-supporting industries to be moved into industry directly contributing to the German war effort. The generals surely did not have good evidence that this bombing would significantly enhance the prospect of victory.

This rule is one which parties to a war might be expected to accept in advance, since following it could be expected to minimize the human cost of war on both sides, and since it does not involve a significant compromise of the goal of victory. The proposed rule, incidentally, has some similarities to the accepted rule cited above from the U.S. Army Manual, that "loss of life and damage to property must not be out of proportion to the military advantage to be gained."

This rule, which I am suggesting only for wars like World War II, where the stakes are very high, may become clearer if seen in the perspective of a more general rule that would also be suitable for wars in which the stakes are much lower. I pointed out above that what is at stake in a war may be no more than a tiny strip of land or national prestige. (The utility of these, may, however, be considered very great by a nation.) Now, it is clear that a risk of defeat which may properly be taken when the stakes are enormous might quite properly be run when the stakes are small. So if the above-suggested rule is plausible for serious wars, in which the stakes are great, a somewhat different rule will be plausible in the case of wars of lesser importance—one that will require more in the way of "good evidence" and will require that the actions more "significantly enhance" the prospect of victory than is necessary when the stakes are much higher. These thoughts suggest the following general principle, applicable to all types of war: a military action (e.g., a bombing raid) is permissible only if the utility (broadly conceived, so that the maintenance of treaty obligations of international law could count as a utility) of victory to all concerned, multiplied by the increase in its probability if the action is executed, on the evidence (when the evidence is reasonably solid, considering the stakes), is greater than the possible disutility of the action to both sides multiplied by its probability. The rule for serious wars suggested above could then be regarded as a special case, one in which the utility of victory is virtually set at infinity—so that the only question is whether there is reasonably solid evidence that the action will increase the probability of victory. The more general rule obviously involves difficult judgments; there is a question, therefore, as to how it could be applied. It is conceivable that tough-minded civilian review boards would be beneficial, but we can hardly expect very reliable judgment even from them.[7]

These rules are at least very different from a blanket permission for anything the military thinks might conceivably improve the chances of victory, irrespective of any human cost to the enemy. In practice, it must be expected that each party to a war is likely to estimate the stakes of victory quite high, so that the rule which has the best chance of being respected is probably the first one mentioned, and not any modification of it that would be suggested to an impartial observer by the second, more general principle.

The reader may have been struck by the fact that these suggested rules are essentially institutionalized applications of a kind of act-utilitarian principle for certain contexts. This may seem inconsistent with the notion of a system of absolute rules themselves justified by long-range utilitarian considerations. But there is nothing inconsistent in the suggestion that some of the "absolute" rules should require that in certain situations an action be undertaken if and only if it will maximize expectable utility.

It may be objected that the rules suggested are far too imprecise to be of practical utility. To this I would reply that there is no reason why judgment may not be required in staff decisions about major operations. Furthermore, the U.S. Army Manual already contains several rules the application of which requires judgment. For example:

> Absolute good faith with the enemy must be observed as a rule of conduct. . . . In general, a belligerent may resort to those measures for mystifying or misleading the enemy against which the enemy ought to take measures to protect himself.
> The measure of permissible devastation is found in the strict

necessities of war. Devastation as an end in itself or as a separate measure of war is not sanctioned by the law of war. There must be some reasonably close connection between the destruction of property and the overcoming of the enemy's army. . . .

The punishment imposed for a violation of the law of war must be proportionate to the gravity of the offense. The death penalty may be imposed for grave breaches of the law. . . . Punishments should be deterrent. (pp 22, 23-24, 182).

It has sometimes been argued, for instance by Winston Churchill, that obliteration bombing is justified as retaliation. It has been said that since the Germans destroyed Amsterdam and Coventry, the British had a right to destroy Hamburg. And it is true that the Hague Conventions are sometimes regarded as a contract, the breach of which by one side released the other from its obligations. It is also true that a government which has itself ordered obliteration bombing is hardly in a position to complain if the same tactic is employed by the enemy. But maximizing utility permits obliteration bombing only as a measure of deterrence or deterrent reprisal. This rule, incidentally, is recognized by the army manual as a principle governing all reprisals: "Reprisals are acts of retaliation . . . for the purpose of enforcing future compliance with the recognized rules of civilized warfare. . . . Other means of securing compliance with the law of war should normally be exhausted before the resort is had to reprisals. . . . Even when appeal to the enemy for redress has failed, it may be a matter of policy to consider, before resorting to reprisals, whether the opposing forces are not more likely to be influenced by a steady adherence to the law of war on the part of the adversary" (p. 177). Purposes of retaliation, then, do not permit bombing in contravention of the suggested general principles.

Special notice should be taken that widespread civilian bombing might be defended by arguing that a significant deterioration in civilian morale could bring an end to a war by producing internal revolution. Our principle does not exclude the possibility of such reasoning, in the presence of serious evidence about civilian morale, when the stakes of victory are high. But we know enough about how bombing affects civilian morale to know that such bombing could be justified only rarely, if at all. The U.S. Army seems to go further than this; its rule asserts that any attack on civilians "for the sole purpose of terrorizing the civilian population is also forbidden."[8] It may be, however, that in actual practice this rule is interpreted in such a way that it is identical with the less stringent rule which is as much as utilitarian considerations can justify; if not, I fear we have to say that at this point the army's theory has gone somewhat too far.

3. *Acceptance of military losses for humanitarian reasons.* Let us now turn to some rules which have to do with what we might call the *economics* of warfare, when the ultimate outcome is not involved, either because the outcome is already clear or because the action is fairly local and its outcome will not have significant repercussions. What damage may one inflict on the enemy in order to cut down one's own losses? For instance, may one destroy a city in order to relieve a besieged platoon, or in order to avoid prolonging a war with consequent casualties? (The use of atom bombs in Japan may be an instance of this type of situation.) It is convenient to deal with two types of cases separately.

First, when may one inflict large losses on the enemy in order to avoid smaller losses for oneself, given that the issue of the war is not in doubt? A complicating fact is that when the issue is no longer in doubt it would seem that the enemy ought to concede, thereby avoiding losses to both sides. Why fight on when victory is impossible? (Perhaps to get better terms of peace.) But suppose the prospective loser is recalcitrant. May the prospective victor then unleash any horrors whatever in order to terminate the war quickly or reduce his losses? It is clear that the superior power should show utmost patience and not make the terms of peace so severe as to encourage further resistance. On the other hand, long-range utility is not served if the rules of war are framed in such a way as to provide an umbrella for the indefinite continuation of a struggle by an inferior power. So it must be possible to inflict losses heavy enough to produce capitulation but not so heavy as to be out of proportion to the estimated cost of further struggle to both sides. This condition is especially important in view of the fact that in practice there will almost always be other pressures that can be brought to bear. The application of such a rule requires difficult judgments, but some such rule appears called for by long-range utilitarian considerations.

The second question is: Should there be restrictions on the treatment of an enemy in the case of local actions which could hardly affect the outcome of the war, when these may cause significant losses? Rules of the army manual forbid killing of prisoners when their presence retards one's movements, reduces the number of men available for combat, uses up the food supply, and in general is inimical to the integrity of one's troops. Again, the Second Hague Convention forbids forcing civilians in occupied territory to give information about the enemy, and it forbids reprisals against the general civilian population "on account of the acts of individuals for which they cannot be regarded as jointly and severally responsible."[9] The taking of hostages is prohibited (U.S. Army Manual, p. 107).

All these rules prescribe that a belligerent be prepared to accept certain military disadvantages for the sake of the lives and welfare of civilians and prisoners. The disadvantages in question are not, however, losses that could be so serious as to affect the outcome of a war. Furthermore, the military gains and losses are ones which are likely to be evenly distributed, so that neither side stands to gain a long-term advantage if the rules are observed by both. So, without affecting the outcome of the war and without giving either side an unfair advantage, a considerable benefit can come to both belligerents in the form of the welfare of their imprisoned and occupied populations. Thus the long-run advantage of both parties is most probably served if they accept forms of self-restraint which can work out to be costly in occasional instances. Such rules will naturally be accepted by rational, impartial people in view of their long-range benefits.

Rules of War and Morality

I have been arguing that there is a set of rules governing the conduct of warfare which rational, impartial persons who believed that their country might from time to time be engaged in a war would prefer to any alternative set of rules and to the absence of rules. I have also suggested, although without argument, that it is proper to say of such a set of rules that it is morally justified (and of course I think that such a set ought to be formally recognized and given authoritative status). There is thus a fairly close parallel with the prohibitions (and justifications and recognized excuses) of the criminal law: certain of these would be preferred to alternative sets and to an absence of legal prohibitions by rational, impartial persons; the prohibitions that would be so preferred may (I think) be said to be morally justified; and such rules ought to be adopted as the law of the land. I do not say the parallel is exact.

It may be suggested that there will be a considerable discrepancy between what is permitted by such "morally justifiable" rules of war and what it is morally permissible for a person to do in time of war. (Nagel mentions dropping the bomb on Hiroshima, attacks on trucks bringing up food, and the use of flamethrowers in any situation whatever as examples of actions not morally permissible; but it is not clear that he would say these would be permitted by morally justifiable rules of war, or even that he recognizes a distinction between what is morally permissible and what is permitted by morally justifiable rules of war.) Moreover, it might be thought that such "morally justifiable" rules of war could not be derived from justified moral principles. It might be asked, too, what the moral standing of these "morally justified" rules of war is, in view of the fact that the rules of war actually accepted and in force may, at least in some particular, be rather different. These are difficult questions, about which I wish to say something.

It is obvious that there may well be discrepancies between what a person morally may do in wartime and what is permitted by morally justified rules of war, just as there are discrepancies between what is morally permitted and what is permitted by morally justifiable rules of the criminal law. For one thing, the rules of war, like the criminal law, must be formulated in such a way that it is decidable whether a person has violated them; it must be possible to produce evidence that determines the question and removes it from the realm of speculation. More important, just as there are subtle interpersonal relations—such as justice and self-restraint in a family—which it is undesirable for the criminal law to attempt to regulate but which may be matters of moral obligation, so there may well be moral obligations controlling relations between members of belligerent armies which the rules of war cannot reach. For instance, one might be morally obligated to go to some trouble or even take a certain risk in order to give aid to a wounded enemy, but the rules of war could hardly prescribe doing so. I am unable to think of a case in which moral principles require a person to do what is forbidden by morally justifiable rules of war; I suppose this is possible. But it is easy to think of cases in which moral principles forbid a person to injure an enemy, or require him to aid an enemy, when morally justifiable rules of war do not prescribe accordingly and when the military law even forbids the morally required behavior. (Consider, for instance, the fact that, according to the manual, the U.S. Army permits severe punishment for anyone who "without proper authority, knowingly harbors or protects or gives intelligence to, or communicates or corresponds with or holds any intercourse with the enemy, either directly or indirectly." [p. 33].)

The possible contrast between morally justifiable rules of war and what is morally permitted will seem quite clear to persons with firm moral intuitions. It may be helpful, however, to draw the contrast by indicating what it would be, at least for one kind of rule-utilitarian theory of moral principles. A rule-utilitarian theory of morality might say that what is morally permissible is any action that would not be forbidden by the kind of conscience which would maximize long-range expectable utility were it built into people as an internal regulator of their relations with other sentient beings, as contrasted with other kinds of conscience or not having a conscience at all. Then justifiable rules of war (with the standing described above) would be one thing; what is morally permissible, in view of ideal rules of conscience, might be another. Rational, impartial persons, understanding that their country may be involved in a war, might want one set of rules as rules of war, whereas rational, impartial persons choosing among types of conscience might want a different and discrepant set of rules as rules of conscience. In the same way there may be a discrepancy between a morally justified system of criminal law and morally justified rules of conscience. And just as, consequently, there may occasionally be a situation in which it is one's moral duty to violate the criminal law, so there may occasionally be a situation in which it is one's moral duty to violate morally unjustifiable rules of war.

It might be asked whether a person who subscribed to sound moral principles would, if given the choice, opt for a system of rules of war; and if so, whether he would opt for a set that would maximize expectable utility for the situation of nations at war. I suggest that he would do so; that such a person would realize that international law, like the criminal law, has its place in human society, that not all decisions can simply be left to the moral intuitions of the agent, and that the rules of war and military justice are bound to be somewhat crude. He would opt for that type of system which will do the most good, given that the nations will sometimes go to war. I am, however, only *suggesting* that he would; in order to show that he would, one would have to identify the sound moral principles which would be relevant to such a decision.

Another question that might be raised is whether a person should follow the actual military rules of his country or the morally justifiable ones (in the sense explained above). This question can obviously be taken in either of two ways. If the question is which rules are legally binding, of course the actual rules of war recognized at present are legally binding on him. But the question might be: Is a person morally bound to follow the "ideal" rules of war, as compared with the actual ones (or the legal orders of his officer), if they come into conflict? Here two possible situations must be distinguished. It is logically possible that a morally justifiable set of rules of war would permit damage to the enemy more severe than would the actual rules of war; in that case, assuming the actual rules of war have the status of an obligation fixed by a treaty, the moral obligation would seem to be to follow the provisions of the treaty (subject to the usual difficulties about older treaties not contemplating contemporary situations). Suppose, however, that a superior officer commands one to do something that is permitted by the actual rules of war (that is, not explicitly forbidden) but which clearly would be forbidden by morally justifiable rules of war. The question is then whether a moral person would refuse to do what is permitted by an unjust institution but would be forbidden by a just one. It would have to be argued in detail that sound moral principles would not permit a person to do what would be permitted only by an unjust institution. I shall not attempt to argue the matter, but only suggest that sound moral principles would *not* permit obedience to an order forbidden by morally justifiable rules of war. It is quite possible, incidentally, contrary to what I have just said about the legal issues, that a court-martial would not succeed in convicting a person who refused an order of this sort and defended his action along these lines.

There is space only to advert to the larger issue of the moral justification for nations being belligerents at all. Presumably, just as there are morally justified rules of war, in the sense of rules which rational, impartial persons would choose on the assumption their country might be involved in a war, so there are morally justified rules about engaging in a war at all, in the sense of rules governing the behavior of nations which rational, impartial persons would subscribe to if they believed that they would live in a world in which the chosen rules might obtain. Not only are there such morally justified rules regarding belligerency, but almost every nation is in fact signatory to a treary abjuring war as an instrument of policy. Moreover, it has been declared criminal by the Treaty of London for a person to plan, prepare, initiate, or wage a war of aggression or a war in violation of international treaties, agreements, or assurances. So there is basis both in morally justified principles of international law and in actual international law for questioning the position of a belligerent. Presumably the relation between these and the moral obligations of citizens and government officials is complex, rather parallel to that just described for the case of rules of war.

Notes

1. Cambridge, Mass., 1971.
2. Thomas Nagel, "War and Massacre," Chapter 23 in this volume.
3. Department of the Army Field Manual PM 27-10, *The Law of Land Warfare* (Department of the Army, July 1956), pp. 17, 18, 21, 35. The Manual specifically states that the rules of war may not be disregarded on grounds of "military necessity" (p. 4), since considerations of military necessity were fully taken into account in framing the rules. (All page numbers in the text refer to this publication, hereafter called the Army Manual.)

Other valuable discussions of contemporary rules of warfare are to be found in L. Oppenheim, *International Law*, ed. H. Lauterpacht, 7th ed. (New York, 1952) and in Margorie M. Whiteman, *Digest of International Law*, esp. Vol. 10 (U.S. Department of State, 1963).

4. It is conceivable that ideal rules of war would include one rule to the effect that anything is allowable, if necessary to prevent absolute catastrophe. As Oppenheim remarks, it may be that if the basic values of

society are threatened nations are possibly released from all the restrictions in order to do what "they deem to be decisive for the ultimate vindication of the law of nations" (*International Law*, p. 351).

5. This summary statement needs much explanation, e.g., regarding the meaning of "rational." It is only a close approximation to the view I would defend, since I think it is better to substitute a more complex notion for that of impartiality or a veil of ignorance.

6. *International Law*, p. 226.

7. If we assume that both sides in a major struggle somehow manage to be persuaded that their cause is just, we shall have to expect that each will assign a net positive utility to its being the victor. For this reason it makes very little difference whether the more general principle uses the concept of the utility of victory by one side for everyone concerned, or the utility for that side only.

One might propose that the general restriction on rules of war, to the effect that in a serious war the use of any force necessary or sufficient for victory must be permitted, might be derived from the above principle if the utility of victory is set virtually at infinity and the probability of a certain action affecting the outcome is set near one. I believe this is correct, if we assume, as just suggested, that each side in a serious war will set a very high positive utility on *its* being the victor, despite the fact that both sides cannot possibly be correct in such an assessment. The reason for this principle as stated in the text, however, seems to me more realistic and simple. There is no reason, as far as I can see, why *both* lines of reasoning may not be used in support of the claim that the principle (or restriction) in question is a part of a morally justifiable system of rules of war.

8. Whiteman, *Digest of International Law* 10, 135.

9. Article 50.

25

War Crimes

Telford Taylor

In his chapter on "War Crimes" taken from his book Nuremberg and Vietnam: An American Tragedy, *the American chief prosecutor at Nuremberg, General Telford Taylor, provides a usefully brief history of the "laws of war." From largely unwritten rules of conduct, to treaties, military manuals, and decisions of military courts, such "laws" remain substantially a body of laws based on custom, growing much as the common law of England grew in preparliamentary times. Taylor also helps us understand the reasons for the amorphous and shifting quality of the laws of war, and the relevance and constraints of what goes under the designation "military necessity."*

—R. C.

What is a "war crime"? To say that it is a violation of the laws of war is true, but not very meaningful.

War consists largely of acts that would be criminal if performed in time of peace—killing, wounding, kidnapping, destroying or carrying off other peoples' property. Such conduct is not regarded as criminal if it takes place in the course of war, because the state of war lays a blanket of immunity over the warriors. This concept is very ancient; it is clearly stated by the 12th century compiler of canon law, Gratian: "The soldier who kills a man in obedience to authority is not guilty of murder."

But the area of immunity is not unlimited, and its boundaries are marked by the laws of war. Unless the conduct in question falls within those boundaries, it does not lose the criminal character it would have should it occur in peaceful circumstances. In a literal sense, therefore, the expression "war crime" is a misnomer, for it means an act that remains criminal even though committed in the course of war, because it lies outside the area of immunity prescribed by the laws of war.

What, then, are the "laws of war"? They are of ancient origin, and followed two main streams of development. The first flowed from medieval notions of knightly chivalry. Over the course of the centuries the stream has thinned to a trickle; it had a brief spurt during the days of single-handed aerial combat, and survives today in rules (often violated) prohibiting various deceptions such as the use of the enemy's uniforms or battle insignia, or the launching of a war without fair warning by formal declaration.

The second and far more important concept is that the ravages of war should be mitigated as far as possible by prohibiting needless cruelties, and other acts that spread death and destruction and are not reasonably related to the conduct of hostilities. The seeds of such a principle must be nearly as old as human society, and ancient literature abounds with condemnation of pillage and massacre. In more recent times, both religious humanitarianism and the opposition of merchants to unnecessary disruptions of commerce have furnished the motivation for restricting customs and understandings. In the seventeenth century these ideas began to find expression in learned writings, especially those of the Dutch jurist-philosopher Hugo Grotius.

The formalization of military organization in the eighteenth century brought the establishment of military courts, empowered to try violations of the laws of war as well as other offenses by soldiers. During the American Revolution, both Captain Nathan Hale and the British Major John Andre were convicted as spies and ordered to be hanged, the former by a British military court and the latter by a "Board of General Officers" appointed by George Washington. During the Mexican War, General Winfield Scott created "military commissions" with jurisdiction over violations of the laws of war committed either by American troops against Mexican civilians, or vice versa.[1]

Up to that time the laws of war had remained largely a matter of unwritten tradition, and it was the United States, during the Civil War, that took the lead in reducing them to systematic, written form. In 1863 President Lincoln approved the promulgation by the War Department of "Instructions for the Government of Armies of the United States in the Field," prepared by Francis Lieber, a German veteran of the Napoleonic wars, who emigrated to the United States and became professor of law and political science at Columbia University. These comprised 159 articles, covering such subjects as "military necessity," "punishment of crimes against the inhabitants of hostile countries," "prisoners of war," and "spies." It was by a military commission appointed in accordance with these instructions that Mary Suratt and the others accused of conspiring to assassinate Lincoln were tried.

In the wake of the Crimean War, the Civil War and the Franco-Prussian War of 1870 there arose, in Europe and America, a tide of sentiment for codification of the laws of war and their embodiment in international agreements. The principal fruits of that movement were the series of treaties known today as the Hague and Geneva conventions. For present purposes, the most important of these are the Fourth Hague Convention of 1907, and the Geneva Prisoner of War, Red Cross, and Protection of Civilian Conventions of 1929 and 1949.

"The right of belligerents to adopt means of injuring the enemy is not unlimited," declared Article 22 of the Fourth Hague Convention, and ensuing articles specify a number of limitations: enemy soldiers who surrender must not be killed, and are to be taken prisoner; captured cities and towns must not be pillaged, nor "undefended" places bombarded; poisoned weapons and other arms "calculated to cause unnecessary suffering" are forbidden. Other provisions make it clear that war is not a free-for-all between the populations of the countries at war; only members of the armed forces can claim protection of the laws of war, and if a non-combatant civilian takes hostile action against the enemy he is guilty of a war crime. When an army occupies enemy territory, it must endeavor to restore public order, and respect "family honor and rights, the lives of persons, and private property, as well as religious convictions and practices."

Rules requiring humane treatment of prisoners, and for protection of the sick and wounded, are prescribed in the Geneva Conventions. While there is no general treaty on naval warfare, the Ninth Hague Convention prohibited the bombardment of undefended "ports," and the London Naval Treaty of 1930 condemned submarine sinkings of merchant vessels, unless passengers and crews were first placed in "safety."

In all of these treaties, the laws of war are stated as general principles of conduct, and neither the means of enforcement nor the penalties for violations are specified. The substance of their provisions, however, has been taken into the military law of many countries, and is often set forth in general orders, manuals of instruction, or other official documents. In the United States, for example, the Lieber rules of 1863 were replaced in 1914 by an army field manual which, up-dated, is still in force under the title *The Law of Land Warfare*.[2] It is set forth therein that the laws of war are part of the law of the United States, and that they may be enforced against both soldiers and civilians, including enemy personnel, by general courts-martial, military commissions, or other military or international tribunals.

Comparable though not identical publications have been issued by the military authorities of Britain, France, Germany and many other countries. These documents, and the treaties on which they are largely based, are regarded as a comprehensive but not necessarily complete exposition of what is really a body of international common law—the laws of war.

Since the mid-nineteenth century, with increasing frequency, the major powers have utilized military courts for the trial of persons accused of war crimes. An early and now famous trial, depicted in a successful Broadway play, was the post-Civil War proceeding against the Confederate Major Henry Wirz on charges of responsibility for the death of thousands of Union prisoners in the Andersonville prison camp, of which he had been commandant. War crimes tribunals were convened by the United States after the Spanish-American War, and by the British after the Boer War.

Following the defeat of Germany in the First World War, the Allies demanded that nearly 900 Germans accused of war crimes, including military and political leaders, be handed over for trial on war crimes charges. The Germans resisted the demand, and in the upshot they were allowed to try their own "war criminals." The trials in 1921 and 1922 were not conducted by military courts, but by the Supreme Court of Germany, sitting in Leipzig. From the

Allied standpoint they were a fiasco, as only a handful of accused were tried, and of these nearly all were acquitted or allowed to escape their very short prison sentences. The German court did, however, affirm that violations of the laws of war are punishable offenses, and in the *Llandovery Castle* case sentenced two German U-boat officers to four-year prison terms (from which both soon escaped) for complicity in the torpedoing of a British hospital ship and the shelling and sinking of her life-boats.

Such was the state of development of the laws of war, as the First World War faded into the pages of history. Twenty years later, as the legions of the Wehrmacht swarmed over Europe, putting the monarchs and ministers of the German-occupied nations to flight, London became the capital city of the governments-in-exile. King Haakon of Norway, Queen Wilhelmina of the Netherlands, Grand Duchess Charlotte of Luxembourg, President Benes of Czecho-slovakia, the emigre ministers of Belgium and Poland, and General Charles de Gaulle of the Free French found British sanctuary in 1940, and the next year were joined by King Peter of Yugoslavia and King Constantine of Greece.

London was not only the lodestone of the forces bent on the liberation of Europe, but their listening-post as well. By myriad means—clandestine radio messages, reports of spies and couriers, dispatches of neutral diplomats and churchmen—the British and their refugee guests were informed of happenings behind the coastal walls of Adolf Hitlers's "Fortress Europe," and the picture thus painted darkened month by month.

Before the end of 1939, the press and radio of the Vatican, on the high authority of August Cardinal Hlond, the Primate of Poland, told their readers and listeners that hundreds of Polish priests had been executed by Heinrich Himmler's SS units. Early in 1940, the United States Embassy in Berlin transmitted news of the wholesale deportation of German Jews to Poland. In the wake of the Nazi conquest of the western European countries in 1940, and of Yugoslavia and Greece in 1941, came a flood of reports describing the roundup of millions of men and women for forced labor in German mines and factories, and occupational regimes of unexampled severity, relying on the taking and frequent execution of hostages to maintain civil order. Soon after the invasion of Russia, the Soviet authorities publicized captured German military orders declaring that the "supply of food to local inhabitants and prisoners of war is unnecessary humanitarianism," and calling for the most far-reaching confiscation of all things of value, down to children's boots. Russian prisoners of war in German hands froze and starved to death by the millions. And in 1942 came the first stories, at first incredible but soon confirmed, of the mass extermination of Jews from all the occupied countries at Auschwitz and other concentration camps in Poland—the holocaust described by the Nazis as the "final solution of the Jewish problem."

Thus horror was heaped on outrage, but what was to be done about it? On October 25, 1941, in separate but simultaneous declarations, Winston Churchill and Franklin D. Roosevelt denounced the executions of hostages in France and other German-occupied countries. Soon other voices spoke more explicitly—those of the governments-in-exile in London. Representatives of these nine governments established an "Inter-Allied Conference on the Punishment of War Crimes" which, on January 13, 1942, promulgated what became known as the "Declaration of St. James." After making reference to the "regime of terror" instituted by Germany in their several countries, the signatories expressly repudiated the idea that the perpetrators of these atrocities could adequately be dealt with "by acts of vengeance on the part of the general public." On the contrary, it was declared that "the sense of justice of the civilized world" required that the signatory powers "place among their principal war aims the punishment through channels of organized justice, of those guilty of or responsible for these crimes."

The following year, with the announced support of the United States, Britain, and 15 other Allied governments, the "United Nations War Crimes Commission" was established in London. The Commission's main functions were to serve as a repository for evidence concerning war crimes, compile lists of individuals accused of their commission, and make plans for the apprehension and trial of those accused.

In the United States, as the defeat of Germany appeared more probable and imminent, the Judge Advocate General of the Army took the lead in preparations for war crimes trials at the conclusion of the war. Late in 1944 his activities were overshadowed by decisions at a higher level, which ultimately led to the establishment of the Nuremberg tribunals. As we will see in a later chapter, most of the prominent Germans and Japanese accused of war crimes were tried at Nuremberg and Tokyo before courts established under international authority, and quite outside the usual channels of military justice.

But those channels remained open and, numerically, the Nuremberg and Tokyo trials were a small part of a very large picture. In Europe, the United States Army judge advocate was made responsible for the prosecution of crimes committed against American troops, or in Nazi concentration camps that had been overrun and "liberated" by American forces. Under this authority, some 1,600 German war crimes defendants (as compared with 200 at Nuremberg) were tried before Army military commissions and military government courts, and over 250 death sentences (as compared with 21 at Nuremberg) were carried out. About an equal number were tried by British, French and other military courts established by the countries that had been occupied by Germany.

Precise figures are lacking, but by the spring of 1948 some 3,500 individuals had been tried on war crimes charges in Europe and 2,800 in the Far East, taking no account of trials held by the Soviet Union or China. It would be a conservative estimate that some 10,000 persons were tried on such charges from 1945 to 1950, and during the past 10 years hundreds more have been, and still are being, tried before West German courts. With a few exceptions, these trials were exclusively concerned with violations of the laws of war, and for the most part the charges related to mistreatment either of prisoners of war, or of the civilian populations of occupied countries.

We have looked back at a period of time of more than a hundred years since the laws of war began to emerge from their ancient form as unwritten rules of conduct, and to take shape in treaties, military manuals and the decisions of military courts established for their enforcement. Despite this century of development, as will be seen, the laws of war remain vague and uncertain in many respects. But a number of basic characteristics are by now manifest, and we should take note of them before examining the application of these laws to the fighting in Vietnam.

The first of these is that the laws of war remain a body of what lawyers call "customary" laws—that is to say, laws that are not created by statutes enacted by legislatures, but develop from societal custom and practice. The reason is very simple: There is no international legislature, and thus no way to give the laws of war statutory form. The laws of war, like much other international law, have grown in somewhat the same manner that the common law of England grew in preparliamentary times, and during the several centuries when very little of the basic civil and criminal law of England was to be found in parliamentary statutes, but rather in the decisions of the English common-law courts—judge-made law based on custom and precedent.

Treaties such as the Hague and Geneva conventions, and military directives such as the army field manual are not, therefore, the *sources* of the laws of war. Official directives may be binding as a matter of national law on the armed forces of the issuing country, and treaties may be binding on the signatory nations. But treaties and manuals alike are only partial embodiments of the laws of war on which they are based. This was clearly recognized in the preamble to the Fourth Hague Convention of 1907, by the statement that questions not covered by the convention should be resolved by "the principles of the law of nations, as they result from the usages established among civilized peoples, from the laws of humanity, and from the dictates of the public conscience." Similar language is to be found in Article 158 of the Geneva Convention of 1949, "For the Protection of Civilian Persons in Time of War," where it is provided that a signatory nation may denounce the treaty, but will nevertheless remain bound to abide by the "principles of the law of nations," which are then described in the same words used in the Hague Convention.

For present purposes, the highly important consequence of all this is that nations are regarded as bound by the laws of war whether or not they are parties to the Hague and Geneva conventions. In fact, not all countries have signed those treaties, and nonsigning countries have sometimes declared that they would nevertheless agree to observe them, and sometimes have said the opposite, or nothing at all. Nonsignatory nations are, to be sure, not bound by the precise wording and detailed prescriptions of the treaties, but, as the 1949 Geneva Convention expressly provides, they are bound by the customary laws of war from which the treaties are derived.

Of course, the reference in the Hague Convention preamble to "civilized" nations suggests what is obvious: that savage tribes may not be held to standards of conduct wholly unfamiliar to them. But the days of Custer and Kipling are over, and in the true tales of those years the colonial soldier comes off little better than the savage. Whether today we are all civilized or all barbarians, the distinction is no longer of much importance so far as concerns the applicability of the laws of war.

A second and very basic characteristic of the laws of war and war crimes is that, as these names indicate, they concern only conduct which is directly related to *war*—to hostilities in progress between organized belligerent forces. When the Nazis killed or assaulted German Jews in Germany, that may have been a crime, but it was not a war crime. At Nuremburg, an effort was made to give such domestic atrocities international significance under the expression "crimes against humanity," and today they would no doubt be covered by the international treaty defining and condemning "genocide," which most nations (not including the United States) have signed. "Genocide" and "crimes against humanity" will be pertinent to the discussion at a later point, but clarity requires that they be distinguished from the "war crimes" with which we are presently concerned.

This does not mean that a war that brings the laws of war into effect must be an international war. It may be a civil war; as we have seen, it was during our own Civil War that the first effort to codify the laws of war was made. But traditional war crimes involve the belligerent relation—between the armed forces of the hostile parties, or between armed forces and the civilian population of the enemy country.[3] The coverage of the Geneva Conventions as amended in 1949 is considerably broader, and extends to all persons "in the hands of" a belligerent or occupying nation of which the persons are not nationals. In Vietnam, where the American forces are operating primarily on the territory of a presumptive ally (South Vietnam), the question whether or not the laws of war are applicable to a given situation may present considerable difficulties.

By now, the reader will surely understand that the laws of war, although a long-established reality with a substantial core of recognized practice, are very fuzzy around the edges. They are also, as we will now see, unstable in the sense that their enforcement is and has always been spasmodic and uneven, and changeable in that the extent to which they are observed may be rapidly altered by the circumstances and techniques of warfare.

In part this is due to the customary nature of the laws of war, and the lack of any authoritative source or means of systematic enforcement. For want of an international legislature, there is no single, authoritative text of the rules, and there are no prescribed penalties for their violation. In the rare instances, such as the Second World War, where hostilities end in total victory for one side, there may be extensive enforcement by the victorious powers against the vanquished. Otherwise, enforcement is limited to proceedings against prisoners of war, or against the enforcing power's own troops. In such an embryonic legislative and judicial context, it is hardly surprising that the effective content of the laws of war should fluctuate.

Even more, however, this amorphous, shifting quality of the laws of war is due to the nature of war itself. Otherwise law-abiding individuals will commit crimes in order to save their own lives; national governments will likewise break treaties and international rules, if necessary, for their own preservation. Intrinsically a desperate and violent business, war is not readily limitable in terms of the means to be used in its prosecution. Especially in modern times, war is a rapid breeder of new techniques, the successful use of or defense against which may be incompatible with the continued observance of rules previously respected.

These characteristics of warfare are epitomized in the expression "military necessity." The men who first undertook to give written form to the laws of war were acutely conscious of the bearing of this principle on the task they undertook. In the Lieber rules of 1863, military necessity was defined as "those measures which are indispensable for securing the ends of war, and which are lawful according to the modern law and usages of war."

This definition, neatly if unintentionally, reveals the great dilemma, as yet unresolved, that permeates the very concept of "laws of war." Is there any measure that by assumption is "indispensable for securing the ends of war" that the laws of war can effectively condemn? Or must we not accept Lowes Dickinson's flat verdict that "no rules to restrain the conduct of war will ever be observed if victory seems to depend upon the breach of them"?[4]

It is interesting to compare what was said about this problem in the army's field manuals of 1917 and 1956. The earlier version declared that the laws of war were "determined by those principles" as follows:

> *First*, that a belligerent is justified in applying any amount and any kind of force which is necessary for the purpose of the war; that is, the complete submission of the enemy at the earliest possible moment with the least expenditure of men and money. *Second*, the principle of humanity, which says that all such kinds and degrees of violence as are not necessary for the purpose of war are not permitted to a belligerent. *Third*, the principle of chivalry, which demands a certain amount of fairness in offense and defense and a certain mutual respect between opposing forces.[5]

Except for the surpassingly vague "principle of chivalry," this is a plain statement of the rule of military necessity; if the use of force is necessary, it is lawful, and if unnecessary, it is unlawful. The 1940 manual was not significantly different, but in the most recent (1956) edition the matter is not at all so clear:

> The law of war places limits on the exercise of a belligerent's power . . . and requires that belligerents refrain from employing any kind or degree of violence which is not actually necessary for military purposes and that they conduct hostilities with regard for the principles of humanity and chivalry.
>
> The prohibitory effect of the law of war is not minimized by "military necessity" which has been defined as that principle which justifies those measures not forbidden by international law which are indispensable for securing the complete submission of the enemy as soon as possible. Military necessity has been generally rejected as a defense for acts forbidden by the customary and conventional laws of war inasmuch as the latter have been developed and framed with consideration for the concept of military necessity.[6]

The later statement surely rings less harshly in the ear, but careful reading only heightens its ambiguity. In any event, no form of words can resolve the essential difficulty, which is that "necessity" is a matter of infinite circumstantial variation. To illustrate the problem in the pragmatic dimension, two examples may be helpful.

Perhaps the most important of all the laws of war is the rule that an enemy soldier who surrenders is to be spared further attack and, upon being taken prisoner, is to be conducted, as soon as possible, to safety in the rear of the capturing force. It is "especially forbidden" under the 1907 Hague Convention "to kill or wound an enemy who, having laid down his arms, or having no longer means of self-defense, has surrendered at discretion." It is equally forbidden "to declare that no quarter will be given." And under the 1949 Geneva Convention on prisoners of war, they "shall be evacuated, as soon as possible after their capture, to camps situated far enough from the combat zone for them to be out of danger."

Now, these requirements are followed more often than not, and for that reason millions are alive today who would otherwise be dead. But they are not infrequently violated; the rules read like absolute requirements, but circumstances arise where military necessity, or even something less, causes them to be disregarded. In the heat of combat, soldiers who are frightened, angered, shocked at the death of comrades, and fearful of treacherous attacks by enemies feigning death or surrender, are often prone to kill rather than capture. Under quite different circumstances, the killing may be done in cold blood, by order of humane commanders. Small detachments on special missions, or accidentally cut off from their main force, may take prisoners under such circumstances that men cannot be spared to guard them or take them to the rear, and that to take them along would greatly endanger the success of the mission or the safety of the unit. The prisoners will be killed, by operation of the principle of military necessity,[7] and no military or other court has been called upon, so far as I am aware, to declare such killing a war crime.

An equally striking illustration of the "necessity" principle may be drawn from the development of submarine warfare. During the First World War, the havoc worked by German U-boats in sinking merchant and passenger vessels (notably the *Lusitania*) led to strong pressure, especially from neutral nations, to limit their depredations. A consequence of these widely held sentiments was the provisions of the London Naval Treaty of 1930, subsequently agreed to by the United States, France, Italy, Japan, Great Britain and Germany, forbidding warships "whether surface or submarine" from sinking merchant vessels "without having first placed passengers, crew, and ship's papers in a place of safety."

Soon after the outbreak of the Second World War, it became apparent that submarine operations could no longer be effectively conducted (if indeed they ever could have been) in accordance with these rescue requirements. Radar, sonar, convoys and long-range aircraft rapidly advanced the techniques of antisubmarine warfare to such a point that it was virtual suicide for a submarine to surface anywhere near its target, let alone to remain in the vicinity for rescue operations. During the war the German, British and American submarine forces all disregarded the rescue provisions of the London treaty.

Nevertheless, at Nuremberg Admirals Erich Raeder and Karl Doenitz, successively commanders in chief of the German navy, were charged with war crimes in that they were responsible for U-boat operations in violation of the London treaty. But the evidence at the trial, which included testimony by the U.S. naval commander in the Pacific, Admiral Chester W. Nimitz, established that in this regard the Germans had done nothing that the British and Americans had not done. The Nuremberg tribunal therefore ruled that, while Raeder and Doenitz had indeed violated the London rescue stipulations, they should not be subjected to any criminal penalties on that account. The plain rationale of this decision was that the London rescue requirements were no longer an effective part of the laws of naval warfare, because they had been abrogated by the practice of the belligerents on both sides under the stress of military necessity.

Other examples of the impact of military necessity on the laws of war come readily to mind. A signal and terrible example during the Second World War was the growing acceptance of aerial bombardment of population centers—from the pre-war Japanese and German attacks on Canton and Barcelona, through London, Coventry, Belgrade, Hamburg and Berlin, to Dresden, Tokyo, Hiroshima and Nagasaki in 1945. On this matter there will be more to say in relation to Vietnam. I mention it here to underline the lesson of all these examples, which is that the laws of war do not have a fixed content, but are constantly reshaped by the exigencies of warfare.

To be sure, there is abundant room for the view that the laws of war should be closer to fixed principles of conduct, less at the mercy of military pressures. If there were an international criminal tribunal, with jurisdiction over all nations, it might then be possible to ban specific weapons or practices as inhumane and unlawful, regardless of their military value. Perhaps one day there will be such a court, but its creation would hardly be possible except in a climate of world opinion in which war itself could be eliminated.

But as long as enforcement of the laws of war is left to the belligerents themselves, whether during the course of hostilities or by the victors at their conclusion, the scope of their application must be limited by the extent to which they have been observed by the enforcing party. To punish the foe—especially the vanquished foe—for conduct in which the enforcing nation has engaged, would be so grossly inequitable as to discredit the laws themselves.

If then, the laws of war are so erratically if not capriciously enforced, and subject to change under the pressure of military practice, are they worth having at all? Might it not be better to junk the whole concept of war crimes, and acknowledge that war is war and anything goes? Indeed, if warring nations were totally uninhibited, might not the very enormity of the consequences revolt the conscience of the world and lend additional strength to the movement for abolition of war?

Support for affirmative answers to these questions has not been lacking, and is perhaps more extensive than the literature on the subject suggests. But such views are, I believe, counsels of desperation with little in logic or experience to commend them. All in all this has been a pretty bloody century and people do not seem to shock very easily, as much of the popular reaction to the reports of Son My made depressingly plain. The kind of world in which all efforts to mitigate the horrors of war are abandoned would hardly be a world sensitive to the consequences.

There are at least two reasons—or perhaps one basic reason with two formulations—for the preservation and continued enforcement, as even-handedly as possible, of the laws of war. The first is strictly pragmatic: They work. Violated or ignored as they often are, enough of the rules are observed enough of the time so that mankind is very much better off with them than without them. The rules for the treatment of civilian populations in occupied countries are not as susceptible to technological change as rules regarding the use of weapons in combat. If it were not regarded as wrong to bomb military hospitals, they would be bombed all of the time instead of some of the time.

It is only necessary to consider the rules on taking prisoners in the setting of the Second World War to realize the enormous saving of life for which they have been responsible. Millions of French, British, German and Italian soldiers captured in western Europe and Africa were treated in general compliance with the Hague and Geneva requirements, and returned home at the end of the war. German and Russian prisoners taken on the eastern front did not fare nearly so well and died in captivity by the millions, but many survived. Today there is surely much to criticize about the handling of prisoners on both sides of the Vietnam War, but at least many of them are alive, and that is because the belligerents are reluctant to flout the laws of war too openly.

Another and, to my mind, even more important basis of the laws of war is that they are necessary to diminish the corrosive effect of mortal combat on the participants. War does not confer a license to kill for personal reasons—to gratify perverse impulses, or to put out of the way anyone who appears obnoxious, or to whose welfare the soldier is indifferent. War is not a license at all, but an obligation to kill for reasons of state; it does not countenance the infliction of suffering for its own sake or for revenge.

Unless troops are trained and required to draw the distinction between military and nonmilitary killings, and to retain such respect for the value of life that unnecessary death and destruction will continue to repel them, they may lose the sense for that distinction for the rest of their lives. The consequence would be that many returning soldiers would be potential murderers.

As Francis Lieber put the matter in his 1863 army regulations: "Men who take up arms against one another in public war do not cease on this account to be moral beings, responsible to one another and to God."

Notes

1. The history of American military practice with respect to the laws of war is covered in Colby, "War Crimes," *23 Michigan Law Review* 482, 606 (1925).

2. Department of the Army Field Manual FM 27-10, *The Law of Land Warfare* (1956). The 1940 edition was in effect during the Second World War.

3. It is interesting to note that while most violations of the laws of war consist of homicidal or other acts involving moral obloquy, this is not universally true, even with respect to conduct capitally punishable. A good example is spying. Of course, if one spies against one's country, then traitorous or even treasonable elements are present. But spying for one's country, though punishable by death under the laws of war (explicitly recognized in Article 68 of the 1949 Geneva Convention on the protection of civilians), is not regarded as ignoble. We think of Major Andre as a blameless, luckless victim of Benedict Arnold's perfidy, and Nathan Hale is honored with a statue on the old campus at Yale and a plaque on the outside wall of the Yale Club in New York City, near where he was hanged by the British in 1776. That spying is not intrinsically criminal is interestingly recognized in Article 31 of the 1907 Hague Convention, which provides that a spy "who, after rejoining the army to which he belongs, is subsequently captured by the enemy, is treated as a prisoner of war and incurs no responsibility for his previous acts of espionage." Thus deterrence of others, not retribution or condemnation, is the object of capital punishment for spies caught in the act.

4. G. Lowes Dickinson, *War: Its Nature, Cause, and Curse* (1923), p. 16.

5. *Rules of Land Warfare*, War Department Doctrine No. 467, Office of the Chief of Staff, approved April 25, 1914 (U.S. Government Printing Office, 1917), par. 9.

6. *Law of Land Warfare*, par. 3.

7. The Lieber rules of 1863 recognized this necessity by providing that "a commander is permitted to direct his troops to give no quarter, in great straits, when his own salvation makes it *impossible* to cumber himself with prisoners." The Hague and Geneva rules and the recent army manuals contain no comparable provision.

26

Superior Orders and Reprisals

Telford Taylor

Continuing with the second chapter, "Superior Orders and Reprisals," from his Nuremberg and Vietnam: An American Tragedy, *General Taylor first discusses whether obedience or the laws of war take precedence, legally, when the two requirements conflict. After surveying the relatively ambiguous legal history of the issue, he considers two ways that a plea of superior orders can be used for the defense in war crimes charges: first, it can be used as an appropriate* defense, *based on* lack of knowledge *of an order's unlawfulness and the presumption in favor of obedience; second, it can be used in* mitigation, *based on the* fear *of punishment for disobedience. The second issue considered is whether reprisals or the practice of taking hostages would constitute a legal justification for what would otherwise be against the laws of war. Taylor briefly suggests some reasons why we might want such a legal position, but then points out that current law forbids taking hostages and restricts the "permissible scope of reprisals."*

—K. W.

Moral responsibility is all very well, the reader may be thinking, but what about military orders? Is it not the soldier's first duty to give instant obedience to orders given by his military superiors? And apart from duty, will not the soldier suffer severe punishment, even death, if he refuses to do what he is ordered to do? If, then, a soldier is told by his sergeant or lieutenant to burn this house or shoot that prisoner, how can he be held criminally accountable on the ground that the burning or shooting was a violation of the laws of war?

These are some of the questions that are raised by the concept commonly called "superior orders," and its use as a defense in war crimes trials. It is an issue that must be as old as the laws of war themselves, and it emerged in legal guise over three centuries ago when, after the Stuart restoration in 1660, the commander of the guards at the trial and execution of Charles I was put on trial for treason and murder. The officer defended himself on the ground "that all he did was as a soldier, by the command of his superior officer whom he must obey or die," but the court gave him short shrift, saying that "when the command is traitorous, then the obedience to that command is also traitorous."[1]

Though not precisely articulated, the rule that is necessarily implied by this decision is that it is the soldier's duty to obey *lawful* orders, but that he may disobey—and indeed must, under some circumstances—unlawful orders. Such has been the law of the United States since the birth of the nation. In 1804, Chief Justice John Marshall declared that superior orders will justify a subordinate's conduct only "if not to perform a prohibited act," and there are many other early decisions to the same effect.[2]

A strikingly illustrative case occurred in the wake of that conflict of which most Englishmen have never heard (although their troops burned the White House) and which we call the War of 1812. Our country was badly split by that war too and, at a time when the United States Navy was not especially popular in New England, the ship-of-the-line *Independence* was lying in Boston Harbor. A passer-by directed abusive language at a marine standing guard on the ship, and the marine, Bevans by name, ran his bayonet through the man. Charged with murder, Bevans produced evidence that the marines on the *Independence* had been ordered to bayonet anyone showing them disrespect. The case was tried before Justice Joseph Story, next to Marshall the leading judicial figure of those years, who charged the jury that any such order as Bevans had invoked "would be illegal and void," and if given and put into practice, both superior and subordinate would be guilty of murder. In consequence, Bevans was convicted.[3]

The order allegedly given to Bevans was pretty drastic, and Boston Harbor was not a battlefield; perhaps it was not too much to expect the marine to realize that literal compliance might lead to bad trouble. But it is only too easy to conceive of circumstances where the matter might not be at all clear. Does the subordinate obey at peril that the order may later be ruled illegal, or is he protected unless he had good reason to doubt its validity?

The early cases did not answer this question uniformly or precisely. There are rigid, absolute formulations, such as the statement of Chief Justice Taney in 1851 that: "It can never be maintained that a military officer can justify himself for doing an unlawful act, by producing the order of his superior."[4] More realistic judicial assessments, however, recognized that often the subordinate is in no position to determine the legality or illegality of the order, and that the very nature of military service requires prompt obedience. "While subordinate officers are pausing to consider whether they ought to obey, or are scrupulously weighing the evidence of the facts upon which the commander in chief exercises the right to demand their services," Justice Story observed in 1827, "the hostile enterprise may be accomplished." Twenty-five years later Justice Curtis made much the same point in a case where the soldier was sued for false arrest: "I do not think the defendant was bound to go behind the order, apparently lawful, and satisfy himself by inquiry that his commanding officer proceeded upon sufficient grounds. To require this would be destructive of military discipline and of the necessary promptness and efficiency of the service."[5]

Much the most dramatic case in American military history which turned on this problem was the trial, already mentioned, of Major Henry Wirz, the commandant of the Confederate prison camp at Andersonville, Georgia. Abundant and virtually uncontested evidence showed that the Union prisoners were herded into a camp altogether lacking shelter, so that they froze in winter and burned in summer; that the stream constituting the sole source of water was constantly fouled by corpses and human waste; that the food was totally inadequate, despite abundant harvests in the country around the camp; that neighboring farmers, hearing of the starvation rampant at the camp, came with wagonloads of food for their relief, but were turned away by Wirz; that the camp was a nightmare of hunger, exposure and disease and that the inmates died at the rate of several hundred a week, mounting to a total of some 14,000 by the end of the war.[6]

Wirz was tried before a military commission of six Union generals and two colonels, presided over by Major General Lew Wallace, a minor but protean historical figure who, apart from his military exploits, was a politician, diplomat, lawyer, and author of the fabulously successful novel *Ben-Hur*. A rigid-minded German Swiss, Wirz defended himself on the ground that his administration of the camp was governed by orders from General John H. Winder, the officer in charge of all Confederate prison camps. The evidence bore out his claim, but the prosecution took the position that Wirz had followed orders willingly rather than under duress, and that Wirz and Winder were co-conspirators. The military commission found Wirz guilty of both conspiring to destroy the lives of Union soldiers and of murder "in violation of the laws and customs of war," and sentenced him to be hanged. Presumably, therefore, it must have accepted the prosecution's contention, though (in accordance with the practice of military courts) there was no written opinion.[7]

Awareness that a problem is an old one is not, of course, the key to its solution. But these cases of many years past are important, I believe, in showing that the idea that under some circumstances military orders ought to be disobeyed is not a novel doctrine first conceived at Nuremberg. Furthermore, while the earliest decisions on the point were rendered by civilian judges, the modern development of the doctrine during the 75 years following the Civil War was largely the work of military men.

The Lieber regulations and the Hague and Geneva conventions are silent on this subject, and the earliest statement of a general governing rule appeared in the German Military Penal Code of 1872, Article 47 of which provided: "If execution of an order given in line of duty violates a statute of the penal code, the superior giving the order is alone responsible. However, the subordinate obeying the order is liable to punishment as an accomplice if . . . he knew that the order involved an act the commission of which constituted a civil or military crime or offense."

The imposition of responsibility on those giving legal orders, but not the secondary responsibility of subordinates who carry out orders known to be illegal, was provided for in the British and U.S. army manuals published in 1914.[8] Both explicitly exempted from liability those whose violations of the laws of war were committed

under orders of their "government" or "commanders," while
declaring that the commanders who ordered or authorized the
offenses might be punished. These provisions raised questions
whether anyone at all could be held liable if the "commanders"
were themselves acting under orders from still farther up the
military chain of command.

At the outbreak of the Second World War, accordingly, military
law on the question of superior orders was in a state of considerable
confusion. The British and U.S. manuals appeared to treat them as
an absolute defense to charges against an accused subordinate, but
was this really intended, no matter how atrocious the order?
Perhaps not, for elsewhere the British manual called for "prompt,
immediate, and unhesitating obedience" only when the "orders of
the superior are not obviously and decidedly in opposition to the
law of the land or to the well-known and established customs of the
army." The German law of 1872 embodied a more rational
approach and, despite all the horrors of the Nazi conquests and
exterminations, it remained in effect throughout the war, and was
reaffirmed in principle by no less a person than Dr. Joseph
Goebbels, the Minister of Propaganda, who in May, 1944,
published an article condemning Allied bombing operations, in
which he declared, "No intentional law of warfare is in existence
which provides that a soldier who has committed a mean crime can
escape punishment by pleading as his defence that he followed the
commands of his superiors. This holds particularly true if those
commands are contrary to all human ethics and opposed to the
well-established usage of warfare."[9]

During the same year (1944) the British and U.S. military
establishments revised the "superior orders" provisions of their
field manuals.[10] The new British language adopted the essential
principle of the German law of 1872, cast in discursive rather than
statutory terms. Members of the armed forces "are bound to obey
lawful orders only"; to be sure, in conditions of "war discipline"
they could not "be expected to weigh scrupulously the legal merits
of the order received," but they could not "escape liability if, in
obedience to a command, they commit acts which both violate
unchallenged rules of warfare and outrage the general sentiment of
humanity."

The 1944 U.S. provision was quite different, for it stated no

guiding principle whatever. Individuals who violate the laws of
war "may be punished therefor," it declared, adding: "However,
the fact that the acts complained of were done pursuant to order of
a superior or government sanction may be taken into consideration
in determining culpability, either by way of defense or in
mitigation of punishment." But *when* should such orders "be taken
into consideration," and what should determine whether the
orders ought to be considered as a defense or merely in mitigation?
It was a most unsatisfactory formulation.

Scrutiny of these efforts of military men to grapple with the effect
of superior orders, as a defense to war crimes charges, discloses that
the problem involves two quite different factors, one of which is
appropriate by way of defense, and the other only in mitigation.
The first is essentially a question of *knowledge,* and the second a
question of *fear.*

Some orders are so atrocious, or plainly unlawful, that the
subordinate must know, or can reasonably be held to know, that
they should not be obeyed. But, especially in combat situations,
there are bound to be many orders the legitimacy of which depends
on the prevailing circumstances, the existence and sufficiency of
which will be beyond the reach of the subordinate's observation or
judgment. The military service is based on obedience to orders
passed down through the chains of command, and the success of
military operations often depends on the speed and precision with
which orders are executed. Especially in the lower ranks, virtually
unquestioning obedience to orders, other than those that are
palpably vicious, is a necessary feature of military life. If the
subordinate is expected to give such obedience, he should also be
entitled to rely on the order as a full and complete defense to any
charge that his act was unlawful. The German law of 1872 was
therefore rightly conceived insofar as it made the subordinate's
liability turn on his awareness of the order's unlawful quality.

But knowledge is not the end of the problem. Suppose the soldier
is indeed aware that the order is beyond the pale, but is confronted
by a superior who is backing his command with threat of stern
punishment, perhaps immediate death. It is one thing to require
men at war to risk their lives against the enemy, but quite another
to expect them to face severe or even capital penalties on the basis
of their own determination that their superior's command is

unlawful. Such a course calls for a high degree of moral as well as physical courage; men are not to be judged too severely for falling short, and mitigation of the punishment is appropriate.

Substantially these rules—that lack of knowledge of an order's unlawfulness is a defense, and fear of punishment for disobedience a mitigating circumstance—are embodied in the army's current field manual, issued in 1956:

> a. The fact that the law of war has been violated pursuant to an order of a superior authority, whether military or civil, does not deprive the act in question of its character of a war crime, nor does it constitute a defense in the trial of an accused individual, unless he did not know and could not reasonably have been expected to know that the act ordered was unlawful. In all cases where the order is held not to constitute a defense to an allegation of war crime, the fact that the individual was acting pursuant to orders may be considered in mitigation of punishment.
>
> b. In considering the question whether a superior order constitutes a valid defense, the court shall take into consideration the fact that obedience to lawful military orders is the duty of every member of the armed forces; that the latter cannot be expected, in conditions of war discipline, to weigh scrupulously the legal merits of the orders received; that certain rules of warfare may be controversial; or that an act otherwise amounting to a war crime may be done in obedience to orders conceived as a measure of reprisal. At the same time it must be borne in mind that members of the armed forces are bound to obey only lawful orders.[11]

These principles are sound, and the language is well chosen to convey the quality of the factors, imponderable as they are, that must be assessed in a given case. As with so many good rules, the difficulty lies in its application—in weighing evidence that is likely to be ambiguous or conflicting. Was there a superior order? Especially at the lower levels, many orders are given orally. Was a particular remark or look intended as an order, and if so what was its scope? If the existence and meaning of the order are reasonably clear, there may still be much doubt about the attendant circumstances—how far the obeying soldier was aware of them, and how well equipped to judge them. If the order was plainly illegal, to what degree of duress was the subordinate subjected?

Especially in confused ground fighting of the type prevalent in Vietnam, evidentiary questions such as these may be extremely difficult to resolve.

The doctrine of "superior orders" as a defense for the subordinate is, of course, the converse of what lawyers call *respondeat superior*—the liability of the order-giver. And in conclusion, it should be emphasized that the consequence of allowing superior orders as a defense is not to eliminate criminal responsibility for what happened, but to shift its locus upwards. It would stultify the whole system to exculpate the underlings who follow orders and ignore the superiors who give them. Indeed, the greater the indulgence shown to the soldier on the theory that his first duty is to give unquestioning obedience, the greater the responsibility of the officer to see to it that obedience entails no criminal consequences.

The superior's responsibility, moreover, is not limited to the situation where he has given affirmative orders. A commander is responsible for the conduct of his troops, and is expected to take all necessary action to see that they do not, on their own initiative, commit war crimes. General George B. McClellan, as commander of the Army of the Potomac in 1861, warned all of his officers that they would "be held responsible for punishing aggression by those under their command," and directed that military commissions be established to punish any persons connected with his army who might engage in conduct "in contravention of the established rules of law." The 1956 army manual provides explicitly that a military commander is responsible not only for criminal acts committed in pursuance of his orders, but "is also responsible if he has actual knowledge, or should have knowledge . . . that troops or other persons subject to his control are about to commit or have committed a war crime and he fails to take the necessary and reasonable steps to insure compliance with the law of war or to punish violations thereof."[12]

This language embodied no novel conception of a commander's responsibility. Ten years earlier, a military commission of American generals condemned General Tomayuki Yamashita to death by hanging, for failure properly to control the conduct of Japanese troops under his command in the Philippines. The *Yamashita* case, and the principles that it exemplifies, are of great importance in establishing the reach of criminal responsibility for episodes such as those said to have occurred at Son My.

Another doctrine, which may be invoked to justify conduct that otherwise would be a war crime, is that of *reprisals*. Today the open resort to reprisals is not as frequent as in earlier times, but the concept is nonetheless of great importance in relation to the conduct of the war in Vietnam.

In origin, a reprisal (or "retaliation," as Lieber called it) was an action taken by a nation against an enemy that would normally be a violation of the laws of war, but that was justified as necessary to prevent the enemy from continuing to violate the laws of war. Thus if one side makes a practice of shooting medical corpsmen or bombing hospitals, the other side may take action by way of reprisal in order to dissuade the enemy from continuing his unlawful course of conduct. The justification for reprisals was the lack of any apparent alternative; the enemy miscreants were beyond the reach of the offended belligerent, and protests had proved fruitless. As Lieber put it, their purpose was not "mere revenge," but rather "protective retribution."

Resort to reprisals in order to bring an enemy government back to the paths of military virtue is still recognized by the laws of war, subject to various restrictions written into the Geneva Conventions and the recent army field manuals. But reprisals of this type are not much used today, partly because they are generally ineffective, and partly because the resort to crime in order to reform the criminal is an unappetizing method. Generally, a nation that deliberately embarks on a course of conduct violative of the laws of war will have taken into account the possibility and effect of reprisals, and will not be easily checked. Then crime and reprisal both continue, and the standards of warfare are debased.

But reprisals of another type, directed not against any enemy government but against the civilian population of territory under military operation, are of great significance in relation to both Nuremberg and the Vietnam War. They were inflicted on a number of occasions during the Civil War,[13] and used extensively by the Germans during the Franco-Prussian War of 1871 and the First World War. One example from many is General Karl von Bulow's proclamation of August 22, 1914, issued in the course of the German advance into Belgium:

The inhabitants of the town of Andenne, after having protested their peaceful intentions, made a treacherous surprise attack on our troops.

It was with my consent that the General had the whole place burned down, and about one hundred people shot.

I bring this fact to the attention of the town of Liège, so that its inhabitants may know the fate with which they are threatened, if they take a similar attitude.

Closely related to the matter of reprisals is the practice of taking hostages. In past centuries, two countries that had made a treaty often exchanged hostages, as mutual security for compliance. In modern warfare, civilian hostages have been taken by armies occupying enemy territory, as a measure of ensuring the good behavior of the local population.

Before the Second World War, the state of the laws of war with respect to the use of reprisals and the taking and treatment of hostages in occupied territory was one of considerable confusion and conflict. The U.S. field manuals of 1914 and 1940, perhaps influenced by the army's experience in the "pacification" of the Philippines after the Spanish-American War, gave the occupying power great latitude for positive action. The 1940 manual included the following:

Hostages taken and held for the declared purpose of insuring against unlawful acts by the enemy forces or people may be punished or put to death if the unlawful acts are nevertheless committed. . . . Villages or houses, etc., may be burned for acts of hostility committed from them, where the guilty individuals cannot be identified, tried and punished. Collective punishments may be inflicted either in the form of fines or otherwise.[14]

To what extent such language reflected international opinion on the point is hard to say. Draconic as it is, the U.S. provision would have fallen far short of authorizing the extensive and ruthless use of hostages and reprisals that characterized the German military regimes in the occupied countries of Europe, especially in the Balkans and Russia. In consequence, these problems were an important part of the subject matter of the Nuremberg trials, as will shortly appear.

After Nuremberg, hostages and reprisal questions were considered in framing the 1949 Geneva Convention Relative to the Protection of Civilian Persons in Time of War, and important reforms were adopted, which were carried into the 1956 army manual. Under these new provisions, the taking of hostages is entirely forbidden, and the permissible scope of reprisals is much more restricted than it was under the 1940 manual.

The trend of the laws of war since the Second World War is in line with Francis Lieber's judgment, expressed in the 1863 rules, that: "Unjust or inconsiderate retaliation removes the belligerents farther and farther from the mitigating rules of regular warfare, and by rapid steps leads them farther to the internecine wars of savages."

Notes

1. *Axtell's case*, 84 Eng. Rep. 1060 (1660).
2. Marshall's statement was made in *Little* v. *Bareme*, 2 Cranch 170, 179 (1804). For parallel decisions, see those of Justice Bushrod Washington in *United States* v. *Bright*, Fed. Cas. No. 14647 (C.C.D.Pa. 1809) and *United States* v. *Jones*, Fed. Cas. No. 15494 (C.C.D.Pa. 1813).
3. *United States* v. *Bevans*, Fed. Cas. No. 14589 (C.C.C.Mass. 1816). The case was tried in the Federal court on the jurisdictional basis that the crime occurred on the high seas. The Supreme Court reversed the conviction on the ground that Massachusetts Bay was not part of the high seas, and therefore the Federal courts had no jurisdiction. *United States* v. *Bevans*, 3 Wheat. 336 (1818).
4. *Mitchell* v. *Harmony*, 13 How. 115, 137 (1851).
5. Story's observation is in *Martin* v. *Mott*, 12 Wheat. 19, 30 (1827), and Curtis' in *Despan* v. *Olney*, Fed. Cas. No. 3822 (C.C.D.R.I. 1852).
6. The proceedings of the military commission in the Wirz case were published in House Executive Documents, Vol. 8, No. 23, Serial No. 1381, 40th Cong. 2d Sess. (1868). There is a vivid contemporaneous account of Andersonville and Libby prisons in A. C. Roach, *The Prisoner of War and How Treated* (Indianapolis, 1865). The play based on the trial, by Saul Levitt, is published by Dramatists Play Service, Inc. Those interested in the subject may also want to read McKinley Kantor's novel *Andersonville*, published in 1955.
7. In the play based on the trial, Wirz's last line is, "I did not have that feeling of strength to do that. I could not disobey." There is an interesting likeness between this language and the statement of the

German Supreme Court in the *Llandovery Castle* case (convicting two naval lieutenants who had acted under superior orders) that: "A refusal to obey the commander of a submarine would have been something so unusual, that it is humanly possible to understand that the accused could not bring themselves to disobey."

8. The British provision is in *Manual of Military Law* (1914) p. 302, par. 366; the American is in *Rules of Land Warfare* (1917) p. 130, par. 366.

9. *Deutsche Allgemeine Zeitung,* 28 May 1944.

10. The 1944 revisions of the superior orders provisions of the British and U.S. manuals are set forth in *History of the United Nations War Crimes Commission* (HMSO 1948), p. 282. The 1940 edition of the U.S. army's *Rules of Land Warfare* repeated (par. 347) the provision of the 1914 manual.

11. FM 27-10, *The Law of Warfare,* p. 182, par. 509, entitled "Defense of Superior Orders."

12. FM 27-10, *The Law of Warfare,* p. 178, par. 501. McClellan's order is quoted in Colby, "War Crimes," *23 Michigan Law Review* 482, at 502 (1925).

13. In 1864, the Union General David Hunter burned many Virginia homes during his advance in the Shenandoah Valley. The Confederate General Jubal Early drove Hunter's forces back across the Potomac and, when Confederate troops reached Chambersburg, Pennsylvania, Early ordered the town burned by way of reprisal. The regimental commander in Chambersburg, Colonel William E. Peters, refused to obey Early's order, and was relieved of his command and placed under arrest, while others did the burning. There is a vivid account of all this in the Confederate General John B. Gordon's "Reminiscences of the Civil War" (1903), in which the author pays high tribute to Peters's courage and chivalry, and states that "prudently and wisely, he was never brought to trial for his disobedience."

14. FM 27-10, *Rules of Land Warfare* (1940) pp. 89-90, par. 358.

27

Can I Be Blamed
for Obeying Orders?

R. M. Hare

Professor Hare is a British philosopher and the author of many books and articles on ethics. He is particularly known for emphasizing the meaning of and relationships between ethical terms before analyzing specific practical moral problems. In this article Professor Hare points out that the argument "This person commands me to do X; therefore, I ought to do X" is invalid unless we add a premise that would tie together the fact of the command and the alleged moral obligation. However, in the case of a command to commit moral atrocities, the clear immorality of the commanded action serves to suggest that whatever additional premise (which would yield a valid argument) might be proposed would be false. At a minimum, such a premise would be false if it logically required that we have an absolute *moral obligation to obey.*

—K. W.

Many people, if asked for the distinctive feature of present-day British philosophy, would say that it lies in the peculiar attention which we tend to pay to the study of language. Perhaps most British philosophers would agree that the study of language, in some sense, is a very potent philosophical tool; and many would say that it is *the* philosophical method—that any problem which is properly philosophical reduces in the end to an elucidation of our use of words. Criticisms of this approach to philosophy are frequently made by those who have not practised the sort of method we use, and therefore do not understand either what the method is, or how fruitful it can be. It is alleged that we are turning philosophy away from matters of substance to trivial verbal matters (as if it were a trivial matter to understand the words we use); and it is also sometimes said that we are to be contrasted unfavourably in this respect with the great philosophers of the past.

The purpose of these talks is to indicate, by means of two examples taken from political philosophy, that both these criticisms arise from misunderstandings of the nature of philosophy in general and of our kind of philosophy in particular. The point could have been made by means of a general discussion about philosophical method; or it could have been made by taking examples out of the works of famous philosophers, and showing how much kinship there is between their methods of argumentation and ours. But I thought it better to take two practical problems of political morality—problems which exercise us currently, or ought to—and to show how a great deal of light can be shed on these by an understanding of the words used in discussing them: an understanding of the sort which it is the purpose of contemporary moral philosophy to achieve. None of the things I shall say will be original; indeed, it is part of the point of these talks that they are not original: I am merely translating into a new, and I think clearer, idiom things which have been said by great philosophers of the past, and thereby showing that the new idiom is a vehicle for philosophy as it has always been understood.

In the first of these talks I shall discuss a problem which arises frequently in wartime and in connection with war crimes trials. The thesis is sometimes maintained that a soldier's duty is always to obey orders; and this is often brought forward as a defense when someone is accused of having committed some atrocity. It is said that, since it is a soldier's duty to obey his orders, and he is liable to blame if he disobeys them, we cannot consistently also blame him if in a particular case he obeys them—even though the act which he has committed is of itself wrong. We may blame his superiors who gave the orders, but not the man who carried them out. Others, in opposition to this, maintain that the individual is always responsible for his own acts.

Can the study of moral language shed any light on this problem?

I want to maintain that it can; and the way I shall do this is by exhibiting the formal features of the problem, as they arise out of the logical properties of the words used in discussing it. I wish to show that these formal features are common to a large range of questions which are not at first sight similar, and that the key to the whole matter is a purely linguistic and logical observation made a long time ago by Hume.

The formal features of this problem are brought out extremely clearly by Kant in a famous passage,[1] in which he is arguing that we have to make our own moral judgements, and cannot get them made for us, without any decision on our part, by God. Suppose that I am commanded by God to do something. The Bible is full of stories where this is said to have happened. Can I without further consideration conclude that I ought to do it? Kant argued (rightly) that I cannot—not without further consideration. For it does not follow automatically, as it were, from the fact that God wills me to do something, that I ought to do it. From the fact that God wills me to do something, I can only conclude that I ought to do it if I am given the additional premise that God wills that and that only to be done, which ought to be done. This additional premise is one which indeed Christians all accept, because they believe that God is good; and part of what we mean by saying that God is good is that he wills that and that only to be done which ought to be done. But we have to assume this, if we are to pass from the fact that God wills us to do something to the conclusion that we ought to do it. So we can indeed, as it were, get out of making the particular moral decision as to whether we ought to do this particular thing, by putting it on the shoulders of God; but only at the cost of having to make for ourselves a more general moral decision, that we ought always to do what God commands (the very fundamental, crucial decision that is made when anyone decided to become, or to remain, an adherent of the Christian or some other religion). This more general moral judgement obviously cannot, without arguing in a circle, be shuffled off our shoulders in the same way.

Yet, if we do not assume that God is good, the only conception we have left of him is one of power without goodness—one, as Kant picturesquely puts it, compounded of lust for glory and domination, together with frightful ideas of power and vengefulness; and to make our duty the obedience to the will of such a being would be to adopt a highly immoral morality. We might rather be inclined to approve of disobeying an evil God, as Shelley portrays Prometheus doing, however appalling the consequences.

I want you to notice that this argument does not depend on its being God's will in particular upon which it is sought to base morality. The same argument would apply were we to substitute for 'God' the name of any other person whatever, divine or human. Kant is here making use of a principle in ethics which was, so far as I am aware, first stated by Hume. The actual passage is worth quoting, both because it is rightly held to be one of the two or three most important observations in moral philosophy, and because it illustrates very well my thesis that the subject matter of philosophy is the use of words. Hume says:

> In every system of authority, which I have hitherto met with, I have always remark'd, that the author proceeds for some time in the ordinary way of reasoning, and establishes the being of a God, or makes observations concerning human affairs; when of a sudden I am surpriz'd to find, that instead of the usual copulations of propositions, *is*, and *is not*, I meet with no proposition that is not connected with an *ought*, or an *ought not*. This change is imperceptible; but is, however, of the last consequence. For as this *ought*, or *ought not*, expresses some new relation or affirmation, 'tis necessary that it shou'd be observ'd and explain'd; and at the same time that a reason should be given, for what seems altogether inconceivable, how this new relation can be a deduction from others, which are entirely different from it. But as authors do not commonly use this precaution, I shall presume to recommend it to the readers; and am persuaded that this small attention wou'd subvert all the vulgar systems of morality.[2]

It is easy to apply this canon of Hume's to our example. The proposition "X's will is, that I do A" (where X is any person whatever and A is any act whatever) is a proposton of fact, an "is"-proposition. It does not matter who X is; in Kant's example it was God; but it might be some human ruler. From this "is"-proposition the "ought"-proposition "I ought to do A" cannot be derived. The first proposition states a mere fact, a fact about what someone wills that I do. From this fact no moral proposition follows. Only if we are given the *moral* premise, "X wills that and that only to be done, which ought to be done" or "Everything which X wills to be done, ought to be done" can we, from this, in conjunction with the premise "X's will is, that I do A," conclude that I ought to do A. This is all right, because we have added to our factual minor premise a moral major premise; and from the two together we can infer a moral conclusion; but not from the factual minor premise alone.

In the example with which I started, X was God. But I wish to discuss the first and most celebrated example of a philosopher who thought that moral decisions could be made on his subjects' behalf by a ruler, namely Plato. Plato thought that, just as there are experts in riding and in other skills, so there ought to be experts in morals. All we had to do, in order to solve all moral problems, was to get such an expert, make him our philosopher-king, and leave him to decide for us what was right and what was wrong. He would make the laws, and we, by obeying them, could be absolutely certain of living morally blameless lives. This program has an obvious and immediate appeal. For moral problems are difficult and tormenting; how fortunate it would be if we could leave them, like problems of engineering, to somebody who could solve them for us! To get rid of one's moral problems on to the shoulders of someone else—some political or military leader, some priest or commissar—is to be free of much worry; it is to exchange the tortured responsibility of the adult for the happy irresponsibility of the child; that is why so many have taken this course.

The flaw in this arrangement is that we could never know whether the philosopher-king really was a philosopher-king. Plato himself admits that his ideal republic might degenerate. The maintenance of the republic depended on the correct calculation of the famous Platonic Number,[3] which was used for determining the correct mating-season to produce the philosopher-kings of the next generation. If the number were miscalculated, a person might be made ruler who did not really possess the required qualifications. Suppose that we are inhabitants of a Platonic republic, and are ordered by our so-called philosopher-king to do a certain act. And suppose that we are troubled about the morality of this act; suppose that it is the act of torturing some unfortunate person. It is perfectly true that if our ruler is a *true* philosopher-king, then, *ex hypothesi*, he knows infallibly what is right and what is wrong, and so we cannot do wrong to obey him. But the question is: Can we be sure that he is the genuine article? Can we be sure that they did not miscalculate the number a generation ago, so that what we have at this moment is not a philosopher-king, but the most wicked of tyrants masquerading as one?

We can tell whether a man is a good man, or, specifically, whether a king is a good king, only by considering his acts. So that it is no use saying of *all* our ruler's acts, "He is the philosopher-king, and the philosopher-king can do no wrong; therefore each and every act of his must be right." For this would be to argue in a circle. It is only if we are satisfied that his acts are right that we can be satisfied that he is a good king. Therefore if he commands us to perform what looks like an atrocity, the only thing we can do is look at the individual act and say, "What about this very thing that he is commanding me to do now? Could a good man command anyone to do this?" That is to say, we have to make up our own minds about the morality of the king's acts and orders.

Governing is different from engineering in an important respect. The engineer as such is concerned with means only; but government involves the choice both of means and ends. If you know no engineering, you have to get the best engineer you can to build your bridge; but the engineer is not the man who decides that there shall be a bridge. Therefore, we can say to the engineer, "We want a bridge just here"; and leave him to build it. We judge him by his success in bringing about the end which we have set him. If his bridge falls into the river, we do not employ him again. Rulers also often have to find means to ends which are agreed upon. For example, it is recognized that it is a bad thing if large numbers of people starve through being unable to get employment; and we expect our rulers nowadays to see to it that this does not happen. The means to this end are very complicated, and only an economist can understand them; but we are content to leave our rulers to employ competent economists, understand their prescriptions as best they can, choose between them when, as often, they conflict, and generally do their best to realize the end of full employment without impairing any other of the ends which we also wish to realize. But in government someone has to decide on the ends of policy. In a democracy this is done by the voters. They do it in part explicitly and in advance, by choosing between parties with rival policies; but in the main they do it implicitly and by results, by turning out of office those parties who do not achieve the ends which the voters desire.

In Plato's republic it was different. The people were supposed to be entirely ignorant both about means and about ends; the rulers decided on both. And if the ruler decides both on the means and on the end, one cannot judge him as one judges the engineer. For one can say to the engineer, "You were told to produce a bridge that stood up to the weather, and your bridge has been blown into the river." But if we have not told our ruler to do anything—if we have just left it to him to decide on the ends of political action—then we cannot ever accuse him of not fulfilling the purposes which we intended him to fulfill. He can always say, "I did what I thought good, and I still think it good." This is the decisive point at which Plato's analogy between the ruler and the expert breaks down. The expert is an expert at getting something done, once it has been decided *what* is to be done. Plato's philosopher-king was supposed to do not merely this—he was supposed not merely to perform a task, but to decide what the task was to be. And this is a thing that cannot be left to experts; it is the responsibility of all of us.

If it is true that we cannot leave the moral problems about political ends to a Platonic philosopher-king, then it is still more obviously true that we cannot leave them to any ordinary human superior. As I said at the beginning, we often hear it said by someone who is accused of a war crime—for example of killing some innocent people in cold blood—"I did it on the orders of my superior officers; I am not morally guilty." If the superior officers could likewise be found and charged they would say the same thing, until we got back, perhaps, to some high-up ruler who initiated in some very general terms some policy whose detailed execution involved the slaughtering of the innocents. But how can the orders of somebody else absolve *me* from moral responsibility? It may indeed absolve me from legal responsibility: that is a different matter, and depends on the law that is in force. But if we are speaking of a matter of morals, surely the man who is ordered to do such an act has to ask himself whether it is morally right for him to do it. It cannot follow, from the "is"-proposition that *X* orders me to kill these people, that I ought to kill them. The people who order these crimes, and I who execute them, are accomplices, and share the responsibility.

In many cases, admittedly, a person in such a position can plead that he is acting under duress; he, or his family, will be shot if he does not obey orders. We do tend to excuse a man in such a position, or at any rate to blame him less. Why we do so is also a matter upon which the study of moral language can shed a good deal of light; but I have no time to discuss it now. Let us exclude duress from the argument by assuming that the subordinate knows that his superiors will not find out whether he has obeyed orders or not: let us suppose that he is the head of a mental home who has been ordered to poison all incurables, and that he himself does the classification into curables and incurables.

Up to a certain point, indeed, a person in this position can plead ignorance of fact; his superiors, no doubt, have access to more information than he has, and can foresee consequences of the omission to murder these people which might not be known to the person who has to perform the act. Up to a point a subordinate can say, "I cannot see the whole picture; I must be content to leave the formulation of policy to my superiors, whose job it is to know what the consequences would be of various alternative policies, and to make a choice between evils." But the point must in the end come when a subordinate has to say, "Any policy which involves my doing this sort of thing (for example, slaughtering all these people in cold blood) must be a wicked policy, and anyone who has conceived it must be a wicked man; it cannot therefore be my duty to obey him." To decide just when this point has been reached is one of the most difficult problems in morals. But we must never banish from our minds the thought that it might be reached. We must never lose sight of the distinction between what we are told to do and what we ought to do. There is a point beyond which we cannot get rid of our own moral responsibilities by laying them on the shoulders of a superior, whether he be general, priest or politician, human or divine. Anyone who thinks otherwise has not understood what a moral decision is.

Notes

1. *Groundwork*, 2d ed., p. 92 (tr. Paton, *The Moral Law*, p. 104).
2. David Hume, *Treatise*, III I i.
3. Plato, *Republic*, 546c.

28

The Laws of War

Richard Wasserstrom

*In this paper, Professor Wasserstrom argues rather uniquely that a view of
the current laws of war that upholds their moral importance and primacy is a
view that is "mistaken" and "morally unattractive." He argues that the laws
of war do not make the important moral distinctions often claimed for them
(most critically they do not appropriately distinguish between combatants and
noncombatants), and secondly, they do not have the beneficial effects
frequently attributed to them. He finds that the doctrine of "military
necessity" too often provides exceptions to rules that might have protected the
innocent, that conduct cannot be labeled criminal if both sides in the conflict
engage in it, and that the conventions in war change to accommodate the
introduction of "important instruments of war." He argues that the
traditional view that the laws of war restrain uses of violence and prevent war
from becoming totally inhuman is not compelling or totally accurate. The
incompleteness and incoherence of the existing laws of war and the prevailing
provision that permits the rules to be set aside when they conflict with an
important military goal together legitimate what Wasserstrom calls "morally
indefensible behavior." He concludes that proper laws of war should make the
methods and instruments of war conform to rules of morality and not the other
way around.*

—M.M.W.

Many persons who consider the variety of moral and legal
problems that arise in respect to war come away convinced that the
firmest area for judgment is that of how persons ought to behave in

time of war. Such persons feel a confidence about dealing with questions of how war ought to be conducted that is absent when other issues about war are raised. They are, for example, more comfortable with the rules relating to how soldiers ought to behave vis-à-vis enemy soldiers and enemy civilians—the laws of war—than they are with the principles relating to when war is permissible and when it is not. Thus, most commentators and critics are uneasy about the applicability to the American scene of that part of Nuremberg that deals with crimes against peace and crimes against humanity. But they have no comparable uneasiness about insisting that persons who commit war crimes, violations of the laws of war, be held responsible for their actions.

I propose to consider several features of this view—and I do think it a widely held one—which accepts the moral significance and urges the primacy of the laws of war. I am not interested in providing a genetic account of why this view gets held. I am, rather, concerned to explicate at least one version of this view and to explore the grounds upon which such a view might rest. And I want also to show why such a position is a mistaken one: mistaken in the sense that this conception of the laws of war is a morally unattractive one and one which has no special claim upon our attention or our energies.

There are two general, quite distinct arguments for this notion of the primacy of the laws of war. One is that the laws of war are important and deserving of genuine respect and rigorous enforcement because they reflect, embody and give effect to fundamental moral distinctions and considerations. The other is that, considered simply as laws and conventions, they merit this dominant role because general adherence to them has important, desirable effects. The former of these arguments emphasizes the contents of the laws of war and the connection they have with more basic moral ideas. The latter argument emphasizes the beneficial consequences that flow from their presence and acceptance.

The arguments are clearly not mutually exclusive; indeed, they are related to each other in several important respects. Nonetheless, it is useful to distinguish sharply between them for purposes of analysis and to examine the strengths and weaknesses of each in turn. Before I do so, however, it is necessary to explicate more fully the nature of the laws of war with which I shall be concerned. This is so because it is important to see that I am concerned with a particular view of the character of the laws of war and the related notion of a war crime.[1] I believe it to be the case that this account constitutes an accurate description of the existing laws of war and the dominant conception of a war crime. That is to say, I think it is what many if not most lawyers, commentators, military tribunals, and courts have in mind when they talk about the laws of war and the responsibility of individuals for the commissions of war crimes. In this sense at least, the sketch I am about to give constitutes an actual, and not merely a possible, conception of the laws of war. If I am right, the criticisms that I make here have substantial practical importance. But I may of course be wrong; I may have misstated the actual laws of war and the rules for their applicability. To the degree that I have done so, my criticism will, perhaps, less forcefully apply to the real world, but not thereby to the conception of the laws of war I delineate below.

I

The system I am concerned to describe and discuss has the following features. There are, to begin with, a number of formal agreements, conventions, and treaties among countries that prescribe how countries (chiefly through their armies) are to behave in times of war. And there are, as well, generally accepted "common law" rules and practices which also regulate behavior in warfare. Together they comprise the substantive laws of war. For the most part, the laws of war deal with two sorts of things: how classes of persons are to be treated in war, e.g. prisoners of war, and what sorts of weapons and methods of attack are impermissible, e.g. the use of poison gas. Some of the laws of war—particularly those embodied in formal documents—are narrow in scope and specific in formulation. Thus, Article 4 of the Annex to the Hague Convention on Land Warfare, 1907 provided in part that all the personal belongings of prisoners of war, "except arms, horses, and military papers," remain their property. Others are a good deal more general and vague. For example, Article 23(e) of the same Annex to the Hague Convention prohibits resort to "arms, projectiles, or material calculated to cause unnecessary suffering."

Similarly, Article 3 of the Geneva Conventions on the Law of War, 1949 provides in part that "Persons taking no active part in the hostilities . . . shall in all circumstances be treated humanely." And at Nuremberg, war crimes were defined as "violations of the laws or customs of war. Such violations shall include but not be limited to, murder, ill-treatment or deportation to slave-labor or for any other purpose of civilian population of or in occupied territory, murder or ill-treatment of prisoners of war or persons on the seas, killing of hostages, plunder of public property, wanton destruction of cities, towns or villages, or devastation not justified by military necessity."[2]

The most important feature of this conception of the laws of war is that the laws of war are to be understood as in fact prohibiting only violence and suffering that are not connected in any direct or important way with the waging of war. As one commentator has put it, the laws of war have as their objective that "the ravages of war should be mitigated as far as possible by prohibiting needless cruelties, and other acts that spread death and destruction and are not reasonably related to the conduct of hostilities."[3]

This is reflected by the language of many of the laws themselves. But it is demonstrated far more forcefully by the way even relatively unambiguous prohibitions are to be interpreted. The former characteristic is illustrated by that part of the Nuremberg definition of war crimes which prohibits the "*wanton* destruction of cities, towns or villages." The latter characteristic is illustrated by the following commentary upon Article 23(c) of the Hague Convention quoted above. That article, it will be recalled, prohibits the resort to arms calculated to cause unnecessary suffering. But "unnecessary suffering" means suffering that is not reasonably related to any military advantage to be derived from its infliction. "The legality of hand grenades, flame-throwers, napalm, and incendiary bombs in contemporary warfare is a vivid reminder that suffering caused by weapons with sufficiently large destructive potentialities is not 'unnecessary' in the meaning of this rule."[4]

Another way to make the same point is to indicate the way in which the doctrine of "military necessity" plays a central role in this conception of the laws of war. It, too, is explicitly written into a number of the laws of war as providing a specific exception. Thus, to quote a portion of the Nuremberg definition once again, what is prohibited is "devastation not justified by military necessity."

The doctrine of military necessity is, moreover, more firmly and centrally embedded in this conception of the laws of war than illustrations of the preceding type would suggest. The doctrine does not merely create an explicit exception, i.e. as in "devastation not justified by military necessity." Instead, it functions as a general justification for the violation of most, if not all, of even the specific prohibitions which constitute a portion of the laws of war. Thus, according to one exposition of the laws of war, the flat prohibition against the killing of enemy combatants who have surrendered is to be understood to permit the killing of such persons where that is required by "military necessity." There may well be times in any war when it is permissible to kill combatants who have laid down their arms and tried to surrender:

> Small detachments on special missions, or accidentally cut off from their main force, may take prisoners under such circumstances that men cannot be spared to guard them or take them to the rear, and that to take them along would greatly endanger the success of the mission or the safety of the unit. The prisoners will be killed by operation of the principle of military necessity, and no military or other court has been called upon, so far as I am aware, to declare such killings a war crime.[5]

Or, consider another case where, according to Taylor, the doctrine of military necessity makes ostensibly impermissible conduct permissible. In 1930, a number of nations signed the London Naval Treaty. That treaty required that no ship sink a merchant vessel "without having first placed passengers, crew and ship's papers in a place of safety." The provisions of this treaty were regularly violated in the Second World War. Nonetheless these violations were not war crimes punished at Nuremberg. This is so, says Taylor, for two reasons. First, the doctrine of military necessity makes the treaty unworkable. If submarines are to be effective instrumentations of war, they cannot surface before they attack merchant ships, nor can they stand around waiting to pick up survivors. The answer is not that it is wrong to use submarines. Rather it is that in the interest of military necessity the prohibitions of the treaty cease to be prohibitions. And second, even if considerations of military necessity were not decisive here, violations of the London treaty would still not have been war crimes because the treaty was violated by both sides during the Second World War. And nothing is properly a war crime, says Taylor (at least in the absence of a genuine international tribunal) if both sides engage in the conduct in question.

> As long as enforcement of the laws of war is left to the belligerents themselves, whether during the course of hostilities or by the victors at the conclusion, the scope of their application must be limited by the extent to which they have been observed by the enforcing party. To punish the foe—especially the vanquished foe—for conduct in which the enforcing nation has engaged, would be so grossly inequitable as to discredit the laws of themselves.[6]

Finally, the question of the legality of aerial warfare is especially instructive and important. Once more I take Telford Taylor's analysis to be illustrative of the conception I have been trying to delineate. The bombing of cities was, he observes, not punished at Nuremberg and is not a war crime. Why not? For the two reasons he has already given. Since it was engaged in by the Allies—and on a much more intensive level than by the Germans or the Japanese —it would have been improper to punish the Germans and the Japanese for what we also did. But more importantly the bombing of cities with almost any kind of bomb imaginable is perfectly proper because bombing is an important instrument of the war.

There is nothing illegal about bombing population centers; there is nothing impermissible about using antipersonnel bombs. To begin with, it is not a war crime because aerial bombardments were not punished at Nuremberg. Nor, more importantly, should they be proscribed. For bombs are important weapons of war. But what about the fact that they appear to violate the general prohibition against the killing of noncombatants? They certainly do end up killing lots of civilians, Taylor conceded. But that just cannot be helped because a bomb is, unfortunately, the kind of weapon that cannot discriminate between combatants and noncombatants. What is more, bombing is an inherently inaccurate undertaking. The pilots of fast moving planes—no matter how carefully they try to annihilate only enemy soldiers— will inevitably miss lots of times. And if there are civilians nearby, they will, regrettably, be wiped out instead,

The general test for the impermissibility of bombing is, says Taylor, clear enough. Bombing is a war crime if and only if there is no proportioned relationship between the military objective sought to be achieved by the bombing and the degree of destruction caused by it.

This collection of specific prohibitions, accepted conventions, and general excusing and justifying conditions is the conception of the laws of war with which I am concerned. I want now to examine the deficiencies of such a view and to indicate the respects in which I find unconvincing the two general arguments mentioned at the beginning of the paper.

II

I indicated at the outset that one argument for the importance and value of the laws of war is that they are in some sense reflect, embody or give effect to fundamental moral distinctions and considerations. I can help to make clear the character of my criticism of this argument in the following fashion. There are at least three grounds upon which we might criticize any particular criminal code. We might criticize it on the ground that it contained a particular criminal law that ought not to be there because the behavior it proscribed was behavior that it was not morally wrong for people to engage in.[7]

So, we might criticize our criminal code because it punishes the use of marijuana even though there is nothing wrong with using marijuana. Or, we might criticize a criminal code because it is *incomplete*. It proscribes a number of things that ought to be proscribed and regards them with the appropriate degree of seriousness, but it omits to punish something that ought, *ceteris paribus*, to be included in the criminal law. So, we might criticize our criminal code because it fails to make criminal the commission of acts of deliberate racial discrimination.

Compare both of these cases with a criminal code that made criminal only various thefts. Such a code would be incomplete in a different way from the code that just omitted to prohibit racial discrimination. It would be systematically incomplete in the sense that it omitted to forbid many types of behavior that any decent

criminal code ought to prohibit. It would, I think, be appropriate
to describe such a code as a morally incoherent one and to regard
this incoherence, by itself, as a very serious defect. The code would
be incoherent in that it could not be rendered intelligible either in
terms of the moral principles that ought to underlie any criminal
code or even in terms of the moral principles that justified making
theft illegal.[8] One could not, we might say, make moral sense out of
a scheme that regarded as most seriously wrong (and hence a fit
subject for the criminal law) a variety of harmful acts against
property, but which permitted, and treated as in this sense
legitimate, all acts of violence against persons. It would be proper
to regard such a code as odious, it should be noted, even though one
thought that thefts were, on the whole, among the sorts of things
that should be prohibited by the criminal law.

As I hope the following discussion makes clear, it is this last kind
of criticism that I am making of the conception of the laws of war
set out above. So conceived, the laws of war possess the kind of
incompleteness and incoherence that would be present in a
criminal code that punished only theft.

The chief defense to the accusation that the laws of war are in
this sense incomplete and incoherent would, I think, rest on the
claim that the laws of war are complete and coherent—the
difference is that they set a lower standard for behavior than that
set by the typical criminal code. Even in war, so the argument
would go, morality has some place; there are some things that on
moral grounds ought not be permitted even in time of war.
Admittedly, the argument might continue, the place to draw the
line between what is permissible and impermissible is different, is
"lower," in time of war than in time of peace, but the guiding
moral principles and criteria remain the same. The laws of war can
quite plausibly be seen as coherently reflecting, even if imperfectly,
this lower but still intelligible morality of war. Thus, the argument
might conclude the laws of war are not like a criminal code that
only punishes theft. Rather, they are like a criminal code that only
punishes intentional homicides, rapes, and serious assaults and
thefts.

Although I do not argue the point at length in this paper, I
accept the idea that even in war morality has some place. What I
do challenge, therefore, is the claim that the laws of war as I have

sketched them can be plausibly understood as reflecting or embodying in any coherent fashion this lower but still intelligible morality of war.

Consider first the less permissive (and hence morally more attractive) conception of the laws of war, the conception that does not always permit military necessity to be an exception or an excuse. It cannot be plausibly claimed, I submit, that this scheme of what in war is permissible and impermissible reflects simply a lowering of our basic moral expectations or standards. The most serious problem, I think, is that the distinction between combatants and noncombatants is not respected by the laws of war—particularly as they relate to aerial warfare and the use of weapons of mass destruction. This constitutes a deviation in kind and not merely a diminuation of standards in respect to our fundamental moral notions. This is so because the failure meaningfully to distinguish between combatants and noncombatants obliterates all concern for two basic considerations: the degree of choice that persons had in getting into the position in which they now find themselves, and the likelihood that they are or are about to be in a position to inflict harm on anyone else. The distinction between combatants and noncombatants is admittedly a crude one. Some noncombatants are able in reasonably direct ways to inflict harm on others, e.g. workers in a munitions factory. And some noncombatants may very well have knowingly and freely put themselves in such a position. Concomitantly, many combatants may have been able to exercise very little choice in respect to the assumption of the role of a combatant, e.g. soldiers who are drafted into an army under circumstances where the penalties for refusing to accept induction are very severe. Difficulties such as these might make it plausible to argue that the laws of war cannot reasonably be expected to capture perfectly these distinctions. That is to say, it would, I think, be intelligible to argue that it is unreasonable to expect anyone to be able to distinguish the conscripts from the volunteers in the opponent's army. It would, perhaps, even be plausible to argue (although less convincingly, I think) that civilians who are engaged in activities that are directly connected with the prosecution of the war can reasonably be expected to understand that they will be subject to attack. If the laws of war even preserved a distinction between soldiers, munitions workers, and the like on the one hand and children, the aged, and the infirm on the other, one might maintain that the laws of war did succeed in retaining—at a low level and in an imprecise way—a distinction of fundamental moral importance. But, as we have seen, the laws of war that relate to aerial warfare and the use of weapons of mass destruction do not endeavor to preserve a distinction of even this crudity.

A similar point can be made about those laws of war that deal primarily with combatants. Here, though, there is a bit more than can be said on behalf of the rationality of some of the relevant laws of war. The strongest case is that for the special, relatively unequivocal prohibitions against the mistreatment of prisoners of war and the infliction of damage upon hospitals and medical personnel. Someone might object that these make no sense, that there is no difference between attacking a wounded soldier in a hospital and attacking an unwounded soldier with a weapon against which he is defenseless, e.g. strafing or bombing infantrymen armed with rifles. Similarly, it might be objected that there is no coherent principle that distinguishes the wrongness of killing (generally) prisoners of war and the permissibility of killing enemy soldiers who are asleep.

Such an objection would be too strong, for there does seem to be a morally relevant distinction between these two kinds of cases. It is the distinction between those who have obviously been rendered incapable of fighting back (the wounded and the prisoners of war) and those who only may be incapable of fighting back.

It would be wrong, however, to make too much of this point. In the first place, for the reasons suggested earlier, distinctions among combatants are morally less significant than the distinctions between combatants and noncombatants. And in the second place, the principle justifying this distinction among combatants is a pretty crude and not wholly attractive one. In particular, it does not very convincingly, I think, establish the obvious appropriateness of using deadly force against combatants who pose no direct threat and who are defenseless against the force used.[9]

Be that as it may, this is the strongest case for these particular laws of war. There are others for which no comparable rationale can be urged. Thus, it cannot be argued successfully that the laws of war concerning combatants can be generally understood to be a reflection or embodiment of a lower but coherent set of standards relating to how combatants ought to behave toward one another. More specifically, it cannot be maintained, as persons sometimes seek to maintain, that the laws of war relating to which weapons are permissible and which are impermissible possess a similar coherence. Someone might argue, for example, that there are some ways of killing a person that are worse, more inhumane and savage than other ways. War both permits and requires that combatants kill one another in a variety of circumstances in which, in any other context, it would be impermissible to do so. Nonetheless, so the argument might continue, the laws of war do record and give effect to this perception that some techniques of killing are so abhorrent that they ought not be employed even in war.

Once again, my response is not a direct challenge to the claim that it may be possible to distinguish on some such ground among methods of killing. Indeed, were such a distinction to be preserved by the laws of war, important and desirable alterations in the nature of war would almost surely have to take place. What I am concerned to deny is that the laws of war that deal with weapons can be plausibly viewed as reflecting distinctions of genuine moral significance. Since it is permissible to kill an enemy combatant with an antipersonnel bomb, a nuclear weapon, or even a flame-thrower, it just cannot be plausibly maintained that it is a war crime to kill a combatant with poison gas because it is morally worse to use poison gas than to invoke the former methods of human destruction.

It must be observed that so far I have been concerned with that morally more attractive view of the laws of war which does not permit a general exception to all of the laws on grounds of military necessity. Once such a general exception is permitted, whatever plausibility and coherence there is to this conception of the laws of war is diminished virtually to the vanishing point. That this is so can be shown in the following fashion.

To begin with, it is important to notice that the doctrine of "military necessity" is employed in an ambiguous and misleading fashion. "Necessity" leads us naturally to think of various sorts of extreme circumstances which excuse, if they do not justify, otherwise impermissible behavior. Thus, the exception to the rule about taking prisoners is, perhaps, a case where necessitarian language does not fit: if the prisoners are taken by the patrol deep in enemy territory the captors will themselves almost surely be captured or killed. They cannot, in such circumstances, be held to the rule against killing prisoners because it is "necessary" that the prisoners can be killed.

Now, one may not be convinced that necessitarian language is appropriately invoked even in this case. But what should nonetheless be apparent is the inappropriateness of describing the doctrine that justifies aerial warfare, submarine warfare, or the use of flame-throwers as one of military *necessity*. Necessity has nothing whatsoever to do with the legitimacy of the aerial bombardment of cities or the use of other weapons of mass destruction. To talk of military necessity in respect to such practices is to surround the practice with an aura of justification that is in no way deserved. The appeal to the doctrine of military necessity is in fact an appeal to a doctrine of military utility. The laws of war really prohibit (with only a few minor exceptions) some wrongful practices that also lack significant military value. The laws of war permit and treat as legitimate almost any practice, provided only that there is an important military advantage to be secured.

The more that *this* doctrine of military necessity permeates the conception of the laws of war, the less intelligible and attractive is the claim that the laws of war are a coherent, complete, or admirable code of behavior—even for the jungle of warfare. Given the pervasiveness of this doctrine of military utility, the laws of war are reducible in large measure to the principle that in war it is still wrong to kill (or maim or torture) another person for no reason at all, or for reasons wholly unrelated to the outcome of the war. But the laws of war also tell us what it is permissible and legitimate to do in time of war. Here the governing principle is that it is legitimate, appropriate (and sometimes obligatory) to do almost anything to anybody, provided only that what is done is reasonably related to an important military objective. It is, in short, to permit almost all possible moral claims to be overridden by considerations of military utility. Whatever else one may wish to claim for the preservation of such a system of the laws of war, one cannot, therefore, claim that they deserve either preservation or respect because of the connection these laws maintain with the idea of morality.

Finally, it should be noted, too, that the case is hardly improved by the condition that a practice which is otherwise prohibited ceases to be so, if the practice was engaged in by both sides. As I indicated earlier, this may not be the way to interpret the argument for not punishing the Germans for, say, engaging in unrestricted submarine warfare. But if part of the idea of a war crime is, as some of the literature surely suggests it is, that an offense ceases to be an offense once the practice becomes uniform, then this, too, must count against the possibility of making the case for this conception of the laws of war rest on moral grounds.

III

As I indicated at the outset, there is another way to approach the laws of war and to argue for their worth and significance. This route emphasizes the beneficial consequences of having and enforcing the laws of war, and is relatively unconcerned with the "intrinsic" morality of the rules. The arguments in support of such a view go something like this.

Despite some real fuzziness about the edges (or even closer to the center), many of the laws of war are reasonably precise. A number of the laws of war are written down and embodied in rather specific conventions and agreements. It is relatively easy, therefore, to tell, at least in a good many cases, what is a war crime and what is not. It is certainly simpler to decide, for example, what constitutes a war crime than it is to determine whether a crime against peace or humanity has been committed. And the fact that the laws of war are more readily ascertainable has certain important consequences of its own.

To begin with, there is first the intellectual confidence that comes from dealing with rules that are written down and that are reasonably specific and precise. More to the point, it is this feature which makes it quite fair to hold persons responsible for violations of the laws of war. The laws of war can be ascertained in advance by the individuals concerned, they can be applied impartially by an appropriate tribunal, and they can be independently "verified" by disinterested observers. They are, in sum, more like typical criminal laws than any of the other rules or principles that relate to war.

A second argument for the primacy of the laws of war also concerns their enforcibility. It goes like this. It is certainly not wholly unrealistic to imagine the laws of war being enforced, even while a war is going on. More importantly it is not wholly unrealistic to imagine the laws of war being enforced by a country against members of its own armed forces, as well as against members of the opposing army. Such has indeed been the case in the United States as well as in other countries. Once again, the contrast with crimes against peace is striking. It is quite unlikely that the perpetrators of crime against peace, who will be the leaders of the enemy, will ever be caught until the war is over. It is surely unlikely, therefore, that the existence of rules making the waging of aggressive war a crime will ever deter leaders from embarking on aggressive war. If they win, they have nothing to fear. If they lose, they expect to die whether they are guilty or not.

The case is more bleak still where the perpetrators of crimes against peace are the leaders of one's own country. While one can in theory imagine the courts of a country holding the leaders of the country liable for waging aggressive war, this is a theoretical but not a practical possibility. While a war is going on the one thing that national institutions are most unlikely to do is to subject the conduct of the leaders of the nation to cool, critical scrutiny. The leaders of a country are hardly likely to be deterred by the prospect that the courts of their own country will convict them of having committed crimes against peace.

The situation in respect to crimes against war is markedly different in both cases. Soldiers fighting on the opposing side do run a real risk of being caught while the war is on. If they know that they may be captured, and if they also know that they may be punished for any war crimes they have committed, this can have a significant effect on the way they behave toward their opponents. Similarly, the knowledge that they may be punished by their own side for misbehavior toward the enemy can influence the way soldiers in the army go about fighting the war. Hence there is a genuine prospect that the members of both armies will behave differently just because there are laws of war than they would have were there no such laws.

What all of this shows is that the laws of war will influence the behavior of persons in time of war. There are additional arguments, connected with those that have just been presented, to show that the behavior will be affected in ways that are both desirable and important.

The first such argument is that, despite all of their imperfections, the laws of war do represent the consensus that does at present exist about how persons ought to behave in time of war. The fact that the laws of war are embodied in conventions and treaties, most of which have been explicitly ratified by almost all the countries of the world, means that we are dealing with conduct about whose character there can be relatively little genuine disagreement. To be sure, the conventions may not go as far or be as precise as we might like. The laws of war may be unambitious in scope and even incoherent in the sense described earlier. Nonetheless, they do constitute those rules and standards about which there is universal agreement concerning what may not be done, even in time of war. And the fact that all nations have consented to these laws and agreed upon them gives them an authority that is almost wholly lacking anywhere else in the area of morality and war.

Closely related to, but distinguishable from, the above is the claim that past experience provides independent evidence of the importance and efficacy of having laws of war. They have worked to save human life. If we look at wars that have been fought, we see that the laws of war have had this effect. Perhaps this was because the participants were deterred by the threat of punishment. Perhaps this was because the laws of war embody standards of behavior that men, even in time of war, thought it worth respecting. Perhaps this was because countries recognized a crude kind of self-interest in adhering to the conventions as a means of securing adherence by the other side. It does not matter very much why the laws of war were respected to the degree that they were— and they were respected to some extent in the total wars of the Twentieth Century. What matters is that they were respected. Telford Taylor has put the matter this way:

> Violated or ignored as they often are, enough of the rules are observed enough of the time so that mankind is very much better off with them than without them. The rules for the treatment of civilian populations in occupied countries are not as susceptible to technological change as rules regarding the use of weapons in

combat. If it were not regarded as wrong to bomb military hospitals, they would be bombed all of the time instead of some of the time.

It is only necessary to consider the rules on taking prisoners in the setting of the Second World War to realize the enormous saving of life for which they have been responsible. Millions of French, British, German and Italian soldiers captured in Western Europe and Africa were treated in general compliance with the Hague and Geneva requirements, and returned home at the end of the war. German and Russian prisoners taken in the eastern front did not fare nearly so well and died in captivity by the millions, but many survived. Today there is surely much to criticize about the handling of prisoners on both sides of the Vietnam war, but at least many of them are alive, and that is because the belligerents are reluctant to flout the laws of war too openly.[10]

The final argument for the preservation of the laws of war concerns the effect of the laws—or their absence—upon the moral sensibilities of individuals. Were we to do away with the laws of war, were we to concede that in time of war anything and everything is permissible, the effect upon the capacity of persons generally to respond in accordance with the dictates of morality would be diminished rather than enhanced. This, too, is one of Telford Taylor's main theses. "All in all," he argues, "this has been a pretty bloody century and people do not seem to shock very easily, as much of the popular reaction to the report of Son My made depressingly plain. The kind of world in which all efforts to mitigate the horrors of war are abandoned would hardly be a world sensitive to the consequences [of total war]."[11]

The consequences for military sensibilities are at least as important, Taylor continues, as are the consequences for civilian sensibilities. The existence of the laws of war and the insistence upon their importance prevent combatants from becoming completely dehumanized and wholly vicious by their participation in war. The laws of war, Taylor asserts, are

> necessary to diminish the corrosive effect of mortal combat on the participants. War does not confer a license to kill for personal reasons—to gratify perverse impulses, or to put out of the way anyone who appears obnoxious, or to whose welfare the soldier is

indifferent. War is not a license at all, but an obligation to kill for reasons of state; it does not countenance the infliction of suffering for its own sake or for revenge.

Unless troops are trained and required to draw the distinction between military and nonmilitary killings, and to retain such respect for the value of life that unnecessary death and destruction will continue to repel them, they may lose the sense for that distinction for the rest of their lives. The consequence would be that many returning soldiers would be potential murderers.[12]

It should not be difficult to foresee the sorts of objections that I believe can most tellingly be raised against these arguments. I will state them very briefly.

It is, to begin with, far less obvious than the argument would have it that the laws of war possess the kind of specificity we typically require of an ordinary criminal law. In particular, the pervasive character of the doctrine of military "necessity" comes close to leaving as unambiguously criminal only senseless or gratuitous acts of violence against the enemy.

Similarly, the fact that countries have been able to agree upon certain conventions does not seem to me to be a matter of particular significance. At the very least, it is certainly a mistake to infer from this fact of agreement that we have somehow succeeded in identifying those types of behavior that really matter the most. Indeed, it is at least as likely as not, that agreement was forthcoming just because the issues thereby regulated were not of great moment. And it is surely far more likely than not that agreement was forthcoming just because it was perceived that adherence to these laws would not affect very much the way wars got fought.

This leads me to what seem to me the two most significant criticisms that can be made against the assertion that beneficial consequences of various sorts flow from respecting and enforcing the laws of war. There is first the claim that adherence to the laws of war teaches important moral lessons (or prevents soldiers from becoming totally corrupt). Just what sort of things about killing do the laws of war (in theory, let alone in practice) teach soldiers; will someone who has mastered the distinctions established by the laws of war thereby be less a potential murderer? It is difficult to see that getting straight about the laws of war will permit someone to learn important moral lessons and to maintain a decent respect for the value of human life. It is difficult to be at all confident that soldiers who have mastered the distinctions established by the laws of war will be for that reason turned away from the path of murder. This is so just because the laws of war possess the kind of incompleteness and incoherence I described earlier. We can, of course, teach soldiers to obey the laws of war, whatever their content may happen to be. But we must not confuse that truth with the question of whether we will have, through that exercise, taught them to behave in morally responsible ways.[13]

The issue is made more doubtful, still, because the laws of war inescapably permit as well as prohibit; they make some conduct criminal and other conduct legitimate. The evidence is hardly all in, either from the twentieth century in general or Vietnam in particular. It will probably never be in. But it surely appears to be at least as likely as not that the laws of war—if they have taught anything at all—have taught soldiers and civilians alike that it is permissible and lawful to kill and maim and destroy, provided only that it will help to win the war. And I do think this constitutes morally retrograde movement.

But this still leaves unanswered what may appear to be the most important argument of all, the argument put forward by Telford Taylor and others that the laws of war are important and deserving of respect because they work. Isn't it sufficient that even somewhat irrational, incoherent, and incomplete rules have the consequences of saving lives? Even if it is permissible to kill women and children whenever military necessity requires it, isn't it important to save the lives of those women and children whose deaths are not necessitated by military considerations?

The argument is both sound and deceptive. Of course it is better to save some lives rather than none at all. If adhering to the laws of war as we now have them will save the lives of persons (and especially "innocent" persons) in time of war, that is a good reason (but not a decisive one) for maintaining these laws of war. If punishing soldiers (like Lieutenant Calley) for war crimes will keep other soldiers from gratuitously killing women and children, among others, in Vietnam, that is a good reason for punishing persons for the commission of these war crimes.

But to concede this is not to put an end to the matter at hand. For reasons I have tried to make plain there are costs as well as gains from concentrating our attention upon the laws of war and their enforcement. There is to put it simply a risk to human life that is quite substantial. The risk is that we inevitably and necessarily legitimate behavior that is morally indefensible, that is, truly criminal. The cost—and it is a cost in human life—is, for example, that the sanitized war in Vietnam that would result from a scrupulous adherence to the laws of war will increase still further our tolerance for and acceptance of the horror, the slaughter, and the brutality that is the essence of twentieth century war. There is something genuinely odious about a code of behavior that says: if there is a conflict between the attainment of an important military objective and one or more of the prohibitions of the laws of war, it is the prohibitions that quite properly are to give way. And there is something dangerous about a point of view that accepts such a system and directs us to concentrate our energies and our respect upon its enforcement. The corrosive effect of living in a world in which we embrace such a code and insist upon its value seems to me appreciably more dangerous than the effect of a refusal to accord a position of primacy to the sometimes bizarre, often morally incoherent laws of war.

The answer is not, of course, to throw out the laws of war with a view toward inculcating in us all the belief that in war anything goes. But neither is it an acceptable answer to take as given the nature of modern war and modern weapons and to conform, as best one can, the laws of war to their requirements. This, it seems to me, is the fatal flaw in the conception of the laws of war with which I have been concerned. The beginning of a morally defensible position is surely to be found in a different conception of the laws of war, a conception sufficiently ambitious that it refuses to regard as immutable the character of contemporary warfare and weaponry, and that requires instead, that war itself change so as to conform to the demands of morality.

Notes

1. For my purpose I treat the laws of war and war crimes as identical phenomena. I recognize that for other purposes and in other contexts this would be a mistake. See, e.g., Richard Falk, Gabriel Kolko, and Robert

Lifton, eds., *Crimes of War* (New York, 1971), p. 33.

2. *The Charter of the International Military Tribunal,* Article Six (b).

3. Telford Taylor, *Nuremberg and Vietnam: An American Tragedy* (New York, 1970), p. 20.

4. Georg Schwarzenberger, *The Legality of Nuclear Weapons* (London, 1958), p. 44.

5. Taylor, p. 36. There is an ambiguity in this quotation that should be noted. Taylor may not mean that the laws of war permit an exception in this kind of case. He may mean only that the law is uncertain, that he knows of no court decision which authoritatively declares this to be either a war crime or a permitted exception. It is sufficient for my purposes if he means the weaker claim, that it is an open question.

A more serious objection to my assertion that I am accurately characterizing the existing laws of war would call attention to the following quotation from the U.S. Army Field Manual, *The Law of Land Warfare,* Chapter 1, sec. I.3:

"The law of war places limits on the exercise of a belligerent's power in the interests mentioned in paragraph 2 and requires that belligerents refrain from employing any kind or degree of violence which is not acutely necessary for military purposes and that they conduct hostilities with regard for the principles of humanity and chivalry.

"The prohibitory effect of the law of war is not minimized by 'military necessity' which has been defined as that principle which justifies those measures not forbidden by international law which are indispensable for securing the complete submission of the enemy as soon as possible. Military necessity has generally been rejected as a defense for acts forbidden by the customary and conventional laws of war inasmuch as the latter have been developed and framed with consideration for the concept of military necessity."

I leave it to the reader to decide exactly what this means. It seems to anticipate, on the one hand, that the laws of war and the doctrine of military necessity can conflict. It seems to suppose, on the other hand, that substantial conflicts will not arise either because the laws of war prohibit militarily unnecessary violence or because they were formulated with considerations of military necessity in mind. In substance, the view expressed in the quotation is not inconsistent with the conception I am delineating.

6. Taylor, p. 39. Once again, there is an ambiguity here. Taylor may mean that it is procedurally unfair to punish the loser but not the victor for the same act. He may also mean, though, that there is a principle at work which legitimizes a practice which was previously proscribed on the ground that the practice has now become widespread. He does not

distinguish these two positions in his book and he seems to me to hold both.

7. I realize that this is vague. For my purposes it does not matter. It does not matter, that is, whether the law is criticized because the behavior is not immoral, or because the behavior is immoral but not harmful, or because the behavior is harmful but not sufficiently so to justify the use of the criminal law, etc.

8. Of course, there is still a fourth possible code. It would make illegal only those things that it is morally right and permissible to do, or that ought, on other grounds, never be made illegal. Such a code would certainly be the very worst of all. I am not claiming, it should be emphasized, that the laws of war are like this fourth possible case.

9. It is, for example, legitimate to bomb the barracks of soldiers who are not at the front lines, to ambush unsuspecting (and possibly even unarmed) enemy soldiers, and to use all sorts of weapons against which the particular combatants may be completely defenseless. At some stage it just ceases to be very satisfactory to insist that this is unobjectionable because the combatants could defend themselves if they chose and because they chose to be combatants in the first place. For both claims about the combatants may in fact be false and known to be such.

10. Taylor, p. 40.

11. Taylor, p. 39.

12. Taylor, pp. 40-41.

13. Unless, of course, one holds the view that teaching persons to obey orders, or even laws, whatever they may happen to be is an important constituent of the curriculum of moral education. It is not a view I hold.

Selected Bibliography

Ginzberg, Robert (ed.). *The Critique of War*. Chicago: Henry Regency, 1969.

Honderich, Ted. "Democratic Violence," *Philosophy and Public Affairs* 2, no. 2 (1973):190.

Merleau-Ponty, Maurice. *Humanism and Terror*. Boston: Beacon Press, 1969.

Levinson, Sanford. "Responsibility for Crimes of War," *Philosophy and Public Affairs* 2, no. 3 (1973):2.

Murphy, Jeffrie (ed.). *Civil Disobedience and Violence*. Belmont, Calif.: Wadsworth Publishing Co., 1971.

Nagel, Thomas. "War and Massacre," Chapter 23 in this volume.

Shaffer, Jerome (ed.). *Essays on Violence*. New York: David McKay, 1971.

Wasserstrom, Richard. "On the Morality of War: A Preliminary

Inquiry," Chapter 20 in this volume.

Wasserstrom, Richard (ed.). *War and Morality*. Belmont, Calif.: Wadsworth Publishing Co., 1969.

Wasserstrom, Richard. "The Relevance of Nuremberg," *Philosophy and Public Affairs* 1, no. 1 (1972):22.

Wasserstrom, Richard. "The Responsibility of Individuals for War Crimes," in Virginia Held, Sidney Morgenbesser, and Thomas Nagel (eds.), *Philosophy, Morality and International Affairs*. New York: Oxford University Press, 1974.

Wells, Donald. "How Much Can 'The Just War' Justify?", Chapter 17 in this volume.

Wells, Donald. *The War Myth*. New York: Pegasus, 1967.

Wolff, Robert Paul. "On Violence," *The Journal of Philosophy* 66, no. 19 (1969):601.

29

On Moral Codes and Modern War

Arthur C. Danto

It is a classical question whether the traditional moral and legal codes that limit the carnage of war have their foundation in natural law or are simply arbitrary agreements (contracts) between nations. Professor Danto takes a new and novel approach: Moral codes that restrict what one can do in war have their roots in the very meaning *of the terms "war," "soldier," etc. For example, the act of killing can be described as criminal murder, war, or slaughter; and the agent called a criminal, soldier, or marauder—though the objective act of killing may have been the same in each case. We decide what has happened as we provide a social context to give meaning to the act. The rules of warfare which make it possible to distinguish criminal-killing from war-killing dictate (1) that wars be fought between nations to reach specific political objectives rather than as a permanent condition of man, (2) that wars be fought within the restraints necessary to establish eventual peace, (3) that prisoners of war and noncombatants be treated humanely and not killed indiscriminately, (4) that violence be directed to military advantage, (5) that the weapons employed do not cause unnecessary suffering or irrecoverable wounds, etc. If one exceeds the bounds of these* contextual *rules, one is not engaged in warfare, but perhaps is acting as a bandit, barbarian, pirate, terrorist, or common criminal, depending on the details of the case. Professor Danto's approach has the advantage of arguing for a* logically necessary *relationship between moral codes and legal conventions regarding war and the meaning of the word "warfare."*

—M. B.

I shall consider war initially from the point of view of attackers, and define a central case of it as the resort to armed violence as a

This article originally appeared in *Social Research*, Vol. 45, No. 1 pp. 176-190 (Spring 1978). Published with permission.

means of modifying political policy. The definition is accommo-
dating enough to include assassination as a degenerate instance,
but to exclude, as it ought, such events as armed riots which only
happen to have the consequence of altering political policy. And
though it normally takes two parties to make war, there is always a
possibility that, because of surprise or immobility or demoralization, no one fights back. If *any* wars can be morally justified, these
wars will be, since no institutions affect the moral quality of life
more than political ones, and these must then put maximal
pressure on pacifists. Of course we must not sentimentalize
politically motivated warmakers, must not allow our thought to be
dominated by the example of the fighter against injustice,
imperialism, totalitarianism, and repression: men have hideous
political ideals they are willing to fight for. But this again must put
pressure on pacifists who will countenance no violent measures in
defending benign political policies and practices.

The pacifist is of conceptual interest in a discussion of moral
codes in war inasmuch as he rejects the morality of war as such and
hence rejects, as morally inadmissible, any armed violence: every
warmaking action is morally out of bounds for him. In assuming
the question of boundaries of violence to be open, I suppose we
must regard the question of the morality of war as itself open. The
question I ultimately shall be concerned with is whether there are
boundaries, the crossing of which even the morality of the war in
which they happen does not excuse. But the pacifist, who thinks
political reasons never justify recourse to war, believes that the
taking of life as a means to political change outweighs in the scale of
moral condemnability any consideration of the moral quality of
life. So in a way he is not of this world. Of course the pacifist would
want violence mitigated: he is not required to suppose one piece of
violence as just like any other, indifferently and uniformly
condemned just because they are violent; but he cannot *ground* his
reservations in the nature of war, as I should want to do. All I want
to insist upon now is that most of us can think of political practices
so inconsistent with our moral schemes that, other avenues of
modification believed closed or too slow and uncertain, no moral
alternative to war is open.

Violence of means, which is entailed by the concept of war, will
not be the only violence we can realistically anticipate in going to

war. Battlefields are not like tennis courts, areas specifically set aside for the enactment of armed contests. Life will be taken and lives brutalized not just as means but as consequences of those means—"secondary effects," as they are termed by theologians of warfare. These may often exceed vastly the primary effects of violence done by soldiers to soldiers as soldiers: 70 percent of the casualties in the Vietnam War were sustained by civilians in contrast with 5 percent in World War I, a horrendous cost even if secondary in the sense that such violence was only the derivative by-product of means used primarily against soldiers and that brutalizing civilians was not regarded as a means—the war was not by intention but merely in fact a war against a people. Moreover, even in the most disciplined of armies, we may expect a coarsening of moral perception and a weakening of moral restraints as opportunities open for the gratification of vile impulses. Though by Nuremberg criteria these will be counted crimes, since they are so considered already by the states the soldiers belong to, by going to war we enhance the frequency of such crimes even if we do not, in modern war in contrast with the Sack of Rome or the Thirty Years War, exploit the potential criminality of our soldiers as a means.

All this is a moral cost we must reckon with, and to which we cannot be indifferent if we suppose ourselves to have gone to war for moral reasons. It is thus that we admire the initial reticence to make war on the part of Arjuna, the great archer and moral hero of the *Bhagavat Gita,* who is prepared to abandon what all would admit as a just war because of the unacceptable distortions it would induce in the cosmopolitical fabric. He is persuaded by Krishna that *not* fighting will induce comparable distortions, and that he will sacrifice his karmic standing in the bargain; fighting becomes a way of life rather than a means to change, all the more so as he is instructed by Krishna that consequences are irrelevant to the quality of his actions and that he should not be guided by them. But then, like the pacifist, Arjuna is no longer of this world. It is consistent with Arjuna's posture that war should be a perpetual state rather than a means to anything, whereas for the class of wars of interest to me, just because they are means they imply an end in both senses.

Nineteenth-century theorists of war thought of war romantically as a wind stirring the otherwise stagnant life, as a prophylactic against corruption, perpetual peace being viewed with a kind of moral horror because of what would happen to the human material. Sorel's notion of the moral sublimity of violence reflects the same thought. But nothing could be more corrupting than perpetual war, where war is a condition rather than a means, and no one who thinks that warmaking might be a morally acceptable act can regard it as a condition without an end. To be *of* the world is to think it possible that the quality of life can justify the taking of life as a means of changing or preserving it. But exactly because the political quality of life can give a moral reason for going to war, those for whom it is a reason cannot be indifferent to the moral boundaries of war and cannot consistently pursue *victory at any price.* When the costs, primary and secondary, of the use of violence are morally less supportable than allowing to stand the practices one went to war to change, the moral quality of one's war is compromised. In war as elsewhere, there is a continuity between ends and means, ends never all by themselves justifying the means. The way in which we conducted the Vietnam War was so tremendously out of scale with the end we envisioned in fighting it that even if we see that end in the most favorable moral light we have to condemn the war. A moral warmaker's hands are always going to be dirty, simply because of the moral perceptions that move him into war. But these also limit the degree of moral soiling he can live with. I think it is immoral as well to undertake a war one believes one cannot win, merely for the sake of fighting. For that is equivalent to perpetual war, where violence is not a means but a way of life—and a violent way of life cannot be morally accepted. That it should end, and that the end be achieved at a moral cost less than the cost of not making the war to begin with, are necessary conditions for a moral war.

Briefly, then, the question of the morality of war is internally related to the questions of morality in war, and when violence in war becomes criminal the war itself is criminal, for no moral end can justify criminal means. In this I am supposing, contrary to the pacifist, that violence is not criminal as such and that use of it can be justified—but not *any* use. So it does not follow that once started on violence there is no justified stopping, no logical friction to keep us from sliding down the smooth slope to utter degradation. Or at best such considerations are psychological rather than conceptual:

the question is whether a line can be drawn, however difficult it may be for us, say out of weakness, to draw it. But even as a psychological thesis it is dubious that to accept violence is already to have weakened one's resistance to its increase, until one resists nothing and becomes callous to anything. "Not at *that* price," was the response of Frenchmen to the war in Algeria and of Americans to the war in Indochina, even when the wars themselves might have seemed justified within boundaries. When the boundaries were crossed the wars were forfeited. Still, I have not said what the boundaries are in saying they must exist, and everything so far must be regarded as exceedingly primitive. I have tried only to begin to block the folk thought that just because it is a war anything goes, that "all is fair." What I should like to be able to do is to derive the morally defined limits from the very concept of war itself, so that if these are broached we no longer have war but slaughter, and whether there are moral limits to slaughter can hardly arise, since slaughter is the other side of moral limits already.

Hobbes speculated that the relations between states are simply the relations between individuals raised to a higher power, and that states in fact stand to one another as men stood to one another in the logically crimeless circumstances of the state of nature. Logically crimeless, in the sense that, though the latter's daily history was black with deeds of violence, the institutional framework through which any of them could be constituted *crimes* was, by definition of the state of nature, lacking. Thus, though there were killings, there were no murders; and though there were violent seizures of objects, there were no robberies since there was no property (an object being someone's property only if he *owns* it, and ownership is not a natural state). By projection, there are no crimes one nation can commit against another, however violent their intercourse may be. Hobbes's thought was that in the state of nature nothing is forbidden, which does not mean that everything is permitted but only that the cluster of concepts in which permission and prohibition have a location are defined as inapplicable here. One can tell a man not to do something, but one forbids only if one has authority to do so, and in nature there are no authorities but only persons with the power they are born with and such amplifications of it as weaponry affords. There is authority only where it is given through law, and the generalized power to enforce it.

It evidently escaped Hobbes's attention that there is no war in the natural state either, only violence and the meeting of violence with violence. But quite apart from whether there is anything between states comparable to government between men, there has for a very long time been a distinction between war and mere violence; there has been a basis for distinguishing war from slaughter as there has for distinguishing armies from mere bands of marauders or pirates. In nature there are no soldiers, orders, desertions, truces, and the like, so the space between states is not quite the institutional no-man's-land required by Hobbes's theory. Something like the distinction just alluded to is an issue in the ICRC draft proposal regarding Article 3 of the Geneva Conventions, which means to extend to all armed conflicts the protections assured by Article 3 to soldiers in international armed conflict—for example, that prisoners be treated humanely, that there be restrictions on the means of conduct, and the like. Many nations do not favor this draft protocol, since it would have necessary application to forces whose aim it is to overthrow them, something we might appreciate if it required us to reclassify arrested members of the Symbionese Liberation Army as prisoners of war and certain of their killings as acts of war rather than as criminal murders, no more crimes than what our soldiers are routinely responsible for in international war. I should think humane treatment of prisoners is called for whether they are prisoners of war or mere prisoners, but I cite the case for purposes of underscoring the practice that the distinction is there as a matter of implicit convention, that there is no war without a convention of war. This is important in case someone should believe, for Hobbesian reasons, that anything goes when violence is enacted between rather than within states. The conventions are ours, and in terms of them we differentiate criminals from warmakers, even if, taken at their absolute magnitude, they equally seize and destroy. To have a convention is to have the power to interpret and change the convention.

It would be interesting to question why there is this convention at all, how we make distinctions between killers and warmakers, and why warmakers should be entitled to special treatment if mere killers are not. The distinction indeed is honored even in wars which fall outside the class I have defined, concerning whose morality as wars there is perhaps no possibility. Even if we regard the war they make as unjust and possibly criminal, the soldiers remain entitled to special treatment as warmakers, almost as if they were players in an unfortunately deadly game. I shall try to answer this question in a way, and I think its answer shows the direction in which we must go to deduce the limit from the concept of war. The question of *humane* treatment I think should in fact be raised in terms of the rights of prisoners, not just prisoners of war, and an obstacle to the acceptance of the ICRS draft protocol would be erased if the countries in question would change the conditions they put their prisoners under. About sixty-four states use torture routinely and cold-bloodedly, and many of their penal practices amount to torture in the end. They are reluctant to abandon this hideous practice, as they would have to do if political prisoners were classed as prisoners of war. I don't think prisoners of war should be treated inhumanely to even things out: but whence derives their special claim to be treated humanely? Why should torture of them be counted a crime when the same ghastly things done to prisoners of conscience or even plain criminals is somehow accepted? Why this respect for soldiers if there is evidently no respect for humans as humans?

The analogy to games is dangerous but instructive. I can touch anyone with a ball, but he will be "out" only if we both are players in a game where there is a rule that a player is out if touched by a ball held by another player, who touches him with it in order that he should be out. Similarly, a man can kill anybody, but this will be an assassination only if the victim is a political figure killed for political reasons. And again, though anyone can shoot anyone, this will not be murder even if there is a concept of murder in the society he belongs to if the victim is an enemy and he is a soldier and shoots the enemy because he is an enemy. Invariantly as to institutionalized embedment, the person in the first example is touched, and the persons in the other two are killed. But the moral coloration of the latter two, when complicated by the institution which gives them this coloration, differs, perhaps to the despair of the pacifist. Suppose we now say: Shooting the enemy is part of the game, the way the war game is played. And the question before us is this: Once it is a war, is anything against the rules? A soldier who happens to kill another, say out of spite and as a matter of vendetta, is merely a murderer, not playing the game. But *within* the game are there any restrictions we might recognize as moral, or is *anything* fair if it is part of the game?

The concept of sport implies matched opponents with an antecedent even chance of winning, a game in this genre losing interest as a game if its outcome is obvious from the start. Thus we do not, unless interested in mayhem rather than sport, match heavyweights with featherweights, or Christians with lions, or grandmasters with duffers, unless the conspicuously weaker opponent is given, through some system of handicaps, what is called a "sporting chance." These are intended to even the odds, moving the chances of either side winning to as close to 0.5 as is feasible, and to distribute disadvantages as fairly as possible. So the concept of sport entails fair play as an analytical component. Cheating, because it biases the outcome, is necessarily inconsistent with fair play and hence with the concept of a game, which opponents as well as spectators must believe is not so rigged in advance that playing it out is a kind of ritual, like reading the written parts in a play. Within these perimeters it is expected that participants will play to win, the reverse being tantamount to cheating; and it is no part of the concept that players help one another out of tight corners: indeed, there is almost a positive obligation not to help others, since avoiding tight corners is part of playing the game.

To say that in war anything is fair is to say that war is not a game. Each side is rather expected to do anything which biases the outcome in its favor. A boxer who crosses the ring before the opening round and knocks the other boxer out not only has not won the match, he has disqualified himself from playing. But can we extend this notion to sneak attacks in war? Surely not, according to this view of pure war. To warn an enemy is to reduce one's chance of winning, and the stakes are high and serious, having to do, in the cases we are concerned with, with the moral quality of life. War is a license for violence, and anything that contributes to victory is legitimate.

I have supposed that anyone who fights what he believes is a moral war cannot accept this view. But I also believe that no one really accepts this view of war, and the reason, in which I think the concept of limits to war is grounded, connects with a deeper game analogy than I have so far stated, namely, that games are not a part of real life. War is not a permanent condition but only a means of political change. The limits of war are determined by the structure of peace, to which it is anticipated the world returns when the war is done. To this I shall revert in a moment.

Discussion of constraints on violence in warfare have often, even typically, been conducted in largely legalistic terms of pacts and conventions in which signatories give their words to honor certain limits. This has almost a Hobbesian ring, as if the signatories surrendered a right to pure warfare and exposed themselves to sanctions if they exceeded the boundaries they compacted themselves to respect. A degree of cynicism here is inevitable, or at least a degree of pessimism, which is supported by the dim history of such hopeful but evidently empty agreements as the Kellogg-Briand Pact, flaunted in the event by totalitarian and democratic powers alike. What I think is insufficiently appreciated is that such agreements embody moral beliefs that are very widely shared. The Hague Convention of 1907, the Nuremberg principles, the four Geneva conventions of 1949, the United Nations declaration on human rights imply a belief that, while war itself may not be abolished, wars terminate and men and nations should in fighting them be exposed to such costs and danger as are consistent with returning to a state of peace in conditions as much like those under which they left it as is consistent with making war, i.e., to take up life again.

For death, obviously, there is no remedy, and the killed do not come back. But it is required by the principle I have just alluded to that only such wounds are to be inflicted as allow a standard possibility of recovery. All wounds are painful, but pain can be reduced by drugs. The issue is whether the weapons are such that they assure irrecoverable wounds. This goes beyond mere humaneness. It has been argued that there are no inhumane weapons, only inhumane uses of weapons, although it is difficult to see what a humane use of napalm might be. It is not, however, that napalm causes wounds of an inhumanely severe order but that there is at best one chance in four of surviving a standard attack with napalm. The M-16 rifle, our routine infantry issue, has been

ruled out on humane grounds for use against big game in all fifty
states. But again it is the difficulty of recovery from wounds caused
by lightweight bullets delivered at high velocities that recommends
the banning of the M-16 rifle. It is, again, with reference to such
principle that our army was required to abandon the use of
defoliants after 1970 in Vietnam, since we now know the
extraordinary slowness with which a land recovers for use after
exposure to these. And perhaps it explains why use even by us of
hydrogen bombs was never made. It explains why saturation
bombings of cities is regarded as criminal, and why destruction of a
people is impossible to justify in the name of war, however lofty its
aims.

Prisoners, thus, are to be maintained at a level consistent with
return to normal life, and for the same reasons are not to be
enslaved, and so on. However pessimistic men may be as to the
likelihood of wars no longer being fought, there is a touching
optimism in their belief that the human condition is not essentially
one of war but of peace. So we limit ourselves, not to annihilate
enemies but only to change their ways. A warmaker who takes the
reverse view is a monster. It was, I think, because it sought to
change the conditions of warfare in these terms that nazi Germany
appears in the eye of the world a moral monster, but also why
retaliation in kind against nazi Germany would have been equally
monstrous. We could not have held our war with Germany as
moral if we emulated our enemy, who set out to enslave the world
and permanently alter the form of peace. And surely it is this that
moved even pacifists to regard that war as just.

It is because nations do not wish to be reckoned monsters that
they may voluntarily subscribe to the codes of war, and hence
imply that they regard wars as parentheses in life. Nations, like
individuals, have a *pour autrui*, an image of themselves in the
consciousness of others. It is important to them that this not be
radically discrepant with the image they may have of themselves as
morally legitimate. This is especially so of the leading powers of the
world who, as it happens, wish to think of themselves as moral
leaders. There are, I think, two avenues through which leadership
can be achieved. One is domination through material power or its
equivalent, and as the world is now structured there is no
likelihood that one nation can dominate without being annihilated

in the attempt, and annihilation on the scales presently available, which are total, cannot be a means of war since there is no recovery from it. The other way is through moral authority. But no nation can claim moral authority whose warmaking is so inconsistent with the conventions of war as to imply a disregard for the primacy of peace. It is almost certain that the conduct of our war in Vietnam seriously if not fatally degraded our moral image, so much so that we came close to subverting the aims for which we ostensibly fought that war by weakening any moral claim we might make for leading the world.

In any case, the sole avenue I can see for effectively limiting the use of violence in war is the sort of moral monitoring to which each nation is susceptible because of the essential commitment to peace as the standard condition of mankind.

My thought then is that peace is not simply the absence of war, as a cynic has defined it, implying that it is the interruption, merely, of a standard condition of bellicosity. And this is so even should it be historically established that more time has been spent in war than not, for the issue is not one of numerical preponderation; Newton's First Law holds even if we only find acceleration in the universe and never uniform velocity. War remains the aberration, and the commitment to peace governs the degree of allowable violence in war, which is why victory at any price is disallowed, even victory over those who imply by their conduct of war the belief that war could be the norm. If it were the norm, there would be no war, only slaughter, and anything then would go. The concept of war implies the sorts of limits I have sketched.

Inevitably, then, war places its makers at a disadvantage relative to the concept of victory at any price, and this will naturally be used by their enemies in the following way: They will attempt to force broaching of these limits by putting the warmaker in positions where, unless he violates them, he puts his enemy at an advantage. Such tactics are unavailing if the warmaker on the other side feels no moral pressures. Let me illustrate. A man will get nowhere with a hunger strike if his captors to begin with are indifferent to whether or not he starves to death. Only if they care can he put pressure on them by making them accessory to his death if they do not make the changes he wants. A strike will be an ineffectual practice if employers are ruthless and will kill whomever interferes with production. It is widely appreciated that passive resistance would not have worked in India had the governors been Nazis instead of the British. Students occupying a building will have no effect or a negative one if the police are used routinely and refuse to accept moral pressure of this order. It is a standard practice of the weak to use the moral commitments of the strong as a way of controlling them, and it is not plain that these tactics implicate them in the immorality of the strong who break their own code, in case they crush the weak. Something like this, I believe, must be in issue when we ask whether a uniform moral code does not induce injustices of its own. And I want to argue now that it does not.

Consider some strategies of the weak. Suppose they take hostages. There are conventions against killing hostages, grounded largely in the fact that usually they are regarded as innocent. But the conventions are availing only against someone who honors them, and if the enemy did not honor the conventions, was callous as to what happened to hostages, the strategy of threatening their lives to wring concessions could not work. Or consider maltreating prisoners or threatening to: to a nation committed to the view that its soldiers come back victorious or dead, the threat is impotent. Or one sets up an artillery post in a clearly marked hospital: this would just be another target to an enemy unconcerned with the weak and wounded. The problem arises in an aggravated way with guerrillas, who, by refusing to wear uniforms and carry standards, employ their indiscernibility from civilians as a kind of moral camouflage. This could give an enemy an excuse to kill everyone, since anyone might be a guerrilla—and we came close to doing that in Vietnam. But it is not clear to me that guerrillas share in the criminality of an action which made the indiscriminate response a viable if morally costly response.

These are difficult matters to assess, but I think the general outline of a fair assessment is discernible. The exploitation of moral constraints by guerrillas is an attempt to have the war fought on their own terms, any other terms requiring the enemy to cross a boundary and expose himself to the moral condemnation of the world. This may strike the enemy as "unfair," but our argument has been that war must be fought within moral boundaries and this cannot be regarded as unfair, moral conduct not being the sort of thing to which unfairness can apply save relative to nonmoral considerations. So we would have been acting immorally in fighting a war in the style of World War II in a situation in which the enemy was of a different order altogether. The conventions of war have the effect of evening the terms of conflict, of matching the sides. And similarly, setting up artillery posts in marked hospitals is a good way, if the enemy respects hospitals, to limit its use of bombs, not an unacceptable tactic if, as in Vietnam, their control of the air was minimal and they had only the unfortunately fragile restraints of their enemies as a possible shield. It is *not* unfair to put an enemy in a position where his choice either is to alter his tactics or behave as a barbarian.

But such strategies have to be taken up case by case. Killing a hostage, for instance, can never be justified; the weak have no option to behave as barbarians either. But in general what we might term a uniform moral code in warfare is going to be disadvantageous to the weak only if they refuse to exploit the opportunities it gives them to limit the conduct of the strong. And it will be disadvantageous to the strong only with reference to an unacceptable standard of victory at any price. So the conventions of war have the effect in the end of transforming wars into terrible games, and are justified only in that without them violence would be unspeakably more terrible and peace unspeakably less controlling a factor in their conduct. The weak are given what amounts to a sporting chance. There is little doubt that the most powerful advantage the Vietnamese had in the face of our awesome armaments was our grudging adherence to the conventions. We might have won, but only by violating the conventions more than we did, or fighting as the Vietnamese did, only better.

Afterword

Since this article was written, the neutron bomb has made its ambiguous entry in the world's arsenals. Billed as a weapon that destroys humans without destroying property, the neutron bomb has been denounced as "the ultimate capitalist weapon." I raised with a student the question of what the ultimate *communist* weapon might be: he wittily proposed a bomb which destroyed only private property. In truth the neutron is not all that benign to real estate: its use is not quite comparable to exterminating roaches, leaving the cupboards intact. The grisly details lie beyond my imagination and competence, but the central argument of this paper would favor development of the neutron bomb over bombs that destroy both humans *and* property. For there will always be survivors, and they must be left shelter from which to recommence life. But I have no argument that favors bombing which, when used against a populace to get them to put pressure on their leaders to sue for peace, has the same moral profile as terrorism, violating the boundaries I have meant to draw.

30

On the Morality
of Chemical/Biological War

Richard J. Krickus

Richard J. Krickus of the Washington Arms Control Project Office, Bendix Corporation, contends that clarification is needed concerning the morality, use, and military implications of chemical/biological (CB) weapons. His study provides a framework for such an analysis. The claim by just war theorists to offer an alternative to "all-out war" or "all-out submission" is the point of departure for considering the morality of CB weapons. After exposing the misconception that CB weapons are illegal according to international law, he notes that many people who are absolutely opposed to CB warfare fail to make a crucial distinction between chemical and biological weapons. Because the former are controllable and usable in a tactical environment, they can be justified from the point of view of just war doctrine whereas the latter cannot. In conjunction with the military versatility of nonlethal weapons, this offers the possibility of making certain types of limited war more humane. But before this or any other possibility can be explored in the required depth, it is necessary to overcome the "CB taboo." Krickus' article is important because it takes a clear step in this direction.
—W. S.

The moral ambiguity and legal uncertainty concerning the use of chemical/biological (CB) weapons has thus far inhibited rigorous and dispassionate analysis of the military implications of CB operations. At the same time, because of this "CB taboo," the arms control and disarmament problems posed by the existence of CB agents have been omitted from the research agenda of the arms

Reprinted from *Journal of Conflict Resolution* 9, no. 2 (June 1965):200-210 by permission of the publisher, Sage Publications, Inc.

control community. Clarification of the "morality" of CB warfare, therefore, is pertinent to an objective analysis.

No definitive statements or final judgments will be offered here. The aim of the present paper is, rather, to give structure to the issue for further research, especially in terms of CB arms control. It is an exercise in which the moral questions posed by the employment of CB weapons will be measured against those principles generally held today by the proponets of the just war doctrine. Military and legal aspects will be discussed, but many components of the problem may be neglected or covered only briefly because they cannot be considered within the framework of this doctrine.

Just War in the Nuclear Age

The crucial issue facing the proponents of just war today is whether modern weapons of mass destruction can be employed within the limits of the traditional precepts of just war, i.e., the immunity of noncombatants, the proportionality of response, and the control of means to redress grievances suffered. The marriage of the modern state's industrial-agricultural complex to the military machine has evoked the assertion that war in the missile age is total, the front is everywhere, and there are no noncombatants. To these commentators, the advocates of total war, just war is a fantasy of the innocent and idealistic.[1]

The just war theorist finds himself criticized from the other direction by the pacifist. The case of the pacifist or ethical absolutist against the just war code may be summed up as follows: "There are perhaps no readily discernible limits to the disparate situations which may be interpreted as coming within the scope of a just war doctrine. . . . In this manner, modern just war doctrines share the fate of their predecessors in becoming scarcely distinguishable from mere ideologies the purpose of which is to provide a spurious justification for almost any use of force."[2]

While the middle position of the just war doctrine invites criticism from both extremes, its adherents reject the escapist epistemological assumptions of their detractors. The pessimist claims war is inherent in the human condition and thus an eternal phenomenon; the absolute pacifist flatly rejects resorting to violence no matter what the provocation or the consequence of submitting to the enemy. Neither of them can aid the statesman in his quest for normative guides to policy in the real political world because, instead of offering standards of action, they opt out of the game altogether.

The proponent of just war argues that he struggles to achieve some semblance of moral order, that he offers some ethical standards upon which national decision makers may reflect and act in an imperfect world. He does not declare that his doctrine is universally applicable to all moral-political predicaments. He believes that the doctrine can guide the statesman, though he acknowledges that military and political considerations legitimately qualify the prescriptions of just war and that the decision-maker alone is responsible for the final choice. On the other hand, he categorically declares that civilians may in no case be killed intentionally, and that war cannot be just if it breeds more evil than the injury to be suffered at the hands of an aggressor.

John Courtney Murray, one of the leading Catholic thinkers in the United States, holds that just war is relevant today despite the possibility of a thermonuclear war. He appends a new condition to the doctrine, however—that the tinderbox nature of the international environment must be taken into account in pursuing even limited military engagements. The just war, he declares, fulfills three functions: to condemn aggressive war as evil, to limit the evils war entails, and to humanize the conduct of war where possible. The doctrine is not an excuse to open Pandora's box; it does not advocate unqualified violence once war has begun.[3]

Accepting the balance of terror as a "necessary evil" and cognizant of the possible tragedy confronting mankind if deterrence fails, the just war theorist maintains that every possible measure should be taken to prevent such a horrible eventuality. Should it come to pass, however, even a nuclear war must be waged justly. It must be controlled and limited to counterforce targets.

War is not deemed intrinsically evil by the scholastic proponents of the doctrine (though the Protestant Ernest Lefever judges war to be the lesser of evils). Murray has observed that a nation needs "force to repel unjust force" and even "an atomic war waged within the limits of military necessity may be not only something we are morally permitted to do; it may be something we are

morally obliged to do."[4] These statements do not, however, erase
the distinction between combatants and civilians. The Protestant
theologian Paul Ramsey speaks for the just war doctrine when he
asserts that modern technology has not eliminated that distinction.
He admits that civilians "are now in far greater danger even in a
justly conducted war than ever before in human history because
there are many more legitimate military targets than ever before
and because the firepower of even a just war has been vastly
increased."[5] Nuclear bombing would be morally justified
then—even if it involved the loss of a large segment of the civilian
population—if an important military target could not be
eliminated by less drastic means. Most Catholic advocates of the
code would agree with Ramsey on this point.

One might ask, however: once you admit that military necessity
may demand the sacrifice of noncombatants, have you not opened
the door to unlimited and unjustified war? Here the traditional
scholastic precept of "double effect" is often introduced into the
argument. If a civilian is killed as a result of a military engagement,
this act is not considered evil provided that the act itself is not
intrinsically evil, i.e., if good was intended and evil resulted only
incidentally. Thus, while Ramsey rejects all-out thermonuclear
war as evil because "the death and devastation contemplated in
the case of all-out nuclear war would be both directly willed and
directly done as a means," he condones nuclear testing because the
"death brought about by nuclear testing as such is only indirectly
willed and indirectly done as one among several effects of the
tests."[6]

John Bennett (1962) has written that he agrees with Ramsey that
counterforce war is moral, but he is reluctant to accept the
principle of "double effect" since it can be used to apologize for a
great deal of thermonuclear killing.[7] Some scholastic thinkers even
reject double effect, i.e., in the nuclear context; Father Ford holds,
"It is my contention that the civil and military leaders—who plan
and execute the dropping of a series of high megaton H-bombs on
an area like New York or Moscow: (1) would not in practice avoid
the direct intention of violence to the innocent; (2) could not if they
would; and, (3) even if they would and could avoid it, would have
no proportionate justifying reason for permitting the evils which
this type of all-out warfare would let loose."[8] Gordon Zahn calls

double effect "a moral slide rule by which almost any act of war can be justified."[9]

The severer critics of just war have asserted that the principles of control, proportionality, and civilian immunity are impossibilities in the missile age. Walter Millis has said, "We are faced with a situation in which any war seems likely to escape entirely from the control of man . . . and one in which the resort to nuclear weapons can never be "indispensable" to self-defense: since so far as we know now, resort to the weapons can never promote defense."[10]

Christopher Hollis strikes another soft spot: "One of the traditional arguments for a just war has always been that a war can only be just if, *inter alia,* it has a reasonable chance of achieving its purpose. . . . Now it may be argued that it is not sensible. Whatever emerges from a new international war, nothing remotely like any of the institutions that began that war would emerge."[11] The institutions fought for would be destroyed in a thermonuclear Armageddon; such is the argument, and it has tormented the just war proponents despite the fact that it is premised on the advent of the worst possible eventuality—the total exchange of nuclear might.

The proponents of just war recognize that they possess no universally applicable ethical system. Nevertheless, they hold the state is obliged to maintain an environment where men live in peace and with dignity, practicing religion and politics in freedom, and pursuing material well-being and intellectual development in common equality; if an aggressor should threaten to destroy this environment, the state may pursue a defensive war. Under such circumstances, the statesman may not always possess the means to make an unequivocal moral choice. Furthermore, with the advent of nuclear systems and ballistic missiles, an attempt to maintain the three principles of control, proportionality, and civilian immunity may quite possibly fail.

Advocates of just war argue, nonetheless, that the extreme alternatives—total war or total submission to an aggressor—are unacceptable; and they hold that, since there are other alternatives (nuclear deterrence or conventional operations), their doctrine is relevant to the statesman's predicament today. Namely, how can a limited war be waged in an era when the lines that distinguish the warrior from the noncombatant are obscured, when the weapons that the belligerents possess are difficult to control and when unrestricted use of these weapons will destroy those values and institutions which one is fighting to preserve in the first place?

It is in this context and in this search for less extreme alternatives that chemical/biological warfare can also be approached. In 1943 President Roosevelt announced, with reference to CB operations, "I have been loath to believe that any nation, even our present enemies, would or would be willing to loose upon mankind such terrible and inhumane weapons. . . . Use of such weapons had been ruled out by the general opinion of civilized mankind."[12] There is a consensus in the West today that CB weapons not only are immoral but also have been ruled out by international law. We may well pause here to examine the legal status of CB.

CB and International Law

Before gas was first used by the Germans in 1915, it was generally thought that the St. Petersburg Declaration of 1868, the Hague Gas Declaration of 1899, and the Hague Rules on Land Warfare of 1907 had outlawed the use of gas in war. But after the Germans employed gas at Ypres, as O'Brien points out, the Allies did not protest the German action and they ignored the rule that, before invoking the right of reprisal, a belligerent is obliged to exhaust all other means of inducing the enemy to desist from the illegal practice. Instead, the Allies proceeded to develop their own gases and means of delivery.[13]

In the aftermath of World War I, Article 5 of the Washington Treaty of February 1922 outlawed the employment of CB agents in warfare. The United States ratified the treaty with the stipulation that it would take effect only if ratification was unanimous. The French refused to sign because they were dissatisfied with the wording of a clause relating to submarines.

A few years later the Geneva Protocol of 1925 was signed by all the world's major powers except the United States and Japan. The protocol prohibited the use of chemical and bacteriological agents in war. The major European powers, however, reserved the right to use these agents in retaliation. The possibility therefore remained of the building up of a *CB deterrent* as part of national armaments.

Despite the success at the Geneva Conference of 1925, H. G. Wells and Bertrand Russell were warning their compatriots on the eve of World War II that they could expect to be showered with gas in the event of another world war. The British public accepted these prophecies as likely to be fulfilled once hostilities began, and there was little confidence in the prewar efforts to ban the employment of CB armaments. Yet, except for limited Italian and Japanese use of these agents in Ethiopia and China, respectively, none of the major powers used CB during the war.

CB and the Just War

In 1960 the American public was made aware of hitherto classified information about CB operations. Opponents of CB declared that the U.S. Army Chemical Corps released the information in order to obtain more funds for research and development of new and more deadly nerve gases and still more demonic biological agents. They argued that it was a campaign to make CB warfare acceptable to the American people. For its part the Chemical Corps said the public was ignorant of the necessity for a CB deterrent because of the "CB taboo." This ignorance was not endangering national security, since the Chemical Corps could not get enough popular support to persuade Congress to approve the necessary funds.

At Columbia University, students and faculty members in the biological sciences signed a pledge not to work on germ warfare. As reported in the *New York Herald Tribune* of February 25, 1960, they said it was a "betrayal of 2,500 years of medical research to stockpile the agents of anthrax, cholera, tularemia, plague, and other diseases which will remain as enemies of man long after the barriers between hostile armed camps have disappeared." Though chemical agents were not mentioned in the declaration, most opponents of CB do not discriminate between biological and chemical warfare, but consider them equally diabolical. This observation leads us to an important point: that a discrimination *may* be made between the two types on a moral basis.

Chemical agents are now deemed tactical armaments. They are more predictable and they can be limited to battlefield use. Biological agents are of strategic significance because there is a time lapse between their introduction and the subsequent infection. However, since biological agents are dispersed over a wide area, it is difficult if not impossible for the users to control the damage they wreak, whether they are intended for humans, livestock, or crops. From the viewpoint of the just war doctrine, then, chemical weapons can be justified but biological weapons cannot.

Ramsey discusses this issue in the following terms: "The distinction between actual killing or not killing, or the relative "humaneness" of such application of power, is not the issue; but rather obliteration of the distinction between counterforce and counter-people warfare."[14] He argues at this point that if CB weapons are used indiscriminately against civilians as well as military personnel they are categorically immoral. Elsewhere, however, he qualifies his position by stating, "Unless the only possible use of these weapons would require subjectively intended and objectively direct action against an enemy population as such, the Christian's action should not be, even symbolically, directed against everything the government may be doing in this manner."[15]

Our discussion of CB warfare thus far has reflected the opinion of civilian commentators; the military case for CB operations will be examined next.

The Military Case for CB Operations

Military decision makers argue that unless they are prepared to wage wars of all kinds—conventional, nuclear, guerrilla, chemical/biological—there is no hope of deterring enemy attacks on the free world. CB weapons, they declare, are fundamental to a "limited war deterrent." Brigadier General J. H. Rothschild (Chemical Corps, Retired) says that communist China, for instance, may be willing to accept a U.S. nuclear strike because she has so few important nuclear targets, while she may be more effectively deterred by a U.S. capability that includes CB weapons.[16]

General Frank Stubbs of the Chemical Corps addresses himself to the versatility of CB operations: "Chemical weapons can be tailored to fit the exact requirements of the changing situation.

They can effect any necessary type casualties from incapacitation to death in minutes. . . . Chemical and biological weapons can reach troops whether they are concentrated or visibly dispersed or out in the open; in concealment or cover; above ground or in . . . underground installations."[17]

With the new emphasis on guerrilla warfare the potential use of CB weapons by insurgents as well as counter-insurgents is considerable. A small group of insurgents having access to these weapons could destroy an underdeveloped nation's food or cash crops, and/or incapacitate its farmers during planting and harvest. Once the economy had been crippled by such tactics, and the legitimate government "embarrassed," the rebels would be in a better position to overthrow that government. Worse yet, if the insurgents had appliances to disperse nerve gas, they could easily rout the forces of the legal government even if they were vastly outnumbered. On the other hand, military experts point out, counter-insurgents could employ tear, vomiting, or nerve gas to flush out rebels while reducing their own casualties in turn. Defoliating agents could clear brush and prevent guerrillas from hiding in ambush in lush forests along vital roads and waterways.

Even more ominous is the possibility that two underdeveloped states might produce or buy large quantities of infectious biological agents and wage a protracted war, aimed at crippling each other's morale, by spreading disease among the civilian as well as the military population. With poor health care and an inadequate supply of doctors and medical materials, such a war would be disastrous for both sides. For all these reasons the army warns that CB warfare must be taken seriously.

Military critics of CB point out that CB agents were withheld during World War II not merely because they were considered immoral by both the Allied and the Axis powers; there were concrete military reasons why gas was not used by the Germans. In the beginning of the war, for example, the *Wehrmacht* would have found it impossible to advance as quickly as it did had gas been used to pave the way. Later on, when the Germans no longer controlled the skies, a gas exchange would hardly have enhanced the security of the Third Reich. Furthermore, the argument goes, both sides concluded that gas was difficult to control and to use in a disciplined manner, as demonstrated in World War I; thus its effective use was considered marginal.

CB proponents among the military answer that, on the contrary, gas attacks during World War I inflicted a great number of casualties. Crudely implemented at first, toward the end of the war these agents proved to be most effective. During World War II the U.S. forces island-hopping in the Pacific might have used gas effectively. American casualties could have been reduced considerably if gas had been employed to flush out the Japanese forces buried in caves and concrete entrenchments, but U.S. generals were not permitted to do so. And who knows what might have been the result if the Germans had met the Allied invasion of France with gas?

Liddell Hart argues that it is very doubtful whether nuclear weapons of any size could be used without such action escalating. Therefore, a nation invaded by an aggressor who has numerically superior conventional and thermonuclear weapons is faced with a grim choice between defeat and the near certainty of national suicide if it used nuclear weapons in defense. Gas, he asserts, permits the victim nation another option.[18]

In considering the delicate question of the humaneness of CB operations, the military advocates contend that CB weapons produce casualties with a minimum of destruction of ancillary targets such as roads, houses, hospitals, etc. The reconstruction of a battered city is thereby made easier, while the suffering of the civilian population is mitigated considerably. British pundits add that in World War I fewer gas victims died of their injuries than soldiers injured by other weapons (though gas inflicted a proportionately greater number of casualties than did high explosives, and was more effective in demoralizing the enemy and reducing his battle efficiency). And the accusation that gas victims suffered greater after-effects, such as blindness and tuberculosis, than did other casualties has been statistically disproved.[19]

General Rothschild attributes the alleged consensus on the immorality of CB warfare to Allied propaganda aimed at the German's first use of gas in 1915. Over the years this campaign, he says, has resulted in the "CB taboo" which may some day prove to be responsible for more deaths and destruction at the hands of conventional and nuclear armies than would have been necessary had CB armaments been employed instead. "For hundreds of years it has been impossible to carry on war without firing hot metal capable of blasting off legs and arms and of leaving men blind or mindless for life." Then, after referring to the horrors of nuclear war, he concludes, "Ironically enough, it can be argued that the only known hope for relatively humane warfare in the future lies in the chemical and biological weapons."[20]

This is not the place to evaluate the military case for CB in detail, but two major points should be emphasized. First, in the light of the myriad innovations in weapons technology since World War II, it would probably be a mistake to belittle the claim of the U.S. Army that it has both lethal and nonlethal CB weapons in variety and in abundance, and that they are capable of being used either tactically or strategically in a genuine environment of war. Secondly, it is doubtful that a moral consensus alone deterred the belligerents from using such weapons in World War II. We might well assume that the Axis and the Allies merely deterred each other from using them. Public opinion in the Allied countries undoubtedly militated against initiating CB warfare, but it is not at all certain that the same was true in the Axis countries. And we certainly cannot assume today that any worldwide moral consensus will prevent the use of CB weapons tomorrow.

CB Arms Control

If, then, we must take CB warfare seriously, it would seem wise to direct more attention toward the arms control and disarmament problems involved in it. The big powers, reluctant to use even "tactical or battlefield nuclear weapons," in fear of escalation, will be forced to consider other alternatives for limited wars. The poorer countries tend to favor nuclear disarmament because a sophisticated nuclear strike force is beyond their means; but CB weapons are both inexpensive and easy to produce, and some of these countries may well reject the international control of such weaponry. To date, research on CB arms control and disarmament techniques and possibilities seems to have been very limited—and one inhibiting factor has surely been the uncertainty and ambiguity surrounding the morality of CB operations.

As has been indicated, present international law offers little in the way of CB arms control. After World War I the European powers agreed not to initiate the use of these weapons, but retaliation was left open. The Geneva Protocol of 1925 remains unsigned not only by the U.S. but also, of course, by newer governments such as that of communist China or the new African and Asian states. Indeed, international law as it is understood in the West is not considered relevant by a great portion of the world's population. The Communists are not the only ones who question an international law developed and codified by the capitalist, Christian states of Western Europe and America. The nonwhite, non-Christian, ex-colonial peoples of Asia and Africa argue that they are not bound by treaties and agreements imposed on them by the Western colonialists. Many commentators who make a case for the outlawing of CB warfare by the Hague Conventions, the Washington Treaty, or the Geneva Protocol have not fully appreciated this fact.

Any attempt to deal with CB warfare as a problem of international law must be preceded by a dispassionate debate of the military, political, legal, and moral problems which this mode of warfare engenders, and it must be worldwide in scope. The debate itself has been inhibited in this country (in part) because the military recognizes that CB is a controversial issue. A public debate could be manipulated by CB's opponents so as to restrict future research and development of CB agents if not to wreck the present program. On the other hand, those who have attacked CB operations on moral grounds have not taken the military and political realities into account. They have assumed a moral consensus in this country against CB agents and have terminated the debate at that point.

Consequently, the arms control and disarmament requirements of CB have been neglected. Specifically, although certain government agencies have been working on the control of CB, they have not been able to benefit from nongovernmental research in this area, notably on political, social, and legal questions. Yet it seems prudent to assume that, in the near future, the proliferation of CB weapons will pose an "Nth-country problem" similar to the nuclear one that threatens the "status quo" today.

Nonlethal Weapons

It seems appropriate to conclude this study by discussing a class of weapons unique to CB warfare; the nonlethal. Nonlethal CB weapons pose a new type of problem for proponents of the just war doctrine. We have already reviewed the difficult problems that CB warfare engenders for the moralist; now we must ask whether specifically nonlethal CB agents are more humane than conventional and nuclear armaments. Is it conceivable that we shall be able, some day, to wage entirely nonlethal war because of these agents?

Not all commentators believe nonlethal CB weapons to be more humane than conventional arms. Representative Robert Kastenmeier of Wisconsin has been a vocal critic of the Army's declaration to this effect. He has said, "Realizing strong opposition to chemical and biological weapons, the Defense Department has developed the novel argument that a war fought with chemical weapons is a more humane war. . . . The generals talk about psychochemicals which make cowards out of brave men and vice versa, while causing temporary madness in the population. The horror of a population stricken with mass madness is a strange conception of humanity."[21]

Proponents of nonlethal agents would probably answer such objections as follows: suppose the United Nations possessed nonlethal weapons that would temporarily incapacitate people. If it had been able to use such weapons in the Congo conflict, for instance, the Katangese army and the white mercenaries could have been subdued while the number of casualties would have been reduced by one-quarter to one-half. Survivors with conventional injuries might well have remained permanently maimed or crippled, while victims of nonlethal weapons would have recovered completely.[22] The question can be put this way: if such weapons are available to us, are we immoral in sticking to conventional warfare?

It seems that nonlethal weapons might well fit within the parameters of the just war doctrine; they also seem to satisfy the two principles embodied in the St. Petersburg Declaration of 1868, for they neither inflict superfluous suffering nor make death inevitable. Yet the judgment of Paul Ramsey may be taken as representative of the just war school on this issue, and he has declared that the use of incapacitants against noncombatants is as immoral as are lethal weapons. We are forced to wonder whether an indiscriminate taboo against all CB agents might inhibit a potential increase in humaneness in the waging of certain types of limited war.

There is perhaps a broader distinction to be made in considering the possibility of nonlethal warfare. John Courtney Murray remarks, "Force is the measure of power necessary and sufficient to uphold the valid purposes of law and of politics. What exceeds this measure is violence which destroys the order both of law and of politics."[23]

Assuming that nonlethal CB agents are available in quantity and are a feasible means of redressing grievances on a limited scale, might we not take the liberty to equate force—the measure of power necessary and sufficient to uphold the valid purpose of law and politics—with nonlethal weapons that only incapacitate; and violence—the excessive use of power where the order of both law and politics is destroyed—with lethal weapons that kill or maim?

Military operations that indulge in the unnecessary, widespread killing of civilians encourage revenge and reprisal and jeopardize the waging of counterforce war as well as a secure peace after hostilities have been terminated. Some day, perhaps, the advent of nonlethal weapons may engender a new kind of war where "force," as just defined, will be the only legitimate means of combat. But even here, once nonlethal agents are used, who knows where such an action might lead? This difficulty is analogous to that of distinguishing between battlefield and tactical nuclear weapons, or between tactical and strategic weapons.

Conclusion

It has been suggested throughout this paper that the "CB taboo," stemming from a widespread feeling that this kind of warfare is immoral, may be inhibiting both an essential discussion and essential research on CB arms control. The just war doctrine has been used here as a viewpoint from which to examine the problem. Some analysts, however, assert that the "CB taboo" serves as a fire-break; and we should not overlook the use of the taboo to secure a CB arms control accord with the Soviet Union. There are several reasons why an East-West arms control agreement specifically banning the production and deployment of biological weapons should be negotiated:

(1) These weapons do not enhance the military security of the United States or the Soviet Union and the present strategic balance would not be destabilized if they were outlawed.

(2) There is a real danger that in the near future they may spread to the underdeveloped world where they could be employed with awesome effectiveness against nations with poor medical facilities and a paucity of doctors. Moreover, insurgents today can effectively employ biological weapons against legitimate governments whereas the latter cannot use biological agents as effectively in counter-insurgency operations.

(3) Under just war, biological weapons are deemed immoral because they are inherently uncontrollable and they cannot be employed in counterforce warfare.

A CB arms control treaty would dampen East-West tensions. It would serve as a confidence-inducing agreement that would bring us a step closer to more comprehensive arms control negotiations. Short of an immediate East-West accord along these lines, the nations of Latin America and Africa should work to secure a regional arrangement that would ban the procurement and deployment of biological weapons, for they are certain to have the most to lose should biological weapons proliferate to Africa and Latin America.

Notes

An earlier version of this paper was presented at the Second International Arms Control and Disarmament Symposium in Ann Arbor, Michigan, in January 1964.

1. The scholastic and Protestant proponents of just war generally agree that a war cannot be waged justly unless seven conditions are fulfilled (see Joseph C. McKenna, "Ethics and War: A Catholic View," *American Political Science Review* 54, 3 [September 1960], pp. 647-658):

(1) The war must be declared by the legitimate public authority and the action must aim at a universal good; it must not be a matter of expediency.

(2) The seriousness of the injury to be suffered must be proportional to the damages war will cause.

(3) The seriousness of the injury to be suffered at the hands of the aggressor must be real and immediate.

(4) There must be a reasonable chance of winning the war.

(5) War may be initiated only as a last resort to redressing grievances.

(6) A war may be prosecuted legitimately only insofar as the responsible agents have a right intention.

(7) The particular means employed to wage the war must be themselves moral.

2. Robert Tucker, *The Just War* (Baltimore: Johns Hopkins University Press, 1960), pp. 42-43.

3. John Courtney Murray, *Morality and Modern War* (New York: Church Peace Union, 1960), p. 13.

4. Quoted in Paul Ramsey, *War and the Christian Conscience* (Durham, N.C.: Duke University Press, 1961), p. 234.

5. Ibid., p. 68.

6. Quoted in William Clancy, *The Moral Dilemma of Nuclear Weapons* (New York: Council on Religion and International Affairs, 1961), p. 51.

7. John Bennett, *Nuclear Weapons and the Conflict of Conscience* (New York: Scribner, 1962).

8. William Nagle, ed., *Morality and Modern Warfare* (Baltimore: Helicon Press, 1960), p. 100.

9. Ibid., p. 111.

10. Walter Millis, "War as a Moral Problem," in Donald Keys, ed., *God and the H-Bomb* (New York: Macfadden-Bartell, 1962), p. 32.

11. Christopher Hollis, "The Two Pacificisms," in Keyes, p. 70.

12. Quoted in Walter Schneir, "The Campaign to Make Chemical Warfare Respectable," *The Reporter*, 1 October 1959 (reprint).

13. William O'Brien, "Biological/Chemical Warfare and the International Law of War," *Georgetown Law Journal* 51, 1 (Fall 1962):23-24.

14. Ramsey, pp. 228-229.

15. Ibid., p. 226.

16. J. H. Rothschild (Brigadier General), *Tomorrow's Weapons* (New York: McGraw-Hill, 1964).

17. Quoted in Joseph Kelly, "Gas Warfare in International Law," *Military Review* (July 1960), p. 36.

18. Basil H. Liddell Hart, *Deterrent or Defense* (New York: Praeger, 1960), pp. 82-88.

19. James Kendall, *Breathe Freely: The Truth about Poison Gas* (London: Appleton-Century, 1938), pp. 62-64.

20. J. H. Rothschild (Brigadier General), "Germ and Chemical Warfare," *Survival* (March-April 1962), p. 30.

21. Robert Kastenmeier, "Chemical Warfare: Pentagon Booby Trap," *The Progressive* (December 1959) (reprint), p. 2.

22. We should note that researchers working with LSD-25 warn that psychochemicals may not harm a man physically but they may do

irreparable damage to his psyche. However, an even more humane weapon may result from present research to perfect an agent that reduces a man's blood pressure and induces unconsciousness if the victim should attempt to remain vertical, while he retains his senses if he stays in a horizontal position.

23. John Courtney Murray, *We Hold These Truths* (New York: Sheed and Ward, 1960), p. 288.

31

Some Paradoxes of Deterrence

Gregory S. Kavka

A moral evaluation of deterrence reveals certain paradoxes which, though absurd or incredible at first glance, are not easily disposed of. Professor Kavka maintains that these moral paradoxes of deterrence call into question some significant and widely accepted moral doctrines that he calls "bridge principles," so named because they are used to form a bridge between the moral evaluation of agents and their actions. By analyzing a class of situations involving nuclear deterrence, he shows that there are serious conflicts between these "bridge principles" and what is required of a rational moral agent in such situations. For example, in certain situations it would be morally right for a rational and morally good agent to deliberately attempt to corrupt himself. Interpreting his findings, Kavka suggests that such conflicts reflect a fundamental malaise in ethical theory, namely, that the principles by which we morally evaluate agents and actions are basically incompatible. Unless we are willing to adopt some extreme position or reject some significant and deeply entrenched beliefs, however, we may simply have to live with these paradoxes.

—W. S.

Deterrence is a parent of paradox. Conflict theorists, notably Thomas Schelling, have pointed out several paradoxes of deterrence: that it may be to the advantage of someone who is trying to deter another to be irrational, to have fewer available options, or to lack relevant information.[1] I shall describe certain new paradoxes that emerge when one attempts to analyze

Reprinted from *The Journal of Philosophy* 75, no. 6 (June 1978):285-302, by permission of the publisher.

deterrence from a moral rather than a strategic perspective. These paradoxes are presented in the form of statements that appear absurd or incredible on first inspection, but can be supported by quite convincing arguments.

Consider a typical situation involving deterrence. A potential wrongdoer is about to commit an offense that would unjustly harm someone. A defender intends, and threatens, to retaliate should the wrongdoer commit the offense. Carrying out retaliation, if the offense is committed, could well be morally wrong. (The wrongdoer could be insane, or the retaliation could be out of proportion with the offense, or could seriously harm others besides the wrongdoer.) The moral paradoxes of deterrence arise out of the attempt to determine the moral status of the defender's *intention* to retaliate in such cases. If the defender knows retaliation to be wrong, it would appear that this intention is evil. Yet such "evil" intentions may pave the road to heaven, by preventing serious offenses and by doing so without actually harming anyone.

Scrutiny of such morally ambiguous retaliatory intentions reveals paradoxes that call into question certain significant and widely accepted moral doctrines. These doctrines are what I call *bridge principles*. They attempt to link together the moral evaluation of actions and the moral evaluation of agents (and their states) in certain simple and apparently natural ways. The general acceptance and intuitive appeal of such principles lends credibility to the project of constructing a consistent moral system that accurately reflects our firmest moral beliefs about both agents and actions. By raising doubts about the validity of certain popular bridge principles, the paradoxes presented here pose new difficulties for this important project.

I

In this section, a certain class of situations involving deterrence is characterized, and a plausible normative assumption is presented. In the following three sections, we shall see how application of this assumption to these situations yields paradoxes.

The class of paradox-producing situations is best introduced by means of an example. Consider the balance of nuclear terror as viewed from the perspective of one of its superpower participants, nation N. N sees the threat of nuclear retaliation as its only reliable means of preventing nuclear attack (or nuclear blackmail leading to world domination) by its superpower rival. N is confident such a threat will succeed in deterring its adversary, provided it really intends to carry out the threat. (N fears that, if it bluffs, its adversary is likely to learn this through leaks or espionage.) Finally, N recognizes it would have conclusive moral reasons *not* to carry out the threatened retaliation, if its opponent were to obliterate N with a surprise attack. For although retaliation would punish the leaders who committed this unprecedented crime and would prevent them from dominating the postwar world, N knows it would also destroy many millions of innocent civilians in the attacking nation (and in other nations), would set back postwar economic recovery for the world immeasurably, and might add enough fallout to the atmosphere to destroy the human race.

Let us call situations of the sort that nation N perceives itself as being in *special deterrence situations* (SDSs). More precisely, an agent is in an SDS when he reasonably and correctly believes that the following conditions hold. First, it is likely he must intend (conditionally) to apply a harmful sanction to innocent people, if an extremely harmful and unjust offense is to be prevented. Second, such an intention would very likely deter the offense. Third, the amounts of harm involved in the offense and the threatened sanction are very large and of roughly similar quantity (or the latter amount is smaller than the former). Finally, he would have conclusive moral reasons not to apply the sanction if the offense were to occur.

The first condition in this definition requires some comment. Deterrence depends only on the potential wrongdoer's *beliefs* about the prospects of the sanction being applied. Hence, the first condition will be satisfied only if attempts by the defender to bluff would likely be perceived as such by the wrongdoer. This may be the case if the defender is an unconvincing liar, or is a group with a collective decision procedure, or if the wrongdoer is shrewd and knows the defender quite well. Generally, however, bluffing will be a promising course of action. Hence, although it is surely logically and physically possible for an SDS to occur, there will be few actual SDSs. It may be noted, though, that writers on strategic policy frequently assert that nuclear deterrence will be effective only if the defending nation really intends to retaliate.[2] If this is so, the balance of terror may fit the definition of an SDS, and the paradoxes developed here could have significant practical implications.[3] Further, were there no actual SDSs, these paradoxes would still be of considerable theoretical interest. For they indicate that the validity of some widely accepted moral doctrines rests on the presupposition that certain situations that could arise (i.e., SDSs) will not.

Turning to our normative assumption, we begin by noting that any reasonable system of ethics must have substantial utilitarian elements. The assumption that produces the paradoxes of deterrence concerns the role of utilitarian considerations in determining one's moral duty in a narrowly limited class of situations. Let the *most useful* act in a given choice situation be that with the highest expected utility. Our assumption says that the most useful act should be performed whenever a very great deal of utility is at stake. This means that, if the difference in expected utility between the most useful act and its alternatives is extremely large (e.g., equivalent to the difference between life and death for a very large number of people), other moral considerations are overridden by utilitarian considerations.

This assumption may be substantially weakened by restricting in various ways its range of application. I restrict the assumption to apply only when (*i*) a great deal of *negative* utility is at stake, and (*ii*) people will likely suffer serious injustices if the agent fails to perform the most useful act. This makes the assumption more plausible, since the propriety of doing one person a serious injustice, in order to produce positive benefits for others, is highly questionable. The justifiability of doing the same injustice to prevent a utilitarian disaster which itself involves grave injustices, seems more in accordance with our moral intuitions.

The above restrictions appear to bring our assumption into line with the views of philosophers such as Robert Nozick, Thomas Nagel, and Richard Brandt, who portray moral rules as "absolutely" forbidding certain kinds of acts, but acknowledge that exceptions might have to be allowed in cases in which such acts are necessary to prevent catastrophe.[4] Even with these restrictions, however, the proposed assumption would be rejected by supporters of genuine absolutism, the doctrine that there are certain acts (such as vicarious punishment and deliberate killing of the innocent) that are always wrong, whatever the consequences of not performing them. (Call such acts *inherently evil.*) We can, though, accommodate the absolutists. To do so, let us further qualify our assumption by limiting its application to cases in which (*iii*) performing the most useful act involves, at most, a small *risk* of performing an inherently evil act. With this restriction, the assumption still leads to paradoxes, yet is consistent with absolutism (unless that doctrine is extended to include absolute prohibitions on something other than doing acts of the sort usually regarded as inherently evil).[5] The triply qualified assumption is quite plausible; so the fact that it produces paradoxes is both interesting and disturbing.

II

The first moral paradox of deterrence is:

(*P1*) There are cases in which, although it would be wrong for an agent to perform a certain act in a certain situation, it would nonetheless be right for him, knowing this, to form the intention to perform that act in that situation.

At first, this strikes one as absurd. If it is wrong and he is aware that it is wrong, how could it be right for him to form the intention to do it? (*P1*) is the direct denial of a simple moral thesis, the *wrongful intentions principle* (WIP): *To intend to do what one knows to be wrong is itself wrong.*[6] WIP seems so obvious that, although philosophers never call it into question, they rarely bother to assert it or argue for it. Nevertheless, it appears that Abelard, Aquinas, Butler, Bentham, Kant, and Sidgwick, as well as recent writers such as Anthony Kenny and Jan Narveson, have accepted the principle, at least implicitly.[7]

Why does WIP seem so obviously true? First, we regard the man who fully intends to perform a wrongful act and is prevented from doing so solely by external circumstances (e.g., a man whose murder plan is interrupted by the victim's fatal heart attack) as being just as bad as the man who performs a like wrongful act. Second, we view the man who intends to do what is wrong, and then changes his mind, as having corrected a moral failing or error. Third, it is convenient, for many purposes, to treat a prior intention to perform an act, as the beginning of the act itself. Hence, we are inclined to view intentions as parts of actions and to ascribe to each intention the moral status ascribed to the act "containing" it.

It is essential to note that WIP appears to apply to conditional intentions in the same manner as it applies to nonconditional ones. Suppose I form the intention to kill my neighbor if he insults me again, and fail to kill him only because, fortuitously, he refrains from doing so. I am as bad, or nearly as bad, as if he had insulted me and I had killed him. My failure to perform the act no more erases the wrongness of my intention, than my neighbor's dropping dead as I load my gun would negate the wrongness of the simple intention to kill him. Thus the same considerations adduced above in support of WIP seem to support the formulation: If it would be wrong to perform an act in certain circumstances, then it is wrong to intend to perform that act on the condition that those circumstances arise.

Having noted the source of the strong feeling that (*P1*) should be rejected, we must consider an instantiation of (*P1*):

(*P1′*) In an SDS, it would be wrong for the defender to apply the sanction if the wrongdoer were to commit the offense, but it is right for the defender to form the (conditional) intention to apply the sanction if the wrongdoer commits the offense.

The first half of (*P1′*), the wrongness of applying the sanction, follows directly from the last part of the definition of an SDS, which says that the defender would have conclusive moral reasons not to apply the sanction. The latter half of (*P1′*), which asserts the rightness of forming the intention to apply the sanction, follows from the definition of an SDS and our normative assumption. According to the definition, the defender's forming this intention is likely necessary, and very likely sufficient, to prevent a seriously harmful and unjust offense. Further, the offense and the sanction would each produce very large and roughly commensurate amounts of negative utility (or the latter would produce a smaller amount). It follows that utilitarian considerations heavily favor forming the intention to apply the sanction, and that doing so involves only a small risk of performing an inherently evil act. Applying our normative assumption yields the conclusion that it is right for the defender to form the intention in question.[8]

This argument, if sound, would establish the truth of (*PI'*), and hence (*PI*), in contradiction with WIP. It suggests that WIP should not be applied to *deterrent intentions,* i.e., those conditional intentions whose existence is based on the agent's desire to thereby deter others from actualizing the antecedent condition of the intention. Such intentions are rather strange. They are, by nature, self-stultifying: if a deterrent intention fulfills the agent's purpose, it ensures that the intended (and possibly evil) act is not performed, by preventing the circumstances of performance from arising. The unique nature of such intentions can be further explicated by noting the distinction between intending to do something, and desiring (or intending) to intend to do it. Normally, an agent will form the intention to do something because he either desires doing that thing as an end in itself, or as a means to other ends. In such cases, little importance attaches to the distinction between intending and desiring to intend. But, in the case of deterrent intentions, the ground of the desire to form the intention is entirely distinct from any desire to carry it out. Thus, what may be inferred about the agent who seeks to form such an intention is this. He desires *having the intention* as a means of deterrence. Also, he is willing, in order to prevent the offense, to accept a certain *risk* that, in the end, he will apply the sanction. But this is entirely consistent with his having a strong desire not to apply the sanction, and no desire at all to apply it. Thus, while the object of his deterrent intention might be an evil act, it does not follow that, in desiring to adopt that intention, he desires to do evil, either as an end or as a means.

WIP ties the morality of an intention exclusively to the moral qualities of its object (i.e., the intended act). This is not unreasonable since, typically, the only significant effects of intentions are the acts of the agent (and the consequences of these acts) which flow from these intentions. However, in certain cases, intentions may have *autonomous effects* that are independent of the intended act's actually being performed. In particular, intentions to act may influence the conduct of other agents. When an intention has important autonomous effects, these effects must be incorporated into any adequate moral analysis of it. The first paradox arises because the autonomous effects of the relevant deterrent intention are dominant in the moral analysis of an SDS, but the extremely plausible WIP ignores such effects.[9]

III

(*P1'*) implies that a rational moral agent in an SDS should want to form the conditional intention to apply the sanction if the offense is committed, in order to deter the offense. But will he be able to do so? Fortunately, he will not be. He is a captive in the prison of his own virtue, able to form the requisite intention only by bending the bars of his cell out of shape. Consider the preliminary formulation of this new paradox:

(*P2'*) In an SDS, a rational and morally good agent cannot (as a matter of logic) have (or form) the intention to apply the sanction if the offense is committed.[10]

The argument for (*P2'*) is as follows. An agent in an SDS recognizes that there would be conclusive moral reasons not to apply the sanction if the offense were committed. If he does not regard these admittedly conclusive moral reasons as conclusive reasons for him not to apply the sanction, then he is not moral. Suppose, on the other hand, that he does regard himself as having conclusive reasons not to apply the sanction if the offense is committed. If, nonetheless, he is disposed to apply it, because the reasons for applying it motivate him more strongly than do the conclusive reasons not to apply it, then he is irrational.

But couldn't our rational moral agent recognize, in accordance with (*P1'*), that he ought to form the intention to apply the sanction? And couldn't he then simply grit his teeth and pledge to himself that he will apply the sanction if the offense is committed? No doubt he could, and this would amount to trying to form the intention to apply the sanction. But the question remains whether he can succeed in forming that intention, by this or any other process, while remaining rational and moral. And it appears he cannot. There are, first of all, psychological difficulties. Being rational, how can he dispose himself to do something that he knows he would have conclusive reasons not to do, when and if the time comes to do it? Perhaps, though, some exceptional people can produce in themselves dispositions to act merely by pledging to act. But even if one could, in an SDS, produce a disposition to apply the sanction in this manner, such a disposition would not count as a rational intention to apply the sanction. This is because, as recent writers on intentions have suggested, it is part of the concept of rationally intending to do something, that the disposition to do the intended act be caused (or justified) in an appropriate way by the agent's view of reasons for doing the act.[11] And the disposition in question does not stand in such a relation to the agent's reasons for action.

It might be objected to this that people sometimes intend to do things (and do them) for no reason at all, without being irrational. This is true, and indicates that the connections between the concepts of intending and reasons for action are not so simple as the above formula implies. But it is also true that intending to do something for no reason at all, in the face of recognized significant reasons not to do it, would be irrational. Similarly, a disposition to act in the face of the acknowledged preponderance of reasons, whether called an "intention" or not, could not qualify as rational. It may be claimed that such a disposition, in an SDS, is rational in the sense that the agent knows it would further his aims to form (and have) it. This is not to deny the second paradox, but simply to express one of its paradoxical features. For the point of (*P2′*) is that the very disposition that *is* rational in the sense just mentioned, is at the same time irrational in an equally important sense. It is a disposition to act in conflict with the agent's own view of the balance of reasons for action.

We can achieve some insight into this by noting that an intention that is deliberately formed resides at the intersection of two distinguishable actions. It is the beginning of the act that is its object and is the end of the act that is its formation. As such, it may be assessed as rational (or moral) or not, according to whether either of two different acts promotes the agent's (or morality's) ends. Generally, the assessments will agree. But, as Schelling and others have noted, it may sometimes promote one's aims *not* to be disposed to act to promote one's aims, should certain contingencies arise. For example, a small country may deter invasion by a larger country if it is disposed to resist any invasion, even when resistance would be suicidal. In such situations, the assessment of the rationality (or morality) of the agent's intentions will depend upon whether these intentions are treated as components of their object-acts or their formation-acts. If treated as both, conflicts can occur. It is usual and proper to assess the practical rationality of an agent, at a given time, according to the degree of correspondence between his intentions and the reasons he has for performing the acts that are the objects of those intentions. As a result, puzzles such as $(P2')$ emerge when, for purposes of moral analysis, an agent's intentions are viewed partly as components of their formation-acts.

Let us return to the main path of our discussion by briefly summarizing the argument for $(P2')$. A morally good agent regards conclusive moral reasons for action as conclusive reasons for action *simpliciter*. But the intentions of a rational agent are not out of line with his assessment of the reasons for and against acting. Consequently, a rational moral agent cannot intend to do something that he recognizes there are conclusive moral reasons not to do. Nor can he intend conditionally to do what he recognizes he would have conclusive reasons not to do were that condition to be fulfilled. Therefore, in an SDS, where one has conclusive moral reasons not to apply the sanction, an originally rational and moral agent cannot have the intention to apply it without ceasing to be fully rational or moral; nor can he form the intention (as this entails having it).

We have observed that forming an intention is a process that may generally be regarded as an action. Thus, the second paradox can be reformulated as:

$(P2)$ There are situations (namely SDSs) in which it would be right for agents to perform certain actions (namely forming the intention to apply the sanction) and in which it is possible for some agents to perform such actions, but impossible for rational and morally good agents to perform them.

$(P2)$, with the exception of the middle clause, is derived from the conjunction of $(P1')$ and $(P2')$ by existential generalization. The truth of the middle clause follows from consideration of the vengeful agent, who desires to punish those who commit seriously harmful and unjust offenses, no matter what the cost to others.

(*P2*) is paradoxical because it says that there are no situations in which rationality and virtue preclude the possibility of right action. And this contravenes our usual assumption about the close logical ties between the concepts of right action and agent goodness. Consider the following claim. *Doing something is right if and only if a morally good man would do the same thing in the given situation.* Call this the *right-good principle.* One suspects that, aside from qualifications concerning the good man's possible imperfections or factual ignorance, most people regard this principle, which directly contradicts (*P2*), as being virtually analytic. Yet the plight of the good man described in the second paradox does not arise out of an insufficiency of either knowledge or goodness. (*P2*) says there are conceivable situations in which virtue and knowledge combine with rationality to preclude right action, in which virtue is an obstacle to doing the right thing. If (*P2*) is true, our views about the close logical connection between right action and agent goodness, as embodied in the right-good principle, require modifications of a sort not previously envisioned.

IV

A rational moral agent in an SDS faces a cruel dilemma. His reasons for intending to apply the sanction if the offense is committed are, according to (*P1′*), conclusive. But they outrun his reasons for doing it. Wishing to do what is right, he wants to form the intention. However, unless he can substantially alter the basic facts of the situation or his beliefs about those facts, he can do so only by making himself less morally good; that is, by becoming a person who attaches grossly mistaken weights to certain reasons for and against action (e.g., one who prefers retribution to the protection of the vital interests of innocent people).[12] We have arrived at a third paradox:

(*P3*) In certain situations, it would be morally right for a rational and morally good agent to deliberately (attempt to) corrupt himself.[13]

(*P3*) may be viewed in light of a point about the credibility of threats which has been made by conflict theorists. Suppose a defender is worried about the credibility of his deterrent threat, because he thinks the wrongdoer (rightly) regards him as unwilling to apply the threatened sanction. He may make the threat more credible by passing control of the sanction to some *retaliation-agent*. Conflict theorists consider two sorts of retaliation-agents: people known to be highly motivated to punish the offense in question, and machines programmed to retaliate automatically if the offense occurs. What I wish to note is that future selves of the defender himself are a third class of retaliation-agents. If the other kinds are unavailable, a defender may have to create an agent of this third sort (i.e., an altered self willing to apply the sanction), in order to deter the offense. In cases in which applying the sanction would be wrong, this could require self-corruption.

How would a rational and moral agent in an SDS, who seeks to have the intention to apply the situation, go about corrupting himself so that he may have it? He cannot form the intention simply by pledging to apply the sanction; for, according to the second paradox, his rationality and morality preclude this. Instead, he must seek to initiate a causal process (e.g., a reeducation program) that he hopes will result in his beliefs, attitudes, and values changing in such a way that he can and will have the intention to apply the sanction should the offense be committed. Initiating such a process involves taking a rather odd, though not uncommon, attitude toward oneself: viewing oneself as an object to be molded in certain respects by outside influences rather than by inner choices. This is, for example, the attitude of the lazy but ambitious student who enrolls in a fine college, hoping that some of the habits and values of his highly motivated fellow students will "rub off" on him.

We can now better understand the notion of "risking doing *X*" which was introduced in Section I. For convenience, let *X* be "killing." Deliberately risking killing is different from risking deliberately killing. One does the former when one rushes an ill person to the hospital in one's car at unsafe speed, having noted the danger of causing a fatal accident. One has deliberately accepted the risk of killing by accident. One (knowingly) risks deliberately killing, on the other hand, when one undertakes a course of action that one knows may, by various causal processes, lead to one's later performing a deliberate killing. The mild-mannered youth who joins a violent street gang is an example. Similarly, the agent in an SDS, who undertakes a plan of self-corruption in order to develop the requisite deterrent intention, knowingly risks deliberately performing the wrongful act of applying the sanction.

The above description of what is required of the rational moral agent in an SDS leads to a natural objection to the argument that supports (*P3*). According to this objection, an attempt at self-corruption by a rational moral agent is very likely to fail. Hence, bluffing would surely be a more promising strategy for deterrence than trying to form retaliatory intentions by self-corruption. Three replies may be given to this objection. First, it is certainly *conceivable* that, in a particular SDS, undertaking a process of self-corruption would be more likely to result in effective deterrence than would bluffing. Second, and more important, bluffing and attempting to form retaliatory intentions by self-corruption will generally not be mutually exclusive alternatives. An agent in an SDS may attempt to form the retaliatory intention while bluffing, and plan to continue bluffing as a "fall-back" strategy, should he fail. If the offense to be prevented is disastrous enough, the additional expected utility generated by following such a combined strategy (as opposed to simply bluffing) will be very large, even if his attempts to form the intention are unlikely to succeed. Hence, (*P3*) would still follow from our normative assumption. Finally, consider the rational and *partly corrupt* agent in an SDS who already has the intention to retaliate. (The nations participating in the balance of terror may be examples.) The relevant question about him is whether he ought to act to become less corrupt, with the result that he would lose the intention to retaliate. The present objection does not apply in this case, since the agent already has the requisite corrupt features. Yet, essentially the same argument that produces (*P3*) leads, when this case is considered, to a slightly different, but equally puzzling, version of our third paradox:

(*P3'*) In certain situations it would be morally wrong for a rational and partly corrupt agent to (attempt to) reform himself and eliminate his corruption.

A rather different objection to (*P3*) is the claim that its central notion is incoherent. This claim is made, apparently, by Thomas Nagel, who writes, "The notion that one might sacrifice one's moral integrity justifiably, in the service of a sufficiently worthy end, is an incoherent notion. For if one were justified in making such a sacrifice (or even morally required to make it), then one would not be sacrificing one's moral integrity by adopting that course: one would be preserving it."[14] Now the notion of a justified sacrifice or moral virtue (integrity) would be incoherent, as Nagel suggests, if one could sacrifice one's virtue only by doing something wrong. For the same act cannot be both morally justified and morally wrong. But one may also be said to sacrifice one's virtue when one deliberately initiates a causal process that one expects to result, and does result, in one's later becoming a less virtuous person. And, as the analysis of SDSs embodied in (*P1'*) and (*P2'*) implies, one may, in certain cases, be justified in initiating such a process (or even be obliged to initiate it). Hence, it would be a mistake to deny (*P3*) on the grounds advanced in Nagel's argument.

There is, though, a good reason for *wanting* to reject (*P3*). It conflicts with some of our firmest beliefs about virtue and duty. We regard the promotion and preservation of one's own virtue as a vital responsibility of each moral agent, and self-corruption as among the vilest of enterprises. Further, we do not view the duty to promote one's virtue as simply one duty among others, to be weighed and balanced against the rest, but rather as a special duty that encompasses the other moral duties. Thus, we assent to the *virtue preservation principle: it is wrong to deliberately lose (or reduce the degree of) one's moral virtue.* To many, this principle seems fundamental to our very conception of morality.[15] Hence the suggestion that duty could require the abandonment of virtue seems quite unacceptable. The fact that this suggestion can be supported by strong arguments produces a paradox.

This paradox is reflected in the ambivalent attitudes that emerge when we attempt to evaluate three hypothetical agents who respond to the demands of SDSs in various ways. The first agent refuses to try to corrupt himself and allows the disastrous offense to occur. We respect the love of virtue he displays, but are inclined to suspect him of too great a devotion to his own purity relative to his concern for the well-being of others. The second agent does corrupt himself to prevent disaster in an SDS. Though we do not approve of his new corrupt aspects, we admire the person that he *was* for his willingness to sacrifice what he loved—part of his own virtue—in the service of others. At the same time, the fact that he succeeded in corrupting himself may make us wonder whether he was entirely virtuous in the first place. Corruption, we feel, does not come easily to a good man. The third agent reluctantly but sincerely tries his best to corrupt himself to prevent disaster, but fails. He may be admired both for his willingness to make such a sacrifice and for having virtue so deeply engrained in his character that his attempts at self-corruption do not succeed. It is perhaps characteristic of the paradoxical nature of the envisioned situation, that we are inclined to admire most the only one of these three agents who fails in the course of action he undertakes.

V

It is natural to think of the evaluation of agents, and of actions, as being two sides of the same moral coin. The moral paradoxes of deterrence suggest they are more like two separate coins that can be fused together only by significantly deforming one or the other. In this concluding section, I shall briefly explain this.

Our shared assortment of moral beliefs may be viewed as consisting of three relatively distinct groups: beliefs about the evaluation of actions, beliefs about the evaluation of agents and their states (e.g., motives, intentions, and character traits), and beliefs about the relationship between the two. An important part of this last group of beliefs is represented by the three bridge principles introduced above: the wrongful intentions, right-good, and virtue preservation principles. Given an agreed-upon set of bridge principles, one could go about constructing a moral system meant to express coherently our moral beliefs in either of two ways: by developing principles that express our beliefs about act evaluation and then using the bridge principles to derive principles of agent evaluation—or vice versa. If our bridge principles are sound and our beliefs about agent and act evaluation are mutually consistent, the resulting systems would, in theory, be the same. If, however, there are underlying incompatibilities between the principles we use to evaluate acts and agents, there may be significant differences between moral systems that are *act-oriented* and those which are *agent-oriented*. And these differences may manifest themselves as paradoxes which exert pressure upon the bridge principles that attempt to link the divergent systems, and the divergent aspects of each system, together.

It seems natural to us to evaluate acts at least partly in terms of their consequences. Hence, act-oriented moral systems tend to involve significant utilitarian elements. The principle of act evaluation usually employed in utilitarian systems is: in a given situation, one ought to perform the most useful act, that which will (or is expected to) produce the most utility. What will maximize utility depends upon the facts of the particular situation. Hence, as various philosophers have pointed out, the above principle could conceivably recommend one's (*i*) acting from nonutilitarian motives, (*ii*) advocating some nonutilitarian moral theory, or even (*iii*) becoming a genuine adherent of some nonutilitarian theory. Related quandaries arise when one considers, from an act-utilitarian viewpoint, the deterrent intention of a defender in an SDS. Here is an intention whose object-act is anti-utilitarian and whose formation-act is a utilitarian duty that cannot be performed by a rational utilitarian.

A utilitarian might seek relief from these quandaries in either of two ways. First, he could defend some form of rule-utilitarianism. But then he would face a problem. Shall he include, among the rules of his system, our normative assumption that requires the performance of the most useful act, whenever an enormous amount of utility is at stake (and certain other conditions are satisfied)? If he does, the moral paradoxes of deterrence will appear within his system. If he does not, it would seem that his system fails to attach the importance to the consequences of particular momentous acts that any reasonable moral, much less utilitarian, system should. An alternative reaction would be to stick by the utilitarian principle of act evaluation, and simply accept (*P1*)-(*P3*), and related oddities, as true. Taking this line would require the abandonment of the plausible and familiar bridge principles that contradict (*P1*)-(*P3*). But this need not bother the act-utilitarian, who perceives his task as the modification, as well as codification, of our moral beliefs.

Agent-oriented (as opposed to act-oriented) moral systems rest on the premise that what primarily matters for morality are the internal states of a person: his character traits, his intentions, and the condition of his will. The doctrines about intentions and virtue expressed in our three bridge principles are generally incorporated into such systems. The paradoxes of deterrence may pose serious problems for some agent-oriented systems. It may be, for example, that an adequate analysis of the moral virtues of justice, selflessness, and benevolence imply that the truly virtuous man would feel obligated to make whatever personal sacrifice is necessary to prevent a catastrophe. If so, the moral paradoxes of deterrence would arise within agent-oriented systems committed to these virtues.

There are, however, agent-oriented systems that would not be affected by our paradoxes. One such system could be called *extreme Kantianism*. According to this view, the only things having moral significance are such features of a person as his character and the state of his will. The extreme Kantian accepts Kant's dictum that morality requires treating oneself and others as ends rather than means. He interprets this to imply strict duties to preserve one's virtue and not to deliberately impose serious harms or risks on innocent people. Thus, the extreme Kantian would simply reject (*P1*)-(*P3*) without qualm.

Although act-utilitarians and extreme Kantians can view the paradoxes of deterrence without concern, one doubts that the rest of us can. The adherents of these extreme conceptions of morality are untroubled by the paradoxes because their viewpoints are too one-sided to represent our moral beliefs accurately. Each of them is closely attentive to certain standard principles of agent or act evaluation, but seems too little concerned with traditional principles of the other sort. For a system of morality to reflect our firmest and deepest convictions adequately, it must represent a middle ground between these extremes by seeking to accommodate the valid insights of both act-oriented and agent-oriented perspectives. The normative assumption set out in Section I was chosen as a representative principle that might be incorporated into such a system. It treats utilitarian considerations as relevant and potentially decisive, while allowing for the importance of other factors. Though consistent with the absolute prohibition of certain sorts of acts, it treats the distinction between harms and risks as significant and rules out absolute prohibitions on the latter as unreasonable. It is an extremely plausible middle-ground principle; but, disturbingly, it leads to paradoxes.

That these paradoxes reflect conflicts between commonly accepted principles of agent and act evaluation, is further indicated by the following observation. Consider what initially appears a natural way of viewing the evaluation of acts and agents as coordinated parts of a single moral system. According to this view, reasons for action determine the moral status of acts, agents, and intentions. A right act is an act that accords with the preponderance of moral reasons for action. To have the right intention is to be disposed to perform the act supported by the preponderance of such reasons, because of those reasons. The virtuous agent is the rational agent who has the proper substantive values, i.e., the person whose intentions and actions accord with the preponderance of moral reasons for action. Given these considerations, it appears that it should always be possible for an agent to go along intending, and acting, in accordance with the preponderance of moral reasons; thus ensuring both his own virtue and the rightness of his intentions and actions. Unfortunately, this conception of harmonious coordination between virtue, right intention, and right action, is shown to be untenable by the paradoxes of deterrence. For they demonstrate that, in any system that takes consequences plausibly into account, situations can arise in which the rational use of moral principles leads to certain paradoxical recommendations: that the principles used, and part of the agents's virtue, be abandoned, and that wrongful intentions be formed.

One could seek to avoid these paradoxes by moving in the direction of extreme Kantianism and rejecting our normative assumption. But to do so would be to overlook the plausible core of act-utilitarianism. This is the claim that, in the moral evaluation of acts, how those acts affect human happiness often is important—the more so as more happiness is at stake—and sometimes is decisive. Conversely, one could move toward accommodation with act-utilitarianism. This would involve qualifying, so that they do not apply in SDSs, the traditional moral doctrines that contradict $(P1)$-$(P3)$. And, in fact, viewed in isolation, the considerations adduced in Section II indicate that the wrongful intentions principle ought to be so qualified. However, the claims of (*P2*) and (*P3*) that virtue may preclude right action and that morality may require self-corruption are not so easily accepted. These notions remain unpalatable even when one considers the arguments that support them.[16]

Thus, tinkering with our normative assumption or with traditional moral doctrines would indeed enable us to avoid the paradoxes, at least in their present form. But this would require rejecting certain significant and deeply entrenched beliefs concerning the evaluation either of agents or of actions. Hence, such tinkering would not go far toward solving the fundamental problem of which the paradoxes are symptoms: the apparent incompatibility of the moral principles we use to evaluate acts and agents. Perhaps this problem can be solved. Perhaps the coins of agent and act evaluation can be successfully fused. But it is not apparent how this is to be done. And I, for one, do not presently see an entirely satisfactory way out of the perplexities that the paradoxes engender.

Notes

An earlier version of this paper was presented at Stanford University. I am grateful to several people, especially Robert Marrihew Adams, Tyler Burge, Warren Quinn, and Virginia Warren, for helpful comments on previous drafts. My work was supported, in part, by a Regents' Faculty Research Fellowship from the University of California.

1. *The Strategy of Conflict* (New York: Oxford, 1960), Chapters 1-2; and *Arms and Influence* (New Haven, Conn.: Yale, 1966), Chapter 2.

2. See, e.g., Herman Kahn, *On Thermonuclear War*, 2d ed. (Princeton, N.J.: University Press, 1960), p. 185; and Anthony Kenny, "Counterforce and Countervalue," in Walter Stein, ed., *Nuclear Weapons: A Catholic Response* (London: Merlin Press, 1965), pp. 162-64.

3. See, e.g., note 9, below.

4. Robert Nozick, *Anarchy, State, and Utopia* (New York: Basic Books, 1974), pp. 30/1 n; Thomas Nagel, "War and Massacre," Chapter 23 in this volume; Richard Brandt, "Utilitarianism and the Rules of War," Chapter 24 in this volume, especially note 3.

5. Extensions of absolutism that would block some or all of the

paradoxes include those which forbid intending to do what is wrong, deliberately making oneself less virtuous, or intentionally risking performing an inherently evil act. (An explanation of the relevant sense of 'risking performing an act' will be offered in Section IV.)

6. I assume henceforth that, if it would be wrong to do something, the agent knows this. (The agent, discussed in Section IV, who has become corrupt may be an exception.) This keeps the discussion of the paradoxes from getting tangled up with the separate problem of whether an agent's duty is to do what is actually right, or what he believes is right.

7. See *Peter Abelard's Ethics*, D. E. Luscombe, trans. (New York: Oxford, 1971), pp. 5-37; Thomas Aquinas, *Summa Theologica*, 1a2ae. 18-20; Joseph Butler, "A Dissertation on the Nature of Virtue," in *Five Sermons* (Indianapolis: Bobbs-Merrill, 1950), p. 83; Immanuel Kant, *Foundations of the Metaphysics of Morals*, first section; Jeremy Bentham, *An Introduction to the Principles of Morals and Legislation*, chap. 9, secs. 13-16; Henry Sidgwick, *The Methods of Ethics* (New York: Dover, 1907), pp. 60/1, 201-204; Kenny, "Counterforce and Countervalue," pp. 159, 162; and Jan Narveson, *Morality and Utility* (Baltimore: Johns Hopkins, 1967), pp. 106-108.

8. A qualification is necessary. Although having the intention involves only a small risk of applying the threatened sanction to innocent people, it follows, from points made in Section IV, that forming the intention might also involve risks of performing *other* inherently evil acts. Hence, what really follows is that forming the intention is right in those SDSs in which the composite risk is small. This limitation in the scope of (*P1'*) is to be henceforth understood. It does not affect (*P1*), (*P2*), or (*P3*), since each is governed by an existential quantifier.

9. In *Nuclear Weapons*, Kenny and others use WIP to argue that nuclear deterrence is immoral because it involves having the conditional intention to kill innocent people. The considerations advanced in this section suggest that this argument, at best, is inconclusive, since it presents only one side of a moral paradox, and, at worst, is mistaken, since it applies WIP in just the sort of situation in which its applicability is most questionable.

10. "Rational and morally good" in this and later statements of the second and third paradoxes, means rational and moral in the given situation. A person who usually is rational and moral, but fails to be in the situation in question, could, of course, have the intention to apply the sanction. (*P2*) is quite similar to a paradox concerning utilitarianism and deterrence developed by D. H. Hodgson in *Consequences of Utilitarianism* (Oxford: Clarendon Press, 1967), chap. 4.

11. See, e.g., S. Hampshire and H.L.A. Hart, "Decision, Intention

and Certainty," *Mind* 67, 1, 265 (January 1958):1-12; and G.E.M. Anscombe, *Intention* (Ithaca, N.Y.: Cornell, 1956).

12. Alternatively, the agent could undertake to make himself into an *irrational* person whose intentions are quite out of line with his reasons for action. However, trying to become irrational, in these circumstances, is less likely to succeed than trying to change one's moral beliefs, and, furthermore, might itself constitute self-corruption. Hence, this point does not affect the paradox stated below.

13. As Donald Regan has suggested to me, (*P3*) can be derived directly from our normative assumption: imagine a villain credibly threatening to kill very many hostages unless a certain good man corrupts himself. I prefer the indirect route to (*P3*) given in the text, because (*P1*) and (*P2*) are interesting in their own right and because viewing the three paradoxes together makes it easier to see what produces them.

14. Nagel, "War and Massacre."

15. Its supporters might, of course, allow exceptions to the principle in cases in which only the agent's feelings, and not his acts or dispositions to act, are corrupted. (For example, a doctor "corrupts himself" by suppressing normal sympathy for patients in unavoidable pain, in order to treat them more effectively). Further, advocates of the doctrine of double effect might consider self-corruption permissible when it is a "side effect" of action rather than a means to an end. For example, they might approve of a social worker's joining a gang to reform it, even though he expects to assimilate some of the gang's distorted values. Note, however, that neither of these possible exceptions to the virtue preservation principle (brought to my attention by Robert Adams) applies to the agent in an SDS who corrupts his *intentions* as a chosen *means* of preventing an offense.

16. See Hodgson, *Consequences*. Also, Adams, "Motive Utilitarianism," *The Journal of Philosophy* 73, 14 (August 12, 1976):467-81; and Bernard Williams, "A Critique of Utilitarianism," in J.J.C. Smart and Williams, *Utilitarianism: For and Against* (New York: Cambridge, 1973), sec. 6.

The Contributors

Elizabeth Anscombe is professor of philosophy at the University of Cambridge. She is the author of *Intention, An Introduction to Wittgenstein's Tractatus,* and a number of other philosophical texts and articles.

Richard B. Brandt is professor of philosophy at the University of Michigan, Ann Arbor. He has taught philosophy at Swarthmore College, was the John Locke lecturer at Oxford in 1974, and has held a number of distinguished national fellowships. He has authored and edited several major works in ethics, including *Ethical Theory* and *A Theory of the Good and the Right,* in addition to authoring numerous articles.

Arthur C. Danto is Johnsonian Professor of Philosophy at Columbia University. He has taught philosophy at the University of Colorado and has held a number of distinguished fellowships including serving as Fulbright Distinguished Professor to Yugoslavia (1976). He has authored a number of books in the theory of knowledge and philosophical analysis including *Analytical Philosophy of Knowledge* and *Analytic Philosophy of Action* as well as works on Nietzsche and Sartre and a number of articles.

Philip M. Flammer is professor of military and diplomatic history at Brigham Young University. He has taught history at the U.S. Air Force Academy. He has authored a volume on airpower and a number of articles dealing with the military critic and the air war over Europe in World War II.

Thomas M. Gannon is associate professor and chairman of the Department of Sociology at Loyola University, Chicago. He has served as consultant to a number of government and private social agencies. The works he has authored include *The Desert and the City* and *The Society of Jesus in the United States: A Sociological Survey.*

General Sir John Winthrop Hackett was Principal of King's College in London from 1968 to 1975. Prior to that time he served in the British regular army beginning in 1931, seeing combat action for several years, especially during World War II, and holding a number of distinguished command positions including that of commander in chief of the British Army of the Rhine and commander of the Northern Army Group, 1966-68. He is the author of a number of articles and reviews, The Lees Knowles Lectures (Cambridge, 1961) published as *The Profession of Arms, I Was a Stranger,* and the very recent *The Third World War: August 1985* (co-author).

Richard M. Hare is White's Professor of Moral Philosophy and Fellow of Corpus Christi College, Oxford. He has been Visiting Fellow at Princeton, Visiting Professor at the University of Michigan and the University of Delaware. He is the author of *The Language of Morals, Freedom and Reason,* and a number of other influential texts and articles in ethics, logic, and philosophical method.

Nicolai Hartmann (1882-1950) was a German philosopher who taught at Marburg, Cologne, Berlin, and Göttingen. His three-volume book, *Ethics,* is the only one of his major works translated into English although he authored several works in ontology and epistemology.

Samuel P. Huntington is the Frank G. Thomson Professor of Government at Harvard University and Associate Director of the Center for International Affairs. He has taught at Columbia University and served as Henry L. Stimson lecturer at Yale University and as Samuel Paley lecturer at Hebrew University, Jerusalem. He has held a number of distinguished national fellowships including a Guggenheim Fellowship at Oxford University and has served in a number of distinguished national study groups dealing with domestic and foreign policy issues. He has been consultant to the State Department, AID, and a number of Department of Defense agencies. His publications in addition to *The Soldier and the State* include a large list of books and articles in comparative politics, political development, and foreign and military policy.

Morris Janowitz is professor of sociology at the University of Chicago. He has taught sociology at the University of Michigan and served as Fulbright Research Professor at the University of Frankfurt and Pitt Professor at Cambridge University. He has been consultant to a number of U.S. government agencies including the State Department, the U.S. Information Agency, and various agencies of the Department of Defense. He is on the editorial staff of a number of scholarly journals and member of a number of national steering committees. He is president of the Inter-University Seminar on Armed Forces and Society and author of a large number of books and articles in military sociology including his well-known *The Professional Soldier.*

Gregory S. Kavka is assistant professor of philosophy at the University of California, Los Angeles. He is the author of a variety of articles dealing with nuclear deterrence, the paradoxes of rationality, and other philosophical issues.

Richard J. Krickus is associate professor of political science at Mary Washington College. He has published a number of articles dealing with ethnic and urban affairs, political development, and national security.

George I. Mavrodes is professor of philosophy at the University of Michigan, Ann Arbor. He has taught philosophy at Princeton and was Visiting Associate Professor at Carleton College. He is the author of several books and articles dealing with the philosophy of religion including *The Rationality of Belief in God.*

Charles C. Moskos, Jr. is professor of sociology at Northwestern University. He has taught sociology at the University of Michigan. He has served as distinguished lecturer at several of the senior professional military schools and as consultant to agencies in the Department of Defense. He is author and editor of a number of books and articles dealing with the armed forces and society including *The American Enlisted Man* (author) and *Public Opinion and the Military Establishment* (editor).

Jeffrie G. Murphy is professor of philosophy at the University of Arizona. He has taught philosophy at the University of Michigan and U.C.L.A. He is author of *Kant, The Philosophy of Right*, edited *Civil Disobedience and Violence*, and authored a number of articles in legal and political philosophy and moral philosophy.

Thomas Nagel is professor of philosophy at Princeton University.

He has taught philosophy at the University of California, Berkeley, and has held Guggenheim, National Science Foundation, and National Endowment for the Humanities fellowships. He is the author of *The Possibility of Altruism, Mortal Questions,* and a number of philosophical articles.

General John D. Ryan was chief of staff of the United States Air Force from 1969 to 1973. He had served formerly as vice chief of staff, as commander in chief of Pacific Air Forces, as commander in chief of Strategic Air Command, and as inspector general for the U.S. Air Force. He holds honorary doctorates from Creighton University and the University of Akron.

Sam C. Sarkesian is professor of political science and department chairman at Loyola University, Chicago. He has taught political science at the U.S. Military Academy and at DePaul University. He has edited and authored a number of books and articles dealing with the armed forces and society including *The Professional Army Officer in a Changing Society.*

Lewis S. Sorley, III, is currently with the Office of the Inspector General of the Central Intelligence Agency. A retired army officer, he previously served on the faculty of the U.S. Military Academy and the Army War College. He has published a number of articles dealing with the current state of professionalism in the U.S. Army.

Frederick R. Struckmeyer is professor of philosophy at West Chester State College, Pennsylvania. His central research interests include the philosophy of religion and Eastern philosophy and he has published articles in these areas in a number of scholarly journals.

Telford Taylor is professor of law in the Columbia University School of Law. At the close of World War II he served as chief counsel for the prosecution at the Nuremberg trials. In addition to *Nuremberg and Vietnam: An American Tragedy,* he authored *Sword and Swastika, Grand Inquest,* and a number of other volumes dealing with history and military affairs.

Colonel Malham M. Wakin is associate dean of the faculty and professor and head of the Department of Philosophy and Fine Arts at the United States Air Force Academy. He is in his twentieth year of teaching philosophy at the Air Force Academy. In recent years, he has been featured in *Notre Dame Magazine* and *People Magazine* as a spokesman for the military profession and as an outstanding teacher. He has authored a number of articles in professional journals, a handbook of the Viet-Cong Infrastructure, and coauthored a symbolic logic text used at the Academy.

Richard A. Wasserstrom is professor of law and philosophy at the University of California at Los Angeles. He has served on a number of distinguished national councils, has been a Guggenheim Fellow at All Souls College, has taught both philosophy and law at Stanford, has served as an attorney, and was Dean of the College of Arts and Sciences at Tuskegee Institute (1964-1967). He has edited several texts including *War and Morality, Morality and the Law,* and *Today's Moral Problems,* and has published a number of articles dealing with moral, social, and legal philosophy.

Donald A. Wells is professor of philosophy and chairman of the department at the University of Hawaii, Hilo. He has served on the faculty of Oregon State College, Washington State University, and the University of Illinois, Chicago. He is the author of *The War Myth* and a number of other texts and articles dealing with religion, ethics, and war.

Major Michael O. Wheeler is currently serving as a White House Fellow. He holds degrees from the U.S. Air Force Academy, Georgetown University, and the University of Arizona. He taught philosophy at the U.S. Air Force Academy and has authored a number of articles dealing with philosophy and the military and values in American society.